ae - p. 32

W9-BTF-505

AMERICAN
TAPESTRY

ALSO BY TOM TIEDE

Calley, Soldier or Killer?
Coward
Welcome to Washington, Mr. Witherspoon
Your Men at War
The Great Whale Rescue (with Jack Findleton)

AMERICAN TAPESTRY

Eyewitness Accounts of the Twentieth Century

TOM TIEDE

PHAROS BOOKS
A SCRIPPS HOWARD COMPANY
NEW YORK

Copyright © 1988 by Tom Tiede

All rights reserved. No part of this book may be reproduced in any
form or by any means without written permission of the publisher.

First published in 1988.

Library of Congress Cataloging-in-Publication Data

Tiede, Tom.
  American tapestry.
    1. United States—History—20th century.
2. Interviews—United States.   3. Oral history.
I. Title.
E741.T54 1988   973.9   88-60376
ISBN 0-88687-359-2

Printed in the United States of America

Pharos Books
A Scripps Howard Company
200 Park Avenue
New York, NY 10166

10 9 8 7 6 5 4 3 2 1

Cover and interior design: Elyse Strongin

Cover painting: "Five O'Clock in Saco Maine", by Janet Munro © 1988
Jay Johnson America's Folk Heritage Gallery, New York City

"Ma (She's Making Eyes at Me)" by Sydney Clare and Con Conrad © 1921,
renewed 1949, MILLS MUSIC INC., c/o FILM TRADES COPYRIGHT
HOLDINGS, INC. All rights reserved. Used by permission.

Pharos Books are available at special discounts on bulk purchases for sales promo-
tions, premiums, fundraising or educational use. For details, contact the Special Sales
Department, Pharos Books, 200 Park Avenue, New York, NY 10166.

CONTENTS

To my parents, who, like all the mothers and fathers of this century, assign the blessings and afflictions of interesting times.

PREFACE

The noted literary critic Malcolm Cowley, eighty-nine, complained that he has lived long enough to become something of a public archive. He says people are ever so often gathering up their curiosities to ask: "Won't you please share your memories?" One hopes he doesn't review the following. It validates his grumble. The men and women herein were born in the kindling of the twentieth century, have survived through most of its entirety, and their shared memories constitute its history. Thank God for it, Cowley; whoever recounts the remembrances of the next century might rather use data banks.

See Brooke Johns. He is the old trouper who initiates the first chapter. He says, "Oh, I love to talk. People don't do it like they used to, yak, yak, yak. I don't know what has happened. Everyone is watching television, and isn't it awful. I am a ham, I admit it; I like to perform face to face. That was the wonderful thing about my day. Go ahead, ask me anything. The songs we had, for example, they were like conversations. 'Let me call you sweetheart/ I'm in love with you/ Let me hear you whisper/ That you love me too.' See what I mean—face to face. I loved it then. I'll tell you anything you want to know."

Brooke Johns died soon after he made those remarks. The comments are carried on these pages in the present tense, however. The same is true for the other commentators. All of them were interviewed within eighteen months of publication. Their average age in 1987 was eighty-six, but there has been no attempt to keep track of subsequent mortalities. Memories do not pass on. If we treat them as if they do we risk losing, as it's been said, the only thing we really own. The playwright Nahum Tate wrote: "The sweet remembrance of the just, shall flourish when he sleeps in dust." He was a wise gentleman.

There are two other things to know about these shared memories. Both have to do with editing. The men and women spoke of many things, usually with simple eloquence, albeit not always in words and sequences that could be transcribed verbatim for print. The recollections have therefore been modified and rearranged for the sake of clarity and readability. The words have also been edited occasionally at the requests of those involved. Studies indicate that elderly people often tend to remember their lives in the best light, but they can slip, and so you shan't be told the identity of the fellow who once pinched Betty Grable on the boob.

1. Potpourri

BROOKE JOHNS

Brooke Johns was a boy of eight when the twentieth century was introduced into what the poets call the deluge of time. And he remembers the occasion with an enthusiasm that he has cultivated through the long years since then. He lived in Georgetown, a neighborhood of Washington, D.C., and he says there was a great deal of celebration in the capital, bonhomie and that sort of stuff—strangers kissing along the avenues, flags waving in the winter air. It was not just a change of numbers; after all, it was a change of history. The United States was coming of age. The nation that John Gunther said was "the only country founded on a good idea" was on the threshold of international maturity. It was big, strong, and inventive; it was bold, adventurous, and pushy. It was also rich.

Gangway, world.

January 1, 1901. The time before men wore earrings and women wore neckties. President William McKinley issued greetings to the American people and expressed his wish that nations would exist in amity during the new century. The Congress of the United States issued a joint resolution concerning its great expectations for the arriving era. And the residents of the citadel of governance took the good cheer to the streets. Washington was not yet cosmopolitan (its population of 230,000 could have stood snugly on the White House lawn), but the telegraphs were busy with happy messages, the railroad trains had whistles to blow, Pennsylvania Avenue afforded something of a view of the fair face of the future, and the present well attended, and young Brooke Johns joined the revelry that consumed the moment:

"Oh, it was elaborate. It was very special. Things like that were done nicely in those days. I am ninety-three years old now, but I will never forget. My mother and father talked about the celebration all through the last months of the old year. The kids were excited because they had cap pistols to shoot. My father toasted the new century with a tin can of beer. My mother baked what we called a 'Washington pie.' That was a concoction! She made it from the stale leavings she bought on sale from the bakery, like day-old doughnuts and jellied pastries. She chopped it all up with a knife and mixed it in a secret batter. I think it was secret. She never told me, and I never asked. She rolled it all out on a pan, added powdered sugar, put it in the oven on a wood stove, and I ate it along with soda pop. Delicious.

"Everybody went downtown to the parade. There were parades in the neighborhoods, too, but not so big. I think it was cold. I'm sure it was. I don't remember any snow. There were fireworks, rockets, guns. It was high-larious. That's the way we said it then, 'high-larious.' Everybody was involved. The churches and my school. I was in a grade school on P Street in Georgetown, and Georgetown was like a little village of its own in 1901. We had to do compositions on the twentieth century. I was not the best of students, but I think I completed the assignment. 'The twentieth century is here,' or maybe 'I wonder if I'll be around for the twenty-first century.' I probably didn't write that. But maybe I should have. Maybe it would have been prophetic. The year 2000 is now only a little ways away, and, if God is willing, I will be around for it."

Well, wait. Johns doesn't mean the year 2000, he means 2001. The turns of the centuries can be confusing. And the confusion is as old as the formalized measurement of time. The ancient mathematicians used to measure months from one new moon to the next, which was less than perfect, and they also numbered their years according to the reigns of their rulers, which was impossibly indiscriminate. The Roman Catholics fixed the months somewhat (their Gregorian calendar is still observed today) and one Catholic, a sixth-century monk named Dionysius Exiguus, created the notion of dating years from the birth of Jesus Christ. Exiguus suggested the years be designated AD, or anno Domini, "in the year of the Lord," and so the first century by way of the Christian viewpoint began in AD 1, the second in AD 101, the twentieth in AD 1901, and the twenty-first will begin in AD 2001.

That determination has for all intents and purposes been universally adopted. It has not pleased the Moslems or the Jews, however. Nor has every Christian been satisfied. William Hillcourt says that European Christians have been particularly critical of the measuring arrangement because it seems to defy logic. Hillcourt, a New York State resident born in Denmark—right in the middle of the arithmetical complexity, as it happened—recalls the argument from the last time around:

"The obvious thing, from a mathematical standpoint and astronomical standpoint, is that a century ends the last day of the year that has two zeros. Because that is the one-hundredth—or the last—year of each century. So our previous century ended on December 31, 1900. But Kaiser Wilhelm of Germany got into the debate and said that was a lot of nonsense. He felt the century should change when either of the first two numbers of a year change—or, in this case, when 1899 changed to 1900.

"I don't think his reasoning had any merit, however. Because when we came to the first of January in 1900 we were only in the hundredth year of that century. It can't be otherwise. I don't know why Wilhelm took such a position. But it's interesting for me, because I was born in 1901, and so now I can claim that if I live beyond December 31, 2000, I will have lived in three centuries, in a manner of speaking. I also claim that in 1987 I celebrated the forty-seventh anniversary of my thirty-ninth birthday; if Jack Benny could get away with it, so can I."

Benny was the same age as Brooke Johns in 1901. The two were to become entertainers, sometimes appearing together. Benny was actually named Benjamin Kubelsky; Johns used his given name all during his career; but they both had humble beginnings, and both became well-to-do as well as widely famous personalities. And that sort of progression was to become the defining apothegm of the 1900s. The great gift of the new century was opportunity. Johns says it was a wonderful time for Americans to get started.

One reason was that the 125-year-old Republic was at last becoming a world power. The status was awarded as part of the spoils of triumph in the Spanish-American War. Officially, the war had been fought (in 1898) to preserve American interests in Cuba. The other story is that it was waged to further the circulation interests of the aggressive mass media of the period. In any event, the battling lasted a mere ten weeks. The United States successfully employed elements of its sixty-ship navy, Spain was forced to sue for peace, and global politics was rearranged. The adolescent had grown up, the United States had become worldly, even damnright imperialistic, and the 1900s, with all the attendant promise, would clearly be America's century.

JANUARY 1, 1901. The population of the United States was 77,000,000. There were forty-five contiguous states, not yet including Arizona, New Mexico, and Oklahoma. The Philippines, Puerto Rico, Samoa, Guam, and the Hawaiian Islands were called colonies, and Alaska was a barely settled possession. Canada had seven provinces then, and several districts, including "Assiniboia" and "Keewatin"; Mexico before its revolution had three gunboats in its navy; and, in 1901, the first year of his second term, popular Mr. McKin-

ley would become the third American president to be killed by an assassin.

The federal legislature contained 447 members. They included ten members of the Populist Party and one from the Silver Republicans (the Bimetallists). The government raised $587,000,000 in revenues in 1900 and Congress authorized $525,000,000 worth of expenditures. Memorial Day was known as Decoration Day; Lincoln's birthday went largely unnoticed; the bureaucracy recorded in excess of 100 "Negro lynchings" per annum; and the law for penny postcards prohibited messages that "contained any threat, offensive dun, or scurrilous or indecent communications." Cards in violation would "not be forwarded."

Lillie Langtry, at forty-eight, was still hubba-hubba. Mount McKinley was measured 140 feet higher than it is today. The nation was still giving benefits to four women who lost husbands in the War of the American Revolution and one soldier who survived from the combat of 1812. The national debt was about 1.2 billion dollars. The approximate amount of private money in the nation was said to be $12 billion (public currency, bank deposits, gold, etc.). The United States had come to regularly export more goods than it imported; there was an average of 12,000 business failures a year; one of the leading causes of death from illness was constipation (102,000 in 1901); James J. Jeffries was the heavyweight boxing champion; and there was an organization known as the Knights of Ladies Honor that operated sixteen lodges and 1100 sublodges and was led by a gentleman whose title was Supreme Dictator.

Henry Ford. Joseph Pulitzer. Admiral George Dewey. Army privates received $13 a month salary. There were diplomatic legations in Washington from Hayti, Persia, and Siam. Carrie Chapman Catt was serving as the president of the National American Woman Suffragist Association. The stage play To Have and To Hold was featured on Broadway; there was a twelve-cent-per-pound tax on snuff; Cassius Clay was ninety, Jules Verne was seventy-two, Andrew Carnegie was sixty-six, and The New York Times, trying to survive as the newspaper of record, cut its newsstand price from three cents to one cent, advertised five-and-dime "muslin drawers," and noted on the front page of a sixteen-page New Year's edition:

> The Century is dead; long live the Century. Yesterday was the Nineteenth, today is the Twentieth. Sometime last night the one died, and the other was born. Here in New York the event took place at midnight. A moment of darkness at the City Hall, an instant's interlude in the singing, a hush among the crowd—and the old Century was buried. The lights flashed, the crowds sang, the sirens of craft in the harbor screeched and roared, bells pealed, bombs thundered, . . . and the new Century made its triumphant entry.

That first day was a Tuesday. In Washington, Brooke Johns was called home in the late afternoon, when the gas lamps were lit, because he had school the following day. He says he disliked school. He paid more attention to marbles than to memorization. He liked the interaction with schoolchildren, however. He remembers playing with Theodore Roosevelt's son when the one-time vice-president took over for the murdered McKinley. He also remembers "an association" with a smallish neighbor named J. Edgar Hoover; most of all, he remembers going to the vaudeville and burlesque shows with friends in tow:

"I think I was twelve when I saw my first burlesque show. My father took me and some other boys. My father was a grocer. He was also a cripple—one of his legs was shorter than the other. He made up for that defect in talent, though. He was a wonderful banjo player. That was a very nice thing way back when. We didn't have radio or television and we had to entertain ourselves, so my father was the show in our house. He played the piano, strummed the banjo, and sang songs. My mother sang along. It felt very nice, singing and carrying on.

"I don't know what was so bad about burlesque. I suppose it was a little blatant for the day, but look what's happened since. Everybody sleeps with everybody right on television. Correct? I got sick when I smoked my first cigarette. That was a terribly bad thing for a young boy to do. Today I read about ten-year-old dope fiends. No, I liked the burlesque. I liked the excitement and the costumes and the music. Dad took me several times. And vaudeville! The theaters in Washington were small, but the performers were good. I decided I wanted to get in the act.

"Dad had taught me how to play the banjo. I did not learn to read music, but I had a feel for the instrument. When I started I could not reach the far ends of the cords [strings], so I cut the neck down to size. It was a mistake; I caught hell, but I kept trying. I did not know what a note looked like, and I could only play in the keys of C and G, but I could get the music across. I could hear a tune and play it like there was no tomorrow. I could not remember the words very well, either, but if I forgot I would throw in a 'honey babe' or something like that. I was a natural, I was loose; that's why I became popular. One time Will Rogers told me it was a good thing I never learned to play the banjo very well; he said it would have ruined my career.

"I was in high school when I turned professional. I was going to Georgetown Prep. My grandmother had married a wealthy sea captain and my family's social position had been elevated. I did worse in high school than in grade school, though. You had to get a fifty-percent average to pass, and I got below that. One day the people who ran the school concluded I would never be an intellect—in other words, I was wasting my time in their institution—and they told my father that he should have a heart-to-heart talk with me. So Dad sat me down. I was worried he was going to talk about the birds and bees, but he asked me what I wanted to do about school. I told him I wanted to quit and get into show business. He said great. Then he told my mother.

"She said no.

"I asked why.

"She said 'The whiskey and women will kill you.'

"My mother wanted me to go into the ministry. She was a pious woman, and I had a grandfather who had been an Episcopal bishop.

"I said 'Mom, I believe in God, but I don't want to work for him. I'm going on the stage. I'll make you proud of me.'

"She cried. I had always been a pain in the butt as a boy, and I don't think I relieved her worries with the boast."

Initially, Johns tried to catch a ring in the Washington circuit. He hung around the Keith Theater, a popular vaudeville stage, but to no good end. He went to New York with forty dollars and straw luggage, he visited the Street of Dreams, he dressed in the power clothes of the day (spats and a derby), but he struck out there as well.

"I stayed in a modest hotel in Manhattan. There were strong smells in the corridors. I didn't have a window in my room, or ventilation. Everyone on the floor shared the urinal. The bed was a cot; there was a single hard-back chair; and I put the chair at the foot of the cot if I wanted to stretch out. There was an unfrosted bulb hanging from the ceiling. I used to yell down to the bartender to see what time it was. And one more thing. The management kept a rattrap in the corner."

Johns eventually got a job in Altoona, Pennsylvania, keeping the audiences amused while the main features changed their costumes. Twenty dollars a week. It beat the ministry. "You could buy a day's worth of groceries for a dollar." *He also played men's clubs, church gatherings, dance crowds, picking notes into huge microphones, standing where the floor wasn't taken, hawking requests:* "Whatta ya like? Whatta ya want to hear?"
Bill Bailey!

Won't you come home, Bill Bailey,
Won't you come home.
I'm standing all aloooone.
I'll do the cookin, honey,
I'll pay the rent,
I know I've done you wrrrrong.

Remember that rainy evenin,
I turned you out,
With nothin but a fine tooth cooomb.
Now I am to blame,
Ain't that a shame.
Bill Bailey, won't you please come hooome?

The old man can still do it. He performs from a wheelchair now, in the living room of his home. Blast the arthritis.

"Look at these fingers. They are made for the banjo. I've always had great hands, long and supple. I'm long and supple all over. Six foot four inches. To tell the truth I used to be too skinny. My clothes fit too quick. I rattled around in a celluloid collar. But that was part of the act. I was billed as the world's tallest banjo player: 'Six Foot Four, the Big Boy of Broadway!' I still have some billboards. They used to put up advertisements [posters] along the highways when I was on tour. I did well. I was in the Ziegfeld Follies and made seventy-two thousand dollars a year. I traveled internationally and made a quarter of a million a year. I can't say I was the best banjo player of the day. But I had an appeal.

"That was the key, getting the people to like you. I worked at it. I learned to know what the customers wanted. They like you to smile, they like you to have personality, they like you to be natural and at ease. Music? They liked that too, but genius was not necessary. I found that the faster I played, the less the individual notes could be scrutinized, and the more the audience approved. Up tempo. I played like a house on fire. I also employed gimmicks. One of them was the 'bouncing chair.' I hooked my feet through the legs of a chair and bounced around the stage as I played, say, 'Hard-Hearted Hannah.' Can you imagine that on the *Gong Show* today? The people loved it. I never missed a note, either. I hit some wrong ones, sure, but vaudeville wasn't a recital. There were no critics attending.

"Florenz Ziegfeld hired me in 1922. He was something of a son of a bitch, but he had the greatest show in the game and he liked me. I had worked for Meyer Davis, I had offers from Oscar Hammerstein, I had played at the Palace, but the Ziegfeld Follies was the top. I was in an act with Ann Pennington, a lovely girl with whom I had a long and bumpy relationship. She was very small, her nickname was Penny Ante, and I was very big. We made a great team. She sang and I played. I think we made more money for Broadway than any other couple. New York Governor Al Smith had a crush on Penny. I did too. A newspaper reporter once asked me to give him a hundred dollars to kill a steamy story about Penny and me. I knocked him unconscious. He then sued me, and I settled out of court for a few thousand dollars.

"I don't remember if the newsman's story was correct or not. It might have been. My mother said I would get entangled with women and whiskey in the theater, and she was right. Not so much whiskey. I didn't drink even then. But there were all these lovely ladies, and there were a string of nasty scandals. One woman in the Follies got very jealous of Penny, and one night she went off the deep end. She came down to the men's dressing room where Paul Whiteman and I were taking showers. Then she took off her robe. I thought it was all great fun, so I threw some ice water on her, and she got mad. She ran out screaming and claimed that she had been molested. The newspapers called me a Peeping Tom, and that wasn't all. What a blow! I didn't need to peep at anyone. If I wanted a look I could get it by asking.

"Then there was the woman who tried to kill me. That was jealousy too. She stabbed me in the neck. Oh, well, I won't say it wasn't worth it. In those days, in the Follies, women were something. They were voluptuous. They had breasts hanging all over the place. They had figures. Today, everybody gets on a diet and looks like that lamp there, with the shade on it. Yes, I played around. But that was to be expected. It was part of the glamour. But a lot of it was also a lot of lies. People in the theater weren't really the rabbits they were pictured to be in the newspapers. Rudolph Valentino did not take everyone to bed. I knew Rudy, by the way; he was much shorter than me. Eventually I got married. Hazel was a girl I met in Washington. She was never in show business, and we've been together sixty-one years.

"Sixty-one good years, I might add. I've had a wonderful life. I played for presidents, you know. I played many times for the Prince of Wales. That was the fellow who would become the King of England and then abdicate [1936] so he could marry Wallis Warfield Simpson. I played for him while I was on tour in England. He came to the theater night after night. He liked that song, what was it, 'There Ain't No Flies on Auntie.' It was a silly tune, but the British went for it. I remember that Prince Edward's parents, the King and Queen, did not approve of his coming to the theater, but he obviously had a mind of his own. One night he asked me to go to his place to play some more. His place was St. James's Palace. It was a great time, and everybody drank from a crock. I went there often after that; I still have his autograph on a banjo.

"Everybody autographed the banjos. I have all of the great names of the twenties. Jimmy Durante, Sophie Tucker, Al Jolson. Fanny Brice. I knew George Burns when he and Gracie Allen were newlyweds. Now he and I may be the last of the old vaudeville stars. He's still a very funny man, but he's not as funny as W. C. Fields. Bill was the champion in that category. I played with Fields in the National Theater in Washington, and one night he came out on stage with his fly open. Now it's true, for a fact, that Bill Fields always wore red underwear, and there he was, with the spotlights on him, and a tuft of red sticking out of his crotch. I tried to get in front of him, but it was too late. The audience went wild. There was a midget in the act then, named Shorty, who tried to fix the fly, and I will never forget Bill wailing out, in that baritone voice, 'Let go of me, Shorty, what in the hell is the matter with you?'

"Bill Fields was the funniest man who ever lived. Think what he would have been sober! But there were so many great talents in the twenties. They are still legends. Paul Whiteman, Ruby Keeler, Gypsy Rose Lee. And those wonderful songs we sang: 'Baby Face,' 'Cuddle Up a Little Closer,' 'I Wonder Who's Kissing Her Now.' Did I mention Eddie Cantor? We worked together for two years. One night I ran offstage and there was this girl, Tessie, she was always messing around. That night I was not in the mood, and I said, 'Tessie, stop teasing me.' Cantor was right there, in blackface, waiting to go on, and he started jumping up and down: 'Brookey, Brookey,' he said, 'I think you're on to something.'

"I said, 'Cantor, keep your hands off this white suit. What do you mean I'm on to something?'

"He said, 'The name for a song.'

"He was very excited. I thanked him for the idea. Later I collaborated with Ray Perkins to write 'Tessie (Stop Teasing Me).' It was a pretty fair hit."

Tessie McKeeser was known as a teaser,
With all her bones.
As soon as she'd land them,
Oh boy how she'd slam them,
But it was only a pose.
She had the fellows jump at her command,
But when they found they couldn't even hold her hand,
They say:
"Aw Tessie, stop teasing me, stop teasing me,
"I'm all a gleam.
"Aw Tessie, please, honest, truly, every day you are unruly.
"Tessie, I'm mad at you,
"You're bad as you can be.
"Honey, just when I think I am due to be kissed,
"You change your mind and forget I exist.
"Tessie, stop teasing me, cause I love yoooou."

Time. It's instructive to note that it has been redefined in the twentieth century. Prior to 1956, a second was measured as the fraction of 1/86,400 of the mean solar day. From 1956 to 1967 a second was recorded as the fraction 1/31556925.9747 of the tropical year at OOh OOm OOs 31 December 1899. The second is presently defined as the duration of 9,192,631,770 periods of the radiation corresponding to the transition between the two hyperfine levels of the ground state of the cesium-133 atom.

Got that?

FRANK FOOLS CROW

Brooke Johns, then, believes that the introduction of the 1900s was a golden moment in the American experience, a new opportunity for every man to catch the new and improved brass ring. Frank Fools Crow might disagree. He was also a young boy when the centuries changed; he also got into the entertainment business, after a fashion; but he was not as able to hear the bugle call to better things. Fools Crow is an Oglala Sioux Indian, a hereditary shaman, as they are called—in other words, a medicine man. He was born in a tepee, he says, forming its likeness with his fingers. The delivery took place so far from Georgetown that the old man doesn't know the date. He is ninety-three years old now, or maybe eighty-seven. In either case, it can correctly be said that he has remained inside the leather skins of the nation all of his life.

Fools Crow lives on the Pine Ridge Reservation near the Black Hills of South Dakota. He wears his hair in braids and watches cartoons on television. He says he does not remember when the 1800s became the 1900s, and he evidently does not care; then he kills a roach on his kitchen table with the thundering flat of his hand. He wears a wristwatch. No, he wears two, but neither of them works particularly well, and it doesn't matter anyway.

The word tepee *comes from Sioux. Fools Crow says the lodgings were the size of motel rooms, as much as 15 feet straight up and 30 feet in diameter:*

"They were used by the buffalo hunters. They could be moved around from place to place. My father was a rancher. The buffalo were all gone then. I didn't see many. I don't remember my mother; she is dead now."

The old man has no teeth. He has large blackheads in the creases of his face. There is a dog barking outside; he says there is always a dog barking on the reservation. He has drooping eyelids. He wears pearl buttons on his shirts. He smiles at the wrong time, laughs for no apparent reason, and in profile looks like he should be on a coin. He remembers Calvin Coolidge, but Ronald Reagan does not ring a bell. His second wife is in a nursing home. He twiddles his thumbs and then his little fingers. He does not speak English. He prefers what the researchers call Macro Siouan, the tongue of his ancestors.

For this interview, he answered questions fielded by his stepson, Joe Paw-nielegging. The latter would ask long questions and the former would give short answers; the transcription here is as faithful as the circumstances allow.

Where were you born?

"Here."

Do you remember what it was like for you then?

"The same."

Fools Crow says he had five brothers and sisters. And he was one of the last of the litter. That would have been shortly after the end of the Indian wars, wars that began when the colonialists landed on the Atlantic Seaboard and end-ed three and a half centuries later at the Battle of Wounded Knee. Fools Crow says his father was at Wounded Knee. The battle took place at a reservation crossroads near his present home. The shaman joins other tribal elders in re-counting the memory of the slaughter:

"It was in 1890. Indians had been defeated everywhere, the tribes had been wiped out by the Army, and so they turned to religion for help. Many Sioux be-gan to practice the Ghost Dance religion: it was supposed to bring back the dead. The Army was afraid of it, however, because it brought the people togeth-er, and that's what led to Wounded Knee. The Sioux gathered there to hold a dance, and the Army swept in to stop it. Sitting Bull was killed first, and then Chief Bigfoot and his followers were murdered later. Three hundred Indians were killed in one day, in winter, and they were left there to freeze solid."

Frank Fools Crow drives past Wounded Knee when he goes to Pine Ridge, the principal town in the reservation. He also passes a large signboard that re-counts the massacre in some detail. The signboard is shot full of bullet holes and is planted in ground that is littered with trash. He says the white man destroyed the Indians, but Indians have destroyed the memory. Carelessness. That's one thing that has changed from before. He remembers the people of his youth as less careless than the people now. They had character that is lacking today. They also had traditions, connections between the generations, stories, and cus-toms. That's why Fools Crow became a shaman, to preserve the old values.

There is the story of lust, for example. It goes back to the early 1900s and it can be told in any number of ways, all of them having merit. One day the

Young Man watched the Old Man gather serviceberry sticks for whittling. When the Young Man asked why, the Old Man said he was making people. He said the big shavings would be men and the little shavings would be women. The Old Man then whittled away and made a good many men and women. Seeing this, the Young Man had an idea. He would whittle some women for himself. He cut off some small shavings, all of which became women, but when he chased after them to seduce them they turned back into serviceberry sticks.

Fools Crow did not become a shaman right away. He first looked around the world for opportunity.

"I heard about Buffalo Bill [William F. Cody]. He had a Wild West show that traveled throughout the United States and into other countries. He had Annie Oakley, overland [Conestoga] wagons, and he had a lot of cowboys and Indians. I was one of the Indians for many years. I was hired in Denver. My job was to ride a horse. We traveled in trains, the horses were in boxcars, and sometimes we went overseas in boats. I did not like the boats. I like to stand on dry land. I got sick on the water when there were storms.

"I did that for many years, I don't remember how many. I rode in on a racehorse; sometimes I wore a headdress. We did not have to stage fights with the cowboys; I don't think so, anyway. Maybe sometimes. I know it was seasonal work. We started the tours in March and stopped in December. I got regular pay for it. I couldn't tell you how much. I was a young man, and I had never been to school, and I just took what they gave me. It was more than I could make at Pine Ridge, I know that. Buffalo Bill was rich. He wore new clothes and his boots were polished by somebody who did it for him."

The Buffalo Bill show was disbanded in 1913. Cody, by the way, had come honestly to that particular kind of theater. He had moved West from Kansas and rode for the Pony Express. He earned his nickname when he supplied meat for the Kansas Pacific Railroad, and he killed a share of red men when he served as chief of scouts for the 5th U.S. Cavalry. He became a celebrity when he became the subject of dime novels, he operated the Wild West show for thirty years, and he died in 1917. Fools Crow was in his early twenties then, back on the reservation, and now on the trail of becoming a shaman:

"I only had a little interest at first. But I learned what I could from the elders. When I was twenty-nine years old, I went to a Vision Quest, which is a ceremony where people communicate with the spirits. I had a dream before that, and it left me in confusion, so I went to the Vision Quest for the answer. The ceremony was held in the traditional place in the Black Hills. I was up there for four days, and I had a vision myself. I talked with the spirits. They told me the answer to my question. I had dreamed that I would become a medicine man; the spirits said that was right. The other people there agreed too. When I came down from the Vision Quest, I was officially a medicine man.

"A medicine man is like a combination priest and doctor. We take care of people's spiritual and religious needs. We hold the sacred ceremonies, and we drive the evil things from their bodies. All of these things are ancient. We use herbs for medicine that have been used for thousands of years. I have herbs for most diseases. They must be properly prepared, but when it is done right they work. I have cured cancer in many people on the reservation. I have kept people from dying time and again. Some doctors from the outside have come here to find out what I'm doing; they have asked me to give them the recipes for my preparations, but I never do. The preparations are secret. It's tribal law: I am not allowed to give them away.

"The herbs would not work without the religious ceremonies anyway. They have to be used together. And only medicine men can use them together. I will give you an example. If a man comes to me with a great sickness, it might turn out that I can only help him by using an animalistic ceremony. That means I have to carry out the ceremony the way the animals would. I might have to speak like a dog or a wolf, if that is the only way to scare away the disease. And that's what a shaman is. He performs a little magic. The doctors on the outside might have their drugs and their machines, but they cannot talk like a dog. You have to bark, and howl, or growl. And that is just one way. There are different things to do for different sicknesses."

He smiles. All gums.

Frank, he is asked, how much are you paid for this?

"Sometimes meat, or a dozen eggs. Sometimes nothing."

And money?

"I don't have money. I don't have anything."

The stepson, Joe Pawnielegging, says that's about right. The old Indian has nothing of material value to show for the twentieth century. He is among the poorest inhabitants of the nation. He is in fact a lifelong ward of the state. He has never had a car, he has never had a new house, he has never had a bank account. He lives on the federal dole and from the leavings of tourists who pay to take his photograph. He says he sees the good life on television and thinks that must be off in the clouds somewhere:

"It was better when I was young. People helped each other then. Now it's everyone for themselves. No one cares any more. People live badly, and they die; it means nothing."

Listen up. This is an exceptional man speaking. Frank Fools Crow may be broke and can't tell the time from a pair of hand-me-down watches, but he has other accomplishments. He is the senior shaman in the Oglala Sioux nation. He is therefore the most venerated member of the tribe. He is the pope of Pine Ridge, and the surgeon general besides. Some Indians say he knows God; others claim he never gets sick; and the story is that he was put on earth to show that great people live among us in anonymity, asking for handouts like everyone else, year after year, century after century perhaps. Who knows? Fools Crow may be the eternal underprivileged. The story goes on to suggest that Fools Crow will never die, he will just make allowance for precedent and then return to grace the people he also serves.

The American people have become indefatigable commemorators in the twentieth century. Special interest groups have created scores of public holidays and thousands of special observances. Most of them have been of arguable merit and hence short-lived. One illustration: Indian Day. The day was created by Congress in 1916 so that Americans would "recognize and honor" the nation's aboriginals, but the celebration was ignored. Some Indians held ceremonies in the states in which they had significant populations—Arizona, California, Minnesota, Montana, Oklahoma, and South Dakota—but even that response was tepid. The grim joke was that the Indians already had a day set aside for them, Memorial Day, and the special observance was eventually dropped.

There has been no such luck with many other commemorations. The American twentieth century continues to be sodden with celebrations that nobody really wants. Sadie Hawkins Day is the first Saturday after November 11 each year. Reformation Day is October 31. Loyalty Day passes with hardly a note on what is sometimes known and normally disregarded as May Day. A Citizenship Day each September 17 has replaced I Am an American Day, which used to be held on the third Sunday in May; there is Bird Day, Forefathers Day, Pan American Day, Child Health Day, Verrazano Day (in New York State), King Kamehameha Day (in Hawaii); and the National Day of Prayer is for some reason held on various days, but never on Sunday.

ERNEST SHAFENBERG

Ernest Shafenberg has never met Frank Fools Crow. But he believes he may have met the shaman's father, tangentially. He says he was a military trumpet boy during a previous life, and he was present at the Wounded Knee massacre:

"I was about seventeen years old," he says, rubbing his forearms with his hands, "and I was with the United States Eighth Cavalry. I knew Sitting Bull and his family, because he had several children about my age. I was very friendly with the Indians. I still can't forget all that killing. My unit had been ordered to Wounded Knee to keep the Indians in line. The government had decided that the Ghost Dance might lead to an uprising, and so it had to be stopped. So we stopped it. I remember the shooting, and seeing the Indians fall. When it was over I was told to go up and down the ravines to see if there were any more Indians around. I only found one Indian alive. She was a squaw, hiding; I could see the hatred in her eyes."

Shafenberg is eighty-one. He lives on the edge of Kingfisher, Oklahoma, along the route of the old Chisholm Trail, square in the heart of Middle America. The men there drive pickup trucks and belong to the Veterans of Foreign Wars. The women still bake bread on Sundays and put up preserves for the winter. There are nineteen churches, at least as many grain elevators, and 4200 residents who are with some exceptions uniform in their designs and habits.

Shafenberg is one of the peculiar exceptions. He stands apart like the stranger in church. He refuses to be sifted through the habit of conformity. He does not think that wisdom can be forced from the crowd like eggs from a chicken. He is, therefore and in short, the grand old man of United States reincarnation. He says the Indians aren't the only ones who believe that someone like Frank Foolscrow may be immortal; the idea that life is recyclable has become an article of faith for many in the 1900s.

Thomas Sherlock said it for the dubious: "We call it death to leave this world, but were we once out of it, and into the joy of the next, we should think it were dying indeed to come back."

Oh, well.

"I have always been spiritual, going back to when I was a kid. It started when my brother died. We lived in Guthrie then, that was the capital of the Oklahoma Territory, and my brother was hit by a switch engine that belonged to one of the railroads. He was two years old; I was ten months, but it's still in my mind. My parents shipped the boy's body to another town for burial, and we all rode in the same car with him. I could see my brother's spirit all the while. He ran back and forth from his body, like he was playing with me. I didn't say anything to Mom and Dad."

"Then when we got to the cemetery, in Cashion, I was distracted by this loud noise. Everybody else was praying, but I heard a clap of thunder. It rang through the heavens and it must have been the signal for the spirits to gather. They started floating down to my brother's grave. I saw forty or more Indian spirits, and also the ghosts of soldiers who had fought in the Revolutionary War. They did not touch the ground. They hovered in midair. People never believe that when I tell them now; but many years later I met a psychic named Polly Estep and she recounted that story psychically, and absolutely word for word.

"I don't care if people don't believe me. The Romans didn't believe Jesus. I take comfort in that. Why would I lie? The lie would be if I denied all these things. Like the vision I had about Teddy Roosevelt, it was one of so many dreams and flashbacks that I've experienced. My family had moved to San Antonio, that was September ten, nineteen hundred and ten. Teddy Roosevelt and his Rough Riders had come to Texas by train. I think it was some kind of tour, and I went down to see him. I remember I had the impression I'd seen him before, in another life, and so I really started thinking about reincarnation."

Shafenberg says he also met Lyndon Baines Johnson in Texas. They rode ponies together in a community called Stonewall. He says his family returned to Oklahoma shortly after that, and he grew up picking mulberries for ten cents a gallon, swimming in horse tanks, and reliving the past in daydreams. He attended high school, went to a small college, played a C melody saxophone for church socials, and served in the army during World War II.

"Just before the war I had a dream about the Russians. I had settled in the town of Kingfisher, and I dreamed a Russian plane dropped a bomb on a grain elevator there. It was very real. Then I had the same dream a second time, so I knew something was going to happen. Sure enough, the elevator exploded. The dust had built up in the headhouse, and it created combustion. The man in the head tower at the time was Olaf Anglin, and he was killed. That was frightening to me, dreaming it like that, and it has happened many times since; it's like looking into a future you don't want to see.

"I was a farmer when I got out of the Army. I started the business during the Great Depression. When the Depression started wheat was a dollar twenty-five a bushel. Then it went to seventy-five cents, then fifty cents, and sometimes I couldn't get anything at all. I survived, though, and when things got a little better I even prospered. I built the first motel in Kingfisher. My wife Helen owned a five-and-dime store. I also had a construction outfit. God has been good to me. I still believe in God, because I think things like parapsychology and reincarnation are Christian in nature. Jesus had two lives, remember; He rose from the dead.

"Maybe he had more than that. I know I have. I've been around so many times I have to keep track of it on paper. Here is the list. I've compiled it from flashbacks and revelations and research. Near as I can tell, I started as a Roman senator and was assassinated in Spain. I came back as a Spaniard and got to the

New World with Hernando de Soto. I was also an Englishman and a French-man for a time, but let's get back to the Americas. I was an Indian chief in Virginia; I was also a Mexican boy at the Alamo. From there I was reincarnated into an Indian scout, and after that I became that boy at Wounded Knee. The boy was killed in 1901. My spirit left my body and watched my funeral. Fifteen years later I was born again as Ernest Shafenberg."

Shafenberg is rotund and wears suspenders. He is married to a woman who says she believes in her husband but does not believe in reincarnation. They own eighty acres east of Kingfisher, hard by what used to be the Chisholm Trail. They used to own the Shafenberg Research Foundation there, for many years one of the nation's most popular centers for the study of holistic healing and life after death. They gave the foundation away in 1985, to the descendants of the psychic Edgar Cayce, and it has fallen into disuse. Shafenberg says the center is now used for country music concerts, 200 seats for $100 a night.

Shafenberg says people are not much interested in practicing old-time spiritualism any more. Like everything else in the 1900s, faith in reincarnation has been colored by giddy change. It used to be enough to think one could be an Indian in one life and an Indian scout in another. Now there must be bombastics as well, which is to say personal and regularly occurring gratifications. Read: whims. The extrasensory perception of the 1930s has been displaced by the ESP of the late century. Psychokinesis takes a back seat to energized channels. Pyramids. Crystals. Ramba, and Shirley MacLaine. Americans will take a chance on any theory, providing it is sexy or inexplicable. There is a new age of consciousness, where the living and dead will meet, and where harmonic convergence must surely take happy root.

Shafenberg says the trend is nonsense. Worse, he thinks, it's commercialization.

"In the first place you cannot reach an understanding of these things by paying money to someone for instruction. This knowledge is a gift from God. I know the preachers don't believe that—I was thrown out of the Baptist church for my views—but I still think that when God created man He created reincarnation to perpetuate man. The Bible says that God lives in each of us who are just, and it's obvious that He can't die. The bodies wither but the God within us, the soul, does not wither. It's transported to another temple, another person. We are born again if we deserve to be born again."

It should be pointed out that in Shafenberg's case he has always been born again to remarkable events. Only as Ernie Shafenberg has he missed the historic doings. He was a colleague of the Caesars and he helped prove the world was round; he fought alongside George Washington and he once spent a wilderness winter with Theodore Roosevelt; he was present at the Battle of the Little Big Horn and he rode for the Pony Express. He also thinks he was in the first chapter of Revelation. But that's another story, for another century no doubt.

Before he died in 1947, the automaker Henry Ford told an interviewer that he had adopted the theory of reincarnation when he was in his middle years: "Religion offered nothing to the point . . . work is futile if we cannot utilize the experience we collect in one life in the next. When I discovered reincarnation it was as if I had found a universal plan. I realized that there was a chance to work out my ideas. Time was no longer limited. I was no longer a slave to the hands of the clock. Genius is experience. Some seem to think that it is a gift or a talent, but it is the fruit of long experience and many lives. . . . If you preserve a record of this . . . write it so that it puts men's minds at ease. I would like to communicate . . . the calmness that the long view of life gives."

JAMES DRUMMOND

James Drummond, slapping his knee, figures that Ernie Shafenberg is a curious dude. Reincarnation. That's to laugh. Every fool knows that you only live once and then go to heaven with Jesus. Still, the whole notion gives one pause. What about the mixing of races, for example? It would be one thing to, say, go from George Washington to Jefferson Davis to George Wallace, but what if the lineage included Crispus Attucks or Martin Luther King, Jr.? Drummond shudders at that. Surely God does not play games. Rhett Butler to Jesse Jackson? No, a thousand times no.

"I can't say I'm against the niggers, or the Jews. I've had them work for me; I've known a good many of them. The trouble comes when they step out of their place. If a man ain't got sense enough to stay in his place the way God intended him to—now I said the way *God* intended him to—if he don't know God and the Bible, he ain't nothing hardly. You don't see you black people in my house. You don't see black pictures on the walls. This is a white section all the way to town, and all the way out."

James Drummond is ninety-two.

"I was born in 1896."

He is a native of Alabama.

"Marengo County, below Selma."

He has a limited education.

"Eight grades."

And he may be the oldest Ku Klux Klan member in America.

He says his first contact with black people was on his father's farm, near a small community called Magnolia. Drummond says the black people picked cotton, yet they were treated well and paid the prevailing wage, fifty cents a day and some groceries.

"It don't sound like much now, but a man could make a living from it then. I only made seventy-five cents or a dollar a day myself. And I picked cotton just like the others. We picked it by hand. No gloves or anything. We picked all day long, maybe three-four hundred pounds apiece. I had a bag that I hung over my shoulder, and I picked with both hands, walking along. Cotton grows in puffy balls. It takes a lot to make three-four hundred pounds."

Drummond says he joined the Ku Klux Klan soon after the turn of the century. His memory may fail him here, for he would only have been nine or ten years old then and, what is more, the Klan was in a dormant stage. The secret organization had come into existence during Reconstruction, when whites moved to preserve their political supremacy in the face of the new black vote. The racists formed dozens of groups at first, particularly in Tennessee and the Carolinas, but they eventually coalesced under the leadership of a Confederate general named Nathan Bedford Forrest. It was then they began wearing robes, burning symbolic crosses, and terrorizing Negroes. They were especially active during election campaigns, when they all too often tortured or murdered people who were opposed to manipulated voting.

The activities of the original Klan were eventually subdued by force. Federal troops were empowered to arrest Klan members and hold them without trial; hence the marauders lost their momentum. The group reorganized in the early 1900s, however, partly because the original clan was popularized in a best-selling novel (Clansman) and in an influential motion picture (The Birth of a Nation). The rejuvenated group reached across the nation; in addition to preying on blacks, the participants became antisemitic, antisocialist, and anti-trade-union. They wrapped their opinions in Golden-Oldie patriotism, which appealed to Drummond:

"It was a long time ago. Too long to talk much about, hardly."

Eighty years, is that right?

"I joined the Klan in nineteen-four, -five, or -six."

What's the reason you joined?

"What's the reason any of us joined?"

Tell me.

"We need to do something to help our country. To Build up the law enforcement and the home. To take care of the home. To take care of white people. It's a white-supremacy organization."

But you said you didn't have anything against black people.

"Well, they lived over here, and some over there. We didn't live mixed up. There may be some low-down who did. Not me."

You didn't associate at all.

"Oh no. We hired them. They'd do what you told them."

What you told them?

"They worked on the farm. The whites told them what to do. There wasn't no mixed-up equal rights or nothing like that."

Were they good workers?

"Some of them was. Or they could go home."

You're saying you were strict.

"The Klan was the law."

The police?

"The Klan was just about everything."

Can you give an example?

"Oh, well, we kept things straight. We kept the niggers from stealing, and, ah . . . the Klan was over all of it."

Did you carry guns?

"Once in a while. I'm not supposed to."

What happened if you caught a black man stealing?

"We'd turn him over to the law."

Anything else?

"I wouldn't say."

Why not?

"We were supposed to be secret."

Yet you did things in public.

"Oh, yeah. The police joined us all the time. We had ministers. The Klan was in Washington, and all down the states."

Washington, D.C.?

"That was a big part of it."

It was. The Klan held a parade on Pennsylvania Avenue in 1925 and some congressmen participated. The group had a membership of more than two million at that juncture, and many politicians gave homage to the numbers. Drummond says the KKK had money as well as forces. It also had a fair public visage. People stood in line to join, women formed auxiliary societies and children asked for miniature robes at Christmas. The robes, by the way, were metaphors of the supernatural; the Klan believed sheets were the gowns of the ghosts.

"I think I paid a dollar and a half to join," Drummond continues.

Do you remember the first meetings?

"They were like big church meetings. There used to be a lot of them, but there aren't so many any more."

Did you wear robes?

"The suits were just about like a white—ah, it buttoned up around the neck, long sleeves, sides on it, and it came down along here. It was a nice-looking bunch of fellows, I'll tell you. It wasn't no cheap bunch. It was the best protection we had in the country—and it still is now, in some places."

Do you remember the hoods?

"They were pointed. I still have one in the house somewhere."

What happened during the meetings?

"Just about everything."

When were they held?

"Mostly at night."

Did you burn crosses, things like that?

"Yeah. Law enforcement."

For the blacks.

"Some whites, too."

What would happen if you caught a black man?

"Doing what?"

Stealing, being with a white woman.

"No telling."

Sometimes they'd string them up, right?

"Sometimes he'd get killed."

Tell me about that.

"I don't know. They might take him up and tell him what to do, make him straight so he won't be about stealing something. Niggers are bad about stealing. Some white fellows the same."

Would the Klan punish a white man for being with a black?

"No, he would be in his class. He could fool around if he wanted. But he better not go fooling around with white people."

I mean being with a black woman.

"Oh, he might be arrested."

I see.

"I didn't go for that. I was raised in a good family. Both of my grandfathers were doctors. I wasn't raised in no riffraff."

Drummond moved to Huntsville from the farm. He married, had children, and took possession of an automobile dealership. He sold out in the 1960s, lost his wife to illness, and lives today in a small, deteriorating house that sits hard by the downtown commercial district. He is short, scruffy, wizened, and amiable. He keeps a picture of General Douglas MacArthur on the wall and one of Ronald Reagan on a table. Reagan is next to a portrait of Jesus. He also keeps a magazine drawing of four bulldogs playing poker.

What's that over there?

"It's an award. I was a soldier in World War One. The Eighty-first Division. We never went overseas. They didn't need us."

And that?

"That's my wife with her sister."

She looks like a lovely lady.

"Oh, she was good."

Drummond still subscribes to the Ku Klux Klan house organ, The Thunderbolt *and he gets literature from three or four different Klan splinter groups. He doesn't know if he's the oldest living member or the member with the most dated membership, but he regretfully observes that the KKK is not what it used to be. In 1987 the Anti-Defamation League of B'nai B'rith reported that membership in the various klans fell to a total of between 5000 and 6000. That was half the figure of only a decade before. Drummond hopes that it may have to do with a reduction in need:*

"I don't hear about it much any more."

What?

"The nigger business."

Has it calmed down?

"A nigger is still a nigger. He belongs in Africa."

He can eat in the restaurants now.

"But they don't mix up with us. There might be a helper in the back there, cleaning up. They know where to stay."

So they don't bother you.

"I can take care of myself."

How about Jews?

"A Jew is a Jew. He should be in Jerusalem."

You don't like them either?

"This is a white country."

It is?

"Sure. You go downtown and see who the sheriff is. He's white. The mayor is white. The president is white. We are the rulers here. The nigger is not."

Nor the Jew.

"The Jew cannot get in the Klan."

Maybe he doesn't want to.

"Well, the Klan is respectable. It's a righteous, good organization. Judges, lawyers, anybody. We have all of them."

Do you still get together?

"I'll do it right here in my house if I want."

Liberty is a wonderful thing.

"The black is not going to run over me. No nigger bosses over white people. That goes for my whole family. I've been in the Klan for years and years. I still am. The niggers, they know who we are, and they know we are going to keep it that way."

A 1987 survey indicated that the Ku Klux Klan was divided into at least eleven separate groups with headquarters in eight states. The major groups included the United Klans of America, Tuscaloosa, Alabama, approximately 2500 members; the Invisible Empire, Knights of the Ku Klux Klan, Shelton, Connecticut, approximate membership 2000; the Knights of the Ku Klux Klan, one faction of which was located in Birmingham, Alabama, with 500 members, and another operated out of Tuscumbia, Alabama, with 500 to 1000 members; the Confederate Knights of the Southern National Front, Fayetteville, North Carolina, approximately 300 members; and the Christian Knights of the Ku Klux Klan, Mount Holly, North Carolina, with perhaps 150 members.

AL KOOPER

James Drummond, meet Al Kooper. He is one of the Jews for whom you say you have no use. And it's difficult to understand why. Like you, he is a small, wiry man; he has worked hard for a living; and he thanks God for a free and independent America. Of course, there are some differences. Kooper is urbane rather than rural. He is also internationally adjusted and, most importantly, he does not savage people for racial or religious reasons, in part because he has had per-

sonal anguish in that sewer. He is a native of Eastern Europe, where he lived through the antisemitic terrors and degeneration of World War II.

Listen:

"I was a young man of thirty-three or thirty-four when the Germans came. I was a member of the Home Guard then, but we could not fight against airplanes and tanks. I lived in an apartment building that was bombed. Ten people were killed in that instant alone. What could you do? They had the advantage. And so when they took over they started gathering up the Jews. They got people from the street, and from their homes, and from their businesses and took them to places, and when they did that they beat you up. They beat me in the head, and I was two weeks in the hospital. This time they hit me in the ear, and even now I cannot hear very well with that ear; it was damaged forever."

Kooper speaks of Warsaw, Poland. He was a small businessman when Adolf Hitler's forces invaded in September 1939, the calculated outrage that precipitated World War II. There were 3.2 million Jews in the nation then, one-fourth of whom lived in the capital, and they were subjected to a Blitzpogrom of intimidation, internment, and murder that became a major element in what is known in Hebrew as the Shoah, the Holocaust.

Kooper is eighty-two.

"I was from a large and fairly prosperous family," he says. "My father was in the lumber business and he also had a flower trade. There were ten children, most of whom were to help in my father's business. I did myself for a while, until I started a business of my own. I imported chemicals for use in curing leather. I had been doing that for about ten years before the Germans arrived. I was also in politics, you might say, because I was a Zionist; I belonged to an organization called Nercaz, which means 'Together,' and we shared the Zionist belief in the establishment of a national Jewish state in Palestine.

"I don't know if the Germans knew about that involvement. Nor do I know if they would have cared if they did. Their idea was to eliminate us, regardless of who we were or what we believed. But I remember I was trying to go to Palestine myself, to work there for a Jewish state, but my father held me up. He needed me for some things and did not want me to leave Poland. So I delayed my departure, and that's why I was there when the war began. There was some fighting around Warsaw as the Germans advanced; the people put up some resistance, but it was not much; and the Germans soon took charge.

Kooper says the discrimination against Jews began instantly. They were ordered to wear blue star armbands for identification. Their possessions were *looted, and they were not permitted to carry more than 2000 zlotys ($50) in cash. Religious services were prohibited, Jewish travel was restricted, Jews could no longer collect debts owed to them, and the Nazis imposed an impossibly severe food ration of 200 calories a day.*

Kooper says the Germans then began building walls in scattered parts of the city. Very soon rumors began to circulate about a plan of "collective confinement." The rumors were confirmed in October 1940, when the Germans announced the formation of what was called the Jewish Residential District, which would otherwise be known as the Warsaw Ghetto. More than 400,000 Jews were forced behind the walls in a depressed area of the city.

"It was a terrible place," Kooper goes on. "They pushed us together, five and six persons to a single room. There was not enough food, there was not enough heat, there was not enough anything. I lived with two or three other people at first. Eating was always the most critical problem. We were starving. The Germans would not allow food to come into the ghetto, and they warned the Polish people against helping us in any way. So we had to buy it illegally and smuggle it in. I was always hungry. Everybody talked about terrible hunger all of the time.

"You cannot imagine it. Even with all of the words that have been written. I ate scraps, nothing more, and by the end of the war I weighed ninety-five pounds. I have a picture of that; I was a skeleton. Hunger was the preoccupation. It seized us. I was a young man, and you know how young men are, but I did not even have a girlfriend in the ghetto. I was too hungry to think about that kind of business. And I was too frightened. If I didn't worry about food, I worried about the Nazis. These people would shoot you if you were out in the streets after five o'clock.

"The sanitation conditions were also very bad. Toilets would not work; garbage piled up. Typhus was everywhere, it was all around the ghetto. Every day I would go out and see dead people in the streets. They were covered with newspapers because if you died, your clothes were stolen. Thousands and thousands died like that, of typhus and starvation. The disease was so bad that it even frightened the German soldiers. And that was at least one good thing. The Germans did not come into the ghetto very much, they were afraid of the typhus.

"My father died of typhus. My mother died of typhus. My brother died also of typhus. There was very little medicine available, you see. The Jewish doctors had brought what they had with them to the ghetto, and some people who worked for the Germans also got small amounts for favors. Otherwise we had to buy it from the Polish people—at very high prices, I might add. The Polish people were not good to the Jews. If we asked them for help, they might turn us in. There were some good ones, but others were just as bad as the Germans.

"I could not bury my father when he died. You were not allowed to travel outside the ghetto, even to go to the cemetery. If you did go out in secret, the Poles would recognize you in the streets and tell the Germans. It was unbelievable what these people did. The Poles and the Jews had lived together for a thousand years, and now they turned against us terribly. I had two brothers who were shot by the Poles. I tried myself to get help from old Polish friends; I wanted them to help me get out of the ghetto, but they would not do it."

So, Kooper continues, events got worse with time. And one reason was that the Germans kept reducing the size of the ghetto. The Nazis would move people out of a sector and put up a new wall, and the Jews would have to relocate and consolidate within the shrinking boundaries. Kooper says the population was also reduced over the months, because of the dying and because large numbers of the Jews were ordered to move to outlying camps such as one in the obscure village of Treblinka.

"We did not at first understand why they were sending the people to Treblinka. When they started doing that, they forced the people to write letters saying that they were happy with the place over there. We did not know the truth until some people came back from Treblinka and little by little, conversation by conversation, we found out what was happening. Can you imagine our horror! To learn about the gas chambers and the slaughter. I had a sister go to Treblinka. Others had entire families. We were dumbfounded—I cannot express it—there was total disbelief.

"I remember watching some of the people march off to the camp before we knew about the gas chambers. I remember watching a group of children, for example. There was this man in the ghetto named Janusz Korczak, he was a well-known doctor who took care of many homeless children. I'm sure you've heard of him. He was very heroic. Then the Germans took the whole lot of them to Treblinka one day; they walked right down the street before my eyes. I thought they were maybe going to a better place; as it turned out, they were all murdered—innocent children.

"We were all very frightened when we found out about Treblinka. I was particularly frightened when I learned they were coming to take me to the camp. I was working as a chemist in a factory, and they came into that factory to take everybody to Treblinka. Luckily, I was able to escape in the confusion. They fired several shots after me, but they didn't hit me, and I hid myself on a roof where I couldn't be seen. It was January, and I was freezing, but I was afraid to come down from the roof. Not for a long time. I did not want to die.

"I thought about leaving the ghetto then and going somewhere they would never find me. That's when I asked my old Polish friends for a little assistance. It was a useless dream, however. No one could really escape the ghetto. We did not have papers; we did not have money; and both the Poles and the Germans would shoot us on sight. The truth was I was trapped—or we all were trapped. We knew by then the Germans did not intend to let us live normal lives again; we could only die from hunger or of sickness in one of the camps.

"That is what led to the Warsaw Ghetto uprising early in 1943. Up to that time we had not fought back very much against the Germans around us. Some people have said that we did not resist at all. I have a son who once wrote a paper on the subject at college, and he came to that conclusion too. I disagree; we did resist all along, but not necessarily with guns. We resisted with disobedience. When they told us we could not educate our children we did it anyway, and when they banned religious services we held them just the same.

"We always had the underground. We had men and women organizing against the Germans. When the underground found out about Treblinka, they decided to strike back once and for all. There was no longer anything to lose, and everybody thought it would be better to take a life for a life rather than simply die for nothing. There were about sixty thousand Jews remaining in the ghetto at the time. I have to say I did not help with the uprising, I was still in hiding from the German soldiers; but I was there when the activity took place."

The activity was planned by a group known as the Jewish Fighting Organization. They built bunkers inside the ghetto, gathered a few dozen rifles and pistols, and plotted escape routes through the sewage tunnels. The JFO initiated the uprising by assassinating Jewish traitors who worked for the Nazis, and they staged attacks on the Germans over a period of four months. The Jews fought with small arms, Molotov cocktails, pickaxes, and stones; the Germans fought back with hand grenades and machine-gun fire.

It's fair to recall that non-Jewish Poles sent at least fifty revolvers to the ghetto fighters. The nationals were not entirely antisemitic. But the Jews could not in any event match the German muscle. The Nazis surrounded the ghetto on April 19, flushed the inhabitants out with flamethrowers, set the streets on fire, flooded the underground escape avenues, and leveled building after building with tank artillery. One month later, Nazi General Juergen Stroop notified Berlin that "The former Jewish quarter of Warsaw is no longer in existence."

Kooper says he saw some of the worst fighting during the uprising. "The noise. The explosions. There were fires and we choked in the smoke." He says he escaped after ten ravaging days. He says the ghetto was more or less divided in two at the time; there was a large section where most of the fighting took place and a smaller area that was more peaceful. The two ghettos were connected by sewers, so Kooper fled that way, one to the other and after that, before all the sewers were blocked, he left Warsaw entirely and took refuge in the forests.

"We became partisans in the woods. We had organizations and leaders; we didn't have many guns, but we could fight back. We sabotaged what we could. We were close to a railway track, for example, which carried German supplies, and we disconnected the track whenever we could. That made them angry, of course. They hunted us day and night. But we knew the woods better than they did, so we protected ourselves by moving around. Still, it was very frightening there. We could see the Germans searching.

"I must tell you that from that time I have hated tree leaves. In the night, when the leaves fell, it was like someone walking. When we were on guard, it was always as if the Germans were all around, sneaking up on us, ready to open fire. It was only the sound of the leaves, we all knew that, but one could never be absolutely certain. I have always hated leaves since then. I do not like to walk in them when they fall, even in my yard.

"I stayed in the forest for eighteen months, until 1945, when the Russians came into Poland. That was our liberation. They came through the forests, and we met them there, and at first they did not believe we were Jews. They thought we were spies. That would have been terrible, yes? To live through the Germans and to be executed by the Russians. But we convinced them. I remember I did not even have a shirt to wear. I had to get one from the Red Cross. But the war was over for us. We could be human beings once again.

"I went to Treblinka later. I wanted to see for myself. I could still hear Adolf Hitler on the radio, I could still hear the Germans marching, and here was all this horror at the camp. The bodies had been removed, but other things were still there. The shoes, the hairbrushes, the personal items. All this in the camp. I was sick afterward. Over 700,000 Jews were killed there, maybe more. Some of them belonged to my family. I lost at least eighty-five close relatives during the war. Of my immediate family, only myself and a brother lived."

Kooper went to England after the war to work in the chemical industry. He decided at that time never to return to Poland, and he never has. Kooper migrated to the United States during the 1950s. He wanted to continue selling chemicals, but he did not have the money to get started in the business. ("I think I had five dollars in my pocket when I got off the plane.") So he became a salesman for a lingerie establishment, and when he learned this new trade he started a competing company of his own. The company did well. Kooper became a well-known international designer. He was called the King of the Crinoline.

He lives now in an upscale section of Forest Hills, a neighborhood of New York City. He is a dapper man, white belt and shoes, who combs what is left of his silver hair across partially barren ground. He is married to a slim and attractive woman who looks a little like Mary Martin. They have a winter home in Florida and are worth more than a million dollars.

How the Nazis would hate it.

And James Drummond, for that matter.

"I do not sleep well," Kooper concludes. "When I was in the forest, on the ground, I slept like a baby. Now I have a bed, king-size, and some nights all I do is close my eyes. I cannot forget. It will always be. That I'm alive is a miracle."

In 1979 the President's Commission on the Holocaust reported that the civilian carnage during World War II "was not a throwback to medieval torture or archaic barbarism, but a thoroughly modern expression of bureaucratic organization, industrial management, scientific achievement, and technological sophistication." The entire apparatus of the German bureaucracy was marshaled in the service of the extermination process.

The churches and health ministries supplied birth records to define and isolate Jews; the post offices delivered statements of definition, expropriation, denaturalization, and deportation; the economic ministry confiscated Jewish wealth and property; the universities denied Jewish students admission and degrees while dismissing Jewish faculty; German industry fired Jewish workers, officers . . . and disenfranchised Jewish stockholders; government travel bureaus coordinated schedules for the railroads that carried the victims to their deaths.

"The location and operation of the camps were based on calculations and accessibility and cost-effectiveness, the trademarks of modern business practice. German corporations actually profited from the industry of death. Pharmaceutical firms, unrestricted by fear of side effects, tested drugs on camp inmates, and companies competed on contracts to build ovens or supply gas for extermination. (Indeed, they were even concerned with protecting the patents for their products.) German engineers working for Topf and Sons supplied one camp alone with 46 ovens capable of burning 500 bodies an hour.

"Adjacent to the extermination camp at Auschwitz was a privately opened, corporately sponsored concentration camp called I. G. Auschwitz, a division of I. G. Farben. This multidimensional petrochemical complex brought human slavery to its ultimate perfection by reducing human beings to consumable raw materials, from which all mineral life was systematically drained before the bodies were recycled into the Nazi war economy; gold teeth for the treasury, hair for mattresses, ashes for fertilizer.

"In their relentless search for the least expensive and most efficient means of extermination, German scientists experimented with a variety of gases until they discovered the insecticide Zyklon B, which could kill 2000 persons in less than 30 minutes at a cost of one-half cent per body. Near the end of the war, in order to cut expenses and save gas, 'cost accountant considerations' led to an order to place living children directly in the ovens or . . . into open burning pits."

BROOKE JOHNS, *continued*

Brooke Johns again. Like Al Kooper, the old vaudevillian has retired into genteel elegance. Unlike Kooper, he did not suffer to get there. He has led a charmed life; he has had every success; he has never wanted for anything, not food, not money, not security; and now he lives in a seventeen-room mansion on the edge of the capital. He says he left show business in 1930, still a relatively young man, because it was changing and because he did not want to become a "hanger-on or a used-to-be-good." He says he bought 200 acres in the Washington countryside for $46,000 and turned it into a riding stable and then into a golf and country club, where he has lived as a reasonably celebrated squire. He says he has 150 chickens, 120 neckties, 61 years of marriage, and that the property is now worth $15 million.

"I don't know why some people are lucky and others are not. I wish it weren't so, but it is. It's certain that God has been very good to me. I never finished school, but it didn't matter. I served in the military during World War I, but all I did was entertain. Think of it. I have had a life full of glamour and gratification. And I didn't even have all that much talent. Girls, there were so many girls, and great moments; I introduced a lot of songs in this country, you know. I was the first one to sing 'I'm Just Wild About Harry' and 'Yes! We Have No Bananas.'

"One night during the 1922 Follies, after the show, I was sitting at Lindy's restaurant with Cole Porter and we were hashing everything over. Then he took out a piece of paper and wrote down a few bars of music. He handed it to me and said, 'Why don't you take this home and think up some lyrics?' So I did, and the number turned out to be "I'm in Love Again." Remember that? *Da, da, da-da-da.* 'I'm in love again, And my heartstrings are strummin', I'm in love again, and the tune I'm a-humming, Is the huddle-up, cuddle-up blues.'

"They called me The Bishop of Broadway. The English called me The Yankee Prince. And I'm proud to say I did not prostitute myself once. I didn't ride coattails, I didn't use anyone, and I didn't get down in the dirt like so many people do today. That was important. Entertainers did not use to have a very good image. One time I spoke to the Kiwanians in St. Louis before a show, and I said, 'Fellows, I've come to town to entertain, and just to entertain. I won't vamp any man's wife. You can attend with no worries.' "

The Johns mansion sits on a hill that overlooks the Maryland suburbs. He rolls around the living room in a wheelchair he inherited from a 1986 stroke. He keeps scrapbooks, copies of RCA Victor sheet music, and a billboard from 1926. The billboard says Stanley and Birnes would introduce a show at New York City's Keith Theater, followed by Robert Kean and Claire Whitney, Joe Frisco, Brooke Johns and Goodee Montgomery, a "few minutes with Jack Benny," and, last, Miss Nora Bayes. "Do you see that?" The old man grins. "I was before Benny. He was not very big then."

Johns says he still plays the banjo when his bones cooperate. He cut a record—a 33, to be sure—in 1981. Old favorites, to be sure: "Shine on, Harvest Moon," "Me and My Shadow," and "Ma (She's Making Eyes at Me)."

Ma, she's making eyes at me.
Ma, she's awful nice to me.
Ma, she's almost breaking my heart
I'm beside her,
Mercy let her conscience guide her.
Ma, she wants to marry me.
Be my honey bee.
Every minute she gets bolder,
Now her head is on my shoulder.
Ma, she's kissing me!

The record spins on. The maid comes through with the vacuum. The phone in the big house goes unanswered.

"You know what I want to do?" Johns says, water in the eyes now. "I want to live long enough to see it all come back again. All the songs, all the guys and the girls. Maybe in the next century. I'd be a hundred and seven then. Whatta ya think? I've been very fortunate so far."

2. Civic Affairs

MARGARET CHASE SMITH

When Margaret Chase fell in love with Clyde Smith in the 1920s, she had not given much notice to government. She was a thin, flinty, small-town business-woman in the backwoods of Maine with no particular politics except for seat-of-the-pants opinions on, well, "this and that, you know, taxes and local elections." She had been born before women's suffrage but had not joined the struggle for equality. She watched some of her high school classmates march off to their fate in World War I, but she did not wonder about the civil meanings of the exodus. She visited Washington, D.C., once, where she shook hands with Woodrow Wilson, explored the White House, and walked on Pennsylvania Avenue, and stood by the Washington Monument, read the inscription on the Lincoln Memorial, and wandered around the Capitol Building, which was a curious place, full of statues and smelling of oiled floors; yet, still, Miss Chase had only passing interest in the ruling system until she met Mr. Smith.

"He was older than me," she says, "by some twenty years, and he became the United States congressman from my district. So, naturally, a whole new world opened up. I met him three or four years before we were married, and during that courtship I started helping him campaign for various elections. He held state offices at first, and I always say that I campaigned with him, rather than for him, because that's how it was. I went around visiting people and talking with them, just as he did. I never thought of running on my own; it never crossed my mind, but I suppose I was learning how to do it. When he won the House seat, in 1937, I went to Washington with him as both his wife and assistant. When he died, in 1940, I was selected to complete his term in office."

Government. Margaret Chase Smith went from total disinterest in the process to complete absorption. And in so doing she joined a transmogrifying drift of her times. Politics have been seized by popularity in the 1900s. Government was formed by the few in the 1700s and dominated by the few for the next hundred years, but the intimacy was not to last. The rank and file have become increasingly involved since the turn of the century, kicking and screaming perhaps, yet there it is: public opinion now rules.

It rules and rules, in fact. The functions of government have at least grown apace with the interest in them. When Mrs. Smith visited the White House as a girl, the federal system was just emerging from institutional adolescence. Government was small in scope and reserved. Laissez-faire was still given currency. Congress met for as few as six months of the year, social welfare spending amounted to $5 million annually, an even dozen places had been designated as national parks, and 155,000 people served in the military.

Then, whoosh! The people decided the lawmakers should assume larger responsibilities in keeping with need, populism, and progress, and government in the United States became the most extensive in the history of the world. Ten thousand pieces of legislation were introduced in Congress in 1985-1986, and 663 became public laws. One-point-six billion units of mail passed through Washington post offices in 1987, and, at this writing, there are more than 300 national parks, battlefields, historic sites, and other set-asides. Five thousand journalists follow the activities in Washington, as do an estimated 15,000 to 20,000 registered lobbyists, and there are twenty-seven columns of leagues, councils, and associations in the telephone directory. The majority vote is no longer just the rhetoric of participatory civics; it has turned into a god.

Thomas P. (Tip) O'Neill puts it another way. He is a former speaker of the United States House of Representatives who has often been both praised and castigated for helping engineer the growth of government. He says that when he entered public life, in the 1930s, half the people in the nation were living in poverty. Twenty-five percent of the workforce was unemployed, and things were not much better for those who had jobs. The police, he says, worked twelve hours a day, eighty-four hours a week, and firemen were on duty for longer than that. For most Americans the workweek was six days, pensions were scarce, social security was unknown, "and there were two classes of people, the rich and the poor"—far more of the last group than the first.

O'Neill claims the government expansion changed that. Margaret Chase Smith will disagree. At any rate, there's no arguing the government's twentieth-century activism. It has been fertile and expensive. The federal system employed 239,000 civilians in 1901, a figure that grew to 3.8 million during World War II. Congress had 447 members and 3000 employees at the turn of the century; now there are 535 and 20,000 respectively. In 1985, a presidential commission reported that the federal bureaucracy had become so large and entangled that it *took as many as sixty people to draft, clear, and handle a single piece of postal correspondence in some departments, and even so the delay in processing the letter was forty-seven days on average.*

As for the expense, the 1901 budget ($524 million) would not buy a fully equipped aircraft carrier in 1988. Furthermore, the $524 million is one-sixth what it costs to run, say, the Railroad Retirement Board for a year, one three-thousandth of the annual deficit in the mid-1980s, and, all in all, it would fit into the 1988 budget almost two thousand times. The Department of Defense alone has spent more than $2 trillion in the 1980s. The bureaucrats who conduct postmortem poultry inspections spend $300 million annually. The United States public debt was thirteen digits into the red as of 1985, the total government liabilities as of 1988 were $14 trillion, and the boggling estimate is that by the year 2000 the federals will be spending almost $5 billion every day.

O'Neill says all this translates into public assistance. That means laws. The Guinness Book of World Records *says the United States of the 1980s has 15.2 million federal, state, and local laws, which may be more than the rest of the nations combined. The* Federal Register *is the government's official record of its regulations. It did not exist when the century started, but it would come to be published five days a week. In 1985 the* Register *printed 50,000 pages of government regulations and presidential documents, enough to stretch around the Capitol dome 4000 times. The magazine* U.S. News & World Report *once offered a terse summary of the phenomenon; it said the legions in Washington have issued several hundred regulations on making a hamburger.*

Thus Maggie Smith, a Republican, differs with Tip O'Neill, a Democrat. She says that, once burgeoning, government got its fingers so deeply into the public pocket it decided to feel all over. She goes on to say that the result is arrogance and abandonment. Particularly in Congress. United States legislators have raised their annual pay from $10,000 in the 1940s to $89,500 in 1986. The total cost of legislating has increased from $20 million to $1.6 billion a year. And arrogance? In 1986, the House of Representatives wrote a tax reform bill that was later rejected; rather than throw it out with the garbage, however, Congress ordered the Government Printing Office to draw a line through each word in the document and print 4500 copies of the crossouts.

Mrs. Smith:

"I did not go to Congress to be a burden on the people. I did not go to abuse my office. I went to help wherever I could. I believe Americans should help one another; that was the way I was raised. My parents were very decent people, with good values. My father was a barber for a long time, and then later he was a caretaker. My mother did special stitching at a shoe factory, which was a very good position in those days. So you see everyone had a part. We all pitched in. When I was twelve years old I went to a five-and-dime store and asked for a job as a clerk. The owner said he'd hire me when I was big enough to reach the tops of his shelves. I went back the next year, when I was thirteen, and big enough, and I've been working ever since.

"I was also a telephone operator when I was a young girl. I was a junior in high school then. The night operator wanted some time off, so she asked if I wanted the job. I said yes I did, because the pay was ten cents an hour. That was when we had crank phones in Maine, and all calls went through the operator. I liked it very much because I could keep up on everything that was going on. I knew who was talking to who, and who wasn't. People would ring me up and say, 'Margaret, get me So-and-So.' Or they'd ask if I knew where So-and-So was. It was great fun, and I came to know everyone's number by heart. I still remember some of the numbers. John Griffith, an insurance man, his number was 31.

"In 1919, I started working on my hometown newspaper. I wrote a little and I worked in the circulation department. I didn't editorialize, though. I belonged to several civic organizations—I was a girl about town—but I did not worry then about the great issues. I was born in 1897, which means I became an adult before women were given the vote, and I remember the campaign to get it, but I didn't participate. I didn't think about it, really. I didn't think I was deprived in any way. I was very active in the community, and I had never been held back because I was a woman, and I wasn't a demonstrative person anyway, so I would not march or carry a sign or get involved that way.

"The other thing is I always thought I was just as good as a man. When I went to Congress I went as a representative, not as a female representative, but just a representative. That doesn't mean I wasn't proud to be a woman, and I was happy to accomplish things as a woman, but I've always felt that women are people. I emphasize it in everything I do. And as far as politics were concerned, I just couldn't separate the sexes. I felt I was elected to serve all of the people, both men and women, and I felt the issues for men and women were the same. War, for example, affects women just as much as men, perhaps even more when you consider that they can lose both husbands and sons.

"So when I was in Congress I expected to be treated like anyone else. I was one of three women in the House in 1940, but I refused to be treated like a woman. I didn't think anything was owed to me because I was a woman. I didn't think I lent anything special to the legislature because I was a woman. Again, I just thought I was a person, a citizen, an American. I demanded everything that I was entitled to as an elected officer, but nothing else. I did not use gender to get any special favors, and I never had any special favors. I did not get them in the House; I did not get them when I went over to the Senate. I was just another one of the members; I insisted on it.

"Now, I didn't forget I was a woman. My trademark, you know, was a red rose. It still is. I have lots of stories about the rose. There was one time, for example, when someone sent a yellow rose every day to my office in Washington. He sent it every morning for twenty-four mornings, and it started everyone talking. No one knew who it was at first. Then *Time* magazine came out and said I had a secret admirer and I was preparing to get married, and the proof was the yellow roses. Later I found out that the roses had come from an automobile dealer downtown; I had befriended and given help to his brother, and he took this way to express his thanks. A very nice way it was, too.

"I wore a rose to every congressional session. I started because I always dressed in suits on the floor, and a rose brightened them up. I introduced legislation to make the rose the national flower at one point, and, if you remember, Senator Everett Dirksen used to introduce legislation to make the marigold the national flower. When John Kennedy was assassinated, Mike Mansfield asked me if I would put a rose on his old desk, and I did. Then when Everett Dirksen died, they asked me if I would do the same thing in his memory. I said I didn't think Senator Dirksen liked roses. So they gave me a marigold, and I put that on his desk. He was a lovely man. The rose, of course, has since become the national flower."

Mrs. Smith spent eight years in the House before changing over to the Senate in 1948. That made her the first woman in history to win elections to both bodies, and she was well on her way to defining parameters of the philosophic territory for which she would become internationally noted: a strong national defense (she introduced legislation to create regular military status for women), a devotion to duty (she would go on to answer 2941 consecutive Senate roll-calls), and resolute integrity.

The integrity would take a dramatic place in history, in 1950. That was a time when Wisconsin Senator Joseph McCarthy held center stage on Capitol Hill, railing against real and imagined Communists in government. McCarthy was a Republican who wrestled with a meat cleaver. No one in the Grand Old Party wanted to tangle with the man whose merest accusation might decapitate a career. Except Margaret Smith, the lady from Maine:

"I had taken all I could from that man and his kind. He was attacking anyone he wanted, and doing it with impunity. He was destroying good people, and he was destroying my idea of American justice. You could hardly go to lunch without fearing that he would get on the floor and denounce you as the newest Communist in Washington. He was a ruthless, ruthless man. He was underhanded and sinister and of course he had congressional immunity. He could say whatever he wanted on the floor and did not have to answer for it. He was a terrible person. I remember the day I spoke against him. I saw him earlier, and he said in his nasal voice: 'Margaret, you look like you've got something on your mind.' I said, 'Yes, Joe. I'm going to make a speech and I don't think you'll like it.'

"When I got to the floor I let him have it. I said, 'Mr. President, I would like to speak briefly and simply about a serious national condition. It is a national feeling of fear and frustration that could result in national suicide and the end of everything that we Americans hold dear. . . . I speak as a Republican. I speak as a woman. I speak as a United States senator. I speak as an American. . . . The American people are sick and tired of seeing innocent people smeared and guilty people whitewashed. . . . I don't want to see the Republican Party ride to political victory on the four horsemen of calumny—fear, ignorance, bigotry, and smear.' The speech took five minutes. I was nervous. I did not mention McCarthy directly. But I think the speech was the first step on the road to his censure."

The speech became known as the Declaration of Conscience. It set Senator Smith's reputation in stone. It likewise subjected her to the heat that follows the light of notoriety. She was immediately condemned for disloyalty by the hard right, she was then belittled by the progressive left for having intellectual limits (she once said John Kennedy was too timid to use nuclear weapons), and much was to be made of her personality and habits.

At length the critics said she was a political loose brick. Her colleagues in Congress denounced her refusal to bend with the realities on important issues. She refused to accept invitations to social events in Washington; she could not suffer the pomp and circumstance of her office; she liked to eat cream cheese sandwiches at her desk (it was a way to avoid the blowhards in the Senate dining room); and she had the temerity to call members of the Senate a "bunch of prima donnas" and to introduce a bill that would have expelled any member who did not meet a minimum attendance record during rollcall votes.

Then there was her vulnerable personal life. She had a long, close, and controversial relationship with a younger man. She refers to him now and respectfully as Mr. Lewis. His full name was William C. Lewis. He was a one-time air force general who became her administrative assistant, the guiding hand of her career, and, some say, her lover as well. They were an item for twenty-four years, until his death in 1982. They traveled together, stayed in the same homes, and were in every way inseparable. She says she remembers traveling between Maine and Washington, time and again, always in an automobile, and he would say "Senator" (she says he always called her that), "Senator, get in the back seat and get some rest," because that's the way he was, helpful.

"Mr. Lewis was a fine man, and a brilliant one. I could not have got on as I did without him. He worked hard, he always gave me sound advice, and he was of course loyal. He had four college degrees; he had a military background; he was a lawyer for the Senate before he came on my staff. I know people thought we were in love—some even said we were secretly married, but that wasn't right. I can't explain our relationship, and I think now that maybe I was the only one in Washington who could have gotten away with it. But there is one thing to keep in mind. Mr. Lewis was fifteen years younger than I; that wouldn't have made a difference to most people wanting to marry, but it did to me."

She pauses to answer the telephone. She still gets several dozen calls a day.

"Now," she continues, "what were we talking about? Mr. Lewis. Yes. I wonder what we would have done if I had been president."

Mrs. Smith ran for the presidency in 1964. She was nominated at the Republican convention and was thus the first woman to be placed in nomination by a major party. She received twenty-seven votes, losing to Barry Goldwater.

"I can't say if I ever seriously thought I would be president. I made my decision very late; I didn't have any money or organization. I knew it was a long shot, but I thought I would make a good candidate. I had a good record, I knew the issues, I was a firm leader, I was always dependable, and people knew where I stood. I also demanded good people around me. That's why Mr. Lewis was always such a great asset, because he had a very fine mind. If I had become president, I would have surrounded myself with top-notch people who would be loyal. Loyalty would be the number-one requirement. Number two, they would be experts in their fields. I think that is the basis of a good presidency and a good administration: excellent people.

"Lyndon Johnson won that election, of course. And I don't think he attracted the kind of advisers that he should have. Certainly not on the war in Vietnam. There's no question that he made fatal errors there, and it destroyed his presidency. I don't think I would have made the same errors. I knew how the French had floundered in that part of the world. I would have called in the reservists, myself, who were paid and trained for this sort of thing, and I would have sent them over to clean it up. If that would not have worked, I would then have pulled out. There is no point in fighting a losing battle. Johnson was stubborn, he was his own worst enemy; he tried to insist on winning.

"I would also have done other things different from Johnson. I don't think I would have tried to create what he called a Great Society. I would have tried to restructure the welfare system in another way, as part of an overall restructuring of the bureaucracy. I would like to have had a study made of the Hoover Commission recommendations for the reorganization of government. I think we would have been able to use the recommendations to our benefit. We could have taken one federal agency at a time, reorganized, cut out the deadwood, and cut everything down to a manageable size. I would have liked to have seen Dwight Eisenhower do that earlier; he could do no wrong in the nation.

"I think I would have made a good president. I certainly don't think a woman could be any worse than the men. I stood for very important matters. I wanted to reduce taxes, balance the budget, fight communism, create a more realistic balance between management and labor, do something positive about civil rights, build bipartisan foreign relations. Most of all, I wanted to convince people that we can't expect something for nothing in this world. That is part of my lifelong belief. People today, they seem to have lost part of their will. They are confused and frustrated, so a lot of them are shrugging their shoulders and letting other people take care of things.

"I'm talking about politics here. People have become frustrated with it, and it's easy to see why. Look at what's gone on in the last few years alone. I think Richard Nixon was one of the most knowledgeable men we ever had in the presidency, and what did he do with his opportunity? He ruined himself and ruined the whole image of government. It wasn't for money. It was for power and popularity. He was a great McCarthyite, of course, so I was never fond of him. I never thought he could be trusted. And that was his downfall. He had everything—he had family, he had position, he had money—but he couldn't be trusted. And after him we had Gerald Ford. I was troubled by that man too.

"I had great hope for Ronald Reagan. But he got stuck as well in the question of trust. And I think the same thing goes for the Senate. I'm still very critical of the Senate. I think the leadership is weak; I think the quality of the members has deteriorated. I try to keep faith in the system, but I lose confidence when the members simply do not do the job for which they were elected. They are out making speeches and shaking hands, and that's wrong. When I ran for president I tried to prove that you can do that and still do your job. I kept right on working in the Senate. I had a commitment to carry out my responsibility and I wish—I think the American people wish—we had more of that today."

Margaret Smith (now rarely called Maggie) remained in the Senate until 1972. She never wavered in her dedication to governmental scruples and self-initiative. And even her political opponents came to compliment her personal stuff. John Stennis is one of the opponents. He is the octogenarian Democrat from Mississippi who has made a career out of various forms of chauvinism. He said a few years ago that until Smith came along he did not want women in Congress. That is high praise from him. "You didn't take Mrs. Smith for granted," he told a reporter for The Washington Post, *"and no one controlled her.*

We tended to treat her as a man, without ceasing to treat her as a woman."

Still, her time passed. In 1972 she was seventy-five years old; she had served thirty-two years in the Capitol; she had worked with or under a half-dozen presidents; and when she tried to win a seventh term in the legislature she was accused of being too old, over the hill, out of touch, a dinosaur, and she was roundly defeated. Correction: not really roundly, more like decisively; she lost by 27,000 votes and did not so much as carry her home town.

"The press said I was very bitter about that. But that's not true. Actually, I did not even want to run that last time. I had been in the Senate for four terms and I wanted to do something else—do some writing, for example. I was disappointed, yes, but not bitter. There were stories that I locked myself behind my doors to weep. That was nonsense. I left office in 1973, when the new Congress began, and I can't say I've ever missed it. I did what I could while I was there; I think I did some good. And, really, I wasn't bitter about losing, that's the democratic way. I'm content, I think. I have no regrets."

She is in her early nineties. She lives high over the Kennebunk River in Skowhegan, Maine (which she pronounces "Skaahagan"), where she continues to cultivate roses. She fell and broke an arm several years ago. She has bluing in her hair. She reads correspondence with a magnifying glass. Neat, prim, very New England, very Republican, very institutional. She lifts her chin when she talks. On second thought, she says, she does have one regret:

"I only spent fourteen thousand dollars on that 1972 campaign. I wish that I would have spent more. I think I would have won if I did."

According to federal election statistics, the average United States Senate re-election campaign cost $3 million in 1986. That means that incumbents serious about retaining their jobs have to raise a minimum of $1350 a day, $10,000 a week, $40,000 a month—half a million dollars each year they are in office. One re-election in 1986 cost $7 million. The total amount spent on Senate and House campaigns that year was $400 million, just short of all tax revenues raised by the United States in 1900.

EARLE MUNN

When Margaret Chase Smith ran for the presidency in 1964 she never got beyond her party's nominating convention; hence her candidacy was at best brief.

Dr. Earle Harold Munn, Sr., however, was chosen to be the standard-bearer for his party that year, and he went on to make something of an avocation out of the quadrennial elections. Munn ran against Barry Goldwater and Lyndon Johnson in 1964; he squared off with Richard Nixon and Hubert Humphrey in 1968; and, finally, he opposed Nixon and George McGovern the year Mrs. Smith was retired from the Senate. He was of course a minority-party candidate in each of those years but he nonetheless received as many as 23,000 votes in the campaigns and thereby typifies something very American about the twentieth century: the notion that if it might not really be correct that anyone can become president of the United States, it is certain that anyone can try.

"I was sixty-one years old when I campaigned the first time. I thought that was a good age to be president. I was also a college executive, which provided me with administerial experience, and I still think to this day that I was on the right side of the issues. I had planks in my platform about containing government and on sociological problems in the nation. I had ideas on various educational matters, and on the principles of morality and teaching that you will find in the Bible. I think I had twenty-two main issues that I addressed. Maybe more. But the issue of drinking was the largest plank in the platform."

The issue of drinking, indeed. Dr. Munn is a longtime member of and representative for the political organization that, as it claims, offers "life at its best," the venerable and seemingly indefatigable Prohibition Party. It was organized in 1869 in the state that was later to christen the battleship Kansas with a bottle of spring water, and it remains today the third-oldest party in the nation. The Democrats and Republicans are larger, the Socialists and Communists are better known, and the Libertarians get more votes. Yet Dr. Munn says the Prohibitionists would rather be right than popular—or in power, as it were—and they continue to believe their time will come.

Actually, their time has already come at least a couple of times. The Prohibitionists were originally organized as a party of radical ideas; they supported woman's suffrage in 1872; they were in favor of social security fifty years before the fact; and they had considerable influence at the turn of the century. Dr. Munn says Prohibitionists held thousands of local offices in the 1800s, and several seats in Congress, and that's when they started campaigning for the Oval Office. The first Prohibition candidate only received 5000 votes, running against Ulysses S. Grant, but by 1884 a man named John St. John got 150,000 votes and thereby tipped a close election to Grover Cleveland.

Yes, Dr. Munn says, there were the hurrahs. Carrie Nation was smashing taverns in the Midwest. Politicians were photographed pouring rum down the drains. And by the first decade of the twentieth century the party was pulling in as many as 250,000 presidential ballots. The Women's Christian Temperance Union was formed as an adjunct. The Anti-Saloon League of America came along. The Prohibitionists then began pressing for government restrictions on alcoholic beverages, and those efforts led to the passage of the Eighteenth Amendment to the Constitution and to the subsequent Volstead Act. Liquor was outlawed from coast to coast for fourteen years, a period when Earle Munn was forming his political conceptions.

"It was a good law. It was ignored too much, and the smuggling and the crime was regrettable, but I was happy with it; my family was happy. I was born in Ohio, and I will say that my father was a virtuous man, he had high principles, and he always voted the straight Prohibition ticket. That's how I began to favor the party as well. I didn't think about it too much as a youngster, but I began to think about it upon graduation from college. I became convinced that drinking was a curse. It drove men from their families; it led to dishonesty and criminal activity; and it was contrary to my religious views. I didn't think that God wanted us to go around drunk and disorderly."

Munn got out of school in 1925. He says he began voting for Prohibitionists ten years later, or sometime after the teetotlers had dropped their designs for radical change. The nineteenth century party of universal unionization and internationl arbitration (that is: One World) had gradually became the twentieth century party of rigid construction and moralistic conformity. The Prohibitionists gave up their support of income tax, for example, to lobby instead for decentralized government, and they were to suffer for it. They lost the liberal vote and were never subsequently able to interest many conservatives.

The party held on to some strength until it became clear that the jewel in its crown, the Eighteenth Amendment, was also sinking, and from there on it disappeared from influential politics. The Prohibition candidate in 1936 drew 37,000 votes, half that of the Communist Party nominee, and there was no recovery. The most votes Dr. E. Munn was to receive was 23,267, in 1964.

"We had our convention in Chicago that year. And my nomination was the end result of a good many years of working for the party. I got into it very strongly in the late 1930s, when Prohibitionists were tussling, trying to recover from the repeal of the Eighteenth Amendment. I joined the staff of Hillsdale College in Michigan, and I became very active in the prohibition work in my state. I then went on to break into the national program in the 1950s. I've held almost every office in the party, and I was the vice-presidential candidate in 1960 before moving along to the presidential nomination in 1964.

"It seems like such a long time ago. I can't even recall the name of my vice-presidential candidate. I think he was from Kansas. Then I think there was another man after that who was from Kansas too, and a third one from Massachusetts, I think. [In 1964 it was Mark Shaw from Massachusetts, in 1968 Rolland E. Fisher of Kansas, and in 1972 Marshal Inchapter of Kansas.] But I remember the campaigns. I conducted them the same as any candidate for that office, except I did not do it as much. I did not do a lot of traveling. I didn't have the time for it: I was holding down a full-time job at the college.

"One thing that should be kept in mind is that there were only certain places where it was profitable for me to go, anyway. The Prohibition Party is not on the ballot in most states. The Democrats and the Republicans have been very successful in squeezing us off the ballots in America. They've done it to other minority parties too. It used to be a simple process to get on the ballot, but the big parties don't want that any more. The only way a small party can get on the ballots in some states now is to go to court. And that's too expensive for the Prohibitionists. So the big parties go after all the votes, and we only go after a few. It's one reason we don't get very far.

"It's too bad. I think we have a lot to give to government. I think I had good ideas when I ran. And I tried to express them to as many people as possible. The Prohibition Party does not just believe in banning alcohol. We want that, yes, but we have a much broader program that we would like to implement. I told people when I campaigned that we want to totally restructure government. We think it's time that it was made to function better. We want to make it more Christian and less costly. I believe we could do that, and I think many people want it done. I don't think people want to be told what to do by Washington all of the time, and I would have tried to change that."

Dr. Munn won a total of 51,000 votes during his decade of campaigning. He also received some notoriety, principally in brief television appearances and tongue-in-cheek newspaper articles. The last time around he finished behind Nixon, McGovern, John Schmitz of the American Independent Party, Linda Jeness of the Socialist Workers Party, Louis Fisher III of the Socialist Labor Party, and Gus Hall of the Communist Party. He says he never fooled himself about his chances, yet he admits to disappointment after a fashion. He says he wishes the Prohibition Party had more to show for its century of activity other than rectitude, of which there is no shortage.

"I'll explain about this. There have been times when people in the party have drifted to other views. One time was in 1932, just before the Eighteenth Amendment was repealed. The Republicans told us then that we should join them in the 1932 elections. The argument was that Herbert Hoover would fight repeal and Franklin Roosevelt would not. Well, I voted for Hoover so that we would be able to save the Amendment. And it turned out that I didn't save anything. Hoover lost, and the Eighteenth Amendment was canceled. So when I thought about what I had done, I decided that in the future I was going to work for what's right, and vote on principle, and stand for what I believe.

"And I've done that. So I don't get discouraged about the party, especially, because I know that we are at least doing what's right. I'm eighty-four years old now, and I've run for many offices. I ran for mayor of my little town, I ran for the governor of Michigan, and, oh, I don't know what all. I never won once. But I kept faith with my convictions. Too many politicians go with whatever way the wind is blowing. They go for the votes. The Prohibition Party is the only party in the nation that stands against immorality; it doesn't change and it doesn't modify. I have always been very proud to be one of its losing candidates."

Dr. Munn retired as dean of Hillsdale College in 1972. He now lives as a contemplative emeritus, where he still adheres to the straight and narrow.
Do you smoke, Dr. Munn?

"No."

Do you swear?

"No."

Can you anticipate the next question?

"As far as I know, I don't believe I have ever had a drink. I have a feeling that I was slipped one once or twice. I'm pretty sure that I attended one function one time where I was dosed with a spiked Coke. But I didn't know, and the general effect of it was that I'll never take part in something like that again."

Statistics compiled by the federal government indicate that 18 million Americans have serious drinking problems in the eighth decade of the century, and this abuse of the bottle costs the nation as much as $117 billion a year in lost productivity, medical bills, and related matters. The government says the per capita consumption of alcohol in 1984 was 2.65 gallons, half of it consumed by the 6.5 percent of adults who were considered big tipplers. Justice officials say a third of the criminals convicted of major legal offenses drink before committing their crimes; medical authorities say booze is implicated in one out of four suicides; and social workers believe 5 million adolescents drink to excess.

AGNES GEELAN

Presidents and senators. It's all very well to be fascinated by the stuff of federal government, but there has been a price to pay. Americans used to concentrate on matters closer to home than Washington—in the town meetings, for example, and in the gatherings of councils, selectmen, commissioners, aldermen, and state legislatures. State government, in other words. Local government. The mayor is the highest-ranking official most people will ever personally know. Municipal elections are in their own way more important than national elections. The city is responsible for trash removal, the county maintains the roads; people do not call Congress when the sewers are slow, they do not go to Capitol Hill to protest rezoning; and the FBI doesn't bother with crime on Elm Street.

Welcome to North Dakota. Home of Agnes Geelan, ninty-one. The first lady of the state's public affairs.

"I've heard that title. One thing about getting old is that people finally say nice things about you. I don't really think I'm the first anything, however. The only thing I've done is to get angry at things that needed to change. I started that as a young person, when I found out that women couldn't vote. I came of age in 1918, which was a year before suffrage on the national level. We were allowed to vote in state elections—women always had that right in North Dakota, even before statehood—but there were restrictions. Women could only vote for women candidates. Men could vote for either men or women, and I didn't like the discrimination. So I didn't go the polls in 1918, because I'd have had to ask for a special ballot. I was too proud. It was the only election I've ever missed."

Geelan says her regret is only natural in North Dakota. The people in the state take politics and government very seriously. It's one of their few diversions, after all. The place is stuck up tight against the Canadian border, where 650,000 residents are scattered over an area the size of all of New England and where three-quarters of the personal income is derived from working the land. The income is often substantial, to be sure. There are 40,000 farms in North Dakota, they produce most of the red spring wheat consumed in the nation, and they also rank high in the trading of barley, sunflower seed, sugar beets, rye, oats, hay, and potatoes. It is the most agriculturally oriented of the fifty states, and, as evidence, 51 percent of its people are rural.

It also has some hard history as evidence. That's one of the reason the politics are serious. Mrs. Geelan says North Dakota was physically devastated and politically sobered by the Great Depression. The state was pinched by falling farm prices long before Black Tuesday (October 29, 1929), and economic mis-

ery was compounded by searing drought and hoards of grasshoppers. The weak joke at the time was that once the grasshoppers devoured the crops, they started chewing on the houses. The joke: A farmer went to a hardware store to purchase hammers for two dollars apiece. He thereupon told the salesman that he was going to sell them for one dollar each to smash grasshoppers. "That's ridiculous," the salesman said. "Do you realize you will lose a dollar on each sale?" "Yes," the customer replied, "but it's better than farming."

Mrs. Geelan:

"It was always hard in North Dakota. Right from the start. People came here when it was nothing more than prairie, and they had to break their backs to make it more than that. For the most part, the state was settled by people taking advantage of the Homestead Act. That was the law that gave free land to anyone willing to live out here. A lot of those people were immigrants, and my ancestors, in fact, had come from Norway. My father was raised in Wisconsin and he came here for the land, riding in a covered wagon, in 1879. He was given a quarter of a section near Haddon, below Grand Forks; he grew wheat. I was one of ten children, two of whom died in infancy.

"Ours was not an immigrant family. My father had been born in this country. But we still acted like Norwegians. I could not speak English until I started school, and then I spoke with a thick accent. When I got in high school, I wanted to be on the debating team, because that was a big thing, so the coach told me I had to do something about my accent. My father had a livery stable, and the coach told him to give me the slowest horse he had, and I had to go out riding every afternoon and practice the *d*'s and the *w*'s, the *j*'s and the *y*'s, and to quit hitching my *s*'s. When I did it, I made the debating team.

"I did pretty well on that team. I suppose it was because I learned something about debating at home. My father was a Republican conservative, and I used to listen to him argue with my uncle, who was a progressive. My father was a wonderful fellow. He was the best loved man in our little town [Haddon], and he made coffee that caused your hair to stand up. He was a simple person—he never got rid of his Norwegian mannerisms, and he did not get further than the third grade in school. But he was very responsible, and very much involved. He was elected clerk of the school board at one time, with only a third grade education; oh, he was so proud of that.

"I did not take after my father politically, however. I came to be more like my uncle. I was an agitator, and I may have gotten that way because of the suffering I saw in those days. Everyone was very poor. We all had lice in our hair at school, for instance, and we had to wash it out with kerosene. Our clothes were old. Our books were worn. We had a tiny schoolhouse that I hated. It was so bad that if you dropped a pencil through a crack in the floor, the boys would have to crawl under the building to get it. We couldn't afford to lose so much as a pencil. There was no running water at school, either, just a pail, one pail, and we all drank from the same dirty cup."

Then the Depression. Mrs. Geelan says things went from bad to exceedingly bad. She had married by then, "to a red-faced Irish farmer named Elric," who like most others lost his job. Two-thirds of North Dakota's banks closed, and a third of the population went on welfare. Ninety thousand people sought relief by fleeing the state, and the average wage of those who stayed was cut in half or more. Mrs. Geelan says it was like an open wound. "If you thought it was bad for you, there were lots of people worse." She says the only way the people survived was to hang on to their faiths, share possessions with their neighbors, and insist on the philosophical revision of state politics.

That revision turned out to be socialism. Mrs. Geelan embraced it. She says progressivism spread from Fargo to the Montana boundary. Public ownership became the order of the time. The progressive Non-Partisan League rose from the fringes to be the most important political party and its standard bearer, the legendary William ("Wild Bill") Langer, was elected governor in 1932. Langer slapped an embargo on farm goods in an effort to raise prices. He ordered a moratorium on farm foreclosures to keep families in business. Wild Bill was a cantankerous brawler who often chewed cigars with the wrapper on, and he was forever deep in legal soup; but he served two intermittent terms in the state house and several in the United States Senate, and Agnes Geelan claims he was the most effective leader in North Dakota history:

"I was so impressed with Bill that I wrote a book about him, *The Dakota Maverick.* He did wonderful things. He went into office when there wasn't a red cent in the state, everybody was going broke, the land value dropped to zero, and I believe he saved agriculture in this state. He set up the state-run Bank of North Dakota so people wouldn't be at the mercy of the private institutions. He helped arrange for a state-owned mill operation. Some of these reforms are still in existence today. We have state hail insurance to protect crops; corporations are forbidden to own farms; and houses on farmland are exempt from property tax. I think he was a man who was ahead of his time.

"I did not appreciate him all that much at first. I was a Democrat back then, partly because my husband was a Democrat. I married Elric Geelan in 1926. The red-faced Irishman. He always told me that 'Agnes, you speak Norwegian, and you speak English, but you have never learned to say no.' He said that because I was a very active person. We lived in the small community of Enderlin, a railroad town, and I got involved in everything that went on. That's where I really got into public affairs. I was an officer with the Lady's Auxiliary of the Brotherhood of Railroad Trainmen, I was a national officer with the American Legion Auxiliary, and then I was elected mayor.

"I ran for mayor because I wanted to do something. Enderlin was in bad shape. It was either put up or shut up. I had complained to the school board, I had complained to the city council. We needed streets, we needed lighting, we needed a new water system. So, finally, people got together and said they wanted me to run for mayor in 1946. When I asked one of them why, he said, 'Agnes, you've bitched so much we are going to let you try it.' I thought it was crazy. Women didn't run for big offices. But I campaigned as hard as I could. I ran against a retired railroad man (I said he wasn't just 'retired,' he was plain 'tired') and when I won I became the first woman mayor in North Dakota.

"I stayed on as mayor until 1954. Some of the men in town used to worry about me at first, but I changed their minds. I promised hard-surfaced roads, I promised street lighting, and I promised a modern water system, and I made good on all of it. And remember, we did it ourselves at that time. We did not get any assistance from Washington, or any help from the state. Everything came from property taxes. But people did not want their taxes raised to pay for everything. I had to talk and talk and talk. I learned a good lesson; when I was in the state senate, later, I sponsored the first law in North Dakota that gave state aid to the cities.

"I'm getting ahead of myself. I didn't get to the state senate until after I ran for the United States Congress. That was in 1948. I had switched my allegiance from the Democrats to the Non-Partisan League, which hurt a little, because I wanted to stay a Democrat, but I then became the first woman in the state to be endorsed by a major party for a federal office. I did not win, but I tried. I got a hundred dollars from a labor organization, I borrowed four hundred more from a bank, and my husband and I campaigned all across the state. I got fifty thousand votes (I came in fourth), but I became very well known and I don't think many people have questioned women in politics here from that time on.

"Right after I lost that election, people said, All right, let's try for the state senate. And I ran from Ransom County. The man I ran against had been in office for fourteen years, but you know what I did, I visited every farm in the county, I visited every home in the largest communities, and I won by sixty-seven votes. I was the first woman elected to the state legislature. Don't think it was an almighty powerful honor, though. The state senate is not like the United States Congress. I did not have a secretary; I did not even have an office. We got a few dollars a day per diem, we had to use pay telephones, and there wasn't anything like free postage. I used penny postcards to contact my constituents.

"There is opportunity in the office, though. You do have some clout, and that is a compensation. I served in 1951 and again in 1953, and I worked on several ideas that I had. One of them was heavily criticized, but that's because it was at the wrong time. Do you remember those candy cigarettes that were popular among the children? I tried to get them outlawed in the state. I thought they were offensive, for one thing, and they encouraged real smoking later on. The press just killed me on that one. I got the heehaw from all across the country. I still think it was a good idea, however. If I introduced the bill today, with the changed attitude about smoking, I'd be a hero."

Mrs. Geelan left the Senate in 1954. She ran for Congress once again; she served eventually as commissioner of North Dakota's workmen's compensation board (another first); she was a delegate to the state's constitutional convention; and she has continued in party politics. She helped arrange the merger of the Non-Partisans with the Democrats, whereupon she became the second highest officer in the combined organization.

She says the merger may have been the most important event in modern state politics. Republicans were the traditional rulers in North Dakota. Now they have slipped almost out of sight. When the 1986 elections were completed, Agnes Geelan reminds, fairly glowing with delectation, the governor was a Democrat, the two senators were Democrats, the United States representative was a Democrat, and Democrats controlled the state legislature.

"Wow," she says.

Elric Geelan died in 1966. Mrs. Geelan now lives alone in an apartment building in Fargo, "eight steps from the ground floor" *behind a two-way security speaker on the door. She remains remarkably spirited. She looks younger than her age. She says she keeps her hands, her mind, and her feet moving:*

"It's been a long life. And not all of it political. May I say something else about Elric? I loved him very much. He was an Irishman, as I said, and I was born a Norwegian Methodist. He never asked me to convert to his religion, but I always knew that he wanted me to. So when he had his first stroke, I was worried he was dying, and I went to a priest to change over. I told the priest that I did not want to leave my old religion, and he said, well, I should think instead that I was bringing it with me. I liked that. I converted then, and do you know, Elric lived for six more years. He said he was that happy. I'm a Catholic to this day, I'm also still a socialist. Especially a socialist."

According to a survey taken by researchers at Rutgers University, there were 1157 women serving in state legislatures in 1986, 15.5 percent of the 7461 state legislative positions. The study indicated that the total had grown in each election since 1969, when the number of women serving was 301, or 4 percent of the total. New Hampshire had the largest proportion of women lawmakers, 138 of 424, or 32.5 percent; and Mississippi had the smallest, with four women among its 174 legislators, or 2.3 percent. Women held twenty-four of the 535 seats in the 100th Congress, or 4.5 percent. Fifty-eight percent of these women were Democrats.

RICHARD STROUT

Richard Strout has the look of a well-seasoned government officer. A diplomat, maybe, or a cabinet secretary. He has a benevolent deadpan, a distinguished mustache, and looks as if he came out of the egg in a necktie. Highbrow, too: it goes all the way over his head. He says he went to Harvard as a young man, and pronounces it with two double a's; and, of course, he thereafter went abroad. But politics? Yes, he has always been interested. Yet no, not as a participant. He says he never wanted to do anything except write. His mother was well read and his father was an English instructor, and so, appearances to the contrary, he went to Washington as a newspaper reporter, something Henry Ward Beecher once called "the schoolmaster of the common people," staying on duty for six decades, observing the tumult of rule and becoming part of it himself.

"The first time I went to the White House was in 1922. My mood was then of a young, bright-eyed boy, and there within touching distance was the President of the United States, Warren Harding. I was with a group of reporters in his office, in front of his desk, and everyone was asking him mean questions. He was standing in his plus fours, and he didn't know the answers to the questions. He was furthermore aware of his inadequacies, and he was pathetic. My thought was the American flag cracking in the breeze, the White House, Abraham Lincoln, and there I was with the President of the United States, and these mean, hateful newspapermen were asking him sharp questions. It was sobering. He said, 'Gentlemen, gentlemen, go easy on me. I just want to go out on the golf course today and shoot a round.'"

That was one side of it.
Here's another:

"Right after the Japanese bombed Pearl Harbor in 1940, Winston Churchill came to Washington to see Franklin Roosevelt. Churchill had been anxious for the United States to enter the war, and now he was here to discuss the mutual effort. I went to cover his press conference. He came in suddenly and started to take questions. I was in the back of the room and couldn't hear him. We shouted 'Stand up, stand up,' and so he stood up on a chair. We said 'That's better, that's better,' and he grinned. It was a marvelous time. All these newsmen surrounding this great man. The snarl in his voice when he said *Nazi*, the excitement and the glory of war, the fate of the free world, and all of that. He was such a commanding figure. I knew I was in the presence of one of the greatest men who ever lived."

Richard Strout started writing in Public School 129 in Cohoes, New York. He went on to the staff of the Harvard Crimson. *He majored in economics at college, but that was window dressing. He knew, as did Wendell Phillips, that twentieth-century America had become a nation of "government and morning newspapers," and he was eager, ooops, eaager, to record his view of it.*

He started in England; actually, it was the vogue of the day. He worked his way over on a grain ship, where he signed up with newspapers in Sheffield and in London. He was there for the first two years of the 1920s. He lived in a settlement house at first, then in a house once occupied by Charles Dickens. He earned from five to eight dollars a week, in British pounds sterling.

"I did not write anything then. I worked on the copy desk. I had to edit stories that other people wrote. That was all right, except they couldn't spell over there. The invented the language, but they had this problem spelling it. They spelled curb with a *k* and tire with a *y*. It was very difficult for me to read copy, ah, as ignorant as they were. But I became bilingual after a while. I'm kidding, of course. I love the way they do things in England. I used to go regularly to Westminster Palace, which is the legislative building there, and watch the proceedings in Parliament. That Dickens house is a museum now; I think they added my name to it when I left.

"At one time I wanted to write novels like Dickens. That was natural enough. But newspaper reporting also seemed a reasonable way to fulfillment. The status of the newsman was fairly low in those days, particularly in England, because the caste system was stronger than it is today. There were the aristocrats and there was everyone else, and newspaper people were everyone else. The pay was not so large . . . but we were sort of accepted as being necessary. You had to have journalists, you know. And some of them could become prominent. Churchill was a war correspondent for a while, and I had a boss, Basil Clark, who was also a war correspondent and a well-known gentleman.

"Basil Clark also wrote a lot from Ireland at that time, about the differences with Great Britain, and that's how I got a break in the business. I ran into

Harold Laski one day—he was a great British political scientist whom I had known at Harvard—and he suggested that I look into the situation in Ireland. He knew the lord mayor of Cork, who was a revolutionary who was in hiding at the time, and he gave me a letter of introduction. So I went to Ireland to interview the lord mayor, and just over the hill was a [soldier] patrol of British Black and Tans. Newsmen were not supposed to interview revolutionaries, it was treason; but I wrote five articles and I sailed for American to sell them.

"I sold them to the New York *Globe*. Then I wrote some other articles on a freelance basis. Finally, I applied in Boston for a regular job. Boston had ten or eleven newspapers, and I got offers from the Boston *Post* and from *The Christian Science Monitor*. I went with the *Post* at first; it had the biggest circulation of any paper in the country but it was also the worst newspaper in the country. My first assignment was to interview the parents of a little girl who had been run over by a truck. I didn't like it. I always wanted to write about government and world affairs, not about little girls run over by trucks. I quit after five days and went with the *Monitor*."

The Monitor *was fourteen years old in 1922. It had been established by Mary Baker Eddy, who also founded the Church of Christ, Scientist, headquartered in Boston. Strout says the newspaper did not ask him his religion (which is Unitarian), nor did it steer him any way editorially except that his writing language was to be morally acceptable. Strout says he was hired on a temporary basis, was dispatched immediately to Washington as a twenty-four-year-old cub, and stayed on the job daily for sixty-two years.*

It may be a record for the media big leagues. Warren Harding to Ronald Reagan. Teapot Dome to the Challenger space disaster. Typewriters had moving carriages when Strout went to the capital. Headlines were set with metal characters. There were 14,000 newspapers in the land, 2200 of them printed daily in English, and neither George Will nor Dan Rather had been born.

"Everything was different then. Congress did not meet all year around, and presidential elections were much shorter. When people held press conferences, they were intimate affairs. Today the president meets the press in an auditorium. The whole atmosphere was also different back then. There were only a few hundred reporters in Washington; we rode around in trolley cars rather than taxis; the town was not so busy; and there was less worry about security. We did not need elaborate credentials to get into Congress or the White House. There was a fence around the White House, but it was not so forbidding as it is now. We could actually walk freely in and out of the building.

"There was also more trust between the officials and the reporters. The newsmen were always after good stories, but it was all handled differently. During the Roosevelt administration, for example, there were two daily press conferences, one in the morning for the evening papers and another in the evening for the morning papers. Steve Early was the [presidential] press secretary then. I went to the evening press conferences. He would give us information and speak to us, and I might say 'Well, can we quote you on that?' Then he might say something like 'Yes, if you will do it in your own words.' There was trust, you understand; he knew we wouldn't betray him.

"I don't think we took ourselves so seriously, either. It was more informal. Calvin Coolidge only answered written questions from the press, and so, one time, we all got together and wrote down the same question. We wanted to know if he was going to run for re-election in 1928. So Coolidge looked at the first question and put it aside. Then he looked at the second and did the same thing. He went through all the slips of papers, I think there were a total of twelve, and on the last one he paused, read it to himself, and went on dryly: 'I have a question about the condition of the children in Poland.' We all smiled. He may have smiled too. And that concluded the press conference.

"Herbert Hoover was the first great man in my life. I thought he was going to be the greatest president we ever had. I met him when he was secretary of commerce. He had that old lousy building on Pennsylvania Avenue for a while, before he built the new Commerce building. We went into the building and up to his suite on the ninth floor, and we sat around a table with him. He had each of us ask our questions, and then he would remember all of the questions and answer them one by one. It was remarkable. 'As for your question, Mr. Strout, blah, blah, blah.' He did it perfectly. I always thought he had a great mind, and he did; of course, he also had some problems later on.

"I covered Hoover when he went to the opening of the first television broadcast between New York and Washington. Hoover was featured because of his responsibilities for commerce. They put a camera on him, and they said people in New York could see his figure on a screen about the size of a postcard. They also brought in a comedian, or something, to do an act. I had Hoover sign a copy of his remarks at the opening. My wife Ernestine always likes to remind me of that first television. She saved a clipping on the broadcast from *The New York Times*. The headline on the clipping mentions the broadcast, and then there was a subhead saying 'Commercial Use in Doubt.' "

Strout says he had his own opinions about the television spectacle but he did not write them. He was a straightaway reporter at the time, and he was not permitted to stray from the who, what, when, why, and how of public affairs.

He had an editorialist's eye for the substance of a matter, however, and during World War II he was asked to write an anonymous column for The New Republic *magazine. The column signature was TRB. The letters had no signifi-*

cance beyond the fact they were the reverse initials of a New York City subway line called the Brooklyn Rapid Transit. TRB became the best-read feature in the publication over forty years. It also turned Strout into a Washington power. He was still a mild-mannered reporter for the Monitor, *but he now carried the additional tonnage of the editorialist.*

"Lyndon Johnson called me in for a talk about one of the columns. I forget what it was but he didn't like it at all. He was the majority leader of the Senate then. I went into his office at the Capitol, and the thing I remember most was this enormous desk. It was enormous. It was big as a room, filled with knick-knacks and whatsoever. When I sat down he gave me the full treatment for about an hour. At one point he said I treated him like a motherless child, and he jumped up and started rocking an imaginary baby in his arms. I was amazed that this man would waste his time with all this. I don't know if he thought he could change my mind; he must have. He didn't, however.

"I probably upset a lot of people with TRB. But I did not purposely set out to do that. I don't think I was ever malicious. The modern trend in journalism has been to attack and cut up, and I don't object to that, as long as the attacks are truthful, yet I was never vicious, like H. L. Mencken. Mencken took pleasure in that. He wrote at the expense of his subjects, like Franklin and Eleanor Roosevelt. I wrote some sharp opinions from time to time. I wrote several columns against Joseph McCarthy, to name one person, but everything I said about him was the truth. That was the important thing. If the element was truth—journalists are historians—then I think it is fair.

"McCarthy got back at me for some of the things I wrote. I wasn't important enough for him to confront me directly, but he did write an article about me. He wrote it for the Chicago *Tribune* during the time he was conducting those famous Senate hearings at which he bullied people about communism in Washington. He said that while the hearings were going on someone made a clever reply to him, which showed he was a liar, I guess, and he said he looked down at the press table to see reporters gleefully shaking hands. 'And there was Richard Strout shaking hands with Gus Hall of the *Daily Worker*.' It was untrue, and a terrible thing to say; I might have lost my job."

Strout did not lose his job until he retired, after a stroke, in 1984. He covered more major news stories than anyone in his newspaper's history, and he covered the federal government longer perhaps, on a day-to-day basis, than anyone in journalistic history. He was taking notes when the Indians were given citizenship; he wrote about the passing of the gold standard; he remembers when the Empire State Building was opened; and he watched as all the banks in the nation closed. Huey Long, Alf Landon, Albert Einstein; Taft-Hartly, Alger

Hiss, the GI Bill of Rights. He took one of the first cross-country airplane flights, for a story; he was at Normandy on D-Day; and he met and did occasional battle with a dozen presidents.

"Some of them were fine men. Hoover was brilliant. Roosevelt was historic. Johnson was a son of a bitch, but he had a compassionate heart. John Kennedy had potential. But we've had a lot of men who have gotten in trouble in the office. When I when to Washington in 1922 Harding was stuck in the Teapot Dome scandal. Richard Nixon had Watergate. Reagan has had several problems of this sort. If you look at the list you will find that five presidents in this century have gotten into so much trouble they virtually lost their ability to lead the country. That's one out of every three. Harding, Hoover, Johnson, Nixon, and Reagan. It's a very serious problem for the nation.

"My own belief is that we should look to the British system for a remedy. I became impressed with Parliamentary government when I worked there in the twenties. I don't think we should change over entirely; that isn't necessary, and it might do more harm than good. But we might borrow whatever we can use. Under the American system, for example, a president can stay in office for four years, even if something has happened where he can't govern. The British, on the other hand, are entitled to have an election whenever the prime minister loses popular confidence. I think that's the better way. The fixed term works all right when things are normal, but things are hardly ever normal any more."

Strout lives with his second wife in a comfortable home in one of Washington's better neighborhoods. They are twenty minutes by taxi from the federal district. He says his politics have always been liberal—power to the people—because he remembers when "Wall Street ran the country." He remains long, lean, an unpretentious and enjoyable man; he is eighty-nine years old. He reads. He drinks wine coolers. He keeps in touch. He says he looked forward all his life to the time when he could write his reminiscences, "and then, goddammit, one morning I woke up and had this stroke. I suppose, though, I've already written everything in other forms."

At least about the government.

TRB in the 1970s: "When I was a child at my grandfather's farm, they used to kill pigs in the fall. They tied them up by their hind legs shrieking and squalling before they slit their throats. Once we children bitterly protested, but the hired man was reassuring. 'They like it,' he said firmly. Today he's in Congress, voting against the poverty programs."

In 1932 a congressman from Arkansas named Claude Fuller introduced a resolution in the House of Representatives that would require every American citi-

zen to memorize the words of "The Star Spangled Banner." He also wanted people to be able to sing, recite, or write all the verses of the national anthem before they could work in government jobs. Mercifully, the resolution died in the Judiciary Committee. "The Star-Spangled Banner" was informally adopted as the Union Army anthem during the Civil War and became the national anthem by an act of Congress in March 1931.

ROBERT ATWOOD

Journalism has been called the fourth estate since the British coined the term in the eighteenth century. Edmund Burke was the first to use it, when he told Thomas Carlyle that the public press constituted a "fourth estate more important by far" than the other three estates of Parliament, which were then the peers, the bishops, and the commons. Thomas Macaulay introduced the term to the United States in an 1828 essay on constitutional history in which he said the newspapers were "the fourth estate of the realm," after the executive, the legislative, and the judicial branches. The comparison is arguable, certainly. But there is no doubt that journalists have played a large role in governments on both sides of the Atlantic. Some, like Richard Strout, have served as observers; others, like Robert Atwood of Alaska, have participated more directly.

Atwood is the eighty-year-old publisher of The Anchorage Times. *He bought the newspaper in 1935, when Alaska was an outback territory, a ward of Washington, not to be taken seriously, and he has labored to see it become both the largest and among the most economically successful states in the domain.*

One: size. Alaska is twice as large as Texas and seventy-five times as large as New Jersey. It stretches from east to west over a distance equivalent to that from northern Maine to southern California, and it covers a similar space from north to south. Alaska also has 5580 miles of coastline, which is more than all the other states (Hawaii included) combined.

Two: success. Alaska's per capita income in the last half of the 1980s was about $17,500 a year, the highest in the nation. It is likewise the largest commercial fishing state and, in January of 1988, it became the largest producer of oil. Since 1979, Alaska has been the only state regularly to produce a budgetary surplus, and part of the excess is by law given back to the residents in rebates.

"Gosh," Atwood says, "it still seems amazing to me. The changes have been extraordinary. When I came to Alaska, Anchorage had dirt streets, there wasn't much business, there weren't many people, and everything from one end of the place to the other was controlled by the federal government. Washington controlled the land and the resources in it, on it, over it, the water, the air—everything was in federal hands. We couldn't even cut a Christmas tree here without getting permission from Washington. We used to go out and sneak around, of course, and bootleg our Christmas trees, and that was kind of fun, but some people didn't want to have an illegal tree at Christmas. They didn't think it was in keeping with the spirit of the season. So one of the things I did as a newspaperman was to go to the government each year and get it to set aside areas where the people up here could get their holiday trees honestly."

Thus it is, then. Bob Atwood has traveled from the days when Washington ran Christmas, more or less, to a time when Alaskans can joke about it. And he says he began the journey as a secondary-school student in Winnetka, Illinois, a suburb of Chicago. He was raised in that area; his father was in the sand and gravel business. When he was in the eighth grade he took a course in printing. That led to an interest in journalism that never flagged. He learned the business early and from the front shop to the back. He joined the staff of his high school newspaper; he worked as a reporter and printer at Clark College in Worcester, Massachusetts; and, once graduated, he went on to jobs at a couple of publications, including one in Worcester.

"I liked it very much. I handled the court beat for the Worcester *Telegraph*, and it was the best job on the paper. I was happy there, and I didn't especially want to leave, but then I went to Alaska for a visit. I had married a girl who had been born in Alaska. Her parents were missionaries up here. So—I think it was in 1932—we came here during my vacation. It was a long trip then. It took three or four days to get to Seattle by train, and then a week on the boat to Skagway. I liked the place immediately. I was a Midwestern boy. The only mountains I had ever seen were the Berkshires, and so I was ga-ga right away. The wilderness was breathtaking. There were endless forests and great glaciers.

"We traveled all around and met a lot of very nice people. I couldn't see where they were going anyplace in life, but they lived in a delightful way and seemed to be happy. Alaska was a territory then. Juneau was the largest city, and it had the largest newspaper. Anchorage had twenty-one hundred people, and Fairbanks was also very small. I believe there were sixty thousand residents all told, about half of them native Indians and Eskimos. There was no transportation to speak of, no roads; if you wanted to go anywhere you had to go by river or dog team. There was no air mail, no telephone service. It was primitive—and exciting. We stayed for a week or so before I had to get back to Worcester.

"When I got back I keep thinking about the place. And my wife told her father about my interest. Her father was then the president of the Bank of Alaska, and he wrote me one day to tell me that the newspaper in Anchorage was for sale, and he asked me if I wanted to buy it. Well, I didn't have any money, I was just a young reporter, and I didn't even have the down payment. I did have enough to buy the tickets, however, and so my father-in-law bought the paper for me. I went up owing him more money than I ever thought possible. I was called the general manager in those days. My wife and I moved with the idea of staying for a few years, five at the most, because we didn't want to get stuck and not be able to fit in somewhere else.

"Naturally, Anchorage was primitive then. There was no pavement anywhere—everything was gravel. There were no sidewalks, either, except a few made of wood. We had a couple of cafés in the downtown with oil cloths on the tables, and there were also some pool halls, but, other than that, there were not many social amenities. We heated with wood. Many people used kerosene lamps. You couldn't even buy a drink at a bar in those days. Anchorage was dry when I got here; the lounges didn't start until later. Some people had automobiles, but they were of limited use. There was no place to go and no roads to get there. We put our cars on blocks in the winter, because we did not clear the snow and ice from any of the streets in town.

"The paper was also small. It was a little tabloid consisting of eight pages daily, and I think the circulation was six hundred fifty. We had five employees. It was set up like a small-town weekly but it had big-town responsibilities. Anchorage was the largest town in the area. It was the place everyone in this part of Alaska came to for services and specialties. We had two railroad doctors. No other town in western Alaska had two doctors. So we had to have national news. The national news was provided by the Associated Press, and it was relayed to us from Seattle by the Army Signal Corps in Ketchikan. It was all done manually, with soldier boys at the telegraph keys, and each time they did it they made errors. We couldn't make heads or tail of some of it.

"There was a war going on in Ethiopia, and the place names were so garbled I got complaints from local schoolteachers. I told them I tried to look the names up on a map to correct them, but sometimes that didn't work either. It was a real mess. We also had to rewrite all of the stories, which added to the confusion. The reason we had to rewrite them was that we paid a cent and a half per word to the Associated Press, and so the stories were delivered in a stripped-down form. The sentences didn't have any prepositions or articles, and code words were used to save money. One of the code words was *upcoming*, which was one word instead of two; then there was *Scotus*, which was the cheapest way of saying the Supreme Court of the United States."

Atwood says the problems of the newspaper were surpassed only by the challenges of the moment. Here he was in the wilderness, but civilization was at the door. Alaska was going somewhere, destination unknown. All in all, it wasn't Worcester. Atwood refurbished The Anchorage Times *during his first year of ownership, nearly doubling the circulation, and he also gave it a new philosophical direction. He says he met so many people who wanted to grow, who wanted to develop their potentials, that he turned his newspaper into an organ for progress. The* Times *became the most influential medium in Anchorage, later in all of Alaska, and, in turn, Atwood became a player in every issue confronting the territory.*

To name one: statehood.

"I think the idea of statehood began seriously during World War II. We realized then that something had to happen. I said before that the federal government controlled everything at the time I arrived, but it got much worse during the Second World War. When the military came up here to defend this area from the Japanese, we were placed under a situation that was very close to being military rule. The commanding general here had the authority to exclude any of us from Alaska if he wanted; he controlled travel; he controlled what supplies we could bring in. The government even censored our mail. And when we went to Seattle, we had to be accepted into the United States. They treated us like foreigners. And this burned us all up.

"I made myself a hero once during all of this. I had flown to Seattle, where I was expected to produce identification to prove I was a citizen before I could leave the airport. When I went to the window, however, I said I did not have any identification. That was not true, but I was trying to make a point. Well, they didn't know what to do with me, so they pleaded with me to produce something—anything—as identification. So I pulled out a permit that I had which allowed me to leave trash at the Anchorage garbage dump. When they let me through on that, I wrote a story about it, printed it on the front page of my newspaper, and from then on lots of people who went to Seattle took along garbage-dump ID to get through the silly gate.

"When the war ended, the talk of statehood began to get serious. It was a gradual thing at first and it was not favored by everyone, but in my case I was persuaded for a couple of reasons. One, I wanted the people in Alaska to get the national respect they deserved, and, two, I argued about it with Ernest Gruening over a period of time and I came to agree with him completely. Gruening was the territorial governor, and a great man in my book, and he was a strong champion of statehood. He said that it would bring about development; he said it would guarantee a progressive future for Alaska; and he said it would also help the people break away from the grip of the canned salmon industry.

"The salmon industry was the most powerful private entity in the territory. And the people who controlled it also controlled all of the economics in the territory, as well as the politics. I think the industry employed fifteen thousand people directly, or something like that, and most of the people who worked in small business were also beholden. The salmon industry did not want statehood, of course. They did not want to lose any of their power. I remember covering the legislature at the close of the war, and there was no doubt Gruening was right. I saw how the salmon industry manipulated the legislators; I saw how it got exactly what it wanted; and from then on I was sold on statehood. We had to have it.

"That put me at odds with a lot of people. All of my friends in the establishment supported the salmon industry and opposed statehood. My father-in-law, the man who lent me the money to buy the newspaper, his bank did a lot of business with the salmon industry. So I was a maverick. And I admit I proceeded cautiously at first. But I did start selling people on the idea, and as I did I got bolder and bolder, and louder and louder, and soon a bandwagon started to form in the territory. I got pretty quick support from newspapers like *The Ketchikan Chronicle*. Bill Baker over there jumped right in. My wife [Evangeline] also made up her mind for statehood, and that was a great personal help. Things had started, we were on our way.

"It took quite a while to get anywhere, of course. Because, there was this powerful opposition. The salmon industry said statehood would hurt business (because the state would then control fisheries), and people were afraid of losing their jobs. *The Juneau Empire* was opposed. *The News Miner* in Fairbanks was opposed; *The Sitka Sentinel* was opposed. Most of the little newspapers in the territory were also opposed, because they were so close to the fishermen and the canneries. We had lots of bad words on the subject. Many politicians condemned it, because that's what they were told to do by the salmon people. Everyone argued about it. Some people didn't know who or what to believe. And, naturally, we didn't have any help from Washington.

"I don't think Washington cared about it one way or another at first. Alaska did not have a lot of political influence there. We had one delegate to Congress, but he was not allowed to vote. So we had to go to Washington to generate interest. Gruening appointed a statehood committee, and the members of the committee elected me as chairman, and one of my principal duties was to go to Washington as many as five times a year to lobby and to peddle the idea of statehood in the House and the Senate. I had to attend hearings and buttonhole officials, and all those things. Meanwhile, the salmon industry was doing the same thing; the industry hired a lot of lawyers and spent big money in Washington to fight us every step of the way.

"I remember the salmon lawyers got to one fellow in particular. He was

Senator Hugh Butler of Nebraska. I never really understood his motives, but he didn't like anything about statehood. He ranted and raved for years. I argued with him so many times that we got to be good friends. The canned salmon people also got to Dwight Eisenhower in the White House. They surrounded Ike with antistatehood people. The secretary of the interior under Eisenhower was antistatehood, and the Eisenhower appointees who administered the territory were antistatehood. Harry Truman had supported us when he was in office, but when Eisenhower arrived we found that all of our normal channels for moving around the federal government were abruptly closed.

"It got so bad then that I decided I had to see Eisenhower personally. We had gotten the statehood bill introduced years before, but it was not going anywhere under Ike's administration. So I asked for and got an appointment. But, technically, it was not to discuss statehood. I was put on the schedule because I was an out-of-town newspaper publisher. When I went to the White House I was delivered to Jim Hagerty, who was Ike's press secretary, and he said to me, 'Now, Bob, I know why you're in Washington, but your meeting with the president is just a courtesy call.' He said I was only there to pay my respects, period, and that I would not be permitted to say anything about anything unless the president mentioned it first.

"Then we went in to the Oval Office. And the three of us were sitting there. I was facing Ike, and Hagerty was at the side, staring at me. He was there to make sure I behaved myself. Well, we started talking. I had known Ike from before, actually. He had been to Alaska, and we had dinner together then, and we had lots to talk about. He started recollecting everything about Alaska, what he'd done on his visits, and that sort of thing. And all of a sudden, out of the blue, he said, 'You know, Bob, about this statehood thing. I'm really for that, but I just can't get out front on it.' Well, I looked at Hagerty, and he looked at me, and everyone sort of relaxed. I guess we spent the next twenty or thirty minutes talking about statehood.

"I came out of the meeting all fired up. That was the first time Ike had mentioned statehood favorably since he was elected. He said that one of the reasons that he was not taking an active role for statehood was that the military had designs in the territory. They were looking around for missile and defense installations and they did not want to have to deal with a state government. So that was the hangup. The federal government needed the unencumbered use of some of the territorial land. I immediately contacted Senator Butler. I also got together with everyone else who had anything to do with the statehood issue. I said that if we could resolve the problem with the military, then Eisenhower would no longer stand in the way of statehood.

"It took a long time to resolve the problem. We had a lot of meetings with a lot of people, and out of this came the so-called Yukon-Porcupine Line agreement. It stated that the new state could not select any of its lands north of the Yukon and Porcupine rivers without special permission from the federal government. That area was where Eisenhower and the military were wheeling and dealing with the defense installations. Well, it satisfied Ike, and after that he became gung-ho for statehood. Then a new secretary of the interior was appointed, who was for our cause, and who incidentally was a newspaperman from Nebraska. A lot of other influential people got aboard, and, after fifteen very long years of trying, that's the way we got statehood."

Alaska was admitted as the forty-ninth state in the Union on January 3, 1959, eight months before Hawaii was named number fifty. The Yukon-Porcupine Line agreement is still in effect. Bob Atwood says the agreement has been modified a little, however. He points out that the military did not put missiles above the line and the area became something of a nuisance for the federal government, owing to surveying problems, and therefore the Bureau of Land Management eventually asked the new state to take some of the land off the federal map. The state thereupon laid claim to a chunk of territory at Prudhoe Bay, which would ironically become one of the largest sources of petroleum in the nation and is one of the defining characteristics of late-twentieth-century Alaska.

Journalist Atwood is another of the defining characteristics. He is big, bold, and, according to some, still largely frontier. He is revered by the forces for growth and commerce in his state and condemned by those who think that the modern revelation in Alaska is to think small. Nobody questions his role as a giant in what used to be the wilderness, however. His paper has become the one of the most effective publications of its size (50,000 circulation) in the country, and, after all these years laboring in the arena of editorial comment, he still relishes a fight. In 1987, as he was walking with his daughter in Anchorage, he was accosted by a thug with fire in his eyes. Atwood was seventy-nine then, and the thug had a pistol, but what the hell! It's not the age of the body it's the age of the heart. He disarmed the young bumbler and gave him over to the police.

For all of the fabled living difficulties in Alaska there are also some handsome benefits, many of them provided by state government. The state abolished sales and income taxes early in the 1980s, for example; it subsidizes mortgage interest rates; it issues low-interest loans to college students; and it takes care of some housing costs for longtime residents who are elderly. The state also puts most of its substantial oil revenues into a special fund and distributes the annual interest earnings to adult citizens; in 1987 the checks amounted to $708 each.

3. War

BENNIE MOREE

There is an opinion that the twentieth century began at the Somme, the river in northwestern France where the traditions of the 1800s gave way to the technologies of the 1900s in one of the most ferocious military engagements in history. The First World War had begun at a moment when the participants still dwelled in a previous age of concerns, but the old ways were overwhelmed by the new on July 1, 1916, when mechanics began to replace tactics in battle as well as society, progress showed a terrible grin, and the new order of things went over the top of the trenches and off the very deep end of man's relations with his own kind. The machine gun came of age at the Somme. The armored tank was used for the first time. Twenty thousand soldiers were killed on the initial day of the fight, and by November, after the Allies won eight miles of territory from the Central Powers on a front that was 123 miles long, 1,250,000 uniformed men had perished.

The argument is that the world is still buried in the litter of that encounter, and of all the war. The wonders, the worries, and even the moralities of today were given birth in the blood at the Somme. The science of destruction was created. Idealism died. Duc Francois de La Rochefoucauld: The violence we do others can ironically be less painful than that which we do to ourselves.

Bennie Moree does not know La Rochefoucauld. He knows about violence, however. He fought in the First World War, and then again in the Second; and, philosophy apart, he says the only thing that counts is to kill the enemy. He was a professional soldier for twenty-seven years; he rose to the rank of First Sergeant; and he doesn't get lost in the rationale of the whole thing. War may be the capital of death's gray land, but is also a consequence of social orga-

nization. Sergeant Moree is one of those willing to deal with it. God bless him. He makes all else possible.

"Do you see what this is? It's a garrote, what is called a garrote. Each one of us had one of these. You carry a forty-five pistol or a machine gun; you carried four hand grenades, tied down, where they won't make no noise. There won't be anything in your mess kit. Nothing on your belt. The idea was to be quiet. You're playing the Indian trick on them. You know what the Indian trick is? You sneak up behind a German, and you slip the garrote around his neck, and you jerk it. That cuts the larynx off, see, and it keeps him from calling for help. All you do is catch him when he falls, see, so he doesn't bang on the ground. You just twist it this a way, and that's all she wrote."

In their small volume Lessons of History, *an afterthought to their monumental work* The Story of Civilization, *historians Will and Ariel Durant wrote that war is one of the constants of the ages. They note that in more than 3400 years of recorded history, only 268 have been free of international or intramural combat. War has thus been acknowledged as the "ultimate form of competition in the human species." Wise men have condemned it universally, and even Dwight Eisenhower said it settled nothing at all. But the Durants wrote that war is the result of the same forces that fuel all contentions in societies—need, pugnacity, and pride—hence the rhetoric about the sin of combat is futile.*

The United States, of course, was born in war. The Durants think that means the contests are not even stayed by good intentions and democracy. The American community has been involved in a major conflict every twenty to thirty years of its constitutional history, it has passed from the eighteenth century, when wars were a contest between aristocracies, to the nineteenth century, when they were distinguished by political adventurism, into the 1900s where, according to the Durants, mechanization and indoctrination have made war "a struggle of peoples, involving civilians as well as combatants, and winning victory through the wholesale destruction of property and life." Civilians indeed; late in the 1900s they've accounted for eight in ten war dead.

The United States has fought four major wars in this century. It's also made several dozen armed incursions of a lesser nature in foreign affairs. The Durants say Americans have assumed the responsibility in the 1900s that Great Britain shouldered in the 1800s, the defense of the West from external danger. And it has naturally been costly. The United States military budget in 1901 was $150 million; it rose to $300 billion in the 1980s. The modern American army expends $5300 just to shoot one kind of conventional artillery round, and, over the century as a whole, the national defense has cost $7 trillion, or enough dollars, put end to end, to reach the moon and back 1400 times.

The nation has likewise paid dearly in human costs. On average, the country has lost 5000 men in battle for each year of the century and had another 13,000 wounded. The figures, according to The World Almanac, *are:* World War I, *4,743,826 participants, 53,513 dead in battle, 204,002 wounded;* World War II, *16,353,659 participants, 292,121 dead in battle, 670,846 wounded;* Korean War, *5,764,143 participants, 33,629 dead in battle, 103,284 wounded;* Vietnam, *8,744,000 participants, 47,321 dead in battle, 153,303 wounded. The total number of participants has been 35,605,628; total dead 426,584 and total wounded 1,131,435.*

The result: two wins, one draw, and a loss. Bennie Moree would argue, however, that the nation continues to stand free, intact, and, when it comes to comparisons, relatively unscathed. The Soviet Union lost 7.5 million battle dead in World War II. The other side lost as many as a million civilians alone in Korea. The United States has not had anyone killed at home in any of the wars of the twentieth century. And there has only been one physical invasion during the time; in 1942, Japanese soldiers seized and occupied two small parcels of the Aleutian Islands off Alaska.

Sergeant Moree:

"I was born September 2, 1900. I'm eighty-seven years old. You know where Akree, Georgia, is; down there on Georgia-Alabama line, there's a little town there called Akrey. I lived just outside the city limits. My old man had ninety acres of land, see; he grew cotton, and peanuts for the hogs—and for the children, ha-ha. I don't think my old man was in a war. He was a farmer. I didn't think about being a soldier, either. We had a big family, there were twelve or fourteen of us. We had a big old table, and a big old oven with one of those cupboards on top to keep the food warm, and, let me think a while, let me think what I want to say, we didn't have a hot water tank, we cooked the water on the stove. We didn't have any electric. No one had electric. We went to the toilet outside with the flies.

"I didn't go to but the fifth grade in school. My old man wanted me to work for him, and that's what I did, see. I got along with the old man all right, as long as I didn't make him mad. I did what he said. Except when I was fourteen years old, and I was a pretty good size, see, and I had an uncle who asked me if I'd pick cotton for him. He said he would pay me money. So I went to my daddy, and I made a deal with him. I told him that if he let me work for my uncle, I would pay him for the work I would have done at home. The blacks around there were picking cotton for forty cents a hundred in those days, and so I told the old man that I would pay him for a hundred pounds of cotton a day. And then I did that, see, I worked for my uncle and paid my dad.

"The first thing I knew the old man started taking all of my pay. So that's how the argument came up about. My uncle gave me change, two dollars a day, and he showed me how to count it out. So I knew my daddy was cheating me. I didn't like that. I was working for nothing, and I quit the job at my uncle's. Then my old man got mad because he wasn't getting the money, and he didn't treat me fair after that. He made me pick the hundred pounds at home, so he could sell it for what he'd been taking from me. One day I got tired of that, see, and I just laid down on a cotton sack and went to sleep. Ha-Ha. And when did I wake up the old man was coming at me with a stick. I knew what he was going to do, he said he was going to teach me to work, and said 'Say, mister, you're going to have to catch me,' and I ran away.

"He hollered after me. He said he'd get me later. And when did I holler back that I was never coming home. I said 'Hey, man, the next time you see me I will have a beard down to there.' I went right over to my uncle's. He was my good friend. They fed me and let me stay. My uncle's wife said 'Here's some biscuits over here,' and they were good too. That was 1917. The war was just going on, I believe. I didn't think about it, though. I went to work from job to job. They had a peach farm there, the Indiana Fruit Company, see, it was right outside of Sylvester, and the owner had a double-story house, and that was a mystery to me, to see a double-story house. It was built in such a fashion, it was so far advanced. I picked peaches. I picked oranges. I never went back home. I joined the Army on June 2, 1917."

Bennie Moree is still more than six feet tall. He is lean as a swagger stick, and his jaw sticks out as if he were marching parade. He chews tobacco. He wears a Combat Infantry Badge on the pocket of his suit jacket. He also has an old bullet lodged permanently in his side. He is almost deaf, a consequence of his years near explosives, and he carried on the conversation here by relay. His son Jim shouted questions in his ear, sometimes only once, and he responded in full, with good-natured asides, remembering details with ease. "My company commander was John A. Hine; he was West Point." *See. Ha-ha. When did I.*

"I didn't have no choice in going to the military. I worked around, but there wasn't much money available. So it was either go into the Army or go hungry. I went to the recruiting station in Valdosta and I asked the guy there, I said, 'Say, don't you need somebody?' He gave me a meal ticket then, and he told me what restaurant to go to, and he told me to come back in the morning, and I said 'Okay.' The next day the train left just about dark, see, and we stopped in Macon when did I had breakfast. I said, boy, this is something, there's plenty to eat. Then we went to Atlanta, and they got us together, and they said strip nekkid ha-ha. I said, well, what's going to happen next, and everybody started hollering, and I was really in the Army.

"I was eighteen. I told them I was nineteen. I've had trouble with that advanced year ever since. But my real age was recorded in a Bible, and everybody believes the Bible. Anyway, they gave us two weeks of training. That's all they gave us, two weeks. They gave me a rifle, an old Springfield, and it was left, right, inspection arms. We trained in Atlanta and after that they sent us to Syracuse, New York, where they took over a fair grounds. They put me in the infantry; I didn't have enough education to figure out the artillery. The uniform had a high collar and it had hooks along with the buttons, and the pants had leggings, and when did I guess I started to look halfway like a real soldier.

"We went to Europe on a German ship they had captured. It was named after the Kaiser's daughter. You heard tell of Kaiser Wilhelm, I suppose, but, when did I, I don't remember her name. There was a convoy we was on. We couldn't tell anyone where we were going. That didn't matter much to me; my mother had died by that time, and neither my father or me could write a letter."

Did you think about the war?

"It was still a long way away."

Were you afraid?

"No. We sang songs: 'Over there, Over there, Send the word, We're coming over, and we won't be back til it's over over there.'

"They landed us at St. Lazare, in France. They made us wash our uniforms with a scrub brush and hang them out to dry. I was a private. I was glad to be a private. I thought I was a big shot. I was a farm boy, you know, now I was across the water. It was by a river, see, I don't remember which one, and then one morning they backed a train right up there, and they put forty men and eight horses in each car. Here we went on that thing, and we wound up in Verdun. That was the first place I went to. It's where the Germans and the French had that big battle in 1916 [and which precipitated the battle at the Somme]. They put my platoon near a bridge; I remember we stayed in trenches that were six foot deep, including the mounds of dirt we threw out.

"That was the first fighting I saw. The Germans used to raid us at the bridge. I remember they sneaked in one morning. We had a trench that run down to the outpost, and they came over and got in behind us in the trench. We didn't have no telephone in them days, and so the outpost didn't even know. The enemy looked just like us, except their uniforms were gray, and they had different helmets. At first, their helmets had spikes sticking out of them. Then Germany got short of steel, and the spikes disappeared. It was close fighting then. We couldn't shoot at them very much, so we threw hand grenades. That was a better way to do it. The hand grenade had a killing range of twenty-five yards. When did I throw them with a twist, thisaway, see.

"Now let me get myself straightened out. I can tell you everything. I was in Company B [Ninth Infantry.] The name of my company commander was Captain Buell. One time when we was fighting at Château-Thierry we had to get word back to Captain Buell, and three of us volunteered to go. We left at ten-minute intervals, so that at least one of us could get through, ha-ha. The other volunteers were John O'Donald and Charles Gustafson. I made it through but they didn't. Everyone figured they were captured, and nobody saw them again. I told Captain Buell that he was ordered to take his men and go to regimental headquarters, and I showed them the way. We had to tie ourselves together with a rope to keep contact, but we made it to headquarters okay.

"I did a lot of that. The only way we could send messages in World War I was to send runners. Sometimes you had to go right through the lines, and that's how I got this here bullet in my side. I was on the Champagne front, see, and when did I take a message directly through the Germans. And the bullets was following me, and I was running as fast as I could, and everybody was hollering at me to 'jump in a hole, Moree.' But when did I, a bullet hit the bank and ricocheted into my side. I've been wounded four times, officially. The first time I was wounded was July 5, 1918. I was wounded one time when I didn't get no Purple Heart because when did I, I didn't bother to go back to the aid station.

The old man pauses. He says he has to go to the urinal. He lives in what he still calls a double-story house in Cordele, Georgia, where he keeps his service garrote looped around a nail on the wall and his dogtags on a shoestring. He has large ears, horned-rimmed glasses, and a military haircut. He has a wine goblet that he says came from a compound frequented by Adolf Hitler. There are barking hounds outside, and squealing pickup trucks; when he smiles, Sergeant Moree shows his lower teeth.

Do you remember the mustard gas?

"Yes. Mustard gas was potent stuff. It was really something. I got burned with that stuff twice, two times."

What was it like?

"You could smell it. That's all you had to do, and you knew it was there. It smelled like rotten hay."

Was it painful?

"Yes, if you were sweating or you were wet. As a rule, they threw it at you when it was sprinkling rain. They wanted to hit you when you were wet, and it would burn all over your skin."

Didn't you wear a gas mask?

"I had one at first, but I lost it. I got burned both times around the face. They shot the stuff when the wind would carry it across the trenches; they knew where we were at all times, see, and you couldn't get away. I got burned both times around the face, and they would give me a little bit of solution on a cotton ball, which didn't do any good. Oh, yeah, it was bad. People would get hit, and then try to walk back for help, and maybe they made it and maybe they didn't. If they didn't make it, the litter-bearers would come around later and pick them up. People were more scared of that than anything. They would groan and cry, and it wasn't good to lose so many; the rest of us wondered if we'd be next.

"We fought back. We used poison gas ourselves. And you got all the ammunition you wanted on the front lines, you know. I used to draw a circle on a piece of paper and shoot at it for practice. Then when they attacked I got better each time. I waited for the Germans to come about two hundred yards and then I'd start working on them. If they got too close, we'd all get out of the trenches and fight them hand-to-hand. They might throw their weapons down then and holler 'Comrade!' but if they didn't everybody would grab everybody or stick them with your bayonet. Or maybe you would get stuck. I don't know how many I killed there; you would just shoot, or throw hand grenades, and hope you could get them before they could get you, ha-ha.

"The war ended at 11:00 A.M. on November 11, 1918. I carried the armistice message up to the front lines. They told me what the message was, and they told me 'Don't you give that to nobody that doesn't got their name on it.' I said 'Yes, sir.' I got up there to one of the people and he was in a shellhole. I jumped in there and I said 'Here's a message they told me to give you.' I went to another place on along a river, where there was nothing but a footbridge across it to the German lines, and there were American officers over there, and I said, 'Hey, you guys, if you want this message you better get over here, I'm not going to give it to anybody on that side.' Then when did I see my old battalion commander and told him that the war was all over.

"They blew the whistle, and right up to that time there was shooting going on. Then everything stopped. And right after that the Germans came a running across the river, see, and they wanted cigarettes and tobacco. They came over to us. And the battalion commander told them to get back over to where they came from. Because there were still a lot of us that wanted to fix bayonets and kill them. I don't know if anybody did. I heard some died after it was over. When I got through delivering the messages, there were still some people in their holes after eleven o'clock, even though everybody else was up and around. I said 'Son, why don't you come out of there?' and he said 'Oh, no, not me,' because he thought somebody was going to fire the last shot, and he didn't want to stand up too soon and catch it."

Moree remained in the army when he returned to Georgia. He married twice, to "the finest women who ever lived," and lost both of them to cancer. He suffered what he calls the indignities of the peacetime service, earned forty-four dollars a month as a corporal, and also watched three of his five children die. He was promoted to sergeant in 1940; he trained troops domestically until 1944; and he was dispatched to his second world war.

What unit did you join?

"The Hundredth Infantry Division."

Where?

"France again."

He grins. He becomes evasive. He says he doesn't want to sound as if he did more than his part. He's also tired. He remembers his wives, and his dead kids, buried in one spot under a marker that says Moree's Babies.

One more war story.

"I went to the lines on November 12, 1944. It was cold as the devil, see, and I was given a platoon in Company A, 397th Regiment, Hundredth Infantry. We were near Bertrichamps, and I killed five Germans one day. So I went up there and there was a lot of fighting going on inside a forest, in the hills, and there was a German machine gun going off behind a big tree. I had some hand grenades, and I crawled up to the tree, and there were some German officers, and right behind them was the machine gun. I threw a hand grenade at the officers, and then I thought, well, I might as well get the machine gun too. I threw another hand grenade, and when I went back to my unit I said to one of the other sergeants, I said, 'Well, check off two of them.'

"Then I heard another machine gun, about twenty or thirty yards on the other side, and I went over there, and there was a staff sergeant there named Knerr. I said, 'Knerr, where is that machine gun?' He said, 'Moree, it's right straight in front of you, thataway.' I said 'Oh, that's just nice, I can throw a hand grenade at it.' He said 'You ought to be able to, you practice enough,' and I said 'That's the reason I practice.' Then I walked up between the trees where I had a clear area and I threw some more hand grenades. When I went back I said I got three more. They said, how do you know there were three, and I said they were thrown all around when I hit them with the grenade, and I could see three pairs of boots sticking up.

"That was the day I got hit myself. I got wounded when I tried to help another man who was shot. I'll tell you what his name was. His name was Lt. Stillwagon. I'll tell you what his first name was, it was John. He was on the ground and I was dragging him back out of the way. I got my hand out there I got ahold of his leg, and I said 'Play dead.' And I just moved him a little bit at a time. I didn't think they would shoot at him if they thought he was dead, ha-ha. Boy oh boy! And just before I got him back the Germans fired, and I raised up and got hit in the face. The bullet came in here near my nose. I put a finger in the hole, and I kept easing back with the lieutenant, and I made it all right."

Sergeant Moree retired from the army on a partial disability. He had accumulated a Silver Star, a Bronze Star, a Purple Heart with three clusters. He still keeps the ribbons on an old uniform. He gets $1397 a month for retirement. He is still military. He is supremely proud. He says he would do it again.

"You want to try this garrote?"

No.

"One time the Germans were just over there, as close as that wall. They said 'Hey, you, why don't you surrender?' and I said 'Maybe tomorrow.' I was an expert rifleman. And then I opened fire. Bang, bang, bang, bang."

In 1940, members of an American Legion Post in Haddonfield, New Jersey, formed what they called the Last Man's Club. They put aside a bottle of Hennessy cognac so that the club's last World War I survivor would one day be able to toast his deceased comrades. Some years later the club charter was amended to allow the last few men to open the bottle, because nobody likes to drink alone. In 1987, four surviving veterans did the honors: Robert Wythes, ninty-six; John William Barron, eighty-nine; Robert Wright, eighty-eight; and Fred Wisner, eighty-eight, Wisner was asked how he felt about the whole thing. "Pretty good," he said, "and I'll drink to that."

BRUCE MEDARIS, GENERAL

The Reverend Bruce Medaris is an ordained minister of God who gives the impression of being slightly out of place in a role that, insofar as convention has it, calls for humility and quiet temperance. Not that he lacks sincerity, of course. He speaks of the Lord with admiration and conviction, as if the Great Spirit is listening in the next room, he also quotes the Bible with a learned familiarity, the result of a lifetime of devotions, and he can marvel at the loaves and fishes with the best of them, telling, for example, of the time the hand of Providence reached into his flesh to cauterize a malignancy that was killing him; he says it felt like current from a battery, and, overtime, the cancer was cured.

For all of that, though, Medaris has a way that belies his calling. He has an arrogance that addresses other interests. He bows only to Jesus. He is vain, egotistical, and short-tempered. He is brusque, dominating, and he does not humor fools. He sniggers at off-color stories; he says he also enjoys hard liquor; and woe be it if one disagrees with his conclusions.

He is, in short, commanding. Before he was an Episcopalian priest he was a military general. Medaris served in two armed forces for parts of three wars, at the end of which he helped develop one of history's most destructive weapons.

Killing and Christianity?

"People ask me about that," he says. "I tell them that some of God's greatest followers took part in wars. The Crusades were fought for the glory of God. I do not personally like killing, and I've never gotten any personal satisfaction out of seeing someone die on a battlefield. But sometimes it has to happen. I don't think the Lord wants us to lay back and surrender. If a nation is attacked it must fight back, and it's moral to do so.

"The commandment says 'Thou shall not kill,' but I believe that refers to murder, and it is different from defending one's country. I don't apologize for my service to my country. I don't think there is any contradiction with my service to God. On the contrary, I think God was there with me in the wars, and I think he stood behind our nation during the wars. The United States is not aggressive, we only fight for peace; as a Christian I am proud of that."

Bruce Medaris is eighty-five. He's also been a businessman and a history-making science administrator during his long life, and his recollections will be carried in another relevant place in this book. His memory is excellent. He says immodestly that the Lord lent him a good mind, and he adds prosaically that he has from the beginning tried to use the gift to advantage:

"I came from Ohio. My family lived near Cincinnati at first, and then we moved to Springfield when my mother kicked my father out of the house. My father was considered to be one of the best lawyers in the state, but he also ran around, apparently, and so I grew up with my mother's side of the family. That family name was LeSourd. They were all descendants of a Frenchman who came to this country with Lafayette's army during the American Revolution. That fellow deserted when Lafayette went back to France, and he married a woman in New York. I also had a Grandfather LeSourd who died of gangrene during the Civil War.

"I was always interested in work, too. We didn't have any money after my father left, and I had to help out. I started by pushing carts in a machine shop when I was nine years old. There weren't any child labor laws to speak of, and I did the same work as the adults. Then I bought a bicycle and got a paper route; I got two routes, actually, morning and evening, and that led to another idea. They still had gas street lampposts in Springfield, and someone had to light them at night and turn them off in the morning. Since I was already out on the streets at those times, on my paper routes, I asked for the job and was hired. I did those things for several years, and then I drove a taxi.

"The war in Europe had started by then, and I wanted to go. I joined the Marine Corps in 1918, when I was sixteen. That was a funny thing. You were supposed to be eighteen to join, and everybody thought that was my age. I go back to these brains God gave me. I was always ahead of my time. When I got out of kindergarten I could read so well that I only spent three months in the first grade before I was kicked up to the second. Then I only spent four months there, and went on to the third. By that time I was thought to be two years older than I was and it stuck with me—I didn't correct the mistake officially until much later—and it enabled me to get into the First World War.

"I trained at Parris Island in South Carolina. And let me tell you the Marine Corps in those days was a tough bunch of monkeys. I started out as a private, I made it to first class private, I made it to corporal, and I made it back again to first class private. I was broken in rank twice for disciplinary reasons. One was for staying out a little too late on a pass and the other was for fighting. I was a squad leader the second time, and the unwritten rule in the Marine Corps then was that you could not hold that kind of position if you could not lick everyone in the squad. Well, one of the other fellows beat the hell out of me, and so I was busted back down to private.

"There was another rule that sticks in my mind. The Marine Corps was entirely voluntary in World War I, and so they only sent soldiers to battle who qualified. You had to pass boot camp in good shape, and you had to be at least a marksman on the rifle range. If you didn't make marksman they would assign you to some kind of duty, but you would not get to go overseas. I saw grown men break down and cry on the rifle range for that. You could also be kept out of the war if you were too good, by the way. That almost happened to me. When I got to the range I fired seven straight bull's-eyes at six hundred yards, and a gunnery sergeant behind me said in a whisper that if I hit one more I was going to be a rifle instructor; so I shot the next three over the hill.

"I really wanted to get into the fight. And I was terribly disappointed when I could not leave for Europe with my training unit. I had been held behind because I was a witness in a court martial. I was just sick about it, but it turned out to be rather fortunate for me. I always say God has made all of the decisions for me in my life, and this was a good example. There were a hundred ten men who went over with that unit, and only three men came back. Everyone else was killed. Two of the three men who returned were permanently crippled. That was the first of many things like that. I have been through a good lot of fighting, I forget how many arrowheads I have [awarded for beach landings under hostile fire], but I've never been wounded, never a scratch."

Medaris went to France just before the war ended. He served as a line soldier in the southern region of the country, principally around the port of Bordeaux. He says the fighting was not always confined to the dispute between the Allies and the Central Powers. Some of the action was at the docks at Bordeaux between members of the U.S. Marines and those of the U.S. Army.

"It was a racial thing. The Army had a contingent of black stevedores who were handling all the cargo at Bordeaux, and the Marines watched them very closely. The blacks did not like the Marine discipline, and they started to waylay some of the Marines along the road leading to the Marine encampment. Several instances of that kind took place, and they got by with it until one night the blacks beat up a popular gunnery sergeant and threw him down a well. When word got back to the Marine camp, the Marines took off and ran the blacks down. It was a bloody mess. There were a number of people killed. I think the casualties out of it were two Marines dead, and twenty blacks.

"So, there was a big investigation, and we were all called to an assembly. There was a general officer named Smedley Butler, who later became a policeman in Philadelphia and who at the time was commander of the Marine forces in Bordeaux. He called us out and stood before us on a platform. We were all in formation, and I was in the front row, and he told us what a disaster the whole thing was and what a disgrace to the corps, and he said 'Now we want to get this settled and get the guilty people, so I want every marine who had anything to do with the riot to step one step forward.' Then I heard him say, under his breath, 'if any of you are stupid enough.' Nobody moved at all."

Medaris left the Marines when he went home. He returned to the service in 1921, this time as an army ordnance lieutenant; he left again later to go into business and succeeded there until the Depression. He lost his shirt and his wife when the economy collapsed. He was forced to sell thousands of dollars worth of securities for $69.50, and he divorced the spouse because she did not want to reduce her standard of living. He worked for the city of Cincinnati through the period, and in 1939 he returned to the military for a third stint.

"I was convinced by this time that we were going to get involved in another war. I was also an ordnance captain in the Army Reserve. So when the War Office decided to ask reserve officers to come back to active duty, I took advantage of that, and I went in as executive officer of the Cincinnati Ordnance District. From there I was called into Washington to head up contract distribution at the office of the Chief of Ordnance. I remember my office was very large, with Persian rugs—it had been built at one time for Black Jack Pershing—and I was told 'Now, look, we are going to send these contractors to come and see you. If they think you are a big shot they will be satisfied. Otherwise, they might come and bother everyone else, and we don't want them.'

"I traveled everywhere on that job. I've probably been in more industrial plants that anyone alive. And I worked with big people and small. I was never intimidated by the big ones, either. I sat across from the president of General Motors once, in his office, and I was discussing something to do with tanks, and he said 'Well, I don't like that idea, and General Motors isn't going to do it that way.' I said, 'I'm sorry, sir, but in that case General Motors is not going to be part of the program.' You'd have thought I struck him with a lighting bolt. No one had ever talked like that to him before. He said, 'You can't do that; you can't cut us out,' and I said 'Certainly I can; we make the rules.' After that we got along much better.

"The Japanese struck Pearl Harbor a short while later, and Washington was turned upside down. Many of the officers in the Army did not even have uniforms to wear. They had a rule in the city before the war that people at the War Department had to wear uniforms at least one day a month, but nobody paid attention to it, and a lot of the senior officers hadn't worn a uniform in years. The day after Pearl Harbor, which was on Monday, the lines to the uniform shops were stretched from here to Atlanta, and the guys were showing up in the funniest-looking things; nothing fit; everyone was going around with tight pants and bulges. We still had the World War I outfits then, riding pants and brown boots, lots of buttons and Sam Browne belts.

"I started begging right away to get to the field. I did not want to spend the war at a desk in the Capital. So I got orders to go to Karachi, which was very disappointing. But it was better than Washington. I was a major then, and I sent a man on before me, and I told him to get us a villa and a supply of scotch. So he went on, and I stayed here to clear up details. When I got on the plane to go myself, however, we had engine trouble and the trip was postponed. Then while I was waiting for another plane, my orders were changed and I didn't go at all, thank God. That's how close I came to being stuck in India. I later got a telegram from the boy who went ahead, and it said 'I've got the villa and the scotch; where the hell are you?'

"I ended up for a while commanding a couple of ordnance battalions at

Camp Blanding, for the Second Corps. And one of them had a reputation for all kinds of trouble. The main thing was that the men were always AWOL. They would get a weekend pass and then not show up until Tuesday or Wednesday. So I gathered them all together for a review. I put on all my remnants from World War I, the riding crop and the medals and all that, and after I gave them an inspection I said, 'Allright, I know about the past troubles here. I want you to know the new rules. If you get a pass and you stay away longer than you are supposed to, you will not get a pass for the next three months.' Oh, how they must have hated me, but they followed the orders after that.

"I finally went overseas in 1943. It was both a happy and sad occasion for me. I was glad to be going, but I was also having personal problems at the time. I had a wonderful wife named Virginia, we had three children; and then while I was at Camp Blanding I fell in love with another woman. It's hard to explain it even now, but when I left for overseas I told Virginia to find someone else. I wrote her a very cruel letter. She broke apart at that. She was bedridden for a time and threatened to kill herself. It was my fault. I struck out at her to ease my own conscience. We patched things up later on—the other woman did not mean very much in the long run—but it's something I don't like to recall, even after all these years. I was wrong.

"I went to North Africa for my first combat assignment. I was a lieutenant colonel, and I became the II Corps ordnance commander. That was in Tunisia, when we took a great beating at Kassarine Pass, on Valentine's Day, and where I had to write to the families of a lot of men in my command who were killed in the Atlas Mountains. George Patton took over II Corps for a while, and Omar Bradley was also present. I liked Bradley from the start. We were to develop a lifelong friendship. He was friendly, and vigorous, and he had a keen sense for detail. I think he liked me because I did not operate by the book. I was an improviser; so was Bradley; and when he took over the First Army in 1944 he asked me to come along for ordnance.

"I'm talking about Operation Overlord now—the invasion of France. I was responsible for twenty thousand of the troops that were formed in four regiments, sixteen battalions, and ninety-six companies. I had four hundred officers under me directing ordnance for the units. It was momentous. D-Day was an act of the Man Upstairs. Five thousand ships or more, one million men from several nations, and twelve thousand airplanes. I landed on Omaha Beach on the second day, but the holocaust raged for weeks after that. Bombs, and fighting, and dying. When we moved inland something touched off a fire in one of our ammunition dumps, and I bring it up because it was an illustration that we had to battle ourselves at times as well as battle the Germans.

"I raced to the fire and found that the officer in charge had become frightened and ran away. He left his men to fend for themselves. I took over—someone had to do something; we needed the supplies desperately and the inferno was such that if it was not extinguished it would attract German bombers at night. The first thing I did was to tell the men to forget about using water on the fire; that would only spread the flames. I said get all the shovels you can find and put dirt over the stocks. I called for bulldozers and drove the lead one myself. There were explosions all around; some of the men were injured, one officer was hit with flying metal fragments, but everybody was a hero; everybody pitched in and we doused it by that evening.

"Then I went after the officer who had run away.

"He was contrite.

"I said, 'You are not fit to serve here. I'm relieving you of your command.' The next day he flew to England and back home."

The war in Europe continued for eleven months after the Normandy invasion. And Medaris stayed in the military as a full colonel after the Japanese surrendered. He says he was denied another promotion for longer than was comfortable (he did not get his star until 1953), but he was by now one of the most experienced ordnance men in the armed forces. He had journeyed from the Springfield rifle to Big Bertha. Thus when the United Nations moved troops into Korea in the summer of 1950, Medaris, then fifty years old, was called on once again to take up duties in a war.

"I was not actually stationed in Korea. But I had a session over there as a troubleshooter. The distribution of ammunition had broken down during the war, and there were very serious shortages on the front lines. I had been in Argentina for a time—I was chief of staff of the military mission there—and I was not very far away from retirement, and when I got back I got a call from Louis Ford [the Army Chief of Staff]. He said 'Bruce?' and I said 'Yes, sir,' and he said 'Don't unpack. I want to see you tomorrow morning.' When I went to see him at his office he said the ordnance problem in Korea had to be resolved. He then made me the head of a task force and gave me all the authority necessary to go to Korea and straighten it out.

"And it was a good thing, too. The situation there was very bad. There were shortages of artillery, there were shortages of rounds for the small arms. You can't fight a war like that. You can't expect the men to throw stones. I made two trips to Korea with the Chief of Staff, and there were some congressional hearings, and I found out basically that the ammunition was available but it was not being distributed correctly. I also found out that the fault went right to the top. To one of our highest-ranking military officers. He lost a son in the war, and I think it affected his competence. At any rate, I threw out the old system and I put in one of my own, so that every bullet could be accounted for.

"Incidentally, speaking of incompetence, I think Korea gave birth to a lot of problems along these lines that are still affecting the military. They started when Harry Truman fired Douglas MacArthur as the commanding general. I think the light of history will say that was the greatest tragedy in the two hundred years of our uniformed services. I realize that the President was trying to maintain discipline, but what it did was that it set up an entirely different method of handling American troops in the field. Military commanders used to be in full control of the troops in the field, but they have not had that control since MacArthur was let go. The troops are now commanded from Washington in detail, by desk soldiers, which is mindless.

"I go back to the D-Day landing. That was the kind of operation the military used to conduct. And the reason was that they were allowed to do it with a minimum of outside interference. The commanders were given an objective; they were told what they were supposed to accomplish; and then it was their job to do it, because they were the professionals who were trained to do it. I'm thinking of the assault on Omaha Beach, the assault against the German batteries on the cliffs. The responsibility was given to the Special Troops. They plotted it inch by inch. They planned it the best way they could because their lives were at stake. No one butted in. The men in the field were left to work it out, carry it out—and they blew the Germans away.

"Now, compare that with what has happened since Korea. When Jimmy Carter was president, the military was asked to go into Iran and get those fifty-two hostages who were being held there. But the whole thing was planned by people sitting behind papers. Now, remember, the job was given to a special military force, just like the one at Omaha Beach. But, if you can believe it, the commander of the special force for Iran was handed his orders forty-eight hours before the strike. Think of it! He was told where to go, how to get there, how many men he would have, everything in detail, everything decided by people who would not be participating, and it was all given to the commander forty-eight hours before. So what happened? The mission failed.

"I think if you look back, we have had many military missions fail since Korea. You can't fight battles in the field from the White House. I don't question civilian control of the armed services. But I think it should stop after the civilians decide when and where our forces should fight. The military should decide how. Military commanders have not really commanded since World War II. You might find it notable that we haven't won anything since then."

Bruce Medaris is a gaunt man with a mustache. He lives in Athens, Georgia, where he is the special assistant to the bishop of the Orthodox Catholic Church. He believes in religious healing, the 96th Psalm, and dry powder.

"After Korea, I set my retirement date. I had a deal with General Bradley, who was then in private industry, to join him. I was ready to get out. But then I got one last assignment. The military was getting into rockets at the time, but we weren't very far along, and the Pentagon wanted to develop a Intermediate Range Ballistic Missile so we could hit the Soviet Union from anywhere in Europe. The Secretary of Defense said it was the highest military priority of the United States. Both the Army and Air Force bid for the job, and they gave it to both of us. The Army took it more seriously, I think, and decided to create an Army Ballistic Missile Agency. So, in 1954, before I could retire, they asked me to be the first director of that agency."

Four years later, just after the Sputnik shock, General Medaris launched the first United States satellite to orbit the earth.
Stay tuned.

One of the most famous members of the 82nd Airborne Division during World War II was a 90-pound boxer dog named Max. He had his own parachute and his photograph and exploits were widely published. Sadly, Max was hit by a truck one day. But it wasn't a complete loss. From then on division recruiting officers began telling prospects that parachuting was safer than crossing the street.

A survey of high school seniors in 1986 revealed that 52 percent could not identify Franklin Delano Roosevelt, the American president during World War II, and most could not identify Winston Churchill, the British prime minister then, or Dwight Eisenhower, the Supreme Allied Commander in Europe.

THOMAS POPE

The Medal of Honor is a five-pointed piece of bronze wreathed in green enamel and held by a star-studded ribbon of blue silk. It is the nation's highest military award for bravery. It was created in 1862, by a congressional resolution directing that it be presented "to such noncommissioned officers and privates as shall most distinguish themselves by their gallantry in action, and other soldier-like qualities, during the present insurrection. The "present insurrection" was the Civil War.
Some people didn't like the decoration at first. They thought it conveyed the kind of unseemly glorification that characterized the medieval militariza-

tion of European monarchies. But, if anything, it was subsequently to become too popular. It was to be imitated extensively, for one thing, so that scores of bogus medals proliferated, and on occasion in the early days, it was also given for questionable performances in one case, 864 men from a single infantry regiment won the Medal of Honor.

The standards for the award were thus revised during the First World War, as was the list of previous winners, and the medal has since come truly to incorporate congressional intent. Three thousand three hundred ninety-four men and one woman have been given the award for gallantry far beyond the usual call of duty (nineteen men have received two medals).

Some 233 survived in 1987.

Corporal Thomas Ambrose Pope, for one.

"I received the medal in a mass ceremony after the war. We were all lined up in ranks, and General John J. Pershing gave the award. The only thing he said to me was 'I'm proud of you.' I should have said to him 'General, you did a good job too.' "

Tom Pope is ninety-four, and one of three men still living who won the Medal of Honor in the First World War. He is six feet tall, has good shoulders, and he wears a string tie secured with a gemstone. He sits on a kitchen chair, and drinks Dad's Root Beer, and occasionally adjusts a hearing aid.

Where did you grow up, Mr. Pope?

"In Edison Park, Illinois, next to Chicago."

And how large was your family?

"I had one brother, who was a very good horseshoe player. We were very close and lived with my grandparents. My mother died when we were young, and my father was always traveling. My father was a stage comedian who used the name Murray K. Hill. I think he was pretty good, too. I saw him perform in Chicago, and I looked around to see if people were laughing. And they were."

Had your father been in the military?

"No, but my grandfather was. He was with [Admiral David] Farragut's fleet in the Civil War. He got a veteran's benefit from that and, do you know, we lived off that money. So I always had a high regard for the military. When I was a young boy, the Thirty-third Division came through our town, and I turned out to see them. One of them was a great big guy, and I asked him 'Can I carry your rifle?' He said 'Sure.' I got a bang out of that."

How about school, Tom?

"I quit in high school. I wasn't a good scholar, let's put it that way. When I was eighteen or so, I was one of those boys who wanted to go west. So I went with two other fellows. We worked our way on the Great Northern Railroad. We got all the way to Montana, and we stopped there to live in a boxcar and to help lay telegraph poles. Every morning we were put on boxcars and taken to places to dig the holes. It was in the mountains and everything was rock, so we had to dynamite the holes. Then we would raise the telegraph poles in place and go home to the boxcar. I met this Indian girl out there, I remember that, and I knew her for a while; she used to watch me play baseball games."

So?

"It didn't amount to anything."

Let's get into the Army. When did you join?

"People don't like me to say this, but I want to tell you the truth. I am of German descent, and I didn't like the idea of the United States fighting Germany, because some of my people were still in that country. So I didn't enlist until I had to."

Had to?

"I found out I was going to be drafted. What are you going to do when they tell you to come in for that? I was a good American. I wasn't scared. I just didn't want to fight my own relatives. But I thought it over, and one day before I was actually drafted, I registered myself and went in voluntarily."

Why do you say people don't want you to tell that story?

"I won the Medal of Honor. They think I should act like it."

Right. Go on.

"I was a good soldier. I trained in Chicago for a while, and then I went to more training at Joliet, Illinois. My outfit was E Company, 135th Infantry Division. We had twelve men there from Edison Park. Two of them were killed in action. Vic Mole and Paul Kendrick, they were both good men. John Fox was also from Edison Park; he was hit in the leg and died later of the wound."

When did you go to Europe?

"In the spring of 1918. We went over to France on a ship, and before we got there we were attacked by German submarines. I was on the deck at that time and I saw this submarine, and the ship bells started to ring. There was an officer standing next to me, and he said I had to go down to my company. I didn't want to go. My company was three floors below the waterline. But I went anyway. I remember there was a little fellow there who was scared to death, and there was a great big sergeant right next to him, and the sergeant said 'Hang on to my hand.' That's all the little guy needed, a little help."

Was the ship hit?

"No. We got them. We had navy gunners on both ends of the ship and they fired I don't know how many shots at the submarine. I don't know. They claimed afterward that we got two of them."

Welcome to France.

"We landed in Brest, in June, and we went from there to fight around Hamel. Now I'm not going to say anything about what I did in the trenches, except that I was cited for extreme bravery."

You don't want to talk about winning the medal?

"No."

Why?

"I don't think it's necessary."

Pope is adamant. He shakes his head and adjusts his glasses and looks at the wall of his kitchen. Alhambra, California. There are earthquake instructions posted near the telephone. There are leftovers on the counter. There is a knock at the door. Pope gets up to get the morning mail, not looking at it, and sits back down to adjust the sleeves on a gray cardigan sweater.

He was cited for actions that took place on July 4, 1918, before the fall of Hamel. The official record indicates that he was provoked to retaliate personally when his company was stopped midfield by hostile machine-gun fire. The record says he went forward from there alone, rushing the machine-gun nest, where he killed several of the crew with his bayonet. He then stood astride the gun and held off survivors in the nest until he was relieved by company reinforcements who took the Germans captive.

"You can say it," he says, "I won't."

He changes the subject. He says Phillip Katz, ninety-nine, is the oldest surviving Medal of Honor recipient. Katz was a sergeant in the war. He won his ribbon near Eclisfontaine, France, for rescuing a comrade left wounded in an exposed position that was being continuously swept by automatic fire. One hundred twenty-three men won the medal in World War I. Alvin York. Eddie

Rickenbacker. John J. Kelly. Katz also lives in California. He and Pope are friends.

Tom, will you talk of other actions?

"I will say that I prayed a lot. I prayed like a son-of-a-gun, because going there, going to the lines, I knew what could happen. I was brought up in religion. I believed in God, and it was a good thing I did. When we first went to Hamel we occupied a German trench. It was just wide enough to sit in. I was laying down, and a shell came over and landed next to the trench. Well, there was a pickax there, and when the shell hit, the ax went way up in the air, and came down at me, and I turned a little, and it went through my pants without hurting me. So I thought I was protected after that: I thought I was being watched over, but I did not pray to be safe, necessarily, and I did not pray to beat anyone; I prayed to conduct myself like a man."

And you did.

"Yes, I think so. There was another incident there that I was kind of proud of. It was also during that fight around Hamel. I came past a dugout with my squad, and we had to be sure there was nobody in there. So I called out and said to come out of there, and I called again, and when nobody answered I threw in a hand grenade. Well, out came twenty-eight men. Now, before that, we had faced a lot of Germans from the Prussian Guard, the elite outfit. But these guys in the dugout didn't seem to be of Prussian Guard caliber. They didn't seem to have the nerve. Anyhow, one of these guys came up to me and tried to tell me about his kids. I felt very bad for him. He was frightened. I put my arm around him and I said 'You're all right, fellow.' He felt better."

That was not the Medal of Honor incident?

"I won't talk about that. I will say this. A man was laying in a trench. A shell came over and exploded right above him, and he was buried by the dirt. One hand was sticking out. A sergeant was next to me. I said 'Sergeant, we got to get this man out.' We dug him out, and he was shell-shocked, and we gave him a cigarette, and we sent him back for medical help. Now I did more in digging that man out than what I've read about other guys who got the Medal of Honor. So that should be sufficient for anyone to realize that I was able to take advantage of the conditions."

You're a modest man.

"I don't like to take much credit on myself. There were a lot of brave people. I'm glad I was able to do what I could do, but there were a lot of good men with me. And it wasn't just the United States, it was some other countries too. I remember those men from England, for example; do you know about them? They took care of the unexploded bombs and artillery; they would go and take all the fuses out. So there were a lot of good people. I think I proved that I wasn't a coward, all right, and I am happy that I was picked out. But, listen, I'm not anything special."

When the armistice was signed, Pope was given a hero's welcome home. There was a parade in Chicago, newspaper attention, and paid trips to veterans' conventions. Following that, there was something less. Pope went into the painting business in the 1920s, where he says he just got by, and he did not work much at all during the Great Depression. He was ultimately hired by the Veterans Administration, where he spent sixteen of his last working years and where he found another outlet for heroic good will.

"I was a contact man for the Veterans Administration. My job was to talk with veterans, find out their problems, and help them however I could. I liked to do that. I believe we should all help one another. And I can honestly say that I was as good in that job as any man they had. Because I was the type of a guy who had been through so much that I could realize what they were suffering. Guys told me their stories, and I listened. A lot of them had trouble with money, for instance, and I told them whatever you do keep your military insurance. 'Twenty-pay life,' and all that stuff. I think a lot of them are thankful now.

"I love these men. But I have to admit there was one or two I wondered about. One fellow came in, and I had an *American Legion Magazine* on my desk, and when I wasn't looking he pushed it into the wastepaper basket. I didn't say anything to him, but a little while later the FBI called me and we got into a conversation about this guy, and the FBI man said, yes, they were watching him. Well, that proved this guy was wrong. I couldn't understand it; he was a veteran, but he must have been against the government. We've had them all over, you know, subversives, left wings or whatever, I could always see it.

"We have to keep patriotism alive. That's what this country needs. I was the commander of my Purple Heart Association when I was younger, and what I do now is still try to help veterans. I'm trying to raise money for veterans' homes. There are quite a few homes for veterans today, and they need money to operate. I'm trying to get the Veterans of Foreign Wars to help me with an idea I have. I want members of the VFW to donate serviceable items to their barracks, and the items will be collected during the annual convention so that they can be resold. The profits will be used to help the homes for veterans."

Tom Pope lives in a small but tidy garden apartment on a street where the flowers always bloom. He has three children, all girls, one of whom served in World War II; two were in Korea. His wife died in 1970, but he is still lively, still ruggedly handsome, and he shares his roof with a somewhat younger, also handsome, lady friend. He is not talkative. He has strong opinions, however, intoned with a full voice:

"I didn't like Vietnam at all. You don't let people at home run a war across the ocean. That's how the Russians got into Berlin, you know. It was politics. The Army was against it all the time."

He keeps his medals and memorabilia in a small study. Plaques and ribbons and photographs of before. Besides the big one, he was given the French croix de guerre, the French medale militaire, the Distinguished Combat Medal of Great Britain, the Italian war cross, something from Belgium, and several others American. He also has postage stamps issued in the names of York, Rickenbacker, and the Vietnam veterans. There is a photograph of Air Force Colonel James Stewart, who became something of a cinema actor. There's a Medal of Honor license plate. And there is the medal itself, kept apart, exactly where it belongs.

You get a special pension for the medal, is that right?

"Yes, two hundred twenty-five dollars a month."

And burial at Arlington national cemetery?

"All that."

Once again, why won't you discuss it?

"You've got my citation. You can print that."

The Medal of Honor is stamped with the likeness of Minerva, the Roman goddess of wisdom and war. The name, grade, and organization of the recipient are inscribed on the reverse side. It is the only American military ribbon that is worn around the neck. It is the only one that military persons of all rank are customarily obliged to salute. According to armed service regulation it is given only in circumstances where individuals perform a deed of personal bravery or self-sacrifice above and beyond the call of duty, so conspicuous as clearly to distinguish them for intrepidity above their comrades, involving the risk of life or the performance of more than hazardous service.

Corporal Pope:

"There have been fellows from the movie studios who have come around a couple of times. The last one who called, I said to him 'Find out how much money you can get for the homes for veterans.' I haven't seen him since."

The oldest living female military veteran in 1987 was Lou Luhrman, 104. She was born in Germany in 1881 and came to the United States on a sailing ship when Chester Arthur was president. She served in World War I as an army nurse, worked afterward for hospitals in the area of San Francisco, and retired to Menlo Park, California, where she says the most important lesson of her service is that the people of the world "must stop killing each other on the battlefields." She says nothing justifies everlasting slaughter, and she says her last great wish in life is that "we have peace, peace at any price."

VICTOR WESTPHALL

Victor Westphall was working the land when the word came. He was in the construction business at the time, building homes in the northern part of New Mexico, and he was moving earth from here to there on the Pacific side of the Sangre de Cristo Mountains. It was the springtime of 1968. That's what the calendar said, anyway. But a winter of national sorrow was also in season. Dr. Martin Luther King, Jr. had been assassinated; Senator Robert F. Kennedy would be cut down as well; the nation was reeling from a confrontation of social and political values unique in the century; and more than half a million American soldiers were engaged in a war in Vietnam that persisted in defiance of domestic confusion and international repudiation.

Dr. Westphall:

"I was developing a subdivision south of Eagle Nest that day, and two Marine Corps officers came into the field to find me. I was operating a backhoe when they arrived, and they informed me that my son had been killed in the war. At first they said 'Victor' had been killed, and I thought there might be a mistake. My son's name was Victor David Westphall, but we habitually thought of him as David. Then they clarified it, however, and I knew there was no error. The officers asked if they could help me down from the machinery. I said no, I could do it. Then I went to the house and told my wife Jeanne what had happened."

David Westphall died as a marine lieutenant serving his second tour in Vietnam. He was at the moment one of 500 Americans being killed each week in the fighting, and his passing was therefore and inevitably given little except family note. The death would eventually be widely recorded, however; when Victor and Jeanne Westphall thought out their grief in the spring of 1968 they decided that David should not die without deference; they believed that all the men in the battle deserved tribute and they went on to build the nation's first— and for a time its only—monument to the participants of its most dissonant war.

This, then, is the story of David's part in the twentieth century.

And that of his father who wants everyone to remember.

Victor Westphall was born in Wisconsin in 1913. The United States was engaged in military adventures then, too—supporting the revolution in Mexico, for one thing, and installing army rule in Haiti—but the senior Westphall did not come to know war personally until he volunteered for World War II.

"I was in the Navy during World War II. I was trained for underwater detection and harbor defense, but I wound up establishing fleet post office facilities and officer messenger centers in forward areas. This was in the South Pacific; I was within five degrees of the Equator for two years; and I was twenty-eight years old when I got there. I did not actually join the fighting, except from a defensive standpoint, but let me say that I did not object to the fighting. I think most people agreed the situation had to be addressed. We did not have the public objection that came later, in Korea for instance and in Vietnam.

"I did start wondering about the futility of World War II, however. I was in Borneo when the cessation of hostilities was announced, and that afternoon I saw a group of Australian and Japanese soldiers riding together in a jeep. The Australians had just released the Japanese, who were prisoners of war, and here they were laughing and joking with each other as if they had been friends all along. This brought home a stark reality to me. What is this all about? One day these men are implacable enemies, and then that afternoon they are having a good time with one another. I went home with that thought in my mind.

"When I got back to the States I wrote a number of letters to politicians regarding my concern. I also wrote to the president. I got back replies that seemed to indicate that nobody was interested in discussing it very much. So I did not push it any more than that, and, in the meantime, I had to get on with my life and so I went on to other things. I met Jeanne and we married; I received a PhD in history at the University of New Mexico; and I got interested in construction. I taught history at the college level, and over the years I built or helped build a couple of thousand homes throughout the state."

Dr. Westphall and his wife also had two children: Victor David and Walter Douglas. He says both were exceptional fellows, as men and boys, but for the immediate purpose he will concentrate on David. He says David was an athlete, a scholar, a musician, a writer. He was five feet nine inches tall, he weighed 175 pounds, he was intellectually and socially active in school, and he once shared the New Mexico state high school record for the 440-yard relay.

Forty-three point two seconds.

"He was an all-around American boy, I guess you could say. He was also a product of his times. He grew up during the Cold War, and he became an anti-communist. He did not like the idea of war—he was the same in that respect as I—but he did feel that there was a definite threat from communism that had to be countered. It was a different time. The feeling of the communist threat was more virulent then, it was more pronounced. So, good, bad, or indifferent, that was what he believed. He enlisted in the Marine Corps in 1960 and afterward, when Vietnam came along, he went back in as an officer.

"I might say we had a difference of opinion here. For me, the threat of communism has never been truly serious or really pronounced. For virtually all of my life I have thought that the most important thing for people to do in the world is to try to get along with each other. I have always seen the need of and encouraged internationalism. I think we should get away from this ancient notion of nationalism. I discussed this with David now and then. Just before he left for Vietnam, actually, we climbed to the top of Wheeler Peak, which is the highest point in New Mexico, and talked about our respective opinions.

"He went to Vietnam in 1967. He had rejoined the Marines after graduating from college, and he volunteered to go to the war. I did not discuss that with him, of course; I felt that he was his own man, and it was his decision to make. He was a second lieutenant when he left, and he received one promotion before he was killed. He was there for about fifteen months. The normal tour of duty was thirteen months, but he extended his time. He was a platoon leader in Bravo Company, First Regiment, Fourth Marine Division, and he took part in a number of battles in the northern part of South Vietnam; that is where the Marines were located.

"We received regular letters from him. I remember they did not dwell on the horrors of the war or the relations between people or the drug scene, or anything like that. David was acquainted with those things, because he was there, but his letters were upbeat, positive, and encouraging. He put a flower in one of the letters. He said it was for his mother on Mother's Day. He said he wished he had had time to send a bouquet, and he didn't want her to think he'd forgotten. That letter was typical. He talked about the countryside and the small things that were happening; his letters were never bitter in the least.

"He did not get into politics very much either. He did say in one letter that he didn't think the United States was any smarter than the French. The French had lost their war in Indo-China, and he drew some parallels. He said the days still belonged to the allies over there, but the nights were ruled by the enemy. He also deplored the leadership in the war; he says the men in the field were not allowed to do things that might end the conflict. Other than that, I think he thought the United States was doing the right thing, and that he was helping as best he could; I think he helped in an exemplary manner, myself.

"He won some citations, but I don't remember what they are. The important thing is that I've been told that he died while dragging a wounded comrade from the field of fire. That was on the twenty-second day of May 1968. His company was on a search-and-destroy mission close to the demilitarized zone that separated North and South Vietnam. It was near a town called Con Thien. The company was just getting ready to stop and bed down for the night when the North Vietnamese staged an ambush. They attacked on two sides, in the shape of an 'L', and David's platoon was on the point—in other words, out in front of the rest.

"One of the soldiers who survived told me later that David was killed while he was dragging a wounded man to cover. The man also told me that it was a characteristic thing for David to do. He was practically idolized by his men. At any rate, the North Vietnam ambush was successful. They killed all of the officers in David's company, and many of the noncommissioned officers. The final count was that twenty-three Marines were killed and twenty-six others were wounded. I'm told that the company was able to regroup and recover and then launched an assault of its own; but by that time it was too late for David."

First Lieutenant Westphall was buried with military honors in New Mexico. It was about the time the Vietnam peace talks were getting started in Paris. It was also when Vietnam opponents received more sympathy than Vietnam participants. Victor and Jeanne Westphall say they could not help in the first matter, but they might do something about the second. Mrs. Westphall made the original suggestion. She said the family could set up a scholarship in David's name. Then, when Mr. Westphall said that would be too ordinary, she countered with the idea of a memorial.

"David had left thirty thousand dollars' worth of insurance benefits," Dr. Westphall continues. "And we owned an eight hundred-acre ranch that we had subdivided for housing development. So we combined both resources. We decided right away that we did not want to build a monument just to David. We wanted to build a chapel to honor all of the people who took part in the war, 'the living and the dead and the maimed in body and spirit.' We hired an architect to design it, and it turned out to be more of a sculpture than a building. We started construction in the fall of 1968, and it was completed as the nation's first Vietnam memorial in 1971.

"We had quite a lot of opposition then. We were criticized for what we were doing. The Tet offensive had just taken place in Vietnam, which was a distinct setback for the United States, and the war was getting more and more unpopular. So building a monument to it was not all that welcome. I don't think we had many complaints on a national basis, but there were a lot of them locally. Some of the people in the vicinity were very hostile to it. I remember that one high-placed state official told a friend of mine, who worked for a newspaper, that we had to have an angle or something, we had to be out for something.

"That official later visited the chapel and changed his mind. And I think most of our opponents did. When the chapel went up it was like an implosion in a hydrogen bomb—the forces came to us from all over the world. The dedication was covered in newspapers like *Le Monde* in France and on the front page of a Tokyo newspaper. In Canada, in Argentina. When that happened, the local people felt, by golly, maybe the Westphalls do have something important. Just like in the words of the Bible, we were prophets without honor in this area; eventually, everyone came to understand, and Jeanne and I are grateful for that.

"The chapel is located below Eagle Nest, which is a small town north of Sante Fe. It consists of three inward-curving walls, shaped together in a triangle. It gives the impression of coming out of the hill on which it rests. Inside, there are declining steps that are reminiscent of those in a Greek theater, and there is a twenty-eight-foot window at the apex of the walls. It is quiet and serene, as a chapel should be, but I want to stress that this is more a memorial chapel than a religious one. We display David's photo on one of the walls, and we also have photos of others who died in Vietnam; we leave David's photo in place, but we change the other pictures periodically, to honor as many as we can."

The monument at Eagle Nest was initially called the Vietnam Veterans Peace and Brotherhood Chapel. In 1977 the Westphalls donated the structure and twenty-two acres of land to an independent arm of the Disabled American Veterans, and the site was renamed the DAV Vietnam Veterans National Memorial. In 1987 the chapel was drawing as many as 300 visitors a day during the summer months.

Dr. Westphall continues to be the director of the chapel. He is now seventy-four, and a world-class bicycling competitor. He rides 8000 miles a year, and holds the United States mark for the 25-mile marathon in the seventy-to-seventy-four age group. One hour and eight minutes.

He also writes, occasionally, against war:

"I have a book I've published that is called *The People's Revolution for Peace*. It espouses an idea advanced by Dwight Eisenhower. He said if the solution to war is to be met, it must be met by people, because government will not do it. He said one day the people of the world are going to want peace so much that government will have to step aside and let them have it."

As for Vietnam?

"I think my son said it as well as possible in that letter I mentioned before. He said we were no smarter than the French."

The amount of money spent by the United States government on twentieth-century veterans is estimated to exceed $500 billion.

The belligerents in the Korean War stopped shooting at one another on July 27, 1953, when North Korea and the United Nations Command signed an armistice. The South Koreans did not participate, however, and other political matters were left outstanding as well, so all sides agreed to continue negotiations at the one-time farm village of Panmunjom, square in the demilitarized zone between north and south, on the 38th Parallel.

The negotiations were still going on in the early part of 1988, thirty-five years after the hostilities ended. The antagonists met irregularly in the Military Armistice Commission Building, which was bisected by a military demarkation line for jurisdictional purposes. Meetings were held over a large rectangular table on which stood the flags of the two nations. By agreement, the North Korean flag was taller, sitting as it was on a base of three tiers, but the South Korean flag had a longer shank.

In 1987, more than 60,000 tourists visited the site from the south. Ten thousand came down from the north. American visitors were cautioned not to smile during their inspections, because North Korean guards would take their pictures for propaganda purposes, and visitors from communist nations were reported to have complained that South Koreans gave them the finger.

All agreed there was no end in sight to the peace talks.

YOSHIYE TOGASAKI

There is a small white obelisk in the wastes of California's Owens Valley, several hundred miles from David Westphall's memorial, that stands as a monument to another melancholy feature of twentieth-century America at war. It does not mark the place of a battle (there have been none in the country in the 1900s); it does not even represent destruction except as it relates to the argument of reason. The monument has been erected on the grounds of what used to be the Manzanar detention center, where the United States government detained Japanese-Americans during World War II. It was one of ten major holding camps established for the wretched purpose, including Amache in Colorado, Gila River in Arizona, Heart Mountain in Wyoming, Jerome in Arkansas, Minidoka in

Idaho, Rohwer in Arkansas, Tule Lake in California, Topaz in Utah, and Poston in Arizona.

More than 112,500 people were kept in the centers. Hundreds of others were detained in smaller places.

Yoshiye Togasaki:

"I am a medical doctor. I have spent my life in the care of people. But during World War II it did not matter. When the rumors of the camps could not be ignored, and when Japanese-Americans started being thrown out of work, I went to the president of the Council of Churches of the State of California to ask for his help, and do you know what he said to me? He said that I was just a traitor. He said, 'How do I know how to trust you? I don't know you from anything—you're Japanese, so you're not trustworthy.' That was the way people thought. There was a hysteria, and we suffered for it."

Let's start at the beginning. Dr. Togasaki says there has been a decided antipathy toward Japanese since they arrived in the United States just before the century began. The nation started importing laborers from Japan in 1884, to harvest the crops and timber on the West Coast, and many Americans resented it when the aliens stayed to put down roots, to buy homes, to originate businesses, to repopulate, and, as the Native Sons of the Golden West put it, to "think they are just like everyone else."

The resentment eventually took the form of a California law (1913) preventing Asians from owning land and of a national law (1924) halting most Asian immigration. Besides these strictures, the Japanese were subject to a much older statute (1870) that prohibited the naturalization of resident aliens of "yellow" race. Orientals born in the United States were entitled to citizenship, certainly, but—hard to believe in retrospect—immigrant Chinese were not allowed citizenship until 1943, Filipinos not until 1946, and the Japanese not until 1954.

Dr. Togasaki is also a woman.

"I have always considered myself American first, Japanese second. I did spend some time in Tokyo as a child, but it was only five months. I am a native of San Francisco. My first home was located where the Geary Theater is now. We had to move later when the great earthquake struck. We were relocated to Post Street, where my father started a grocery business. He later went into the import-export business downtown, where he dealt with things like Japanese foodstuffs and ceramics—*setomono*, as they used to call it, or dishwear. I had eight brothers and sisters. Two of the sisters became doctors, like me, two became nurses; and my brothers all went into some kind of business.

"Everything considered, we all did rather well. When I was a child most white people thought Japanese people should work in the fields or in restaurants or something like that. It was difficult to overcome the discrimination. We could not go to public swimming pools in San Francisco, and they tried to segregate the schools, you know. It was not quite the same discrimination as the blacks in the South experienced, because we were not excluded from most public facilities, but we were definitely set apart. We might have white friends in school, but they did not socialize with us outside of school. We did not date whites, we did not go to parties or dances with them.

"They thought of us as inferior, at least many of them did. We were called J-A-P-S. And of course there was the problem that nobody recognized you as a citizen. So we had to struggle that much harder to reach our goals. I certainly had to do my share of struggling to become a doctor. But that was my dream. When I was a young girl my mother used to take in pregnant women so they would get home care while they were having their babies. Then when I was in school I used to accompany Japanese women who had to go to doctors for office visits. The reason I did that was that the women could not speak English, and I acted as an interpreter. I got very close to health care, doing that.

"Women did not think of becoming doctors in those days. But I applied for premedicine at four colleges and was accepted at the University of California in Berkeley. I graduated in 1931 and went on to Johns Hopkins in Baltimore, Maryland. I may have been the first woman to get a degree in medicine there—I'm not sure one way or the other—but it was an unusual event. The way I understand it is that Johns Hopkins had gotten an endowment from some Quaker women who said that if the school did not admit women it would have to return the money with compounded interest. The professors didn't want women or blacks or Japanese. They made snide remarks to me, but I got my degree in 1935.

"I went to Los Angeles for [medical] internship, and that is when I began to see another kind of hatred of Japanese. Not many white people would go to a Japanese doctor, for one thing. And when we sent Japanese-American patients to the hospital, they were never put in rooms with whites. It was also quite hard for people like myself to get a job in the white institutions. When I completed my internship and decided that I wanted to go into public health, I took the civil service examination at every level—city, county, and state—and I was turned down every time. I wasn't even accepted for postgraduate training at a hospital, and so, in September of 1941, I had to open my own practice."

Three months later Japanese carrier aircraft struck Pearl Harbor in Hawaii without warning, killing 2400 Americans, wounding 1170 others, and devastating the United States Pacific Fleet. Dr. Togasaki says she was ashamed. The majority culture was outraged. The Federal Bureau of Investigation made a sweep of the Pacific Seaboard, two days after the bombing, and arrested hundreds of resident aliens identified in a "presidential warrant." The FBI said the residents were enemy aliens now; in fact they were Japanese community leaders, and they were the first of the lot to disappear into the dark temper of the time.

"That was the start," Dr. Togasaki says. "We did not know where it would lead to, but it did not look good. I personally was optimistic. I thought the initial shock would go away, and that would be that. But what happened was that emotions were kept high, in the newspapers, primarily. They would print stories of spies running around, and there was talk of people having radio communications with Tokyo. It was all completely unfounded, but a lot of it came from William Randolph Hearst's papers—they specialized in yellow journalism. So the idea developed to 'do something about the Japs,' and after a month or so we started to hear that we could all be sent away to concentration camps.

"Then navy intelligence agents began contacting people in the Japanese-American communities, and I was asked to attend a meeting in the first or second month of 1942. The announcement was made that there would be a curfew. People of Japanese extraction were no longer to be allowed on the streets after dark. They also set a limit on our movements. I didn't pay any attention to it, because I had to travel to see patients, but we were not supposed to go more than three, four, or five miles from our homes, something like that. It was all very frightening, you can imagine. People were losing their jobs, people were being threatened, but there was nothing any of us could do.

"Some people wanted to help us. I had doctor friends who said, 'Togi, let me know if there is anything I can do.' But there wasn't much they could do. One day the army removed all of the Japanese fishermen from Terminal Island, in San Francisco [Bay], and I think they took them to New Mexico. We had no rights. My father was a constitutional scholar, but when he brought that subject up, no one would listen. There were a few Japanese-Americans who demonstrated in the streets on an individual basis, but they were usually arrested. We were helpless. Today you could go to the newspapers, or to the television, to get some support, but that wasn't the way it was in 1942; no one cared."

To be sure. Californians believed the Japanese-Americans constituted a potential fifth column, and Americans of all persuasions, fair or prejudicial, demanded containment. Earl Warren, the California attorney general who was later to become Chief Justice of the United States, said that anyone who thought the Japanese residents were loyal was "living in a fool's paradise." Henry McLemore, a widely read syndicated columnist, wrote: "Personally, I hate the Japanese, and that goes for all of them." In this atmosphere, the California congressional delegation called for the removal of all Japanese-Americans to detention points where they could be monitored.

That suggestion was not altogether unprecedented (the U.S. Army isolated 30,000 prostitutes during World War I, see page tk), but it was nevertheless flagrant and raw. The United States attorney general warned that evacuation would be contrary to law, and United States Senator Sam Ervin (North Carolina) was later to say that it "the most blatant violation of the Constitution in our history." But popular fear was myopic and regional pressure convincing. President Franklin D. Roosevelt signed the enabling document (Executive Order 9066) on February 19, 1942. The government said the mass detention was a military necessity.

"The announcements were printed on leaflets and posters, and put in store windows and on telephone poles. Everyone had to comply or go to prison. The rule was that everyone was evacuated who was at least one-sixteenth Japanese. I don't know how that determination was made, but that was it. Status didn't matter. You could be very young or old—everyone had to go. Sometimes we were given a few weeks to get ready to leave, sometimes a few days; it was complete upheaval. People had to sell what they could not take with them, or abandon it. The government stepped in to take my father's home on a rather casual basis, and it was then occupied by strangers who were to pay a small rent.

"I never received orders to leave. It was inevitable that I would, but, before it happened, I volunteered to go. I knew I would be needed because of my medical background. I took ten girls with me, and we were allowed to go in my car; we did not have to go in trucks and train like most others. I went to Manzanar, which was located on the eastern slopes of the Sierra Nevada Mountains, not too far away from Mount Whitney. That is desert country, very desolate. Death Valley is to the east. The camp was under the control of the military at first, and then it was later turned over to civilians. I got there in the early days; when it reached capacity there were ten thousand people.

"It was built from scratch by the military, and so it resembled a military place. They set up a central sanitary facility, a bathhouse and laundry in one building, one side for men and one side for women, and the barracks were constructed around that. The barracks were sectioned off into quarters. There was also a central dining room. And later on a hospital was built. It was cheaply built, very poorly planned, and not a good place for families. Families had no privacy, and they were split apart. I was particularly upset with that aspect of it. A mother and children might be in one place, the father in another, and maybe teen-age daughters would be thrown in with four or five bachelors.

"It was also a very dirty place. Manzanar at one time had been a pear orchard, before Los Angeles took over all of the water rights of the area. When that happened, the orchard went dry, and the place became very dusty. The wind would blow from the south, and then it would turn around and blow from the north, and it was a very fine grit that covered everyone and everything. It was in the beds and in the food. We took showers, of course, but that was an unpleasant task. The showers were all open, and you can imagine how the women were embarrassed with that; the people eventually set up a traditional Japanese bath, called a *furo*; it was unsanitary, but people preferred it to the showers.

"I had the responsibility of setting up the medical arrangement. And I tried to do it according to my belief in preventive as well as so-called curing medicine. I wanted to keep people from getting sick, in other words. Avoiding food epidemics, for example, keeping the kitchen utensils clean. I was by myself in this for the first few months, and there were very real problems to confront. We did not have medical equipment at first, and the military did not have many of the medicines we needed. They did not have anything for pregnant women or for the babies we delivered, and we had to do the best we could. The state and federal governments did start sending things as time went on.

"There were the usual kinds of diseases. Tuberculosis was a worry, because there was no cure; the antibiotics were not in use until the postwar period. Childhood diseases spread rapidly. Diabetes has always been prevalent among the Japanese. Pneumonia. High blood pressure. All of these things were made worse by the conditions. There was the psychology of it, too. Many of the older people had lived in the United States most of their lives, and the nisei (second-generation Japanese-Americans) were full citizens. They were law-abiding people, they were hard-working, they loved the United States, and now they were treated like traitors; depression is also an illness.

"The people did what they could to keep the spirits up. We set up our own leadership, and it was tolerated according to the personality of the government administrator in charge. We also made improvements in the conditions where we could. The food was not to anyone's liking, I recall; it was not Japanese, so the people set up systems where they could bring in things like rice and tofu. Those things were part of our culture. If we didn't have them, then things were even worse than they were. Again, a lot of this depended on the government person in charge of the camp at a given time; we had a few good ones, who understood, and we had at least one who was a very bad apple.

"I would say all in all that the government people were mostly fair. They did not seem to be malicious, and it seemed to be a case of just doing their job. You could even disagree with them on some matters. I protested many of the things that went on, for example. On the other hand, everyone understood the things that went on, for example. On the other hand, everyone understood the relative situation; there was a definite line not to cross. The people in charge would not allow any criticism of the United States; they did not want 'agitators' or 'troublemakers.' There was some rioting at Manzanar during one period, and the leaders were dealt with quickly. Some of them were taken away to other places, or they would wind up in the stockade in our own camp.

"All of Manzanar was a stockade, actually—a prison. We were in jail. There was barbed wire all around, there were great big watch towers in the corners, and there were spotlights turned on during the night. You could not cross the boundaries, unless you were authorized on a work detail or something. The guards carried rifles. There was a teen-ager at Manzanar who walked out into the desert one day. He was not running away, he just walked in plain sight. Who in God's name would try to escape in broad daylight? He was mentally deranged. And he got shot. They shot him in the back. So we all knew exactly where we stood."

The detention camps remained in operation for almost two years. The Supreme Court by then ruled the indefinite detention was without legal foundation, and, besides, the interned Japanese-Americans had proved their loyalty in a variety of ways. Fifteen hundred Nisei men volunteered for military duty and joined 2700 Japanese residents of Hawaii to form one of the outstanding units of the war, the 442nd Regimental Combat Team. Six hundred eighty of them were killed during seven major campaigns. The team won one Medal of Honor, 52 Distinguished Service Crosses, 588 Silver Stars, and, because of multiple injuries, 9486 Purple Hearts. Douglas MacArthur said the Japanese-American soldiers "saved a million lives and shortened the war by two years."

Dr. Togasaki says some of the detainees were welcomed back to the West Coast. Others were told to stay away, particularly from California, because of the potential for racial violence. In all cases, the Japanese-Americans had to start rebuilding their lives all over, at an average age of about fifty. Very few left the country, however. Despite their imprisonment, they still had faith in the nation. They were Americans before, and after.

The doctor completed her career in the California public health service. She lives in Lafayette, east of Berkeley. She is eighty-three.

"You know the government has never apologized for this thing," she says. "There are many Japanese-Americans who have fought for compensation, and God knows they deserve it, but after all these years I think that a government apology would be enough for me."

[Author's Note: In August 1988 Pres. Ronald Reagan signed legislation authorizing a payment of $20,000 to each of the 60,000 internees still living; the law acknowledged that the internment program was a "grave injustice."]

4. Law and Order

FREEMAN COLLINS

Prisoner 19555 is escorted into a small room at the West Virginia State Penitentiary and told to sit down in a straight-back metal chair. He looks around quickly, noting everything but acknowledging nothing, a habit of his kind. His name is Freeman Collins. He is thin and bony. The skin on his face is stretched so tightly the veins pop through like braille. He has one tooth in the upper right side of his mouth. He wears a tie without a shirt collar. He has a red jacket, gray trousers, and pale blue eyes. He lights a cigarette, blows his nose into a desperately soiled handkerchief, and then fetches an aluminum butt can with his foot. "I'm going to spit," _he says._ Ping.

The escort says, "This is the writer, Freeman."

"Oh?"

"Mind you don't bore him now."

Slim chance. Freeman Collins claims to be the oldest inmate in the West Virginia penal system and perhaps in the nation. In 1987 he had been locked away for a total of fifty-two years, and that too may constitute a state record. He has only been convicted of committing three crimes in his life, but two of them have been murder. He originally entered prison in 1930, about the time silent films were taking leave, and, according to the demands of the law, he is scheduled to be incarcerated until he dies.

"I got out one time a few years back. I was paroled, ah, in 1972. It was not the same as it was. Big stores, and the cars were faster. Everbody had a lot of money, too. I seen TV in my cell, so it wasn't new. Everthin' else was. I got whiskey and I got drunk, and there were the women in their fine things, and jet planes, and the highways, and everthin' outside was changed."

Indeed. The world has become a different place since prisoner number 19555 was incarcerated in the first part of the century. The world of crime included. When Freeman Collins killed his first victim, in 1923, there were 7500 other murders reported in the nation. In 1987, there were more than 20,000.

It's true that criminal activity has always enjoyed prevalence in the United States, and for some reason resigned acceptance, but at least it used to have the capacity to shock. Collins was given a stiff belt because his offense was still comparatively peculiar. Thomas Carlyle was right: Today is not yesterday. And Heraclitus: There is nothing so permanent as change.

The change in American crime can't be measured precisely. The compiling of reasonably accurate statistics on crime is a relatively recent development. Police departments kept records in the early 1900s, but they were notoriously unreliable, and prone to political manipulation. The FBI started compiling national figures the year Collins went to stir, yet they necessarily incorporated the local abuses and are still subject to suspicion. There's no doubt about the statistical direction of crime, however; there were 130 legal executions in the year 1901 and 130 reported lynchings, the only two categories in the criminal justice count that have declined.

The following are crime totals (rounded) for 1960 and 1986:

	1960	1986
MURDER	9,000	19,000
RAPE	17,000	90,000
ROBBERY	107,000	542,000
ASSAULT	153,000	730,000

The numbers are skewed somewhat by the differences in reporting techniques that were employed during the respective years. And the figures merely represent crimes that were recorded by police, not the total (perhaps three times as many) that actually occurred. In any event, the statistics boggle. The number of murders doubled in the twenty-five-year period; the number of rapes grew by a factor of five. The FBI says that crime has increased at an average annual rate of 10 percent in the 1980s alone and that by 1987 there was a serious crime committed in America (murder, rape, robbery, assault, burglary, theft, or vehicle theft) every two seconds.

The city of New York recorded more crimes in 1986 (635,199) than did the entire of urban America in 1936 (600,000). The FBI says one out of every four households in the union was touched by crime in 1985. The city of Detroit had twice as many murders in 1986 (58 per 100,000 inhabitants) than died in London from German bombardments during World War II. And, in 1986, the *nation had to employ 475,853 police officers in 12,132 large and small agen-cies, to apprehend more than 10 million suspected crooks.*

Do not be encouraged by that arrest total: It includes every illegality from addiction to vagrancy. The fact is that most serious offenders commit their crimes with impunity. The FBI reports that, in 1986, only 21 percent of the 13 million serious crimes reported were cleared by arrest, and, on average, police authorities believe that only a third of the people they apprehend are ultimately sent to jail. This means that in the 1980s thugs have an 80 percent chance of getting away with crime, and the odds on being jailed for it are one in sixteen.

Also: There would be no place for the rest of the criminals even if they were brought to justice. The state and federal prison population grew from 196,400 to 546,000 between 1970 and 1986 alone, and the institutions became impos-sibly jammed in the process. The 120-year-old penitentiary in West Virginia is an illustration. More than 2000 prisoners live in 872 cells at this stone-walled slammer, including Freeman Collins, age eighty or 107.

"I was born in 1890," Collins says.

The records say 1907.

"I mined coal for twenty-six years."

Ping.

"I quit school to work in the mines. I was raised in the mountains of West Virginia, and everybody did it where I'm from. My dad was a miner. Everone I knew was in the mines. I was about ten or eleven, I got out of school in the fourth grade, and you had to earn money. It was deep minin', there weren't no strippin' going on, and I worked nine hours a day, about three-four-hundred feet in the hole. We had oil lamps to see. I used to help blow the seams; we used black powder in them days, and it was risky. I got caught in a couple of drops [cave-ins], but I never did get hurt. Others did. Lots of them. They only paid us a dollar a day or somethin', but you got to work, which was okay.

"I did it off and on. I was in the mines the first time until I was about thir-teen, and then I got caught up with this girl who was about twelve. I never mar-ried, now, because I always thought it was better just to shack up, but me and this girl wanted to get married. We went around for a few weeks, and then told the families what we wanted to do. Our folks said no, and so the girl said we should just run off. I quit the mine and I went to Charleston to get train tickets to get us to Cincinnati, which was nine dollars, I think. We got up there that night, and we got to Vine Street in Cincinnati, where we got a room for seven dollars and a half a month. The girl's name was Queen; I called her Queen.

"I went out and got a job in the city. It was the Baltimore and Ohio railroad company. I worked on the train between Cincinnati and Baltimore, close to about two years. Then we had a wreck one day and I was sent home. I came into the apartment and, what do you know, Queen had a guy in bed with her. I pulled out a gun in the room, and I threw it on them to scare them. I did that for a while, and I said, 'Well, you guys ain't worth shootin'.' I kept the gun on them, though, and I said, 'Now, you are gonna take this girl, and take care of her.' I said, 'You are gonna get married.' I saw them again about a year later, on Market Street, and they took me at my word; they were married."

Ping.

Collins says he carried a gun because that was the practice. Particularly in Appalachia. Most particularly in the climate in which he lived. He says he carried two of them, revolvers with six-inch barrels, and it was legal to have them showing. He claims he didn't use either one, however, not when he was young at least. He insists that he followed the law as much as he was able when he was a boy, but admits he lost the way as a man.

"I went into the moonshine business first. I come to Charleston and bought me a fifty-gallon still. You could get them made for about fifteen dollars, for a whole copper still, and I set mine up under a bridge. I was on a clear creek there, I had good water, and I could take fifty pounds of sugar and maybe twenty-five pounds of cracked corn and make good whiskey. I sold it for two dollars a pint. That was usually a hundred proof, or one-ten, but I could make it as much as a hundred twenty. I did right well except when the police came around. They came around ever six months or a year. I knew when they were ready. And I stashed my gun. I was arrested once and got thirty days in jail. I guess I made moonshine under that bridge five years."

Was that your first arrest, Mr. Collins?

"Yes."

And when were you arrested again?

"Not until that man died. Perchie Jarrell. Now there's been a lot of stuff about that, so let me tell you the way it happened. My dad had three or four hundred acres in Boone County, and the Jarrell people had three or four hundred acres right next to it, and the Jarrells tried to claim more. They pulled up one of Dad's corner stones one night, and a argument started. My dad was a good man, he was a hard-workin' man, he worked in the mines all day and then he would come home to saw wood or somethin'. He didn't bother no one. He wouldn't let the Jarrells take his land, though; no one could blame him for protectin' his property.

"I knew my dad was in the right about the land. I helped him set that corner stone. And I saw the Jarrells move it out of the ground. There were some oil wells in the area, you see; it wasn't much but I guess the Jarrells wanted to get their hands on everythin'. They fussed about it for a while. My dad tried to talk to them about it. I watched them talk for about two hours once. One of them had a gun stickin' out of his hip pocket. Then the big trouble started a week later. My dad was shot while he was gettin' down off a train. There were about five of them; they shot him in the back; I guess he fired back and got at least one of them, but that was all, and he was killed.

"I didn't like that at all. I thought about it and it wasn't right. So some time later the Jarrells had a party at their place. They had some money and they put out barrels of lemonade, lots of food, and moonshine. I went there to see what was going on, and I met this Perchie Jarrell. We started to talk, and we walked along together, and he offered me some beer. I wouldn't drink beer—I drink whiskey—so I got to drinkin' pretty heavy; there were a lot of pretty girls around, you know. I must have had a quart. Perchie was all along friendly and kept offerin' me more, and after a time I got pretty high.

"Then this Perchie Jarrell brought out a knife, and he said, 'Collins, I got you where I want you.' And I had a pair of steel knuckles in my breast pocket, and I reached down and I grabbed these steels knucks, and I hit him in the jaw, and I kicked him in the balls. I took his knife away from him then—it had a long blade—I took that knife and I hit him across the neck with it. Some people said later that I had an ax. There was a guy sittin' there, he had an ax, and he was half crazy anyway, and I don't know if he hit him afterwards or not. But I didn't hit him with no ax. I hit him with the knife, like I told you. The way it was, he was goin' to get me, so I had to go after him."

Collins was tried in the circuit court of Boone County. He says he had a court-appointed lawyer and the proceedings took six hours. He was found guilty on August 4, 1930, of "willfully, maliciously, deliberately and unlawfully" killing Perchie Jarrell, and he was ordered to be conveyed to the state prison and "confined for the period of his natural life." He was issued the administration number he still wears. The records say he was twenty-three.

He says the penitentiary was undergoing alteration when he got there. But not for esthetic reasons. The prison had long been one of the most forbidding in the nation, and the expansion would not help. It was established in Moundsville, West Virginia, in 1866 and has always been a six-acre enclosure surrounded by a wall that measures twenty-four feet high and seven feet wide at the base. It looks like perdition today. The same as in 1930.

"They were building on the walls then. And there were a lot of trees and underbrush around, and we had a lot of Indians in them days who did the work. I remember we didn't live so good as now. They didn't put the lights in until later, and the only thing we had at first was burning lamps. They didn't have a dinin' room, either, and we ate outside, with spoons we cut out ourselves, rain or shine. They didn't even have cells for a long time, or not many of them anyway, and a bunch of us lived together on the north side, in a—what's it called—a cabin. There was forty-nine of us there, all stuck together in that place.

"You could see people strung up from the dormitory. They were hung in the left side, and we were high up, so I could lay down on my cot and see them hang. You could see their heads jerk as they fell, ha-ha, yeah. They didn't have the electric chair then. They didn't put the electric chair in until, ah, 1940s or 1950s, when was it? I remember the hangin', though. They would throw a rope over a bar, and tie the other end to a horse. Then they would put the noose around a man's neck and shoo the horse. I've seen a lot of them hung, a thousand at least [prison officials say ninety-four people have been executed at the institution].

"I've also seen a thousand people get killed here too. There was a lot of it when I first came. The guards killed the prisoners and the prisoners killed the guards. There was this one time on the north side when some of the old boys were gamblin'. There was plenty of money around here then. And the guards seen it, and they went over there and moved in, and I guess they tried to get the money. The prisoners wouldn't let them and mowed them down; they killed six of these guards. Then they got into this old car and drove outside the walls and kept going. That happened all the time. They escaped.

"We had women here too. All kinds of women around. Nice women. We used to mix with them when we could. I one time took a load of apples to the women's side, and the guard there, she told me to take the apples around to each of the cells. So I went around and when I got to the upper end of the block, there was this old gal in cell 59, or 29, or somethin' like that. Good-looking gal. She said 'Man, I could do it right through the bars.' So she grabbed me and pulled me up to the bars. Yeah. She was inside and I was outside. It went on all the time. That was all right, you know; but the women ain't here no more.

"There were some rapes. But if you got out of line like that you'd go to the dungeon. The dungeon was way underground, and it had bars you could hardly see out of. You'd go there if you got smart or didn't do your work or hurt a woman. They had a big flat log in there, and they had a big barrel that they would fill full of water. Then they'd give you a little cup, held about a half of pint, and they would make you sit on the log and dip water out of the barrel all day long. When you emptied it out, they filled it back up again. That was the punishment. They could hit you too, but the dungeon was the worst thing."

Collins served forty-two years on his first sentence. He says the judge who sentenced him said that he would be released in five, but nevermind, he re-

mained in the penitentiary until he was paroled in 1972. He was sixty-eight years old then; his prison record was fair to good and the state believed that since he had paid an extraordinary debt and his life was in large part spent, he could be released without any risk to the society at large.

Un-huh.

"The warden called me in his office, and he asked me where I wanted to go to. I said it didn't make no difference. He said 'Wanna go to Charleston?' I said 'Might as well.' I think I took the Greyhound. I was okay, I had about a thousand dollars I had won gamblin', and I got a bottle of Old Grandad to take on the bus. I got off on Sixth Street, to spend the night in Parkersburg, and I checked into a roomin' house. I went up on the second floor, and there was a whole bunch of ex-convicts. There was Charley Overstreet, and Willie Frazier, and the Wade boy. There were about six or eight of them; we drank five gallons of booze.

"I went on to Charleston the next day. And like I said it was all different, but I settled in. I got a job, workin' for a guy in a carnival. I got girls for the military boys. I got around, I raised a little hell. I got in this automobile accident when I was out, and broke my collarbone. That's why my head tilts sideways. I can't straighten it up no more. I was in the hospital for a piece. Fifty nurses. I didn't even come to for a couple of days. They were going to operate to fix everythin' up, but they didn't. Here, feel right along in my shoulder. You can still feel that it's all messed up.

"All right. I stayed out from 1972 to 1977, and there is a story to that too. Pauline is the one that got killed, you know that. She was my parole officer, and I worked for her sister; I did lawns, pruned grapes, picked up trash. And one day we were all in this car, a white Cadillac, and we were goin' around, Dogtown, Dunbar, Carter's Creek, ha-ha, yeah. We came back that night, and I think what started this whole trouble was we picked up two girls and went out of our way to take them where they wanted to go, and it was gettin' dark, and then Pauline got out of the car with a snub-nosed pistol and drew it on me.

"I don't know why she did that. I think she was drunk. I slapped her, so she would drop the gun; I did not hit her hard. I picked the pistol up and I gave it to someone else until Pauline sobered up. That's what I did. I left the rest of them after that, and I went over to a friend's house to get me a drink of whiskey. I got the drink of whiskey, and I walked to my apartment; I had an apartment, 412 was the number. I stopped at the state store first to get a couple of pints. My old bones were a-hurtin' so I got pretty high, and I went to bed, and I laid in the bed there. I was about half asleep, you know.

"The police broke the door open. I had the screen door locked, and they cut through it I guess, and they came on in there. All I remember is that I woke all the way up and blood was runnin' out of my head, they hit me, someone did, and my billfold was lyin' over on the floor. I had just cashed a check, and the money was gone, six hundred dollars altogether. They grabbed me out of the bed, and drug me down through the driveway, and put me in a patrol car. I was bleedin' like a hog, and that's when they said Pauline had been killed. That was the first I heard it; I didn't remember nothin' about it, no, and that's a fact."

Ping.

Collins was judged guilty of murdering his parole officer and returned to the penitentiary at the age of seventy-two or thereabouts. He says he is innocent and thinks the policemen who arrested him were the culprits. He has served the time since with no chance of parole. Prison officials say he forfeited his opportunity for mercy when he killed the second person, and the only way he can get out now is to be pardoned by the governor or expire.

Some people think the old man is happy with that. They say he has become comfortable and secure as prisoner number 19555. He proclaims that he wants another chance at freedom and scratches the days from his calendar to that end, but at the same time he knows the score. He knows—everyone knows—that Freeman Collins, a fourth-grade dropout, makes a better convict than a citizen.

He lives in a secluded cell by himself. The state gives him seven dollars a month, and he says the food and the medical treatment are good. There are the drawbacks: he thinks the drugs and the homosexuality are disgusting and getting worse.

"But I don't get involved. I keep to myself. I have my television. I am allowed to get a snack in the kitchen. Sometimes I go to bed early. Maybe I won't go at all. They don't watch me so close now."

He breaks the tip from a cigarette. He says the cotton in the filter is unhealthy.

"I miss the whiskey. I miss the girls. I remember that party at Perchie Jarrell's. I had a pretty good time there at first."

There were 20,000 murders reported in America in 1986. The Federal Bureau of Investigation said they were committed with the use of 8460 handguns, 788 rifles, 1296 shotguns, 22 unknown firearms, 815 cutting or stabbing devices, 3957 blunt instruments such as hammers and clubs, 1310 personal weapons in the manner of hands, fists, and feet. In addition, 14 people were blown up, 230 were burned to death, 23 were killed with narcotics, 49 were drowned, 341 were strangled, 160 were suffocated, and 677 were dispatched with other weapons too numerous to mention, including ropes, rocks, acids, animals, airplanes, and motor vehicles.

HAROLD WEISBERG

Like many other people who were around at the time, Harold Weisberg precisely remembers the first time he heard the news that John F. Kennedy had been assassinated. It was November 22, 1963, shortly after 1:30 in the afternoon, Eastern Standard Time. Weisberg was a professional farmer in those days, he raised chickens on a spread in the rural reaches of Maryland, not far from Washington, D.C.; and says he was gathering eggs in the henhouse. He kept the house divided into four sections, identified as D-E, D-W, U-E and U-W, down and up, east and west, and he had just started the downstairs collection on the eastern side, where he recalls that he had come to the second nest on the line:

"I had a small transistor radio with me, I wore it around my belt, and I listened to a good-music station. I like good music, I also like jazz, and, anyway, the regular programing was interrupted with a flash from Dallas, Texas. The President had been shot. I believe it was the first bulletin broadcast. Naturally I was stunned. I gathered the eggs as fast possible, rushed up to the house, and turned the television on. I stayed there for hours. I had other chores to attend, but I went back to the TV all through the day, and followed as close as I could."

Weisberg kept following for several days. As he did his initial horror regarding the nation's fourth presidential assassination was transmuted into a concern for what would be the subsequent administration of justice. He thought the news reports were beginning to interfere with the constitutional guarantees of fair trial. He felt politicians and law-enforcement officers were fostering impossible legal prejudices. He wondered why the government was allowing wholesale coloring of critical evidence.

"That Sunday morning I got up early to get my farm work out of the way, and when I finished I went in to have breakfast and watch the television again. They were rerunning things then: the motorcade, the hospital scenes, and pictures of Lee Harvey Oswald being brought into the police station. My wife was there with me at the table, and I turned to her and I said, 'Dear, I think the poor son-of-the-bitch [Oswald] is going to get killed.'

"She said, 'Why do you say that?'

"I said because Dallas is not a jerkwater town, it's a major city. There is a federal prejudice. The have an FBI office, and it knows what it's doing, it invented the business, and they are doing everything they can to make it impossible to make use of what they claim is the evidence. I said I couldn't understand why, except to close Oswald's mouth. And there is only one way to close his mouth, and that was to do away with him. Well, that was about seven-thirty in the morning, November twenty-fourth. We kept watching the television, and later that day we saw Jack Ruby shoot Oswald."

So began Weisberg's fascination and consternation with what has become journalistically recorded as the crime of the century. It led him into an odyssey of truth that he says will occupy the remainder of his life. He does not in the least believe the governmental findings as to Jack Kennedy's homicide, that Lee Harvey Oswald acted on his own to plot and carry it out, and he has devoted his energies to the proposition that the murder was in fact a conspiracy that was painted over by the government.

He's not alone in that assessment. Americans have been suspicious of assassination investigations ever since officials fumbled many of the facts about the last hours of Abraham Lincoln, and faith suffered all the more in Dallas. Scores of books have been written to condemn the Kennedy probe, whole groups have organized to advance other theories, yet while most of the critics have moved on to other things and most of the doubts have been buried in time, Harold Weisberg, the one-time chicken farmer, is still searching for the answers.

One question is why.

"My parents were both immigrants from southeastern Europe—my father was from the Ukraine and my mother was from Bessarabia—and I'm a first-generation American. I'm the first member of my family, back to antiquity, to be born into freedom. You know what Robert Frost said about promises to keep and miles to go. I was born with a debt that I wanted to try and pay. I believe that for all of its failings, we have the best system that has been devised. The problem is to make it work. Some of us can help make it work, some of us can try and fail, and some of us just don't give a damn. I'm doing what I can to make it work, at least to try to make it work, instead of the alternative."

Weisberg is seventy-four. He is a rumpled man, moderate in manner, and well-spoken. He grew up in Philadelphia, three blocks south of Connie Mack Stadium, where it might be said that he became a student of the American system for more reasons than birthright.

"Like everyone else, I was influenced by the big events of my youth. In my case they were the Great Depression, some service in government, and the Second World War, in that order. I was hit economically by the Depression, of course, but I also learned a little about how society looks at different crimes in different ways. You know, during the Depression the newspapers would run stories about men who were sentenced to twenty-five years in prison for stealing loaves of bread for their families. But I personally knew a man in Kentucky whose father was a banker who robbed his bank, and he served a year and came out with a quarter of million dollars stashed away. So it became obvious to me that the system was not working.

"It was not working when I was with the government, either. I was an investigator for the United States Senate in the last half of the 1930s, and we investigated 'Bloody Harlan.' Harlan is a mountain town in Kentucky, I think you know, and there was terrible abuse in the coal-mining industry there. The coal companies had everyone in their grip; they ran company stores, they distributed scrip for which they charged fifty percent, and the trade association in the area was actually in business to perpetuate that control. Legitimate unions could not get started. Thugs were hired to eliminate people who tried. There were more murders in Harlan at that time than there were in New York City.

"Then there was World War II. I was in the Army intelligence branch in the 1940s. I wasn't a spook, I was an analyst, and I was not happy with what they gave me to do. The problem was there was no independence of thought connected with the work. We had people in my unit who did not seem to be able to do a single practical thing. We had foregone conclusions that we were suppose to justify after the fact. In other words, they gave you a conclusion to start with, and then you were supposed to prove it. I often wondered how the people in charge could wipe their own asses; they could not get interested in anything original at all. Here again, you see, the system was not working.

"So, after the war, I just said to hell with everything and I became a farmer. I had a small operation, and I did everything myself. I hatched the eggs, raised the chicks, killed the fryers, and I dressed them and delivered them. I also gave my customers cookbooks so they would know how to cook them. I taught a lot of young women how to cook in the Washington area. I used a cookbook put out by the Agriculture Department, called *Aunt Sammie's*. I was a pretty good cook myself. I won a national barbecue championship; I'm the one who made it popular to use marinade as a barbecue sauce. Absolutely. I did pretty well with the chickens. I was in business for almost twenty years. I was just getting out of it, actually, when Kennedy was killed."

Weisberg says his background on the farm was not to help his involvement in the assassination controversy. He would be ridiculed intellectually by many of those who believed the subject was for experts only—whatever that meant.

When he wrote his first book on the case, Whitewash, *he could not find a publisher to take him seriously, and he was forced to purchase the printing himself. The book was ultimately hailed by some critics ("important," "convincing," "historic") and over time 300,000 copies were distributed around the world.*
Weisberg:

"I did one thing in the *Whitewash* book. I proved there was a conspiracy to kill the President. Quite separate from that is who conspired. I was not then, and I am not now a conspiracy theorist. By that I mean I have never tried to theorize who was guilty. I'm not chasing a who-done-it. My goal has been to show that a conspiracy existed and that the body that investigated the killing, the Warren Commission, made the wrong conclusions. I've done that. There was never any reason not to believe it, actually. A conspiracy simply means that two or more people get together to do what the law says is wrong, and in this case it was impossible for Oswald to commit the murder by himself.

"I don't think the government were necessarily involved in the assassination. I don't think the Dallas police was involved, either. And I certainly don't think the FBI had anything to do with it; never did, never will. But there was an different kind of conspiracy and it was definitely a government conspiracy. I wrote about that in my second book, which was subtitled *Coverup.* The government covered up what actually happened in Dallas; the people involved set out purposely to present the facts in their own way, to their own ends; and what they wanted to do, and what they did, was to draw an official conclusion that, one, Oswald did it, and, two, he didn't have any help.

"Now I think I can understand their lying, or being less than truthful. I don't think the conspiracy to cover up was sinister in purpose. Think back about the first few days after the shooting took place. The president was dead, the nation was in shock, and government leaders had real worries. Was Kennedy the victim of domestics who were starting an invasion? Was a foreign power involved and did that mean an invasion would follow? They also had to be concerned about whether the killing was a single act or if others were also to be assassinated. So there was some excuse during those first few days. I don't think it could be excused after that, but at first they had their reasons.

"I have a document here which will show you what I mean. It's a memorandum from Nicholas Katzenbach, who was then the United States Attorney General, and it was written to Bill Moyers, who was a ranking assistant to the new president, Lyndon Johnson. Look at the date on the memo. November 25. That was three days after Kennedy died, and one day after Oswald was shot.

"I quote the memo:

" 'It is important that all of the facts surrounding [President Kennedy's] assassination be made public in a way which will satisfy people in the United States and abroad that all the facts have been told and that a statement to this effect be made now.'

"And here it goes on:

" 'One, the public must be satisfied that Oswald was the assassin; that he did not have confederates who are still at large; and that the evidence was such that he would have been convicted at trial. Two, speculation about Oswald's motivation ought to be cut off, and we should have some basis for rebutting thought that this was a Communist conspiracy or (as the Iron Curtain press is saying) a right-wing conspiracy to blame it on the Communists.'

"There are other things like that in the document. There are eight paragraphs altogether. But you can see how Katzenbach was shaping the evidence. The evidence had not even been collected at that time. The Justice Department could not know if Oswald acted alone; it could not even know for sure if Oswald had any responsibility whatsoever. Yet here was the attorney general of the nation already deciding on a conclusion that was in the best interest of the country. Justice didn't matter. The truth was not important. He said later in the note that the administration needed to do 'something to head off public speculation or Congressional hearings of the wrong sort.' In short, he was forming a conspiracy with the Executive Office."

Weisberg says has uncounted documents of the kind. He keeps them in a basement office that he believes is one of the largest archives in the nation addressing the Kennedy homicide. Rows of filing cabinets. Piles of boxes. Books, films, newspaper clippings. He has an FBI paper that points to Oswald as the lone culprit before Oswald was even charged; he has another FBI paper that emulates the Katzenbach memo before it was written; and he has a J. Edgar Hoover directive, dated November 26, that says "wrap up the investigation" because the basic facts were known.

"I might say here that the cover-up was a conspiracy on two levels. Some of it was spontaneous, and the rest was planned out. Part of the FBI involvement was probably spontaneous. Anybody who works for the FBI has a pretty good idea what is expected of him, or he doesn't make it. The first law in the bureau is to cover the agency's ass; the second is to cover your own ass. The records I have, and Hoover is the source on this, is that Hoover reached his conclusion on the killing at about the time Kennedy's corpse was taken to the navy hospital a few hours after he was shot. He decided that Oswald was the lone assassin, that was the line, and the Bureau had to go along with it."

"I have one more document in this regard. It's a report of an FBI agent in

Dallas, commenting on a set of films and pictures that had been taken of the President's motorcade. People took a lot of pictures that day, and the FBI reviewed some of them. I quote now from this report: 'Films taken . . . fail to show the building from which the shots were fired [the Texas School Book Depository]. Film did depict the President's car at the precise time the shots were fired. However, the pictures were not sufficiently clear for identification.' So they had pictures of the President being killed, but they say it's not worth a damn because it does not show Oswald standing in the window doing it."

Weisberg says the investigation was thus flawed from the beginning, almost from before the beginning, and consequently the Warren Commission did not have the tools to do its job accurately. He doesn't think the commission report was purposely in error, necessarily, nor does he know if any of the people involved, on any level, sat down to cook up a malicious lie. His claim is merely that authorities in the government did not do as much as they should have to be thorough and accurate, they were wrong and probably knew it, and the end result was illegal conspiracy.

The result also is that history may have been forever twisted and that the real offenders may have escaped all penalization. Who are the real offenders?

"As I said, I don't know who killed Kennedy."

Someone in government?

"As an official act, no. Otherwise, it's possible. It's possible someone could have been involved on their own."

High up?

"Not Lyndon Johnson, if that is who you mean. I don't think he could have been involved. He benefited from the assassination, that is true, but if he had arranged for someone to do it, others would have known, and he would be in jail the rest of his life."

And how about Oswald?

"No, it wasn't Oswald. He may or may not have been involved, but I have no reason to believe that he fired the shot. He was at the Texas School Book Depository that day but he was on the ground floor rather that at the window higher up. There were witnesses to that, you see. And I have a photograph that is prima facie evidence of Oswald in the doorway at the time of the shooting. It was taken immediately after the assassination. The FBI says the picture is of a man named Lovelady, but Lovelady was wearing a different shirt that day, his wife told me that. The shirt in this photo is Oswald's. I went to the National Archives to compare it with the actual shirt there. They match exactly.

"There are some other things most people don't know with respect to Oswald. The Warren Commission went on and on about what it said were his connections with Russia; he traveled there, he lived there for a while, he brought home a Russian wife. That makes it look like he was some kind of dupe and an ideologue who didn't like the United States, a zealot. I think most people remember that image of him. The fact is it might not have been true. I don't want to get into it very much, for reasons of my own, but I did quite a lot of research on Oswald—I talked to people who knew him quite well—and I can give you a little different picture of him, based on what I know personally.

"He may not have sympathized with the Communists, for one thing. He may have been the opposite. He had the highest security clearance while he served in the Marine Corps. I believe his work was also connected with the Central Intelligence Agency while he was there. I don't think he made a move in the Marine Corps without the CIA. So here you have a presidential assassin with this kind of record? When Oswald came back from the Soviet Union, the KGB asked him not to speak too harshly of the country. He hated the Communists; he called the Russians 'fat, stinking politicians'; he said the American Communist Party betrayed the working class. We're speaking about a man who was said to be subversive."

Weisberg says he sympathizes with this representation of Oswald, because he has been accused of subversion himself. When the Warren Commission report was published, the government did not take kindly to some of its critics. Weinberg says the FBI in particular did him dirt. He says Lyndon Johnson may have set the deeds in motion when, in November 1966, he asked the FBI to compile reports on people who said the government findings were a lie.

One of the things the FBI told Johnson was that Weisberg and his wife regularly celebrated the anniversary of the Russian Revolution. Weisberg had Russian parents, after all. The whole thing fit. The FBI said thirty-five people would gather at the Weisberg farm to join in the festivities. The Bureau also said that Weisberg had a personal relationship with a USSR national, and the whole of the data was distributed to various government agencies.

"It was unmitigated evil," Weisberg recalls. "The accusations were hogwash, and the only reason they were made was to defame me. They could not refute my book, my conclusions, so they had to destroy my character so that no one would pay any attention. Maybe to teach me a lesson. They wanted the criticism to stop."

Weisberg went on to write seven books in all about the Kennedy assassination. He also wrote a book on the murder of Dr. Martin Luther King, Jr. He lives with his wife in Frederick, Maryland, amid 320,000 assassination papers. He has a bad leg, a good eye for detail, an excellent view of the limitations in Washington, and he offers one concluding, studied, albeit pessimistic, determination regarding the crime of the century:

"When I started to criticize I was very naïve. I thought if I pointed out the errors, something would be done about it. Now I know better. I regard that assassination as the greatest subversion of our society in this century, it is the closest we have come to a coup d'etat, and so I felt I was obligated as a citizen to get to the bottom of it. But I don't delude myself any more. I don't think the government is ever going to admit any fault. I don't think it's possible. Where are you going to reopen the case? How can you get an impartial body? Who are you going to get to stand up to the FBI and the CIA? The government failed us. The system failed. I'm afraid that's it."

We will never know who killed John Kennedy?

"Not unless they confess. I don't look for that, either."

There is at least one other murder that has been known as the crime of the century. And the killing of twenty-month-old Charles Lindbergh, Jr. has been debated almost as hotly as that of John Kennedy. The official version of the case is that Bruno Richard Hauptmann kidnapped the infant in 1932, then killed him for unknown reasons. Shortly after Hauptmann was executed in 1936, however, critics began to say that he had been framed. There were suggestions that the police had arrested him in a desperate attempt to appease an angry public clamor for revenge and that the prosecution covered up major evidence damaging to the cause.

One of the critics was and is Anna Hauptmann, the widow of the convicted. She is eighty-seven as this is being written; she lives alone in a Philadelphia suburb; and she has maintained her husband's innocence for more than fifty years. She says he was not the kind of man who would harm a child; and, besides, "he was with me at the time the kidnapping took place." Authorities have never believed her. It's unlikely they ever will. But she says she will never give up hope. "The last words Bruno spoke to me were 'auf Wiedersehen—I see you again.' Sometimes I wake up even now, and I think that today he is going to walk in my door."

NICHOLAS PETTE

Nicholas Pette is one generation removed from the customs of the Adriatic and, at age ninty-six, he has a bit of the courtly demeanor and a lot of the vocal characteristics of Marlon Brando portraying Don Corleone. The resemblance to the dark side of Italian heritage goes no further, however. Pette is a giudice *rather than a* padrino—*a judge, not a godfather. He sat on one bench or another for forty years in New York City before retiring to the private practice of law, and also to a smart apartment in midtown Manhattan where he now reposes near the illumination of a professionally decorated Christmas Tree, this late week in December, to say that expediency and justice may not always be on speaking terms, as Harold Weisberg insists, but, more often, when both sides are fairly heard, reason triumphs.*

"I was in court in Flushing once, that is in Queen's County, and I had before me a landlord-and-tenant case. The tenant had not paid his rent for three months, and the landlord (as was his right, of course) brought him into court to force him to pay up or get out. Under the law, the landlord could not evict the tenant unless he could get a judge to give the order. So the landlord took the stand to tell his story, and he told it; he told about three months' back rent and he said he was entitled to the money.

"Then it was the tenant's turn. He took the stand, and I asked him if he owed the rent. 'Judge,' he said, 'I owe the rent. But I don't think I should pay it. Because I have been miserable living in this house. I live on the first floor, in the front, near a little yard, and the yard is filled with crickets.' He felt he had the right to stop paying until the situation was corrected. He said he played the tuba in his apartment, and the crickets made so much noise that he could not do it right.

"I said, 'That's interesting, I'll think it over.' And when I did I decided that the tenant was not the only one who wanted to make music at the apartment. The crickets were also musicians. They played tunes by rubbing their legs together. I felt the crickets had just as much right to enjoy their sounds as the tenant did his, and in fact they should have enjoyed each other. Therefore I wrote my opinion in favor of the landlord and ordered the tenant to move somewhere else within fifteen days."

Learned Hand, the great twentieth-century jurist, said justice is the tolerable accommodation of the conflicting interests of society. And the animal kingdom? Nicholas Pette chuckles. He is a practiced chuckler. A friend says he is also shrewd; his wife says he is also modest. He wears a brown suit and a pair of hearing aids this evening; his tie and his handkerchief match. He has been alive since before the Ellis Island immigration center opened in the East River, a short distance from his home.

"My father came here from Naples—that was before I was born—and we lived in Williamsburg, in Brooklyn, which was a very poor neighborhood then. My father began as a cobbler, but he had ambition, and that's why he came here, to look for opportunities. He went to night school to learn English, and he was to open a real estate office, right opposite a park where George Washington made his headquarters during the Revolutionary War. My father was a popular man; he was a patriotic man; and he got into politics, where he helped other immigrants take advantage of this great country and make better lives for themselves.

"My mother died when I was six. My stepmother died a few years later. That was way back when. They did not have subways in New York at the turn of the century; there were trolleys. They were five cents a ride. You could go from Williamsburg to the Rockaways for a nickel. It would cost a dollar today to make the same trip—more if you had to transfer. There wasn't very much crime, either. We moved to Jamaica when my father started to work his way up, and I don't think I remember hearing about a single murder in Queens. There were no muggings to speak of; you could walk the streets any time with safety. We had the Ku Klux Klan around. They were gangsters, but there was no crime like it is today.

"The courts were filled with minor things. My father got involved in that. You did not have to be a lawyer then to go into one of the minor courts to represent someone, and my father helped people that way. He found a judge that he could sort of depend on—all he had to do was bring him a jug of wine—and so he did all right there. My father became very interested in the legal system, and he always wanted me to get into the business. We used to go to magician shows together, and I was always amazed, and I declared to my father that that's my future, I'm going to be a magician. But he said 'I have other ideas for you; when I get the money I am going to send you to law school.'

"He sent me to prep school first. That was in Germany, where I studied different languages. One week we spoke nothing but German, the next week it would be Italian. I was there for several years, and when I got back to the United States I went on to Brooklyn Law School. In those days you did not need a college education to get into law school in New York State; you could do it with a prep- [high-] school diploma. I went into law school when I was seventeen and I graduated in 1912. It was a very small school and we had a very small class. All the others have died since then. I have for many years been the only surviving member of the class, the only one. What do you think about that?"

Pette's wife Ruth touches his knee. She acts as an assistant guide on this trip through time. She is younger than the judge, a slim woman, statuesque; call her a grande dame. She wears her hair above her ears, swept up in a hundred-dollar-a-pop dressing, and she is Big Apple. Bloomingdale's. Name-dropping. The judge is reserved and shy; she is fashionable and talky. True love.

Judge Pette's career in law had an auspicious start. It was delayed at first by World War I, to which he went as a buck private in the infantry and from which he returned as an intelligence officer. It was delayed again when he was discharged and was promptly asked to run under Republican colors for a seat in the New York State Assembly. He spent a pair of sessions there and during that time opened a practice.

"Curiously, one of my first cases was against Teddy Roosevelt, the former president of the United States. Teddy Roosevelt had been involved in an automobile accident, in which he was driving one of the vehicles, and I represented a plaintiff who was suing for several thousand dollars in damages, something like that. So after a time I got a call from Roosevelt's lawyer, who wanted to settle out of court. So we met and he asked me how much my man wanted, and I picked a number—it wasn't very much—and he said 'Settled!' One week later I received a photograph from Teddy, inscribed *All regards to Nicholas Pette*, and I've kept it always.

"I had a couple of bills passed in the legislature. There was one about fares on the Long Island Railroad. The people who rode it from Long Island to Manhattan said the fare was too high, and I wrote a bill to have it reduced. I didn't think it would pass, actually. But it went through the Assembly, and then it got by almost unanimously in the House. The only other thing was the governor's okay. Al Smith was governor then, and I thought he would veto it. One day he called me and asked me to come to his office. I thought he was going to chew me out or something, but it turned out he just wanted me to witness the signing.

"I did not run for the legislature after two terms because I became an assistant district attorney in Queens. That was an interesting time. The Volstead Act had been passed; the district attorney's office was charged with the responsibility of prosecuting violators. We had people running rum down from Canada, for example, and then some of it was being made in cellars right in the city. The speakeasies were illegal too; there were beautiful speakeasies in New York, and I was very busy. The police arrested hundreds of violators and I prosecuted scores of them, and I did not win a single case.

"The reason was the law was so unpopular. People thought the rumrunners were providing a necessary service. Anyway, after I lost a lot of cases, one right after another, one of the judges said to me, 'Nicholas' (he called me Nicholas) 'is your heart and your mind in your duty in prosecuting these cases?' He thought I wasn't doing my best. He was a teetotaler, you see. I said, 'Judge, I'm doing everything I can, but nobody wants these people to go to jail.' And they didn't. I've never been much of a drinker myself, but everybody drank during Prohibition, everybody was guilty; my first wife Gertrude did it all the time."

And you, Judge?

"Wine, maybe. I'm Italian."

Pette moved from prosecuting to judicating in 1928, when he ran for and won a slot in the municipal court of New York City. The court had jurisdiction over civil litigations up to $1000, the most common matters in the American courts—the ebb and flow of everyday trespass, giving every man his own, as Aristotle put it, hearing the tuba player complain about crickets; justice lives where each person has a dependable opportunity to claim redress.

"One day I heard a case about a customer who had been hurt in a barber shop. The testimony was that the customer was getting a shave and the barber was telling a joke at the time. When the customer laughed at the joke, he also threw up his hands, as people will do, and he was cut with the razor. The customer said the barber was at fault because he was in control of the situation, he was holding the razor, and so forth. The barber denied that and said that as far he was concerned it was a freak accident. There were other people in court that day, and they were all laughing by then, so I reserved my decision.

"I liked that kind of case, by the way. Because there was some humor in it, and you don't get much of that as a judge of law."

Yes, but what happened?

"I found in favor of the barber."

Why?

"I thought he had a right to tell the joke."

Ruth Pette says her husband stayed in municipal court for eighteen years before he was promoted to the supreme court (which, oddly, ranks third from the top in New York State judicial system). He was later appointed to the appellate division, number two in importance, where he finished his career on the bench.

The wife says Pette was one of the best-regarded judges in the upper reaches of the system. "He always had nice things to say, even to the people he ruled against." *He also had an affinity for the unfortunate, the poor, the under-privileged, the luckless, and the people protected by the weight of the law and good sense.*

Judge Petty squints his eyes. He is getting tired.

"There was a case I heard in the Supreme Court that had to do with a jockey who was killed during a race at Aqueduct race track. The jockey had fallen from his horse and landed against an unprotected cement wall. The race track was sued for negligence. It was a trial by jury, and the jury ruled against the track. They felt the track should have covered the wall with some kind of padding, like they do in the baseball stadiums. I think the jockey's family got three hundred thousand dollars, and I agreed with every penny. The race track got rid of the hazards after that; the owners changed the track; they knew they had been in the wrong."

Did you often feel sorry for people like the jockey?

"Yes, I followed the law, but I did sympathize. My father had a great heart, and he was very much interested in small people. I followed him in that respect. Wherever I can do anything for someone, whenever I can come to their aid, I try to do it."

His head nods.
The judge retired from the courts in 1968, at age seventy-six, after forty years. He went into private practice, where he argued in court until he was eighty-five. He is now a special counsel to a firm of attorneys in Queens and, when asked by the courts, he arbitrates cases that might otherwise languish for lack of sitting judges to hear them. He is a small gentleman, smiling widely, his hands folded on his knees, and he chooses his words as if they will be reviewed by a higher tribunal. He is the oldest practicing lawyer in the state of New York and one of the oldest in the country.
Ruth Pette takes over when the judge rests:

"Nick and I met at the Emerald Ball, which is a big social affair in the city. His first wife had died of cancer, and my late husband passed away with a heart attack. I really didn't know the judge, except I had heard his name, because my husband used to say he was a nice man, for a Republican, and too bad he wasn't a Democrat. So I didn't pay any attention to Nick that night. But then there was an early breakfast we both attended at one-thirty in the morning, and he said 'Hello,' we talked, and he asked for my telephone number. Well, I got home at five A.M., and the judge called two hours later. He asked if I wanted to go to the Stork Club for lunch, and I said 'Yes,' and that was it."

Mrs. Pette opens a scrapbook. It is filled with the stuff of the privileged. A personal photo of Tom Dewey. A reference to the billionaire entrepreneur and friend Donald Trump. Mrs. Pette had been close to former Mayor William O'Dwyer. The judge knew Nelson Rockefeller. Page after page. Ninety-six years. When the judge started practice in Queens there were still farms on the Island and people were arrested for stealing crops.

"Now they aren't arrested for stealing anything," Mrs. Pette says editorially. "You can't even go to Bloomingdale's without seeing it. I was there a month ago, and someone took my wallet out of my bag without my knowing. I am very conscious of how I hold my bag—I do it defensively—but, somehow, they got to the wallet anyway. They took my credit cards and sent the wallet back to me through the post office. Within one day whoever did it charged twelve thousand dollars to one card and they put another eleven thousand on American Express; they got both cash and merchandise.

"The funny thing was that when I got the wallet back in the mail, I noticed that there was somebody else's Social Security card inside. It wasn't mine. I thought the thieves might have put it in there by mistake or something; it might provide a lead; at least there might be some fingerprints, so I told the police about it right away. When I called the station house, the man said no, he couldn't do anything about it, and said to notify the Social Security office. No one cared. No one did anything. That thief may still be at Bloomingdale's today."

The judge is not yet asleep. A final verdict, then:

"There is a great disrespect for law and order. Time was, when I was a young man, people went to church and people in the neighborhoods looked after each other. That's gone. Now there are changes in relations, the churches and the neighborhoods don't mean so much any more, and people look out for themselves. The country is too busy making money. Crime is a natural result."

Nicholas Petty earned an estimated $1500 the first year he practiced law (1918). In 1987, some large New York City firms offered first-year attorneys as much as $1500 a week.

Officials at the National Center for Juvenile Justice report that children under the age of fifteen constitute the fastest-growing segment of the criminal community during the eighth decade of the century. From 1978 to 1983 the rate of referrals to juvenile courts rose 37 percent for thirteen-year-olds, 38 percent for twelve-year-olds, 22 percent for eleven-year-olds, and 15 percent for ten-year-olds. In 1985 the FBI said that youths fifteen and younger committed 381 cases of murder and non-negligent manslaughter, 18,021 aggravated assaults, 13,899 robberies, and 2,645 rapes; children twelve and under were said to be responsible for 21 of the killings, 436 of the rapes, and 3545 of the aggravated assaults.

AL ("WALLPAPER") WOLFF

When Paramount Pictures held the premiere of the movie version of The Untouchables, *in the spring of 1987, studio executives invited a longtime Chicago resident named Albert H. ("Wallpaper") Wolff to critique the screening. Well, he said, in gravelly vocals, taking it all very soberly, actor Kevin Kostner did all right as federal agent Eliot Ness, and the street scenes and gunplay were entertaining, but he objected to the scene where Ness engaged the gangster Al Capone in a profane discussion of changing times, government intent, and law and order. Wolff said it was true Ness hated Capone, the Windy City crimelord, but the bombastic confrontation was an invention. Ness was too quiet and reserved to waste himself in a public debate, Wolff explained, and Capone would not have bothered with the flapdoodle either.*

The Paramount executives didn't like it.

"But I said what I had to," Wolff recalls. "I always tell the truth. I don't just go along with things; I'm an honest man."

That almost goes without saying. Wallpaper Wolff is, at eighty-five years old, the last of The Untouchables. *He worked for the prohibition enforcement arm of the United States Justice Department during the term of the Eighteenth Amendment and was assigned to the Ness force when it was formed; he did not get his due in the news copy that accompanied the Chicago gangbusters, because he labored in large measure under cover, but he has outlived both his friends and his enemies of the day, and that is a consolation.*

"The trouble with that scene in the movie is that you didn't just bump into someone like Capone on the street. In all my time in Chicago I only met him once, and that was in Hot Springs, Arkansas. I used to take the baths there, for fifty-some years—arthritis—and one time he was there too. I was walking down the street and there he was. Someone pointed me out to him. He came over and said, 'So you are Wallpaper Wolff.' And I said to him, 'So you are Robin Hood.' The newspapers used to call him that because he gave charity baskets out at

Christmas. When I said that he replied that he had heard some nice things about me.

" 'Oh,' I said, 'what's that?'

"He said, 'I heard you don't frame nobody.'

"I said, 'No, I wouldn't want to be framed myself.'

"He said, 'And you let the guys you arrest make bond?'

"I said, 'Sure, I'm not the judge and jury.'

"Then he said, 'I'd like to have a man like you with me.'

"And I said, 'You can't have me because I want to live.'

"He laughed at that. I told him, 'Listen, I don't know you personally, but I can't condone what you're doing because I'm a federal agent.' He said, 'You're right; you've got your thing, I've got mine.' So I can't say much else about him. I didn't like what he did, and he couldn't buy me. That was it."

Al Wolff was born the first son of a Jewish immigrant from Germany. His father was a Hamburg physician who taught him the virtues of veracity. Wolff says he got interested in the good guys versus the bad while reading about cowboy justice in the frontier West (it had only recently folded into history); he was introduced to government service during World War I; he studied accounting and constitutional law at Northwestern University; and he entered law enforcement as a bailiff's assistant in Chicago.

"My job with the bailiff was to collect judgments awarded by the courts. If somebody was sued for bankruptcy, say, and lost, we would go into the company and take whatever merchandise we could to pay off some of the debts. We'd take everything we could, and I suppose most of it was sold for the cash value. That's where I got my nickname. I was very thorough on those assignments. When I went in I would seize anything in sight, big and small; it didn't matter, you follow me? After a while people started to say I took everything but the wallpaper, and it was true. People have called me that ever since. Police, thieves, everybody. Like Capone said: 'So you're Wallpaper Wolff.'

"I worked for other local agencies too. I was with the park police for a while, and I was also with the Secret Six. Do you know what the Secret Six was? It was an investigative body in Chicago; it's now called the Crime Commission. I don't know why they called it the Secret Six. Maybe there were only six at one time. Albert Jamie was the fellow in charge of it. He was related in some way to Eliot Ness. I started to do secret work with that organization. We got informers, we tapped people's telephones; it had a lot to do with bootlegging then, but we also handled prostitution, extortion, and all the rest of it. There was a lot of crime element in Chicago then. Still is.

"I took my federal examination in 1928. I was twenty-six, or around there. I went right in with what they called the Prohibition Department and I became a revenuer. I worked in the hills of Kentucky; I worked across the border in East St. Louis. There were times I slept in the woods with the rattlesnakes, waiting to raid a still at dawn. I didn't like it. I was a big-city boy. But I did it. The law was the law. You could not make, sell, or transport liquor, so we would bust it. I'll tell you, it could get rough; they'd wait for us in the trees with squirrel guns. I'd rather go after Capone; the guys in the hills had no respect, they didn't care if we were federal agents.

"They weren't really terrible people, some of them. They were backward and ignorant. They had been making booze in Kentucky all of their lives, it was part of their ways, and they just fought for that. It was bad stuff, however. I always said bathtub whiskey would make you swear off alcohol. I used to see dead rats in the stills, and clumps of other stuff I couldn't recognize. The garbage didn't bother them. I think they used it as seasoning. They sold a lot, though. They had people in the mob in St. Louis who took all they could manufacture. It wasn't just a harmless little thing; that stuff would turn up all over the country, and it helped create organize crime."

More, it helped create the institutionalizing of organized crime. Structured criminal societies were formed in the United States in the final years of the 1800s, but they were relatively small in scope and influence until the passage of the Eighteenth Amendment created new outlets for illegalities. People wanted spirits; gangsters supplied it; and the Mafia, et al., came to be looked on as an expedient and even merciful malevolence.

The acceptance is what led to the formation of The Untouchables. The police also looked on Prohibition as repression, and that was a justification for treating the mobs lightly. Al Wolff says police officers often joined others in cooperating with rather than struggling against the crime syndicates, and it got to the point in 1927 at which the Justice Department decided that it had to organize a entirely new force to regain credibility in Chicago.

"I was assigned to The Untouchables. Nobody asked me if I wanted to go; it was just another duty for the Prohibition Department. I might have been recommended by Albert Jamie, who was an important man, and I think he was Eliot's brother-in-law. I didn't meet Ness until I was sworn in, along with some other fellows, which was late in the 1920s. That is another thing about that movie they made. They only had Ness and three other guys in the picture, but there were a lot more than that. I knew fifteen people on The Untouchables, and if we needed other people we would get them out of the police department.

"I liked Ness. I got to know him very well. He was a very passive fellow around me, I guess because he knew that I had more experience that he had. He grew up in Chicago, I think, same as me, and he also worked for the Justice Department, but he had never been on the enforcement end of it. I had been in enforcement with the bailiff's office, and with the Secret Six, and I had more time on-line. Ness relied on that. And he knew he could trust me. I am a Jew, you know, and sometimes I had more trouble with that in police work than with the bootleggers, but I don't think it bothered Ness, he never brought it up.

"He put me under cover right away. People started to talk about The Untouchables, agents that couldn't be bribed—the newspapers said that right from the start—but nobody knew I belonged. My family didn't even know. I never told anyone. My wife thought I was still just a revenuer, and all my kids knew was that I was some kind of cop. I led a very normal life at home, you follow me? I kept my guns hidden out of sight. I took everybody on picnics; we went to the movies. We lived on the North Side, 57 North Spaulding Avenue. I never had to worry about my family, which was helpful. I took out all the insurance I could afford, but I did not think anything would happen; I was under cover.

"The way I worked, I would get assignments. Ness might call me at three in the morning and tell me someplace to go. I would go, and I would buy booze, and I would put some of it in a bottle I kept in my coat. That was the evidence. You had to be able to stand up in court. I had the stuff analyzed, and then I'd go back to the place and make my arrest. I knocked off six places like that during one week alone. One time they called me about a boat in the Chicago River, a floating saloon. I went aboard, made some solid buys, and I seized the boat; I showed them my badge, and I took everything and everybody on the boat.

"Sometimes it was not so easy as that. It was always very dangerous. People didn't always surrender passively. I had a partner get shot right alongside of me, during one raid. That was on the South Side of Chicago. A fellow was running a load out of a warehouse there and he tried to get us, and he shot the fellow alongside of me. He only hit him in the leg, however; it wasn't bad, so I fired over the gunman's head and we arrested him. I didn't want to hit him, or I would have hit him; I was a expert shot in those days. I had several weapons; I had a Lugar, a Mauser, a Smith and Wesson; I shot the long barrels.

"I never got hit myself. I did have a shotgun put to my head one time. On Dempster and Waukeegan Road. I ran into a truck that had a load of beer; I got the tip from an informer. I didn't like to use informers, but I had to use them. When I blocked the truck, the driver thought somebody was heisting the load—the bootleggers fought among each other, you know. The truck belonged to a very bad gang, and the driver was one of the gang leaders, and he picked up a shotgun from the seat and pointed it right at my ear. I pulled out my badge and said, 'Go ahead, if you want more trouble,' and he put the shotgun down."

Wolff says he remained under cover until his reputation grew. He says word got around the criminal community that he was not only a square cop but also an honest person, and he could no longer act incognito. He joined Ness in the full-

scale raids on storage facilities; he began to see more of the operation; and, frankly, he says he was not altogether happy with everything he observed.

He says Ness was changing, for one thing. He thinks the agent-in-charge started to make mistakes as The Untouchables matured. Ness might have suc-cumbed to the pressures to succeed, or to the realities of the time. Whatever, Wolff thinks "Eliot started to break laws himself," *making illegal arrests that would not survive court scrutiny and that were not healthy for the group:*

"There may have been some other dishonesty too. Police corruption is as old as the world, and I think The Untouchables had some. I don't say there was definite corruption, because I did not see it myself, but things happened. For example, my cover was broken once and for all when one of the agents took my picture during a raid, and it was distributed. We also had leaks, I think. I think things that we planned were sometimes getting around. I had problems with that personally. I told that to Ness, I told him what I thought was going on, and he got into it, he did what he could about it; he investigated some of the agents, and he put tails on a few of them under suspicion.

"I hit a brewery one time at Sixty-second Street and Cottage Grove. It was a big warehouse and at that time it was in a beautiful neighborhood. The brew-ery was on the two top floors. We heard about it and we set it up; you had to plan it out, you follow me? But when we got there we didn't take no god-damned prisoners. We didn't find anybody working there. They should have been on the job, or at least watching the place, but they were all gone, and we didn't make any arrests. In other words, there were leaks; you understand? There must have been. I don't say it was any of the agents, because I don't have proof, but a lot of agents in the office knew what was going to happen.

"You have to realize this was all big business. The bootleggers had plenty of money to spread around. I earned twenty-three hundred dollars a year as a federal agent, plus five dollars a day per diem when I traveled. Ness made twen-ty-eight hundred. I don't say any of The Untouchables sold out; how can I say it if I didn't see it? But the leaks happened, they took place. I know at least one of the agents was going to be arrested one time. Ness found out about him, and the guy got wind that he was going to be arrested. He didn't work with me, but I know all about the case. He was on somebody's payroll, that might have been it. He got in his car one night and turned the motor on with the windows up and committed suicide."

Al, you're saying some of The Untouchables were touchable?

"It was there, it was done. That's all I can say."

Did anyone try to get to you?

"They knew it wouldn't work. These people knew who would give information and who wouldn't give information, and they knew where I stood. I couldn't be corrupted. I wasn't born to sell out; I wasn't built that way. The pay wasn't good, that's right, but I wasn't forced to go on the job, I was happy to go on the job. I never forgot that I was Jewish. That will tell you something. There weren't many of my kind in the department in that era, and I was proud of it. I was somebody, understand?"

Wolff worked for the federal government through the 1940s. He did undercover narcotics work in New York at one period, and during World War II he pretended to be a grocery butcher so he could nab people who misused ration stamps. He says he had to quit so he could go into business to make a living.

Eliot Ness quit the civil service too. He wanted to go to the FBI, but Wolff says a jealous J. Edgar Hoover would not take him. Ness became city manager of Cleveland for a while; he later worked for the surgeon general on a campaign to combat venereal disease; he died in Pennsylvania, forgotten, at age fifty-two.

WW: "I live in Lincolnwood today, that's in the suburbs, and I live alone. My wife died. Her name was Hannah, a good biblical name; we were married sixty years, two months, and eighteen days. I took her to Florida when she got sick, but she could not take the humidity, so I came back, sold the place in Chicago, and moved to a condominium. I have a congressman in the building, and the former sheriff of Cook County lives here. I'll tell you something else: some of my neighbors are the sons and daughters of people I arrested in the twenties—they are nice people now.

"Don't ask me names. I won't even talk about who I arrested. I don't think that would be right. I took an oath to crack down on them in those days, even though I did not like the law myself, and that's what I was supposed to do. But I think they paid their debt to society; I don't want to drag them through the mud after all this time. I told you I met Capone. I didn't like what he did for a living, but I won't even criticize him today. I don't know if he was as bad as people say, I just don't know. I like all good people, and I suppose I feel sorry for the others.

"Now we have plenty of the others. And today it's all drugs. When I worked in government I saw it coming. I said this was going to be the worst thing that ever happened in the country unless we set up clinics for the addicts, like we have bars for the people who drink, so that when they needed a jolt they can come in and get it. You know what I was told? I was told to stick to undercover work. I still believe it in, however; I think if addicts could go to clinics to get relief, they would not have to turn the crime to get it. We saw that during Prohibition. Nobody broke the law after liquor was legalized."

Wallpaper Wolff says he is still keeps a toe in the crime-fighting business.

For one thing, he advises an association of federal agents about his experiences. He says he speaks about the old days and, what else?—how to be an honest cop.

"There is another thing about that movie that bothers me. In one scene they have Eliot Ness killing Frank Nitti. Nitti was Al Capone's second-in-command, and in the movie he was supposed to have killed one of The Untouchables, and so Ness chased him down and threw him off a roof. That never happened. It's not honest to say it did. I like to be honest. Nitti committed suicide."

The oldest active peace officer in America as of 1988 is United States Marshal Clint Peoples. The seventy-seven-year old Texan is also one of the most experienced lawman of the century. He started as a deputy sheriff in 1930 and has since worn nine different badges in almost six decades of service. In addition to his first and present employments, he has been a chief deputy sheriff, a chief deputy constable, a highway patrolman, a Texas Ranger, a Texas Ranger captain, and a Texas Ranger senior captain.
He is also six feet tall and tips his hat to the ladies.

"I got into the business when we still rode horses in this part of the country, and, oh, it was rough all right. You killed or you were killed. You had to fight to keep living. I saw them all: Bonnie and Clyde, Pretty Boy Floyd, Machine Gun Kelly, they were hard cases. But maybe it wasn't so bad at that. We used to know the bad guys because they had their pictures in the post office, but today you can't tell. The guy in the next car. The kid on the street. Anybody you meet might blow you away."

ROBERT AGNEW

Robert Agnew didn't like it in the least when one of his best friends mistook him for a burglar once in the 1970s and then compounded the faux pas by calling him a thief. Agnew demanded an apology, and when he didn't get it he sued the accuser for slander and won a $1000 judgment. The friend now thinks Bob Agnew is a very hard fellow. So do scores of others who have been subject to the septuagenarian's extraordinary penchant for taking his complaints to court. Agnew holds to the notion that crime shouldn't pay, in particular when it's committed against him. He has been suing people for most of the twentieth century (he's filed more than 200 actions in all); he furthermore acts as his own attor-

ney, *normally, so the vengeance extracted has that much more of a personal characterization.*

Yes, a hard fellow.

"I don't liked to be wronged is all. And you can't hit people in the nose, you know. I had a person once, a woman, who I lent money. I don't remember the exact amount, fifty, a hundred, a hundred and a quarter. Whatever it was, she did not pay it back. I didn't go for that, so I filed a suit against her. I had proof that I lent her the money, and she wouldn't repay; she didn't have a chance. The judge garnisheed her wages seven times, and he gave me possession of an old car that she had.

"Then she sent her son over here to my home, he broke in, and he damn near killed me. When he left he turned on all the gas in the house. I don't use pilot lights, so if the valves are turned on it's raw gas. Fortunately, I woke up in time, I dashed out, went next door, called the cops. The cops came out and turned off the gas. We got the guy the next day. I had recognized his voice in the house, and he left fingerprints; we went to court, of course, and the guy got nine years in the penitentiary.

"That wasn't all. The mother had gotten snotty again during the son's trial, and she really started messing around. This time she called me up to make threats. I recognized her voice—I had talked to her many times—and she said 'If you testify against my son, you better watch out; you won't be alive very long.' Well, there she was wrong again. I took out a criminal complaint against her for a felony, trying to dissuade a witness from attending; she got three years in the penitentiary."

Agnew laughs. There may be a question about the social decorum of suing one's friends and neighbors, but the old man does not much care. He says there are two courses of action open when one is injured: forget it or fight it. And since he does not believe in turning his cheek in most instances, or rapping people on the beak, as he says, he journeys to court.

Alone, remember. He is a litigious layman.

"I didn't have a chance to go to law school myself. I did go to high school, but there wasn't any money beyond that. I was born in St. Louis; my family came west when I was two years old, and we were always poor. We ate bread and gravy a lot of times. We ate jackrabbits. I remember one time when we lived in San Diego, my mother put white rabbit on the table. I said, 'Mom, where did you get the white rabbit?' She said, 'Never mind, we got it, that's the important thing; go ahead and eat it.' I said, 'Mom, it isn't my pet rabbit, is it?' I went outside, looked in the cage, and, sure enough, my rabbit was gone. I let out a scream, and I won't eat white rabbit to this day.

"When I grew up I went through the Depression. Still no money. I was taught how to be an electrician, but I couldn't get a job doing it. When I did get work, it was for an attorney in Los Angeles. I started out doing small things in the office, but the attorney was a wino and he was so damn drunk all the time that I wound up handling everything for him. I couldn't go to court, of course, because I wasn't a licensed lawyer, but I did everything else. The wills and the documents and that. I read all of his books, and I got familiar with the precedents. I worked there for three and a half years, until the lawyer died, and it was about the same as university experience.

"When the Depression ended I found I could use the experience for myself. I think the first suit I ever handled myself was when I had a pickup truck seized for falling behind in the time payments. I had gotten into the wood-cutting business, and I bought the truck on credit. When I missed the payments, the creditor took it away. So I sued on the grounds the truck couldn't be seized because it was a 'tool and implement.' I used to jack the truck up when I worked, put a belt on the tire, and sawed wood that way. The law said tools and implements were exempt from repossession, because that's how people made their living, and so the judge reversed on my appeal.

"Meantime, the creditor had to post a bond to pay service fees for holding my pickup. They had to hire a lawyer too, and they were hurting, they were spending a lot of money on this, and they decided that it wasn't worth it. So they came to me and they said, 'All right, Agnew, we'll release your truck.' And I said, 'Oh, no, I am going to file a cross complaint. You damaged me. I've suffered hunger and other losses. I couldn't use my truck while you kept it, I couldn't work, I couldn't make money, I couldn't feed myself, I suffered from nerves, my emotions; no way.' So I ended up as a collection agency. They gave me my truck, and they also gave me four hundred dollars to get rid of me."

Thus it began. Robert Agnew has since sued everyone and everything from his employers to city hall. He once sued his sister because he says she cheated him. He's also sued his brother because he says he insulted him. He's taken on an agency of the federal government; he's battled large corporations and wealthy individuals; he's been to the California supreme court three times; he almost took a traffic citation to the Supreme Court of the United States; and, as many of his opponents groan, he has succeeded in an estimated 75 percent of his actions.

"I worked in Saudi Arabia once. I got one of my big wins in a case that started there. That government is very strict, you know, and it got mad when my roommate flirted with an Arab woman. They didn't do anything to my roommate, but they arrested the woman for flirting with a 'Christian dog.'

That's against the Koran. They ordered her buried in the sand alongside a road, and she was stoned to death. It was the most terrible thing I ever saw. I wrote a letter about it to my general manager, complaining, and I was fired for criticizing the government.

"I decided to sue for breaking my contract. I had a contract for two years, and there was no penalty in it for criticizing the government. The company was dishonoring its word; I had them by the hair; and I was going to sue in an Arab court. But then they said I could not sue because I was going to be sent home. They would not give me my passport and I could not stay in the country by myself without it. They took me to the airport and gave my passport to the airline captain. I demanded he turn it over and let me off, but I was flown from there to Europe.

"When I finally got to Los Angeles I sued both the company and the airlines. I had a long list of complaints. Breach of contract. Conspiring to breach a contract. Intentional infliction of emotional distress. Damages occurring to a labor dispute; there was a labor dispute over there, and I had them under California law. There were seventeen causes of actions. I even filed for false imprisonment and conspiring to falsely imprison, because when I asked the airline captain to let me off the plane, he would not do it and kept me against my will.

"Then I had to figure out how to prove it. I had to use law, and what's the law in Saudi Arabia? It's the Koran [a Moslem book of religious principles and admonitions]. So I had to get a guy versed in the Koran. And I was in court for a full year. Let's see, we had a total of about fourteen defendants there, and each one had a lawyer. And I was broke by then. I didn't have money for a fried egg; I got to the point where I couldn't even buy legal paper. But I prevailed in the end. The other side offered me ten thousand dollars, and I grabbed it; it was a satisfactory settlement."

It wasn't Agnew's best settlement, however.
He says he's won half a million dollars through the years.

"Most of the money has come in smaller chunks. But there was one other bigger one. That was when I fought against a big Los Angeles attorney. I was working as an electrician, and I had a contract to wire his restaurant for three hundred and some odd dollars. No, seven hundred and some. He put a lot of extras on while I was doing it—a large percolator, and this and that. But when I presented him with the bill he said, 'Well, I think you're charging too much for the extras.' I said, 'Horseshit, you know better than that.' Then I said, 'Look, just give me the original three-fifty,' and we'd argue about the extras later; I told him he could turn his side of it over to his lawyer.

"Then I found out his lawyer was this well-known fellow. And I knew I was in trouble. The lawyer immediately stopped payment on the three-hundred-fifty-dollar check, and so I had to sue for the check and the extras both. After that the lawyer went down to the court to find out about me, and he discovered that I had a unpaid debt of my own. I had bought a car off a woman, and it turned out to be no good, and I wouldn't pay. She sued me and prevailed, but I still didn't pay. So the lawyer went to her and they made a deal to garnishee the money I was owed by the restaurant owner. They didn't notify me, however, because they knew I was sharp enough to claim my rights to an exemption of the garnishment.

"When I found out about that I tore my hair out. And I added another cause of action to my suit: conspiracy to deprive me of a statutory right, to wit, to have claimed an exemption when the garnishment was won. My case had suddenly become much stronger. I lost one of the first rounds, regarding the exemption part, but that was reversed on an appeal. When the jury got ahold of it, they gave me ten thousand dollars. I was not satisfied with that, however; I thought I should get more. So I palsy-walsied the judge, made a motion for a new trial, and it was granted. I empaneled a second trial a little while later, and this one gave me fifteen thousand. It was the most I ever won, and I collected every last penny."

The old man lights a cigarette. He says he has emphysema, but he can't break the habit. He says he "used to be an awful drunk" as well:

"I had to have liquor while I was in court, because I'd get nervous and my hands would shake. So I used to hide whiskey behind the toilet in the courthouse rest room and go out for a drink during recess. I remember rushing to the toilet one time and couldn't find it: some sonofabitch had stole the bottle."

Agnew is lean and angular. He has sparse hair, large ears, and he squints even in the darkened front room of his modest home. He prepares his cases in the room, working on a cluttered table: Agnew, Agnew, Agnew and Worn Carpet, Esq., Beaumont, California.

The police:

"I don't sue many cops. They know who I am and they don't bother me much. But there was one, some years ago, who stopped me for what he said was a traffic offense. He said I ran a stop sign. That was not true. At least, I did not run a legitimate stop sign. There was a contractor at the time who was paving the street, and he had put up a bootleg sign, a sign of his own. I looked up the statute, and California law says that road signs must meet certain specifications, certain shapes, certain-size lettering, certain colors, and so forth. Besides that, the arresting cop was rude; he told me to get in my car and go home. I told him I didn't have to go home; I went to court instead."

City Hall:

"The politicians in Beaumont raised the sewage and garbage fees back in the late seventies. Nobody liked it, but I was the first one who sued. I sued on the grounds that a state law, Proposition Thirteen, forbade the raising of taxes over a period of years. The rate was seen as a tax then, you see, and so I won, or rather I settled; they removed me from the rate rolls completely. I was lucky for that, though. A couple of other people sued on the same thing later, just as the state supreme court was ruling that the rate was a fee instead of a tax, and localities had every right to raise them if they wanted. I was the only winner, therefore; I still don't pay for trash collection and sewage."

The ultimate try:

"That came out of that problem with the policeman I mentioned before. I did not win my case, and was fined fifty dollars in municipal court. I appealed all the way to the Supreme Court. I appealed to the appellate department of the California superior court first and disqualified three sitting judges who I thought would be prejudiced. I got three others who turned out to be worse than the originals. Two words: 'judgment affirmed.' They laid for me, and they got me that time. So from there you can't go to the court of appeals or anything, you have to go to the United States Supreme Court. I did, by mail, and I got a stay of execution. I didn't get a hearing, though, because they denied my petition."

So you lost?

"Not really. The matter went back to the municipal court, and they forgot to collect the fifty dollars. I'd call it a draw."

What about those judges you say laid for you?

"I've had trouble with some judges. They think I'm a smarty pants, or they think that I'm a threat to the system. I don't have so much trouble any more, because I know how to handle them. For example. If I think I have someone on the bench who is going to be a problem, and let's face it, they don't know everything, I may aggravate him and make him angry at me. Then I'll tell him that I think he has formed a prejudicial opinion as to my credibility; I won't be able to get a fair trial. That's grounds for disqualification, and it works. They have to step down."

The laugh again. Robert Agnew delights in the leveling effect of his efforts. He says law is the armor of Everyman. He thinks it is the political religion of a just society. He does have one regret in his use of it, however. That is his reputation. He says he has neighbors who won't so much as say hello anymore, "thinking I'll get mad and sue." He says that's an exaggeration:

"I am not so mean as they make it out. I just believe in my rights under our form of government. I believe in other people's rights, the same, and I've been known to do what I can in that respect too. I met an old woman once in a rest home, and she told me she didn't like it there. I said, 'Why don't you leave?' She said 'I can't, my son won't let me.' So I helped her go home. She packed, and while we were leaving somebody tried to stop her. I said, 'If you stand in her way, I'll make a citizen's arrest for illegal detention, which is against the law and a felony.' We left then, and she was a happy woman.

"I don't want to make it sound as if I was acting as the lady's lawyer. I wasn't. The difference is that I was not helping her for a fee. The bar associations have been trying to pin something on me for years; they would love to haul me in for practicing without a license. But they can't. I have talked to a lot of people. I get calls from people I don't even know, but I never charge a cent. There was a woman in Florida, if you heard about it, she was going to open up a law practice without a license, and she was stopped cold. Lawyers are very jealous of the profession; they don't want anyone else getting in.

"I think other people should get in. I think it should be allowed. Why should someone have to go to a licensed lawyer and pay five grand for two hundred dollars' worth of paperwork? We should allow people to do it for the legitimate two hundred. Now, I would not advocate letting unlicensed lawyers represent someone in court; there is too much risk in that. But I do advocate this: Let an unlicensed lawyer prepare papers and take a fee from a client, provided the client waives your responsibility for any injury that occurs from the representation. But the bar associations don't even want that; they've got a pretty good racket going.

"I could have gotten into the racket myself, at one time. I don't think there's a doubt I could have passed the bar. But I've never liked the sitting-at-the-desk crap. I am also getting older, too. If you are a lawyer, you have to get up in the morning, and get to court at eight o'clock in the morning; it was ten o'clock in the old days. If you aren't there, or you show up late, then you are in contempt. No, God, not for me. I'm seventy-eight. I wouldn't be able to stay in bed as long as I want. I would be at somebody's beck and call. I work hard on my own behalf, but it would be different for every Tom, Dick, and Harry."

Are you hinting you are ready to retire?

"Oh, no. I believe in it too much. Everybody should learn how to sue. If they did, people would treat each other different. There'd be less trouble. We'd have a better world."

5. Human Rights

MODJESKA SIMKINS

When the newly settling colonialists in South Carolina wrote down the precepts of their government in 1712, they prefaced the codes with a preamble that, among other things, noted the presence of black inhabitants. The Negroes, the preamble said, were of "barbarous, wild, savage natures, and ... wholly unqualified to be governed by the laws, customs and practices of this province." The people of color therefore required a special status "as may restrain the disorders, rapine and inhumanity to which they are naturally prone ... and may also tend to the safety ... of the people of this province and their estates."
Modjeska Simkins raises her hand and turns down a thumb.

"When I was a child," she says, "my father was one of the best black brickmasons in this state, and a lot of the white trash hated him because he got jobs and they didn't. They didn't like him because he did fine work, they didn't like him because he was a good-looking brown-skinned gentleman, and they didn't like him because he didn't care if they liked him or not. So one night they came by and shot up our home. They just opened up, bam, bam, bam, and we were all in there, my family, and my mother said: 'They're shooting in on us.'

"Most people might have just cowered and then moved away the next morning. But my father was an exception, and each night he used to set his guns out in case of trouble. He always put his rifle on one side of the door and the shotgun on the other. I can hear him tell my mother to throw down a quilt, I can see that quilt falling in the moonlight, and we got down on it on the floor. Then my father opened the door and shot back. All he had to do was hit one, and the rest of them ran away. The next day he went right back to work as always; he was a fearless man."

Simkins adjusts her shawl. She speaks with such animated conviction that she intermittently slips out from under the wrap. Who really has the "wild, savage nature" in South Carolina? she inquires, without expecting a response.

"My father never hurt a soul. He never caused trouble, and he obeyed all the laws. He stood up for his rights, though, and that was the wrong; the ordinary Negro, you know, his life is one risk after the other."

Rights. The word is listed right after bigotry in the civil lexicon of the twentieth century, and bigotry is defined as the assertion that God made a mistake when He brought some people into being. Blacks are one illustration. There is not a nation or a people on earth that has fully appreciated them, and blacks themselves are guilty of splintering and looking with contempt on one another. When the slave trade was originated in Africa, the enterprising marketers would employ one set of natives to round up other sets of natives. When they were brought to America, the black slaves were sometimes purchased by black plantation squires. There is an argument that the blacks bought the blacks to keep them from the whites; that purifies the inexplicable.

The first African slaves came in the early seventeenth century, so far as is known. A Dutch warship carried a cargo of twenty "negars" to Virginia, where they were put alongside the white servants who had previously worked alone in the East Coast tobacco fields. The new advantage was immediately recognized. The blacks had no rights. A million of them were brought to the American South in the next hundred years, six million more arrived in the 1800s; and these are merely estimated figures. Some historians believe as many as fifteen million Africans were enslaved in America, legally or illegally, before the enactment of the Thirteenth Amendment.

A good many of them were domiciled in South Carolina. Just before emancipation, half the white families in the state owned slaves, a percentage that was the highest in the nation. Abolitionists said South Carolina had "a Roman reverence for bondage," and, in fact, the owners cited the Romans for justification. Slavery was the right of the civilized, and the betterment of the superior world. It was likewise humane. The Greeks would have slaughtered the people they conquered, had they not made them slaves; by the same token, South Carolina offered an alternative to the paganism of African existence.

Similar excuses were made when blacks won their liberty in South Carolina, but not their rights. They had to be protected from the worst fate of their own inferiority. Modjeska Simkins says that "being free did not mean we were white, it only meant we were no longer slaves." She says when she was born, in 1899, blacks could not hold office in the state, they could not vote in many counties, they were not allowed to work in any meaningful government position, and segregation carried the force of law. A turn-of-the-century governor called Negroes "the wool hat boys." There were forty-six verified Negro lynchings in the state between 1900 and 1914. When a black man was accused of putting his hands on a white woman in 1911, Cole Blease, the governor, said that "the sooner the nigger is buried the better."

Mrs. Simkins says South Carolina was one of the last states to reconstruct. And it did not easily become a model of fellowship. The state did not want to accept the Declaration of Independence because it maintains that all men are equal. The first shot of the Civil War was fired at Fort Sumter, in Charleston Bay. State Democrats had no black political candidates until 1948. And Porgy and Bess, the folk opera, was not produced in South Carolina until 1970, fifty years after it was written by state native DuBose Heyward.

Mrs. Simkins takes a deep breath. She prepares to lose her shawl again. She is seated in a reclining armchair, drinking intermittently from a bottle of water, putting Mentholatum up her nose. She is eighty-eight; she is a wiggler and giggler; and, more, she is a living legend, albeit a controversial one, the undisputed Great Old Soul of South Carolina's black liberation struggle.

"I am a little white; should I mention that? My grandfather was white; he was a well-known South Carolina attorney. My grandmother was as black as your shoes, and she worked in his home, and as the old people say she was 'ruined,'—that means she got pregnant by this man. They never married. He took advantage of her; it was the kind of thing that used to be done all the time here. Everybody knew it; the man gave us his last name, so it was all right to go to bed with a black woman as long as you didn't take her to dinner or something. That's how my father came into this life. It's something I've never understood: if a white dog mates with a black dog you get a spotted pup, but if a white man mates with a black woman, you don't get spotted babies.

"I was the firstborn, or the 'oldest rat in the barn.' My parents named me after a Polish actress named Helena Modjeska. I had seven brothers and sisters, and we lived on a farm. My father put a special significance in that farm. He was a man of strong moral character, as far as sex and money were concerned, and he never forgave his mother for what she did with the white man. So he moved us to the farm because he wanted his children to work, to learn the value of a dollar, and also because he did not want us working in white houses. And, yes, I remember my grandfather—his name was Walter Monteith—and he used to come to see us. He used to rub his hands on our heads, because he thought he could tell our worth by the shape.

"My mother was a teacher by profession. She taught school before I was born, and then she taught us at home. The blacks could not attend the white schools, naturally, and there were not many black schools around that were any good. The black schools did not have enough money to stay open nine months a year, and they closed after three or four. That meant a black student only got half the education of a white, not to mention the fact that they had to go to school two years to pass one grade. The black schools did not have the eleventh and twelfth grades, either, and they had to scrounge to get decent teachers. The Negro parents would get together and have fish fries to raise the salaries for teachers. The salaries were fifty dollars a month, tops.

"I waited until I was nine before I started school formally. The Yankees opened Benedict College as part of reconstruction, and I went from the first grade on until I got my degree. Benedict was a Baptist college; there was a lot of religious instruction, but I remember the teachers were very dedicated. They were all white; they came down to work for nothing, in some cases; and they meant business. The idea was to teach the 'freedmen,' and by God they were going to do it. Classes started at seven-thirty A.M., sharp. If you had an assignment you did it that day, and if you didn't you stayed in school until you did. No talking. No fooling around. Just learning. I had to bring my Bible every day, too; the Yankees were strict about religion.

"My mother supplemented that education. She was the first to teach me about race relations. Neither of my parents talked about it directly, but they passed it on in other ways. My mother used to read newspapers and magazines to the family. She didn't hold back anything. She read about all the lynchings, and the Ku Klux Klan, and the black people shot by police. It was a broad exposure. It's how I learned I was black, and what that was, and other people were white, and what that was. We had a magazine called *The Voice*. My mother took it, and read to us about people in Africa. They were working in the gold mines, and if they didn't dig enough gold they were punished. They'd lose part of a finger. My mother even showed me the pictures.

"I also learned about blacks and whites from the experiences of my father. He traveled around in his work, laying bricks, and he saw all of these things, and he'd tell us what was going on. One time he was in Huntsville, Alabama. He was laying a chimney for a new factory, and these white fellows came in where he was working and they said a black man had just been hung in the town. The white fellows said they had seen it, and to prove it they showed my daddy a piece of the victim's body. Well, they did that to scare him. And I think maybe they thought they wanted to hang him as well. But my father didn't back down. He told them to get the hell out of his way or he was going to break their heads.

"That's the kind of man my father was. He was just as damn good as anyone. And I learned that. That's the kind of background I'm from. My father should have been shot a dozen times, but he did not knuckle under. I remember him working near Ridgeway one time. He was asked by a company to finish a project that had been started by a white man who died on the job. My father said okay, and he was put in charge, and that irritated some of the whites who then had to work for him. He didn't boss them, but he did tell them what to do, and they resented it. So they said, 'Old man, you don't know the way you been talking, the Klan is liable to come over and get you.' You know what my father said? He said: 'So what, they're just made of meat, ain't they?' "

Mrs. Simkins moved to Columbia when she graduated from college and became the second teacher in her family. She taught algebra at Booker T. Washington High School, then married a wheelwright named Andrew Simkins, adopting his five sons in the process. A film called The Jazz Singer *was introducing sound to New York movie houses. The first liquid-fuel rocket was launched. O. E. Rolvaag was publishing* Giants in the Earth. *And one-third of the people in South Carolina were black.*

"It sounds terrible to talk about those days now. But it was matter-of-fact then. You could not go to a white restaurant; you sat in a special place at the movie house; and, Lord knows, you sat in the back of the bus. It didn't make any difference if you were rich or poor, if you were black you were nothing. You might have a hundred dollars in your pocket, but if you went to the store you would wait at the side until all the clerks got through with all the white folks, no matter if they didn't have change for a dollar. Then the clerk would finally look at you and say 'Oh, did you want something? I didn't see you there.'

"They did want our money, that was true enough, but otherwise we were dirt in the street. If you'd go in to get some shoes, some stores would not let you try them on before you bought them. If you wanted to have a new hat, they might make you put a handkerchief on your head before you tried it out. They thought we were dirty; they thought we leave stains, maybe that was it; and they didn't want to drink out of the same water fountain. There were women who would go into stores to buy a fur coat but they couldn't use the rest room. Now think about that! The whites were fools . . . asses. But they were in power.

"They kept power through the politics. By politics I mean Democratic politics. The Republicans weren't big enough to do anything. The Democrats held all of the offices in the state, on every level, and they did it by completely excluding blacks from their primaries. The Democrats said the primaries were not under state control; they were private functions of the party, and they could make their own rules. So the rules were that blacks could not run in the primaries; they could not vote in the primaries; and when the general elections came around, and some blacks could vote, there was no one to vote for but whites.

"It used to make me so mad. The whites simply did not care if we lived or died, and I mean that literally. If you were sick, say, they still treated you like an animal. We had a serious flu epidemic during the First World War, and I went to the drugstore to get some medicine. I was sick myself, and so were others in my family. Anyhow, I asked the druggist for the medicine, and when he went to get it I sat down on one of the chairs at the soda fountain. I was weak. I needed to rest. When he came back he said, 'You can't sit there, you know you don't have the right to sit there.' So I had to get up, shaking, and I left.

"It was things like that made me know that I had to fight back. I was like my good-looking brown-skinned daddy. I didn't want to be pushed around. Like when the white trash would call you by their pet names. They called the women 'Auntie' and they called the men 'Uncle.' It was very arrogant, and they did it to keep you down. I just refused to accept it. There was one time during World War II—my husband had a liquor store then—and this big old fat soldier came in there and called me 'Auntie.' And I just looked him right in the eye, and then I said, 'Honey, I didn't know I was kin to your mamma.' "

Mrs. Simkins says a lot of blacks began talking back during the war. Attitudes were changing in both races. One reason was that Northern industries were moving into the South, and they were not so reluctant to do business with minorities. And then there were the Southern soldiers returning from the combat, now re-educated in the ways of the larger world, and not any more willing to accept the dead-ended insult of racial subjugation.

"I had already been active in civil rights—for a long time, actually. People say I was in the movement before there was a movement, and that's pretty close. I think the first time I did something was for my daddy. He was a member of one of the Negro brickmasons' union, and they had a reunion, or some kind of an affair, and they were looking for someone to make a speech. My father said why don't we have my daughter give it, and so I did. I don't remember what I said. But it was a start. That was way back in the nineteen-twenties, thereabouts. I've been active now for sixty years or more. Martin Luther King, Jr., he was wonderful, but he wasn't even born until sometime in the 1930s.

"The early days were very difficult. Black people wanted better things, but they were cautious. The usual thing was that they would have these little meetings at somebody's house, about once a month, and talk about things like unpaved streets and better funding for the schools. They didn't demand anything, though; the most they would do is make appeals to the city. Then the city would take the complaints under advisement and forget about them. The early black movement always reminded me of a little dog we had in the country. He'd go out at night, get up on a potato bank, and bark at the moon. That's what the blacks did; they just barked at the city, and that's all the good it was.

"I was more confrontational. I always believe in being direct and taking chances. I'll give you an example. It's about a man and woman I knew. This was down around Orangeburg, and things were always rough there. The man and woman both worked for a white man in the community, and they got in trouble with him when they attended a meeting about integration. The white man said he didn't want his employees going to things like that and he said they would have to do what he said or be fired. So the man and woman picked up their things and left. Now that took a lot of courage. Those people lost their jobs! They could have caved in, yet they did not, and that's the way I believe my own self.

"Maybe the caution among some of the blacks was related to the church. The preachers have always told the Negro to be patient, wait for the by-and-by. That's one of the reasons I had to leave the church. My daddy wasn't much for it, either. I believe in religion, I was educated by the Baptists, I follow the teachings of Jesus Christ, and I believe in a supreme being. But I also want to think for myself. I don't want to listen to a preacher, or a Negro leader, who cooks up a bunch of pap like gruel on the stove and tells me I'll get my reward in Heaven. I don't think we're going to have it unless we grab what we can right here.

"We started in that direction when we formed the National Association of Colored People in South Carolina. That was in the middle 1930s. My mother had been a member of the W. E. DuBois Niagara Association—which, if you look at your history, was the forerunner of the NAACP. The changeover took place in 1910, and there were NAACP chapters in this state after that, and we brought them all together. I was one of the first members, I still am a member. I was secretary of the group for a number of years and I think we were largely responsible for integrating the schools here, raising Negro pay, and all of that. We went to court on several of the equality issues, and won each time.

"Put another way, we used what I call audacious power. We didn't just bark at the city, we didn't plead with the power structure. We seized our rights. We challenged officials to debates. We held demonstrations. We packed the city-council meetings. We did not accept anything less than what was fair. One of the local newspapers used to have a double standard when it wrote about blacks and whites. It would refer to the whites as Mr., Miss, or Mrs. It would refer to blacks as 'the colored preacher' or 'that Simkins woman.' I battled the editors for years; they kept saying they will do whatever they wanted; then one fine day they quietly relented and that was that."

Modjeska Simkins served as secretary to the NAACP into the 1950s. And her combative ways raised heat in the kitchen. She subsequently came to the attention of the Federal Bureau of Investigation for what the agency insisted was excessive radicalism. Rumors spread. Stories were published. The suggestion: the Great Old Soul was associated with Communists.

"I don't think anybody accused me of being a Communist. They knew that hell would be their portion if they did. But I did associate, yes; I have had Communist friends. My husband and I used to keep the doors open at our place, where people would come to discuss race, politics, and anything else they wanted. Sometimes the guests included Communists. I met Herbert Aptheker there, for example. Aptheker was the director of the Institute of Marxist Studies in New York. I liked him. He is one of the finest men I ever met. People say he is a Communist, however, and I was blasted from pillar to post for it.

"One thing that happened was that I was asked to leave the Democratic Party. I was a candidate for the state house of representatives at the time, and the mucky-mucks told me I was no longer wanted. I didn't leave the party, of course. And I didn't disassociate myself from Aptheker. I still think he is a gentleman and a scholar, and I believe he has contributed to the betterment of the Negro people in America. I am not a Communist. I have never studied Marxism, but I will be friends with whom I please. I won't let people tell me who I can have in my home, and I will invite anybody I think is on the Negro's side.

"See what I mean about being confrontational? I know it bothers a lot of people, but I can't help it. I lost my job with the NAACP for it. One morning I showed up at a state meeting in Rock Hill, and I found I was being replaced. They didn't even say thanks for doing a good job. They didn't even acknowledge me in the audience. I think they just decided that I was too outspoken. I don't know any other way to be in this movement. I get up, I shake my finger, and I stand fast. That has always worried the white establishment, and I think it brought pressure on the NAACP. Anyway, I was let go. I was sorry about it."

Mrs. Simkins formed a citizens' association after that and has remained active in civic affairs. She is widowed today and lives alone. She feeds the pigeons in her yard. She visits prisoners at the jail. She helps the mentally ill. She is stooped at the shoulders, her glasses are low on her nose, and she bends forward to lead the guffaws when she favors a companion with a blue joke:

"There was an older man in a hotel with thin walls, and he could hear a pair of young marrieds in the next room. 'Hurry,' the bride said, 'you get on top.' Then after a bit the groom said, 'All right, now you get on top.' Finally they decided 'We should both get on top.' Well, hearing that, the older man went outside to peek in the window, and they were closing their suitcase."

She covers her mouth with her hand.
Did you win that campaign for the legislature, Mrs. Simkins?

"No."

Have you run for other offices?

"Twice. Just to protest. I lost those times too."

And how do you spend your time now?

"I keep in touch with things. I'm still a member of the NAACP. I get a lot of invitations to go to this function or that function, but I don't do it much. I don't like social things. I don't make myself miserable to make others happy."

Ever the rebel.

"There aren't many of us left. The pickets have disappeared. The power structure got rid of Martin Luther King. Many of the black leaders now are what I call black misleaders. A few years ago I got into an argument with the city government—I forget what it was about—and I got up and I said, 'All right, listen, Christmas is coming, you got all these stores stocked up in town, and if this thing ain't straightened out by the fifteenth of December, I'm going to get the black people together and we're going to tie up Main Street in a hard knot.' Now I knew I couldn't do that, I didn't have the organization, it was just a bald-face lie. But the city got scared and they came around. That's how you do it, you see. You scare the hell out of the peckerwoods. Otherwise we'd still be looking for our rights in South Carolina."

The first black person elected to a state office in the nation was Alexander L. Twilight, who took the Orleans County seat in the Vermont legislature in 1836. The first black placed in a federal office was Hiram R. Revels from North Carolina, who was named to complete an unexpired term in the United States Senate in 1870 from his adopted state of Mississippi. The first black man elected on his own to a national post was Joseph H. Rainey (South Carolina), who was voted a vacated seat in the House of Representatives near the end of 1870 and was thereafter elected through the end of the decade.

In 1987, the Joint Center for Political Studies reported there were 6681 blacks holding elected positions in government. The total included 23 in the House of Representatives, 417 in state legislatures, 724 in county offices, 3290 in municipal positions (among them 303 mayors, including those from six of the ten largest cities), 728 in judicial and law-enforcement posts, and 1547 in education. There were more than 81,000 elected offices in 1987; blacks therefore held about 8 percent of them, which is not far from their representation (26 million) in the population.

JOSEPHINE GARBER

It's been proposed that the measure of a society is its estimate of woman. If that's true, the United States was wholly lacking before the 1900s—all the way back, in fact, to the beginning of the Republic. When the early Americans wrote the Constitution they did not discuss women at all; they argued about the place of other minorities (Negroes and Indians come to mind), yet the group that comprised almost half of the population was not mentioned. The framers did make a last minute decision that would serve women well, they wrote that "The House of Representatives shall be composed of members [the original draft said men] chosen every second year by the people of the several states," yet they left in references to the president as he, and to the president's duties as his, and there is no doubt they meant to deliberately exclude their wives, mothers, and daughters from the right to participate in the new government.

Josephine Garber:

"I was not allowed to vote until I was twenty-five years old. Women were not thought capable of voting. But I did participate in other ways. My father-in-law was a state senator in Montana, and I was at least permitted to help him campaign. He asked his wife to do it, but she didn't think it was right, then he asked his own daughters to do it, and they were just as leery as his wife. So he finally turned to me and asked if I would like to help, and I said 'Sure, I'd love to.' I was always ready for anything. I was never one to stay in the background and play with the dolls. I was criticized for that, but it didn't matter.

"The campaign went on for several weeks, and this was in the horse-and-buggy days. There were no television debates or billboard advertisements; we had to go around his district door to door and visit with the people one by one; and a lot of people thought it was not the thing for a woman. They thought I was impudent, which sounds funny today, but that was back in 1916. There was one home—it was very run down—and the woman said she wanted me to have dinner, but she didn't like to ask, because she thought I might be embarrassed to eat there. I said 'I'd love to have dinner,' and I helped to set the table.

"The dinner turned out to be important. There were nine young men in that house, all of them were registered to vote, and the next day was the election. The men said they were so pleased that I had stayed to dinner, and helped their mother, that they were all going to support my father-in-law. They said they were going to vote for him just as soon as the polling place opened. And they did, all nine of them. They came to the hall early; they voted for John D.

Garber; and when the ballots were in Dad Garber won by about five votes. He said the nine men made the difference, and I won the election for him."

The men who wrote the Constitution did not specifically withhold the franchise from women. That was left to the customs of the states. And no one thought much of it for the next half-century. The first formal consideration took place at a meeting of women in Seneca Falls, New York, in 1848; real agitation began after the Civil War, when suffrage was suggested for black males. Susan B. Anthony became the leader of the cause, and she was able to convince thousands of other women—including Jo Garber—to stand and be counted.

Mrs. Garber is ninety-two. She is small, smartly attired, and wears a "Senior Power" lapel button. Her hair is thin on top. She has a purple visor over her brow, decorated with flowers matching her blouse. And eyeshadow.

"I mentioned the horse-and-buggy days. I remember the first car I saw. I was eleven or twelve years old, eleven probably, and my family had a farm in Wisconsin. My dad and I were going into town on our buggy, with a load of grain, and the car came chugging up from behind us. It was just a buggy itself, but it had a motor in it, and it scared the horses. That worried my dad, of course, so he grabbed one of the horses and I grabbed the other, around the neck, you know, to hug them and keep them quiet. Then the fellow in the car stopped alongside and asked if he could help us, and my dad looked at him and said 'Yes, you can get that blankety-blank devil's wagon out of here.'

"My father was a lumberman at one time. He was part owner of a mill in Duluth, Minnesota. They had to lock the mill during a depression in the early 1900s, and we started to move around. He got the hundred-sixty-acre farm in Wisconsin for a while, and after a while we came west and settled in Idaho, where I finished school. I went through the twelfth grade. Some women went on to college from high school, but not many. I went to work. I lived in a small country town where they had a railroad depot, and one day the dispatcher told me about telegraphy work. Well, it was strange for a woman to become a telegrapher, but in 1911 I took the test, and I went to work for the railroad.

"That was the Northern Pacific. We had a lot of trains running then, and there was a station every seven miles, all across the country. That's how we sent our messages, from station to station. I would call the next station down the line, [that] was the way to tell them that a train was coming, and they would block all other traffic until it came by. I worked 'extra,' which means I was sent all over. That was considered a man's job, and I was young besides, seventeen at the time, and so it led to some problems. When I first went to work I called the station at Sand Point to ask the agent to block a train on the way, and he refused. He said he would not work with 'kids or women.'

"I loved the job. Telegraphy used to be very exciting. That was the only way we could talk with each other around the country. We started to get telephones later, to back us up, but at first everything depended on the telegraph key. We used the Morse code, which is something that has almost disappeared today, and we had to learn how to hit the key correctly. Everyone had a different touch. We all knew how to identify each other by listening to the touch. I've forgotten a lot of it now. There were three dots to a dash, a dot was a dot. SOS was three dots, three dashes, and three dots. I can still do it: dot, dot, dot—space—dash, dash, dash—space—and dot, dot, dot."

The struggle for woman's suffrage had some early triumphs. Several of the states saw the light fairly quickly. Wyoming gave the vote to women in 1869 when it was a territory. When it became a state in 1890 Wyoming was the first to grant women suffrage, and three other states changed their eligibility laws by the year 1900. The federal government stayed out of the argument as much as possible, but women won the right to vote in eight other states by 1914, and two years later Jeannette Rankin of Montana became the first woman in history to be elected to the United States Congress (the lower house).

"I was very excited when she was elected," Mrs. Garber says, shuffling through the memories she keeps on paper. "But I'm not sure it helped the fight for the vote. Some men claimed that I was too bold, because I did things most women didn't do, but then they turned around and said that Jeannette Rankin was too meek. The reason was that when she was elected, the country was getting into the First World War, and she voted against our going. And she cried when she did it—that was the story anyway—and so a lot of men made a to-do about it; they said that it proved women were not fit for politics or for voting because they did not have courage and were too soft to make hard decisions.

"I didn't agree in the slightest. I thought women should be in politics ever since I got interested in it on my own. I've been a Democrat all my life. My father was a Republican, but I never liked that party. The Republicans were in office when I was young; I read quite a bit about them. I thought they were cruel to working people, and I became a Democrat. I talked with my father about it, and he was not happy, but he came to change his mind. He was a Teddy Roosevelt Republican, and when Roosevelt bolted the party in 1912, my father said that if the GOP was not good enough for Teddy Roosevelt, it was not good enough for him, and he became a Democrat from that day forward.

"I met Roosevelt one time. It was in 1913. He came through Sand Point; that was after he formed the Bull Moose Party, and he was running against Woodrow Wilson. He made a whistle stop, and we all went downtown to see him at the railroad station. I was just in my teens, and I have always been small and dainty, and when I went over to him there he picked me up in his arms and lifted me straight up to the platform. He was a very strong man, very powerful.

It was nothing for him to do it. Then he looked at me, grinning like he did, and he said 'Now I know why all the young men go west.' Everyone laughed. I was beside myself; he was the first president I ever saw in person."

The fight for the vote went down and dirty in the latter part of the 1910s when the National Women's Party organized mass demonstrations and hunger strikes. The women formed a permanent picket line outside the White House, for one thing, whereafter some of them were arrested and thrown in a Virginia lockup where they were threatened with rape by guards. The direct tactics were heavily criticized even by women, but the seemingly endless struggle for suffrage finally attracted legislative attention.

"I did as much as I could for suffrage. I was working, and I had small children, but I did quite a bit. I argued with my husband, for one thing. We held regular debates about it. He was a good Democrat and a good union man besides, so I don't think he really objected all that much, but we talked about it. I also talked about it with other women I knew. Many of them were opposed. Some women still are. I still meet women my age who think we should have stayed strictly in the home. I respect their opinion, but I have never had it myself. I handed out leaflets, and everything; I wanted to vote."

Congress proposed the Nineteenth Amendment on June 4, 1919, and it was ratified by a required thirty-six state legislatures within thirteen months. Some states refused to go along. Georgia rejected it, for instance, after a legislator argued that anyone who voted for the Nineteenth Amendment was also ratifying the Fifteenth Amendment, and "any Southerner [doing that] was a traitor to his section." Otherwise, the new rule was certified August 26, 1920.

AMENDMENT XIX

1. The right of citizens of the United States to vote shall not be denied or abridged by the United States or by any state on account of sex.

2. Congress shall have the power to enforce this Article by appropriate legislation.

"What a wonderful thing! We were living in Green Lake, Washington, that year, which is next to Seattle, and I was suddenly a first-class citizen. I can't tell you what it meant. I should have been able to vote in the presidential election of 1916, because I was twenty-one then, and I also should have been able to vote in the congressional election of 1918. But now I was eligible at twenty-five. I waited a long time. I remember going down to the courthouse to register. I nearly flew off the ground. I was so nervous I could hardly sign my name.

"Then I read everything about the election I could get my hands on. I think that is a voter's responsibility. Warren G. Harding was running against

James M. Cox in 1920, and I studied everything they had to say. My husband and I also talked over the congressional candidates, and the local ones, so we could agree on who to choose. We didn't want to cancel each other out. We chose Cox in the presidential race, as you might imagine; he was the Democrat. I think I voted in a library that year, on a paper ballot. And I never missed an election after that."

Twenty-six million people voted in 1920. That was nine million more than in the previous presidential election, but it was largely a disappointing increase. No one could determine if the additional votes were cast by women alone or if they were also due to a larger turnout of men who were worried about females taking control of the election. It is known that half the people eligible to vote that year did not do it, and perhaps two-thirds of the adult women failed to follow J. Garber to the polls.

Mrs. Garber says the election also raised concerns of another sort. For a Democratic woman at least. Harding won by seven million votes, perhaps in part because he was a handsome man who wooed many of the newly enfranchised. The Republicans were to win again in 1924 and 1928, but Mrs. Garber says that she has had better moments over the long term, voting for each of the eight Democrats who held the White House between 1933 and 1981.

In all, she has voted in thirty-two national elections, now from a base in Seattle. She lives in a nursing home managed by the Masonic Lodge, where she keeps a picture of Harry Truman on the wall of her apartment, not far from one of her late husband—which, alternately, is close to a shot of Jimmy Carter.

"I still plug for my party, whenever I can. But I have to watch it a little. Most of the Masons I live with are Republicans."

Eleven of the twenty-six amendments to the Constitution have been en acted in the twentieth century. Only three of them have had truly significant consequences. The income tax amendment was passed in 1913, women's suffrage in 1920, and, in between, in 1913, ratification of the Seventeenth Amendment overturned the power of state legislatures to select members of the United States Senate and gave it instead to the crucible of the popular vote.

BUCK LEONARD

Shortly after the War Between the States ended, in 1867, and four million newly emancipated blacks were more or less released into the general course of the

American community, the National Association of Base Ball Players convened to decide how to deal with the eventuality, and struck out. The NABBP was the first organized league of any stature in the nation; as such it was the ruling body of the commercial side of the pastime at that juncture; and the question before the convention was what to do with the former slaves who were now showing interest in professional games. The answer for the white sportsmen was to obey self-interest. Negroes remained widely detested; most people would not pay to see them line up with the traditional stock; and the NABBP unanimously decided to exclude from its ranks "any club which may be composed of one or more colored players."

Buck Leonard was born forty years later.

"When I was young I heard about Babe Ruth and Rogers Hornsby, and those guys. But they were white guys. The real heros were Josh Gibson and John Henry Lloyd and Cool Papa Bell; they were black. I started playing baseball when I was ten or eleven. I played until I was almost fifty, but I was never on a white team. The closest I came was in Mexico, where they didn't care about race. They couldn't speak English there, but they weren't prejudiced."

Buck Leonard sits stiff and wary in the trophy room of his home in Rocky Mount, North Carolina. It's as if he were still waiting for the crack of the bat. He is surrounded by the mementos of a lifetime in baseball, which are also the relics of a sad time in America. He is a mostly unknown sports legend; his extraordinary talents were buried by bigotry, but he says he had his innings; the nation might have ignored his name, but it cannot now hide his record; and the fact is that when he took the field as it was, the odds stacked impossibly against him, he scored more often in baseball and in life than did most of his opponents.

WALTER F. (BUCK) LEONARD

HOMESTEAD GIANTS

HALL OF FAME

When did you start playing baseball, Buck; that is, at what age?

"I was ten or eleven, I suppose. It was here in Rocky Mount, on the other side of town from where I am now. We played barehanded, nobody had much money to buy gloves, and it was pick-up. Here and there. It was all black kids."

And your father did what?

"He worked for the railroad. Rocky Mount used to be a big railroad town. Railroad and tobacco. My dad got me a job in the railroad shop. He didn't encourage me in sports, he didn't buy me a bat or nothing, but I didn't want to work on the railroad forever; I figured I would play baseball for a living."

Even then?

"Oh, yeah. I never thought nothing else."

You were good enough?

"I got pretty good round about thirteen or fourteen years old. I played in high school then. At least we called it high school; it wasn't much. I got out in 1921, when I was fourteen. I went to work at the railroad, I hung out, and I started playing semi-pro baseball."

What do you remember about it?

"We played anybody we could in this part of the state, Greenville, Golds boro, two or three times a week. My first team was called the Rocky Mount Elks, and then it became the Black Swans. I got two dollars and ninety-three cents a day at the railroad, and about a dollar and a half for a game. We played on the high school grounds—they got a park over there now that is named for me. I was center field then. We had Jimmy Rim at third base, Tooby Thomas second base, and I was also the manager of the team."

All black people?

"Yes."

Did you play any whites?

"It wasn't done."

Leonard became a first baseman. He was left-handed, an inch shy of six feet tall, and one hundred eighty to one hundred ninety pounds. No Ozark Ike, though. More like Roy Hobbs. Leonard was not discovered in his teens and propelled into the higher ranks of black baseball; he waited until he was twenty-six before searching for better things with his hat and bat in his hand.

"I started to play professional ball in nineteen and thirty-three. I had to get going when they started cutting jobs at the railroad. I went up to Virginia and started with a team in Portsmouth. I think the name was the Fire Fighters. I played there and then went to Baltimore. Now, wait a minute; let me tell you exactly how I played. I went to Portsmouth for fifteen dollars a week and board and lodging. I left there and went to the Baltimore Stars for about the same money, and then the Stars went to New York to get bookings, and I went along.

"I got a little raise in New York. Three, four dollars a day, and I lived in Harlem with ten guys in one hotel room. The club bought our uniforms and the equipment, but it was not very good. We played with one ball as long as we could, and we had somebody go after the home runs. The uniforms got dirty, and I don't know when we cleaned them. We had a couple of automobiles to get from town to town; we didn't get enough bookings, though, we couldn't pay the agent; once the hotel sold the two cars to collect the money for our rent.

"The team broke up after that. We didn't have no way to travel. So I ended up with a team called the Brooklyn Royal Giants. I played there for the rest of the summer, and then I thought I was going to go to Puerto Rico in the winter. A guy said he had room for fifteen players there, if I would hang around. Then after I hung around, he said, 'Sorry, I only need fourteen players.' That's the way it was. That was my first professional season. I played on three teams and I didn't even have enough money to get back to Rocky Mount. I had to borrow from a woman I knew to go home."

The next year Leonard returned to New York and the Brooklyn Royal Giants. His luck would be better. He had a good arm, a smooth swing; he was dependable at first base; and, on average, he got three hits in every ten opportunities. Someone directed him to Pennsylvania, where he signed with the Homestead Grays, arguably the greatest team ever in organized Negro baseball.

You were on your way?

"Oh, yeah, I played with Homestead for seventeen years."

In Pittsburgh.

"We played games in a colored stadium and in Forbes Field. Later on we played at Griffith Stadium in Washington, D.C."

And you usually won?

"We won the title practically every year. The Negro National League. We won the championship nine years with that team."

Why is that?

"We had the best players. Not at every position, but we had Smokey Joe Williams, we had Josh Gibson, we had Sam Bankhead."

And you had Buck Leonard.

"I was all right."

Batting?

"Oh, yeah. Josh Gibson was the best black hitter I ever seen, and me and him were number three and four in the lineup. They said we were the Babe Ruth and Lou Gehrig of Negro baseball. Gibson could hit anything, any time, and I was usually around three-fifty."

What was your best season?

"Nineteen forty two. I was three-ninety-one and forty-two home runs."

And lifetime?

"I don't know. We didn't keep many records. I know Gibson hit seventy home runs one year, they were easy to count, and everybody always talked about Babe Ruth and sixty. Other than that, we didn't have statisticians. And we didn't have the same kind of schedule as the white teams. The Pittsburgh Pirates would play the same number of games, year after year. We played so many one year and something else the next. People try to compare black players with whites back then; you see, you can't do it that way."

Are the comparisons favorable?

"Some are. We did not have top players at every position, like they did on the white clubs. But Josh Gibson was as good as they came, white or black, Cool Papa Bell was the best outfielder I knew, and Satchel Paige, no argument about Satchel Paige."

What was he like?

"He played for Homestead one year. Good pitcher. Nice guy. I don't know if he did it or not, but black pitchers had this trick they used, where they scratched the ball on one side—roughed it up, in other words. If the pitcher threw it with that side up, the ball would drop. I don't know if Satchel did it."

Ha.

"We followed the rules. We had umpires. You wanted to win, however. That's why you got paid. I made eighty-five dollars a month when I started with Homestead, and then one-twenty-five. There was a time after the war [World War II] I got a thousand dollars a month. That was big money. Not like today. If I started today I'd make like a million a year. I was born too soon."

Leonard says Homestead was the class of black baseball. The players had lockers at the ballpark; they sometimes traveled by rail; they took spring training in Florida, if you please, after which they would work their way back north by barnstorming. They did not get general recognition, though. Leonard says the team was regularly covered by the black newspapers, and the players became celebrities among their own, but, with some isolated exceptions, they were normally ignored in the larger community.

Major league baseball stuck to the NABBP rule for more than three-quarters of a century, long after the NABBP was quaint history. The game tried to integrate once, briefly, in the late 1800s, when a pair of brothers were hired by the Toledo Mudhens, but it was a disaster. One pitcher named Cap Anson, who was to be inducted into the Hall of Fame, made a sport out of trying to bean the brothers, and they were eventually dismissed.

You mentioned the Pirates, Mr. Leonard, did Homestead play them?

"No."

Did Pirate officials ever come to your games?

"What for?"

To scout?

"No. They would not hire us no matter how good we were."

Was there any talk along these lines?

"We heard rumors. Some owners on the white side said things from time to time. Some of us were called in to see Clark Griffith one time—he owned the Washington Senators—but all he did was talk about how he couldn't integrate. The fans wouldn't like it. That was about 1940. Griffith said it would probably happen some day; he didn't make no offers to anybody."

Did that bother you?

"I didn't worry about it."

Did you ever play with whites?

"I played against them, barnstorming and things. I also played against major league players. We had Negro All Star teams every year; we had Marion Barker, we had George Jefferson, we had Jackie Robinson, we had Roy Campanella, we had Gibson and myself, and we played the American League All Stars in California."

Did you beat them?

"Yeah."

Did you play the National League All Stars?

"Yeah."

Did you beat them?

"Yeah."

When was this?

"In the 1940s. For a few years. Judge [Kenesaw Mountain] Landis was the baseball commissioner, and he stopped it. He said the American and National League teams had everything to lose, nothing to gain."

Buck Leonard played thirty-three years in commercial baseball. All in the Negro or Hispanic leagues. He was still with Homestead when Jackie Robinson broke the color barrier in 1947, but by then he was forty and too old to become a big-league rookie. He continued to play for Homestead until it went out of business in 1950, partly as a result of major league raids, ironically, and he finished his career on a menu of Mexican and South American teams, returning permanently to Rocky Mount in 1955, at age forty-eight.

He worked for an undertaker for the first few years, driving a hearse, working on bodies, and then he was hired by the city as a truant officer. He says he rounded up kids for the black schools while a white man rounded up kids for the white school, and so what else was new? Blacks were now in the same sports together, but not in the same classrooms; he retired from the government in the middle 1960s, aging, obscure, and forgotten.

Ted Williams was chosen for the Hall of Fame about that time. At his induction, he spoke about men like Buck Leonard. He said he hoped Cooperstown would one day enshrine Satchel Paige, Josh Gibson, and the like "as symbols of the great Negro players who are not here only because they weren't given the chance."

In 1971, Paige became the first black man in the Hall of Fame.

"I got a call the next year from Monty Irvin," Leonard recalls, "and he asked me to come up to New York. I said why, and he said he wanted me to sit in on a meeting that was selecting a team for the Hall of Fame. So I went, and when I got there, the baseball commissioner was there, Happy Chandler, and he got up to say that he had a special announcement to make. He said Josh Gibson was going to be put in the Hall of Fame. Well, Josh was dead, you know, and when you name a dead one, that's all. But then the Commissioner said Buck Leonard would also be put in Cooperstown."

Lighting, huh?

"I never thought it would happen."

Leonard became a celebrity in Rocky Mount. White people shook the hands that held the bat that went to Cooperstown. The area newspapers, which once would not print pictures of black athletes, now put him in headlines. Rocky Mount, Home of Walter F. (Buck) Leonard. Former boy. Present member, Hall of Fame.

Any grudges, Buck?

"Naw."

You're not bitter? All those years?

"It just wasn't our time."

How about bad memories?

"Oh, yeah, plenty of those. One time we played in Newport News. When we got out to the stadium the guy said we couldn't change clothes there. I said, 'Man, we're with the team,' and he said, 'It don't matter, you can't change your clothes here.' So we had to go to somebody's house to put on our uniforms."

Why did you take that?

"You learned. You played the game and you left. That's all."

Buck Leonard stares at the plaques on his wall. Team pictures of the Homestead Grays. Baseballs in plexiglass signed by Johnny Mize, Casey Stengel, and Joe DiMaggio. A Louisville Slugger bat. A Big Dipper mitt. All good wishes from Mr. Joe Garagiola.

"One time we were playing in South Bend, Indiana, and we went uptown to eat. We were walking around, walking around, and we looked in a restaurant. There was a white man sitting in there and we knew, uh-uh. We went down the corner to decide what to do. Well, we had a Puerto Rican with us, and we sent him back with a list. It was the only way we could get something to eat.

"Now let me tell you. Someone once asked Ted Williams how he was so successful. He said he kept his eye on the ball. That's what we did, you see. We didn't like things, we knew it was wrong, I won't say otherwise; but we kept our eye on the ball."

And won.

Howard Wallace was a black man who worked as gravedigger in Williamsburg, Virginia, until he was nearly ninety years old. He was small, slight, but inexhaustible, and he insisted on digging graves by hand. He said machines did not have sentiment; new things were no good; and thus he would start early in the morning, equipped with a shovel and a jar of water, and he would dig without a meaningful break until the job would be finished at midday.

"It ain't nice to stop until the grave is done," he would say. "This is a place where somebody is going to sleep forever, and I don't take time out to eat a sandwich, or sit under a tree, because I got more respect than that. I don't work too fast, either. You make mistakes when you hurry. The thing is to be steady. I myself get a rhythm started—down, up, over, down, up, over—and I keep it going by singing. I sing to the people who are here, and to the new one coming."

Wallace died in the middle 1980s. His last wish was to be buried in the cemetery where he had worked, but it was not granted. The grounds were owned at the time by people who worried that they might lose business if a low-caste Negro were admitted to an upscale white sanctuary, and Wallace was hustled off to a graveyard for minorities, where he was put to rest without much ado, but where he is still remembered with joy by a writer on whom he had made an enduring impression.

W. DORR LEGG

If the twentieth century had no other distinction it would at least have to be known as the time when America discovered sex. Catholic bishop Fulton John Sheen used to sigh that while Victorians did not recognize its existence, moderns recognize nothing else. Oh, lust. Or, put more delicately, love. The nation has broken it into its parts, as it has found the leisure and attitude to do so, and obsession has been bred apace. In the early 1900s men were counseled to preserve their semen, if they did not want to make intercourse obsolete. More recently there has not seemed to be enough of the stuff to go around. Imagination and proliferation, there is the reality. And here is the scope. Roget's Thesaurus (St. Martin's Press) pages 559-560:

pet, pamper, caress, fondle, dandle, stroke, pat, tap, pinch, osculate, kiss, buss, embrace, enlace, enfold, clasp, squeeze, press, cuddle, snuffle, nestle, nuzzle, play, romp, wanton, toy, trifle, dally, spark, lick, fawn, ogle, leer, flirt, nibble, bite, and, as concerns related matters, seduce, prurience, promiscuity, nymphomania, adultery, concubinage, wenching, whoring, amourette, front, back, this way, that way, fellatio, cunnilingus, sadism, swinging, panderism, bestiality, three's company, and, deep breath, orgy.

One hesitates to mention W. Dorr Legg after this. Others, less kind, may think it fully appropriate. Legg is one of the founding fathers of the homosexual-rights movement in the United States and therefore he has been assailed by critics for much of eight decades. The practice of homosexuality, he says grimly, was once and is in some places still considered to be a most serious crime against the natural order of humankind:

"When I was a youngster, it was against the law in all the states in this country. In some places the act even carried the death penalty. If two men in Los Angeles were caught together in bed, naked, they could be arrested. If they were in pajamas, that might be a mitigating circumstance, but they could still be arrested. I myself have seen the police rush into a gay bar and break a nightstick over someone's head. The victim was not doing anything wrong. Being in the bar was enough. It was fascism.

"This was the mentality. And it had a long history. It goes back before the Bible. Anthropology shows us that at the very beginning, when society was formed, people began to say 'This is the way to do this, and this is the way to do that.' Then religion came after that, and so God got into the picture. After God cracked down, the law was formed. And finally, when all of these elements could not could make everyone conform to orthodox sex, science was called in to condemn the deviants as perverts."

William Dorr Legg was born in Ann Arbor, Michigan, in 1904. He says his family has been in America since the days of Cotton Mather. Good people. Educated, industrious, and also patriotic. His forefathers fought at Bunker Hill. The Leggs observed the creation of the nation, and, more importantly, of its Constitution. The right of people to be secure in their persons. The right of people to retain protections not formally secured.

"I was a bookish child. It think it's correct to say my entire family was very much oriented in an educational direction. My father could quote verbatim whole scenes from Shakespeare. I remember my mother reading to me from Marcus Aurelius at God knows what age. The University of Michigan was in Ann Arbor, of course, and still is. That is where I finished my formal schooling. I earned three degrees there. I got an AB in 1926, and I had a BM in 1928, and simultaneously I had a MLD in 1928. The AB was a general bachelor's degree. The BM was a bachelor of music (piano). The MLD was a Masters in Landscape Design.

"I developed my first interests in homosexuality from this educational atmosphere. It was a rather atypical development, I would say, because I did it methodically. I read everything I could find on the subject. I also read about everything else at that age, and discussed things, and argued them with other educated people. We had a regular open house in our home, every Sunday afternoon, where friends gathered to discuss political and other issues. By the time I was in college I knew exactly where I stood on the matter, intellectually, because I had a complete academic background in homosexuality.

"I don't want to say I talked myself into it. I was born this way, and I knew it from the first. I had dated girls in high school; I carried on a regular social life, and I went to parties and dances and so on, and I was not at all uncomfortable with that. I was fortunate in growing up in a fine home environment, and I did not have any trouble relating to anyone, including the opposite sex. But at the same time I did not have physical attraction to females. There was some kissing, maybe, but hardly even that; I just wasn't interested in it then or now. I had no question whatsoever about who and what I was.

"The books were a great help in that. They introduced me to aspects of the subject that I did not know or understand. You have to understand that homosexuality was not the subject of discussion that it is today. It was a taboo, like incest or even rape. Most people did not talk about it. Even the word *homosexual* had hardly come into usage then. For instance, in the medical books I read, the word did not appear. There was *inversion*, or *perversion*, or things like that, you see, but the word *homosexuality* was an invented word; it was coined in Europe, and it was just coming into this country back then.

"Actually, the subject was so taboo that I did not even hear anything bad about it. Not in a small university town. People were too broad-minded for that. We had hippies, or what would be called hippies today, when I was in my teens. We had people from Europe, people from all over the world. And among them there were homosexuals. There was one woman, I recall, a medical doctor, who always dressed in a tweed suit, wore a felt hat, and carried a walking stick. She was different, but everyone accepted her as just another 'individualist.' There was no ostracism there—which, of course, was fortunate.

"So this was my training. Ann Arbor was a place of tremendous openness. I was raised to think I could be whatever I wanted to be. And so when I was nineteen, and I had read all of the books about homosexuality, I decided that I had enough of that and it was time to do my fieldwork [on a Florida vacation]. I won't go into details; I just arbitrarily went out and spotted someone that I decided would be my first 'victim.' He was an older man, and I went up to him and asked: 'Are you a homosexual?' He thought that I was just trying to be funny, but I said I was serious, and I wanted to know what it was like to be with a man."

Was he a homosexual, Mr. Legg?

"Yes. I wasn't so dumb."

And you've continued this way since?

"Yes. I've never known a woman, or wanted to. I left the university as a landscape architect—my parents had moved to Florida by that time—and I got a job in Tampa, where I joined a fascinating and very cosmopolitan community of homosexuals. Again, I should say I was atypical in this respect. So many people have had to endure the lifestyle in hostile surroundings. They are dragged through the seedy places and in the back streets, so to speak. But the community in Tampa was not that way. It was ongoing and completely social. There were people of all ages, people of all races, and I feel that it was wonderful to begin in such a natural way. It was utterly irrelevant if any of the people in the circle had any sexual connection with one another; that did not matter. We simply met regularly on weekends, had picnics, and went to the beach."

Legg says the circle in Tampa was not involved in the issue of sexual rights. This was the 1920s, and no one yet raised that question. Homosexuality was beginning to enter the national conversation, but not certainly in a positive way. Legg and those of his sentiment were called fruits, fairies, and the like. The word lavender *(as it applies to homosexuals) may have been derived from the color of pants worn by Oscar Wilde, who professed his love for an English lord, among others;* lesbian *may have been taken from Sappho of Lesbos, a female bisexual poet; and after a while the word* gay *was applied, by homosexuals themselves, first as a code.* Gay, *by the by, was used early on as a cockney term for very young prostitutes.*

Legg was a landscape architect for thirty years. He also taught the subject at Oregon State College. He says his homosexuality was never brought into question at the school—not that he knew, at least—but as he grew into middle age and moved from one part of the country to the other, he began to see widespread ridicule take place, as well as raw injustice. As homosexuals multiplied, so did at-large intolerance. People lost their jobs. They were excluded from military duty. Heterosexuals were taught that the gays were out to sodomize children, and, worse, there was the legal problem.

"I'll give you another example of the laws of the time. People of the same sex, who were of different races, were automatically considered to be homosexual. If a white man walked down the street with a black man in Los Angeles, they might be arrested. If white and black women were together in the same automobile, they might be stopped and yanked out. Well, I found that horrifying, and I wanted to put a stop to it. Here I was, I guess, supposed to just stand by and do nothing. But I was an American, I had relatives in the Revolutionary War, and I could not tolerate the idea of policemen running around like Nazis.

"I started out to reform things in the late 1940s. By this time I was well established in landscape work, and my parents had passed on, so I was free to get into new things. And it may be significant that I did it in the way I had always been trained, systematically. I began by trying to find the best place in the country to start a movement of this sort. I went from city to city and kept charts on each one. I ruled out New York because it was no good. San Francisco was also very uptight in those days. I didn't like Los Angeles either, but it was so big and so spread out that there was a lot of laissez-faire, and it may have been the only place in the nation to start something.

"So I stayed here. And in going about and meeting people, in theatrical circles and so on, I met a very interesting and very brilliant black man who told me that he had been thinking about forming an organization. So I said, well, 'What for?' And he said, to stop the police from harassing black and white homosexuals and to do something about the difficulties that interracial homosexuals have in jobs, and in housing, and in other areas. He said it was terribly unfair and it should be illegal. And of course I agreed with him completely, and I said I wanted to help however I could. That was in 1950, and we then formed a Los Angeles group we called Knights of the Clocks.

"The name was purely a nonsense title, to cover up what we were doing. But the group was the first ongoing homosexual-rights organization in the nation. I might point out that before that, in 1924, there was a rights group formed in Chicago, but it did not last very long and everybody in it was put in jail. Then there was another group that formed in 1947, in Los Angeles, and it was headed by a wonderful woman who published a magazine called Vice Versa. But hers was not so much an organization as it was a publication. So in terms of continuity, the Knights of the Clocks was the first. It was indisputably the first legally incorporated group, and I was one of the incorporators.

"Basically, the Knights was a social service organization. You might say that it was the forerunner of all of the gay community centers of today. We were concerned with helping people with their employment, and with housing, and with all of the other problems of homosexuals. We also got into the idea of keeping families together. Half of our members were men, half of them were women, which was very unusual in those days, and we got their families to participate as well. We sponsored parties, for instance, where we had guys dancing with each other, girls dancing together, Mom and Dad standing by, watching, and little children running around, back and forth to the food table.

"I recall we had a party for one of our black members. A birthday or an anniversary or something. And, remember, a lot of our black members worked as maids and butlers for the rich people in the city, and so the employers sometimes brought them to the parties and waited to take them home. Anyway, there was one of these big Cadillacs sitting outside this time, and one of these big Beverly Hills guys was waiting, and so we asked him if he would like to come in. It was so funny. He wasn't upset, but he was nervous, and he said, 'Oh, no, thank you anyway.' Now somebody in New York might have knocked us down for that. But this is what I mean about Los Angeles; we got away with it here.

"After that the movement began growing. Beachheads were established in other cities, I did some missionary work in Berkeley along those lines, and then other groups began to form on their own. One of the first after the Knights was the Mattachine Society, which grew nationwide. Now, the Mattachines turned out to be completely different from the Knights. The members were all what you would call semi-kooky intellectuals who were very interested in politics, which was largely Marxist politics. The Knights were very social, but the Mattachines believed in direct action through political means, and therefore, when you think about it, things were beginning to move."

Not fast enough, though. Legg says the laws remained abusive even in Los Angeles. Homosexuals could be thrown out of restaurants, denied entrance to movie theaters, monitored in hotel rooms, and, of course, arrested with the certainty of an automatic conviction if they were nabbed between the sheets. As a result, Legg decided to pick up the pace of the defense. In October 1952 he organized a rights group of his own.

"It started when I called a meeting of friends in my home. The subject of discussion was police harassment and entrapment. Many people were still willing to let it go on; they didn't like it but they didn't think anything could be done. Yet I knew something could be done. So we formed another organization for that purpose. We didn't know what to call it at first. We knew what we wanted to do but we didn't have a name. Then one of the members found a line in *Bartlett's Quotations*. Carlisle said that 'A mystic band of brotherhood makes all men one.' We took it from that. It fit perfectly. We called it ONE, Inc.

"Do allow me a little puffery here. I think I should say that when I decided to organize ONE, I also decided to get into the homosexual-rights movement on a full-time basis. I founded ONE at the same time that I belonged to the Knights and to Mattachine, and I was also working full time in landscaping. Well, I had to cut back. And I didn't want to cut back in the movement. I said to myself, either I believe completely in the movement or I don't. So I walked out of my profession without having an idea in the world how I would get along. I think I was therefore the first true homosexual-rights professional.

"ONE, Inc. has continued ever since. And the difference between ONE and the other early groups was that the people in our gathering believe primarily in education. The Knights were social, Mattachine was political; we are educational. We believe in the social part and in the politics, but we leave that to others. We used to have a very successful outreach program in the country, in Chicago and places like that. And for many years we published what I believe was the first continuing homosexual magazine, *One* magazine. It was on newsstands around the nation when it started; it was quite an innovation.

"We had some interesting trouble with the magazine. It was not a very explicit publication by today's standards, but in 1954 the United States Post Office said it was obscene. And they seized our October 1954 edition and said we couldn't mail it. And so we told the postmaster, whose name was Olesen, we said, 'Sonny boy, we are going to take you to court.' The case was listed as *ONE Incorporated* vs. *Olesen*. We lost the first round in a Los Angeles court; we went from there to the court of appeals, where we also lost. Well, the United States Court of Appeals is a big deal, you know, so we were disappointed.

"But we continued. We said there was just no way that we were going to stop and back down. We said nobody was going to take away our right to publish, absolutely no one. And so we went on to the United States Supreme Court, where we won in 1958. It was quite a victory. And it was unprecedented. Up until that time, it was illegal to publish anything about homosexuality unless it was medical, or 'correctional.' You couldn't print a love story, you couldn't print a poem, you couldn't print a discussion of its normalcy. That was obscene. So our victory opened the door for publications to distribute popular material about homosexuals.

"I tell people now that I'm sort of sorry we won. There is so much junk in the magazines today. At any rate, we closed our magazine down eventually and we got away from the outreach programs. We are focusing now on our educational institution. It's called ONE Institute. We have a four-acre campus in Los Angeles. It is the only one of its kind in the country. We are authorized by the state of California to grant masters' and doctors' degrees in the subject of homosexual behavior. I am the dean. I also teach some of the classes, particularly in history. Rather grandly, we call ourselves the Cal Tech of our field."

A PhD in the gay experience?

"Yes, that's right. We have a wonderful research library; there is nothing like it anywhere else. We have fine instructors, some of whom we have trained ourselves. And we have become the people who make the statements about this subject. We correct the outside errors, we re-educate the scientists, we contribute to the textbooks. We also tour the world. We take our students to study gay communities in many other countries—Thailand, Holland, Morocco, Peru, and everywhere. We only accept people who are serious about this. We give some undergraduate courses to two hundred or three hundred students a year, and we normally have about ten people enrolled in advanced studies. It takes up to three years to get a PhD. We call it a doctorate degree in homophile studies, and it is accepted by the board of education, state of California."

W. Dorr Legg has been a practicing homosexual for sixty-five years. He has been with his present lover for twenty-seven years, and they own their home together. He has lived from a period when homosexuals could be committed to mental institutions for "deviancy" to a time when they have become one of the most energetic and successful subcultures in the Union. To be sure, twenty-four states still have laws against gay activity (1987), yet no other minority group, not even blacks, has come so far in the space of one century.

Two more questions, Mr. Dorr.

"All right."

One. What causes homosexuality?

"We had a speaker at the Institute once, and he was asked that question. He said if you ask what causes homosexuality, you have to ask what causes heterosexuality. And we just don't know."

And two. Are there more of them today than before?

"Some people believe that. I don't. I think homosexuals are a substratum in society, like a substratum in geology; it may be more visible from time to time, but it is always the same size."

6. Activism

BENJAMIN SPOCK

Bertrand Russell believed that the fundamental defect of fathers is that they want their children to be a credit to them, and insofar as that is correct it might be said that Benjamin Ives Spock, wherever he is, might be somewhat surprised by his son, Benjamin McLane Spock, wherever he is. The first Spock was said to be a man of reserved attitudes, narrow social concerns, and black-and-white politics, which is to say an establishment lawyer; he was a New England puritan and a Calvin Coolidge Republican, and he might naturally have wanted his boy to follow his prints through an America of unbending tradition, a nation resolute in orthodoxy, a place where the good and the deserving honor the perfections of the perpetual rectitudes even before they may believe in them.

And for a long time the boy did just that. Young Ben kept his nose and his record clean well into middle age. He went to Yale University, he voted for Herbert Hoover, he started work as a medical doctor, and he became a bit of a commercial success. We are speaking of Dr. Spock now. He wrote the parental primer called Baby and Child Care, *in which he told mothers to trust their own judgments in this business, and he would sell 32 million copies altogether, become wealthy, and take a comfortable and also privileged position as one of the country's most recognized and respected personalities.*

Then he rebelled.

His father, God rest him, might say he got naughty.

"I was born to a conservative family. I was raised in a conservative time. And I received a conservative education. It took me a long time to realize there were other ways to think. When I did realize it, I also recognized that the American people have been sold a bill of goods throughout the nineteenth and twentieth centuries: that anybody can get rich if they work hard enough, that in fact anybody can be president in this system, and that individual initiative is the glorious key to personal and national achievement. It's an illusion. It's kept alive to keep people in line. So I became an activist when I was in my sixties, and I became a radical and then a Socialist after that."

Dr. Spock in the streets? The news photographs of the occasions are among the most improbable icons of the 1900s. They likewise represent one of the century's most significant peculiarities. Civil dissent is an attempt to persuade a society to accept an opposing point of view; early man invented it when he defied the tribes; later people have cultivated it by turning against the state; and it has, in some lights, become the taproot of the American commitment. The Pilgrims were activists, as were the Founding Fathers, as is everyone who wants a share of the responsibility. Henry Thoreau said that when conscience is abused by established order, conscience is the higher law.

Of course, Thoreau may also have been a disappointment to his father. For all their charm, activists can be exacerbating. They are forever prattling about duties and standards, and throwing bombs into sacred affairs. "The giant chicken-eating slug will soon be extinct if we don't take action now" (Playboy magazine). "We demand that the government stop cluttering up our billboards with highways" (The Abominist Manifesto). "Undermine the structure of society by leaving the pay toilet door ajar, so the next person can get in free" (Taylor Mead). "Plastic, aluminum, these are the inheritors of the universe; flesh and blood have had their day, and that day is past" (Green Lantern Comics).

Jimmy Durante once asked plaintively "Why can't everyone leave everyone else the hell alone?" The activist's response is that if we don't survive we don't do anything else. Other than this, Americans simply enjoy participation. In 1985, a Gallup opinion poll determined that 89 million men, women, and children volunteered their services to one or more public endeavors. That figure represented 48 percent of the population (51 percent of the females), and in excess of sixteen billion hours, or almost two million years, of participation. All in all, the service was said to have an annual dollar value of $110 billion.

And make no mistake, this is what activism is: volunteering. No other definition need be applied. Those who belong to the Rotary Club are as much a part of the distinction as those who picket the president. The difference is that the pickets of this century have gotten more notoriety, in part because they have taken advantage of modern communications to nourish their complaints. Women did not win suffrage until newsrooms were connected by telephone; unionists made their largest gains with the advent of radio; and Martin Luther King, Jr. might have gone the way of hundreds of his obscure predecessors were it not for the television camera.

So: You Are There. Angry military veterans demand bonus money during the Great Depression. Coalminers walk out of the mines on the orders of John L. Lewis. Moralists protest everything from the Kinsey Report to abortion on demand; worrywarts charge the gates of a nuclear power plant; and, from placards to pacifism, from wetbacks to Woodstock, here is a short hint of the scope of the organizational grump: American Association of the Aging, Air Pollution Control, Bald-Headed Men of America, the Child Welfare League, National Association of the Deaf, Young Americans for Freedom, Group Against Smokers Pollution, the Humane Society, United Jewish Appeal, Literacy Volunteers, the PTA, SCLC, NOW, NRA, AFL, CIO, the Stuttering Project, and SANE.

SANE is an organization opposing atomic armament. Dr. Spock is a past president. How his father might have sighed at the retelling:

"I was raised in New Haven, Connecticut, and, as I mentioned, it was a conservative time in a conservative place. My father was a lawyer for the New Haven Railroad; my mother was from a very stuffy family in Boston. It was so stuffy that when my father courted my mother, her parents tried to shoo him away. He was a self-made man, but only middle-class, and they didn't think he was good enough for her. I followed him in those days; I was very straitlaced, very much a goody-goody. As a matter of fact, my biggest problem throughout my youth was that I felt like a namby-pamby, a mother's boy. I didn't feel that I could stand up to the tough boys or to the more regular fellows.

"I felt I got out from under that when I started at Yale. I gained more self-confidence when I made the Yale crew. I got on through something of a fluke, however. The crew had a new coach that year, and he did not have any use for the English style of rowing, which was the way it was done at most Eastern schools. His style catered to tall people, and I happened to be six feet four inches tall, so that gave me an advantage. I rowed number seven in the boat; I was on the junior varsity and then on the varsity from the time I was a sophomore. The varsity crew went to the Olympics in 1924, in Paris, and we won a gold medal, and I felt quite a bit better about myself.

"The Olympic victory was directly responsible for my being asked to join a secret society at Yale. The Scroll and Key. So I was beginning to be my own man. Not politically, however. I still followed my father in that. My father said Mr. Coolidge was 'the best president the country ever had,' and I believed it. The reason my father liked Coolidge was because he was a corporation lawyer, and Coolidge was the one who thought that 'the business of America is business' and 'the less government interferes with business the better.' My father loved that. I imagine I did too. I never thought about taking another position then. Actually, I didn't think it was any of my concern.

"I started to change a little when I was in medical school and I transferred to Columbia University in New York City. That was the place where I first heard that people could be Democrats, or even Socialists! My father told me that Republicans had created all of the advances, and all of the wealth in the country, and that Democrats were rather sleazy people who were incapable of doing anything like that; they were only capable of taking the fruits of progress. When I was in New Haven it never occurred to me that what he said might not be true. But there was a good deal of variety at Columbia; the students were from all walks of life, and some of them were not Republicans.

"I began to argue politics there. I did it with Democratic classmates and Republican friends. During the day I would argue strict conservatism with the classmates, never yielding an inch, and then in the evening, when I was with my Republican friends, I would argue liberal or radical. I did that for four or five years, and I provoked a lot of people. I was testing things out. It's like a man who has a new car that he likes. He knows it is nice and he made the right choice, but he wants to get someone else to confirm that he made the right choice by buying the same kind of car. That's the way I was. And it was the way I got the courage to drop out of the Republican Party and became a moderately liberal Democrat."

Spock's initial revolt was limited. Yet he was on his way to the barricades, and he would go there in style. He says one of his early insubordinations was to break ranks with medical tradition and become the first pediatrician of the day to take psychiatric and psychoanalytic training, and, as it happened, that shift became the foundation for his decided capitalistic success. He also married in 1927, and had two children. Nothing rebellious about that. He was a Democrat, but in a tight collar and three-piece suit. He practiced pediatrics in Manhattan; he was an attending physician at New York Hospital; and a pediatrics instructor at Cornell.

"Then that horrible nightmare took place. The civil war in Spain [1936-1939]. I would never had enlisted with the Americans, who were going over there in the Abraham Lincoln Brigade, but I was involved emotionally. Here were Benito Mussolini and Adolf Hitler supporting Generalísimo [Francisco] Franco, along with the industrialists and a good section of the Spanish hierarchy, and the United States just piously said that it would maintain neutrality. I used to leap out of bed every morning, rush to the front door, and grab the newspaper for the latest news. It seemed to me that all the good was on the side of the republican government, and all the evil was with Mr. Franco.

"I started paying attention to wars after that. World War II was next, and then Korea. I did not oppose them, as I did the one in Spain, but I eventually came to have my suspicions. I believed in World War II, for example; I believed that we had to stand up to Hitler and the Japanese militarists, but I think now that it did not have to happen. If the United States would have had the wisdom and the integrity to get into the League of Nations and work cooperatively with the democracies in Europe, we could have easily curbed Hitler. The same thing is true for Korea; I know now that the South helped to provoke that war, and we wound up supporting a corrupt and repressive regime.

"That's not to say I am a pacifist. I have never been a complete pacifist. If the country was attacked from the outside, I would be willing to play my part in any way I could to fight back. But I would have to know the background of the attack. And it would be awfully hard for me to imagine a war in which the United States was not to blame. I can't think of a single war like that in which we've been involved. Vietnam was only the best example of what we've been up to. We have taken part in several illegal and immoral invasions this century—in Lebanon, in Grenada, and more recently in Central America. We are the ones causing the trouble, and I won't support that."

The book Baby and Child Care *was released in 1946. It was an immediate sensation. It would be put through thirty printings, published in thirty-one languages, and made Dr. Spock famous. He would write nine other books, seven of them about raising children, but who has heard of, say,* Problems of Parents, *or* A Teenager's Guide to Life and Love? *Dr. Spock says the first book made publishing history because* "it is friendly to parents, and it does not scold them or alarm them," *but, whatever the reason, he likes to think that he has turned the response into something more constructive than success.*

"When the book became popular, I did as well, and the political people started to come around. I was a New Deal Democrat by then, and I was asked to come out for Adlai Stevenson when he campaigned for the White House. I was glad to do it, I suppose, but I'm not sure in retrospect that it was justified. I thought Stevenson was an idealist at the time I supported him, but later on he made an ass of himself at the United Nations. Lyndon Johnson was partly responsible for that—he just did not tell Stevenson what was going on. But when Stevenson found out that he'd been betrayed, he just kept on doing what he had been doing in the United Nations. To me, that is far from admirable.

"At this same time I was being invited to join SANE. I was asked three times, but I kept saying that I did not know anything about radiation and that I was in the business of trying to reassure rather than to scare parents. But I was finally persuaded in 1962. Homer Jack was the executive director, and he got through to my conscience. To put it specifically, he convinced me that if we didn't have a nuclear test ban more and more children around the world would die of cancer or be born with physical defects. He persuaded me to join for the sake of children, and I came to see it as an extension of pediatrics. Vitamins and calories are not enough; we must have a safe world.

"SANE was not a radical group. The national board was a self-selected, and the membership was merely liberal. In fact, when Joseph McCarthy came along and there was a suggestion that Communists may have infiltrated SANE, the board got scared and joined the red-baiters in the country. When some of the student members in the universities took radical positions, SANE stopped recruiting on the campuses. And when the FBI began snooping around and became intimidating, SANE drew up a loyalty oath. It was the most disgraceful thing the members have ever done.

"In 1964 I was asked by the Democratic National Committee to support Lyndon Johnson for president. I went on radio and television for Johnson, and when he won he called me up to thank me and to say 'Dr. Spock, I hope I prove worthy of your trust.' And I said, 'Oh, Mr. Johnson, of course you will.' Well, three months later this man who promised that he would not send Americans to fight in an Asian war did exactly the opposite. He started the bombing of North Vietnam, and the buildup of combat troops there. I was absolutely outraged, and that did it for me. I was radicalized and politicized, and I cast aside the cautiousness of my whole life."

Spock thus joined the most vociferous rebellion of his time, the peace and anti-Establishment movement of the 1960s. He was sixty-two, a ripe fruit among the hippies, the yippies, black power, gray power, the Age of Aquarius, the greening of America, Jane Fonda, Baba Ram Dass, for goodness' sake, and Granola bars. Quote: "Don't be shocked when I say that I was in prison. I am still in prison. That's what American means—prison." (Mr. Malcom X).

"It was very embarrassing to go into the streets. Especially for a professional man. I was embarrassed to picket; I was embarrassed to shout the slogans; I was embarrassed to have interviewers stick a microphone in my face and ask me mildly insulting questions like, 'Doctor, why are YOU here?' But I gradually got used to it. I felt the young people wanted to have the support of older people, and that made me more comfortable. I started to speak at the universities, eight hundred of them at one stretch, and I joined the others who were speaking out against the war, and the draft that was sending all these boys to die."

Instantly, Dr. Spock became the most celebrated dissident in the Union. In addition, he became a particular legal dilemma. He was investigated by the government for his advocacy of civil disobedience; the federals questioned him in his apartment at one juncture; and in 1968 he was indicted with four other antiwar activists for acts that were said to have been committed in conspiracy.

"The 'conspiracy' part was very interesting. There was Michael Ferber, Mitchell Goodman, Rev. William Sloane Coffin, Marcus Raskin, and myself, and most of us had never met one another. But the trial judge said conspiracy is merely breathing together; the government only had to prove we were on a parallel course. Of course, the conspiracy laws were never designed to suppress political dissent. They were designed originally to catch industrialists who were conspiring in restraint of trade, and they were also designed to catch gangsters who could not be otherwise prosecuted. But they tried us for it anyway.

"The charge was that we had counseled, aided, and abetted resistance to the military draft. None of us had actually gone around and counseled young men to do that. So it came down specifically to a document that was prepared by several intellectuals that was called 'A Call to Resist Illegitimate Authority.' That document pointed out that the Vietnam war was completely unworthy of the United States, that it was completely illegal, and that anyone who was sent there was asked to commit war crimes and crimes against humanity. Therefore people were obligated to refuse to carry out those orders.

"I signed that paper. I still believe it today. And I never had any feeling of guilt during the trial. They asked, 'Did you sign the paper?' and I said of course I did. And they asked, 'Did you distribute the paper?' and, of course, there were movie films showing that we had. I remember that when they pulled down the shades to show the films, I used to go to sleep. Well, the trial dragged on for three weeks, and in the end four of us were found guilty. The interesting thing is that Raskin, who was one of the primary authors of the paper, was let go. I was sentenced to serve two years in jail."

That sentence was later overturned, and the convicted parties were spared. Dr. Spock says he has gone to jail at other times, however, always all for civil disobedience. The last time was in 1987, when he was hustled off to the can after climbing over a fence at Cape Canaveral, with 150 other noncomformists, railing against the military designs on outer space.

"I don't want to sound as if the only thing I do is go around committing civil disobedience. I vote, I vote thoughtfully; I write letters by the hundreds; I lobby in Washington; I complain to the newspapers. And I'm also still uneasy about picketing. I remember the first times at the Pentagon, for instance, I wondered if the soldiers had live ammunition in their guns and might do a Kent State on us. But when I feel I'm getting nowhere and the cause is justified, I will break the law, yes."

Dr. Spock ran for the presidency in 1972, sponsored by the People's Party. He says he did not want to do it, but he explains that he was the only member who could afford to pay his own campaign expenses. Spock was on the ballot in ten states and received about 80,000 votes—which, if multiplied by the states in which he did not appear, suggests a national rate of 400,000.

He divorced his first wife in 1976 and married a woman forty-one years his junior. He joined the Socialist Party when he was seventy, and now, at eighty-five, he lives aboard a pair of sailboats, one in Maine during the summer, the other in the Virgin Islands when the weather turns. He also has a house in Arkansas. Hither and yon. He continues to speak and to frequent political demonstrations.

He is an easy, affable individual. He dresses fastidiously, but he enjoys simple things. He is as generous with his time as he is short with conceit. He can laugh at himself. There is a sense that he knows he is a circumspect agitator; he would make a hopeless urban guerrilla; he would misplace his ticket to the revolution; he does not have the capacity to hate. But justice? It's common sense. No one can question Dr. Spock's common sense.

"When I ran for president it was very educational to me to find out how unready most people are to take a socialist position in America. I gave one speech, over and over, because the press was not paying attention anyway and I felt it was a good speech. My aim was to make people feel that it's all right to get radical, and to turn against capitalism, and to make the government more humane. When I finished I would always get long applause, and then people would come up to the platform to shake hands.

"And every time—I mean *every* time—there was always one young man who would come up and say, 'Dr. Spock, that was a great speech, and you have got me convinced that we have to have a different economic system.' Then he would add 'But of course I can't vote for you, because I would not want to waste my ballot.' Well, I translated that into the young man's belief that the government may be rotten but he expected to do all right anyway, and he did not want to cut himself loose from the mainstream."

Youth. Benjamin Spock remembers.

"It's no wonder. We grow up with our parents telling us don't get into politics, don't get into radical groups, that's not important. The important thing is to get ahead and make money."

Seventy-year-old Ruth Leger Sivard started to chronicle a radical and quite remarkable look at political priorities in 1960. She was an economist with the United States Arms Control Agency then, and began issuing an annual publi-

publication, "World Military and Social Expenditures," that turned out to be an impassioned indictment of international values. The government dropped the publication in 1973, ostensibly because of budget reductions, but Mrs. Sivard has continued to work on it privately out of her Washington home, where she compiled the following statistics in a very worrisome 1987-1988 edition:

The governments of the world have participated in 471 wars [of at least 1000 deaths] since 1700, and 101 million people have been killed in them. The world has spent $15 trillion on military affairs since 1960, in 1984 dollars, during which time 81 majors wars were fought, and 12,555,000 people were killed. There were 22 wars in progress at the beginning of 1988, an astonishing 84 percent of the casualties were civilian, 142 nations were spending $1.8 billion a minute on defense, and, in all, 26.6 million men and women were uniformed under arms.

Meantime, Mrs. Sivard says, human needs have gone unmet. She says one-fifth of mankind lives in privation in 1988. One hundred million people do not have shelter; 770 million do not get enough food to sustain working lives; 400 million in the most deprived nations are unemployed or underemployed; 880 million adults are illiterate; 14 million children die annually of hunger-related causes; the poorest fifth of the world population has 2 percent of its economic product (the richest fifth has 74 percent); and 1.3 billion people do not have safe water to drink.

ODILON LONG

Odilon Long, like Benjamin Spock, got into social activism late in life. But under different circumstances entirely, and not at all so contentiously. Long joined the United States Peace Corps when he was sixty-five. He says it was a viable alternative to playing cribbage in a senior citizen's center, and if the duties of, say, constructing privies for the poor in the Third World has not been as publicly noteworthy as leading political revolts in America, it has nevertheless had its distinctions. Denge fever, for instance. No running water. Open sewage. Crawling specimens in the breakfast food. Also blowing dirt, oppressive heat, ominous smells, and, for agreeable relief, quaint native customs.

"When I first went to Haiti, I was assigned to a village in the southern part of the country called Petit Trou de Nipps. I think it was named for a vessel that used to haul bananas to the United States. Anyway, the village people put me up in a small house, and then they sent a girl over to keep me company. She was young—in her teens or early twenties, I guess—and I asked someone what I was supposed to do with her. They said whatever I wanted. They could not see a man without a woman, so they sent her to sleep with me. Well, I said thank you, but I sent her back. I had a lot of work to do in that village, and I didn't want any problem like that; I wanted to keep a clear mind."

Well, let's not start with the wrong impression here. There was another, more typical, time when O. Long was involved with a village woman:

"That incident took place where I am now, in Costa Rica. There is a piece of land that was taken over by the government after the last earthquake, and there was this woman who had squatted there. Her husband had died; she wasn't able to get work; and she lived in a tent, and she didn't have any water, or lights, or anything like that. So I helped her out. I could not get Peace Corps money for it, because the funds are not available for such things; but I spent some of my own, and everything worked out."

Odi Long is eighty-five. He was as of 1988 the oldest Peace Corps volunteer on the planet, and, with twenty years of duty, one of the few who has made a career in the service. He does not seem large enough in size to compete with the mosquitoes in the third-world nations where he labors (he is five foot two), but he is a big man in other regards. He is considered a man of miracles in Togo; he is the only foreigner to receive the prestigious Order of Roekel in Sierra Leone; and it goes without saying that he is something of a saint to that woman he rescued in Costa Rica.

All this after sixty-five. Productive aging.

"I grew up in the far North, in the state of Maine. My hometown is Fort Kent, right on the border with Canada. It is still as much Canadian there as it is American. A lot of French-speaking people settled in the area when it was still a part of England, all along the Saint John River, and most of them stayed where they were when the boundary was set. The boundary was fixed in 1865, using the river, and so the area is surrounded on three sides by Canada. The French culture was very strong when I was a child, and it still is. You can go back in the woods there, and it's more like French-speaking Canada than it is the United States.

"I learned French before I learned English. My father was from New Brunswick; he spoke French and passed it on to me. I knew a little English, but there was no one to speak it with. I did not know it well until I started school, and even there we were taught some things in French. As I remember, they split the day in two ways. In the morning we had everything in English—geography, arithmetic, and all that. Then in the afternoon we had French religion and literature and grammar. Overall, we had more English, but the other language was very strong.

"I went to primary school, and then finished a couple of years after that. I had eight years in all, but I started then to learn things on my own. I was a carpenter at first, at about fifteen, because that was my father's trade. And I did everything else I could to earn money. I was a lumberjack for a few years; the area has a large lumber industry, you know. I swamped the roads for one logging outfit, and I was a chopper. I did not earn much money at it. Nobody earned anything then. But I got what I could to help support my [ten] brothers and sisters.

"When I was eighteen I joined the military. I was too young for the First World War, but I got in right after. I was sent to the Third Division after it came back from overseas, and I helped muster some of the men out at Camp Pike, Arkansas. I re-enlisted after two years and spent the second two years with an artillery unit in Panama, in Central America. The Panama Canal had just been completed, in 1914, and I was with a coastal defense force. We protected the ships passing through. Panama was still in the jungle, and we were paid in gold.

"That was my first trip out of the United States; I was still a kid, and I was very impressed. It was a wild place, and primitive, but I was living at the American base, which was comfortable. The streets were in, and there were flowers all over. I used to like to look at the royal palms, because the only thing I ever saw in Maine were pine trees. I always thought I'd like to get back to Panama when I got out of the Army. I never did get back; but I've been to a whole lot of places just like it, still looking at the royal palms, all over the world."

Long went to work for the American Telephone and Telegraph Company in 1926. That was but eleven years after Alexander Graham Bell and Thomas A. Watson held the first coast-to-coast telephone conversation (and, incidentally, one year before the first television picture was transmitted by telephone wires). Long was a lineman, then a clerk, finally a supervisor. He married in 1928, was widowed in 1957, and says he joined the Peace Corps within twenty-four hours after retiring from AT&T in March 1967.

"I had read about the Peace Corps, and I had considered it for a long time. I had been married for twenty-nine years, now I was single, I wasn't working any more, and I did not want to just sit down alone and do nothing. So I decided to commit myself to a new career. I had talked it over with friends; they encouraged the idea. The Peace Corps did not take many older people at first—it was mostly a younger organization—but I felt I was qualified. I had done everything from farm work to home construction, and I was in good physical condition, and I went down and signed up.

"There were forms to fill out. And we had to have a security check. There were quite a lot of requirements. I think I was the only one over sixty. I may have been the only one over twenty-five. This was during the Vietnam war, and a bunch of young people were getting in so they could stay out of the war. That led to some problems in the Peace Corps. A lot of the kids were not as dedicated as they might have been, and some of them didn't work out. We had to get rid of three of them at one place I was working; one of them for dope, and I forget the other troubles."

The Peace Corps was then six years old. It had begun conceptually in 1960, when a presidential candidate spoke of his plans at Ann Arbor, Michigan. John Kennedy had just completed a televised debate with Richard Nixon, he was exhausted and running late, but he decided to make one final campaign pitch (at 2:00 A.M.) to 10,000 students at the University of Michigan: "How many of you are willing to spend ten years in Africa or Latin America or Asia working for freedom?" he said. "How many of you who are going to be doctors are willing to spend days in Ghana?" He then said the future of free society depended on the answer.

The rhetoric was overmuch, the warning perfectly silly. Yet the challenge was accepted. The Peace Corps went into business in 1961, with 400 volunteers already in waiting. The mission was to send Americans anywhere there was a need plus an official invitation, and by 1966 more than 15,500 enthusiasts were working in at least fifty countries. Those numbers were to shrink in time, but, when Odi Long volunteered, the Peace Corps was still at the zenith of its calling: seeking peace though service to others.

"I started in Gabon. That is on the west coast of Africa, below the horn. It used to be part of French Equatorial Africa, so I suppose they sent me there because I could speak the language. The country got its independence in 1960, and it was just getting started on its own. One of the nice things about the place was that it wanted to do that, it wanted to do things on its own. I didn't go there to do it for them; I was just helping. Gabon also had some things to build on. It is not dirt-poor like many other countries in Africa; there is oil there, and the petroleum revenues made it kind of an African Kuwait.

"That doesn't mean that there were great comforts all over the place. This was twenty years ago. I worked in town at first, but then I went into the countryside. There wasn't much electricity, and like everyone else I got my water from a well. I lived in the area where Albert Schweitzer put up his medical facility, in a place called Lambaréné. That's where I got sick for the first time in the Peace

Corps. I got a bad case of dysentery. I went on to worse things that than. I've had malaria twice, pneumonia six times, and I was very sick once with denge fever. You get very weak with denge fever, and get headaches and a rash.

"One of my jobs in Gabon was to move a depot that was located on the banks of the Ugooué River. The depot was where the Agency for International Development stored many of its materials. We had lumber there, and—oh my gosh sakes alive!—I forget how many vehicles. We had seven dump trucks. So I had to move it to another location, in the southwest. I also built a couple of bridges in Gabon and participated in some other constructions. I don't want to say I built them myself. The people built them and I helped supervise. The Peace Corps does not take over; that's not the idea, and I wouldn't do if it was.

"The people there were very industrious. They were not afraid to work, and that was necessary because the population was not very large [fewer than 400,000 at the time]. Also, people were spread out. You know how it was, it was like any country with plenty of open space. A man would get himself a woman and go out in the bush and start a clan, and after a while there were clans living in poverty all over Gabon. Then when the country won its independence, the government brought the clans to new villages so they could help them. Then they burned the old places. That's where I came in; I helped in the new villages.

"I think they appreciated the help. But there were some problems; there were bound to be some problems. I had a big argument with a chief mechanic at one time. He was working for AID, and he had been in charge of the depot I was preparing. Well, that meant a lot of money was going through his hands, and I found out that he was keeping some of it in his pocket, so I had to cut that off. I told him to stop it and I reported it to my people. He got very sore at that. He said I should mind my own business, and then he said he was going to speak to the police. He said, 'I will have them take care of you.'

"Nothing happened. People are always saying things like that where I've been. But it never goes beyond the threats. I have never been frightened in any country. I'm not that way. Even when the politics heat up. I was in Haiti until just before Jean-Paul Duvalier fled the country, when the Tonton Macoutes [secret police] were running around, but nobody bothered me. I have been asked to leave a few countries. That happened first in Gabon. I only stayed there for six months before there were some political difficulties. The government changed the set-up there; it became restrictive, and they kicked us out of the country."

The Gabon government imposed a one-party system in 1968. That led to objections by some Peace Corps volunteers and, concomitantly, ruptured relations. It also led to an American rethinking of the Corps and budget reductions. When Richard Nixon entered the White House he decided that the Kennedy agency was little more than a haven for left-wing troublemakers. And there was some truth to it. Vice-President Spiro Agnew was hooted by Corps members in Afghanistan, and several governments complained of militant volunteers.

Odi Long says it was an unsettling period. The Corps lost credibility at home and abroad. The service was cut back. The staff shriveled. Good aims seemed to be going up in marijuana smoke, and host nations became sensitive and skeptical. Members who hung on, like Long, found it all the more trying.

"I went from Gabon to Sierra Leone; I was there for more than two years, and I worked on a slew of projects. The government was very happy with the work, but I had some more problems as well. They tried to throw me out at one time. It was nothing political. It was just harder then to work with some of the people. There was one case in the north end of the country, for instance. I was doing some work on a hospital there, and I got into a squabble with one of the local administrators. He had the keys to the AID vehicles and he refused to turn them over for our use. I had to quit the job for that. I was afraid we'd argue more and it would lead to an international incident.

"But that was not the worst thing in Sierra Leone. Another time I had to expose one of the members of parliament. That was really something. That was a cutie. It started when I decided that I had to raise some money for a project. I often raised money like that, when the regular funds were not available. So this guy, the MP, he said to me, 'Say, listen, I can get you all kinds of money.' I had a good record in the country, with everything I had built, and he said he would collect money on that record. I said, 'All right, go ahead,' and he started to collect it. He collected quite a bit, in fact, but the thing was he did not turn it over to us, he kept it for himself.

"So I went to see him in the capital [Freetown] and he wouldn't let me in his office. Then I went to the Catholic Relief Office and talked to their project manager, and I asked him to call the MP for an appointment, and we went to the MP's office together. When we got there I asked the MP for the money, and he said, oh, he didn't know I was looking for him, and he said, 'Just give me your bank account number and I will deposit five thousand dollars within a week.' Don't worry, he said, don't worry. Okay. I agreed. I gave him the number, and I waited a week, I waited two weeks, I waited three weeks, and finally I waited a month, and he didn't deposit a penny—nothing of what he owed to us.

"Well, I had to expose the MP. My gosh sakes alive, what a shock it was! I sent copies of my charges to the high commissioner, to the CARE office, and I also sent one to the MP's office. Now I marked all the other letters personal, but I didn't do it on the one to his office, because I wanted his secretary to open up the doggone envelope. I figured she'd have it all over Freetown in two hours' time. And she did! Everybody heard about it. Naturally, the MP was furious.

He came up to where I was working, 275 miles from the capital, and he came up with a colleague of his, a young MP, and his bodyguard, who was a killer. They all came at me together, and arrested me.

"They didn't take me away. They said it wasn't necessary for me to go to jail, but that I would have to leave the country because my visa had expired. That was just an excuse, of course. And it didn't bother me because my visa didn't mean anything. I had been personally invited into the country by the vice-president of Sierra Leone, and I was there on his acceptance. So I didn't say anything when they arrested me. But when they left I sat down and wrote a long letter to the vice president. I told him everything, just exactly what happened, the man keeping our money and everything. And I said: 'Mr. Vice-President, am I going to regard it as a fact that I will be expelled for this?'

"You know what happened? The MP was forced to write a letter of apology about it. Then he had to apologize in person before the American ambassador and the Peace Corps director in the country, Rudy Watkins. So that was what happened there. The vice-president sent someone to investigate my charge. That man told me that it might just wind up being my word against the MP's. But no, I had proof. When I went to see the MP I took the project officer of the Catholic Relief Service. He was there when the MP admitted he owed the money and would deposit it in my bank account. In other words, he was the best witness I could possibly have, and the cutie MP did not stand a chance."

Any retaliation, Mr. Long?

"No, he was finished."

What about his killer?

"I'm still alive so far. Anyway I stayed in Sierra Leone for some time after that. I completed one project that was probably the largest I have ever done. There were serious storms on the coast one year, and they destroyed a number of school buildings. It was the reason the vice-president asked me to come to the country in the first place. I drew up a design for new classrooms that were well lighted and had plenty of ventilation. I supervised the construction of 185 classrooms like that, using prefabrication techniques. Before I left the president of Sierra Leone made me an Officer of the Order of Roekel; I don't know what the MP had to say about that."

Long has an impish chortle. Like that of Walter Houston in the filmed version of "The Devil and Daniel Webster." When he left Sierra Leone, he went on to serve the Peace Corps in Togo, Upper Volta (now Burinka Faso), Haiti, and he is now on assignment in Costa Rica. He works in the highlands there, on the Pacific Ocean side, and in 1987 he was helping residents build new housing with funds they borrow themselves at low-interest loans.

The Peace Corps has recovered somewhat from the nosedive of the 1960s and 1970s. In 1987 there were 5500 volunteers working in more than sixty nations. The budget was $130 million. Corps officials said it cost $20,000 to keep someone like Odi Long in the field for a year, versus $100,000 for a comparable worker from AID. The average age of Peace Corps volunteers has gone from twenty-five to twenty-nine over the agency's first quarter-century. During the same time, more than 125,000 volunteers have served in 100 countries.

Odi Long lives in San Isidro, Costa Rica. Looking back, he says it is all to the good that he did not accept that young woman who was offered in Haiti. She could never have kept up with him.

"You have to stay busy. You're no good to anyone if you don't. I remember when I wanted to build latrines in one country. The ground was so rocky that the people said they could not build the pits. So I designed an alternative that went completely on top of the ground; I called them *gratte ciels*."

There's the devilish chortle again.
Gratte ciels *means "skyscraper."*

When the concept of the Peace Corps was initially proposed in Washington, in 1960, some members of the Immigration and Naturalization Service raised a question in jest. Why should the United States start going to help the people in other countries, when so many of the people seemed to be coming here to help themselves? Fifty-five million immigrants have settled in America since the 1700s, and the total is said to be higher than the immigration statistics for all other nations combined.

The figures have been particularly impressive during the twentieth century. Nearly nine million foreign-borns took residence between 1901 and 1910, according to INS accounts, and at least that many will arrive before the latest decade (1981 to 1990) is over. The numbers for the intervening years were generally smaller, but, added together, the INS says almost 40 million people have immigrated between 1901 and 1988, and at least 10 million more will be here by the year 2001.

PHILIP BART

Midway in the century a Democratic member of the United States House of Representatives, William Munford Tuck, rose on the floor of the chamber to

*warn of what he believed to be an unprecedented peril in the country. He assert-
ed that the red flag of Vladimir Lenin had been planted in the bastion of freedom. The followers of international totalitarianism were at the gates of domestic peace and security. Reading from text, shifting in cadence from one foot to
another, he said: "Communists are running rampant through the land. They
are fomenting strife and discord and are inciting racial and religious rancor and
hatred, resulting in riots, bloodshed, death, and destruction. They are undertak-
ing to demean and denigrate the good people of America and our government by
spitting on ... and burning ... [our] flag."*

*That was news to Philip Bart. He was a member of the Communist Party
at the time, he remains a member today, and he maintains that he has never fo-
mented hatred, never incited death and destruction, never spat on the national
banner, and, in fact, has always been most loyal and devoted to the Republic:*

"I did not become a Communist to destroy the United States. My motives
have always been to preserve it and make it better. The idea that we want to
hand the government over to the Soviet Union in absurd. I cannot conceive of
such a thing. It is against everything I believe in. It's against everything the
Communist Party believes in. It's against everything the Soviet Union believes
in. I think that the Soviet Union really and honestly seeks peace in the world.
Even if one disagrees with their tactics. So I don't see a country wanting to
achieve peace by trying to take over a country like ours. I could never think that
way. I could never support such a thing.

"I am a Communist because I believe it is the next stage in human development. I read and I studied, and I decided that the collective system is the best
and most humane for all men and women. I think the capitalist society resolved
problems that previous [feudal] societies did not resolve, and the Communist
goal is to resolve problems that capitalism has not handled. For example, production under capitalism is still in the hands of the few, and communism wants
to put it in the hands of the many. Capitalism has created private industry, and
communism wants to create worker control of private industry. If we give them
the chance, the workers will develop a system only dreamed of today.

"This doesn't mean war, or violence, or spitting on the flag—the Joseph
McCarthy charges. We believe in peaceful transformation. However, we do
not ignore the fact that when you have a majority for revolution, the minority
may have certain military or police powers that it will use against you, and then
you will have to struggle. That was the case in the American Revolution. That
was also what happened when the nation resolved the issue of slavery. So we are
not in favor of violence, but we don't control that. It's kind of like the old story
where a policeman grabs a man during a political demonstration. The man says

'Don't hit me; I am an anti-Communist.' And the policeman says 'I don't give a damn what kind of Communist you are.' Bop."

Philip Bart is eighty-five. He is of Polish descent and came to America during the waves of mass immigration in the early 1900s. A million or more immigrated every year from 1905 to 1914; they were Jews like Bart or Slavs, Sicilians, and Greeks for the greater part, and they were not always greeted with warmth. Jobs were scarce. Tradesmen were jealous. Real wages averaged less than they did in the late 1800s. Hence there was a consequent political swing to what was to be called the Progressive Era.

Progressives believed in the perfectibility of man. On one level the movement was no more than an extension of the idealistic principles of Thomas Jefferson and Abraham Lincoln. Beyond that there was a growing interest in public control of the national destiny. The widely ignored Socialists of the nineteenth century came into sudden prominence; intellectuals began reciting "the gospel according to St. Marx"; and communism—Socialists in a hurry, yuk-yuk—was to closely follow.

Phil Bart: "I started as a Socialist, and it was on my own. My father was a shirtworker, he worked in a clothing factory, and he was rather conservative politically, because of his Jewish religion. I would say he voted as a Democrat. He brought us to the Lower East Side of New York City, however, between Seventh Street and Fifteenth Street, and that was a Socialist community. Consequently, I became liberal; I favored Woodrow Wilson because he promised to keep us out of war. When he didn't, I became disenchanted, as did many others, and at the age of sixteen I began to attend Socialist meetings and become active.

"The Communist Party was just getting started, but the Socialists had been around for a long time. The first Socialist organization in this country was formed in 1852, and the idea was spreading rapidly when I was a boy. One reason was the economy. It was a difficult period. A lot of us saw the need for change. I came from a family that was poor; I had to quit school and go to work at an early age. In those days you could get working papers at sixteen, and that's what I did. I left school and became an errand boy. Later I got into the trades. I worked first in printing—I was a printer—and then I went into upholstery.

"At the same time I started to become more involved politically. I joined the Upholsterers International Union, and I became secretary of the largest local in New York, Local 76. I also continued to work for Socialist interests. We held meetings at a big church on Second Avenue and Fourteenth Street that was, and still is now, known as the Labor Temple. We were very active. I did a lot of legwork, distributing leaflets and materials and promoting candidates in the elections. We elected the first Socialist member of Congress, Meyer London, Sixth District, and we got five Socialists into the state Assembly.

"Socialism did not have a severe stigma attached to it then. It was radical, but it was generally accepted as just another political system, particularly in the urban areas. There were a number of Socialist mayors in the country; young people formed clubs at the universities; and the movement was encouraged by many celebrities. My own feeling was that Socialism was a step up from capitalism. I favored the idea of state control of services, for instance. As I grew a little older, communism took root in the country, and I decided that if Socialism was higher than capitalism, communism was the highest form of all."

The Communist Party was born out of the Bolshevik revolution in 1917 Russia. It was created on the Karl Marx promise of an "economy of abundance" and on his vision of the abolishment of private property, and by 1918 it became the chief export of the Union of Soviet Socialist Republics. The movement was given subterranean birth in the United States, and, even under cover, it was bothered by massive public fear and government repression.

"The party was organized here by veteran Socialists. And it was illegal for the first few years. This was right after the First World War, and the relationship between the United States and the Soviet Union was not in the least bit close. The government did not like the Bolsheviks; it did not like the Soviet influence over international Socialism. You could lose your job for being a Communist then. You could be put in jail. The government was worried that the Reds would come here and take over the country, and so the only thing to do was to put them outside the law.

"This was a long time before Senator Joseph McCarthy. This preceded McCarthy by thirty years. The Red-baiting campaign began when the Communist Party began. In 1919, for example, there was a committee set up by the New York state legislature. They launched an investigation of communism, and wrote the findings in three large volumes. Those books are still in the library today. They say the Communists were up to no good, and nobody was safe. Oh, yes, it was vindictive. It was not a good idea at all to be a Communist in 1920; you said you were a Socialist instead.

"There is an interesting commentary on the findings of that New York state committee. The materials were valuable to me in becoming a Communist. You see, there were very few works by Karl Marx in America then, and one of the basic books we lacked was his *Communist Manifesto*. That is the fundamental platform statement for the international workers' movement, but we could not buy it in this country. Then the New York state committee wrote this terrible document into their record, and that's where I was first able to read the *Communist Manifesto*."

Bart says the fear of the Communist movement led to savage consequences in 1920. That was when Attorney General A. Mitchell Palmer, acting on orders from President Wilson ("Palmer, do not let this country see red!"), staged a series of raids on private homes and labor buildings, trashing legality in the process. More than 4000 suspected Communists were arrested during one twenty-four-hour period alone in thirty-three communities; many of them were held in jail, on fictitious charges, and some of them were promptly deported. Not long after, the New York state legislature expelled those five Socialist assemblymen Bart helped elect.

That spring, Palmer overplayed his hand. He said the Communists were plotting to bring down the government on May 1, and National Guard units and police were mobilized. When May Day passed without event, the oppression of communism was somewhat relaxed.

"The Party formed a legal organization in 1921. It was called the Workers Party. A few years later the name was changed to Workers (Communist) Party of America. Eventually it dropped the word *Workers* and became the Communist Party of the United States (CPUSA), the name that it still uses today. I began to be active in the party during all that name-changing, in 1924. I was twenty-two years old. I was still in the upholstery business and in my trade union, and then in 1928 I went with the Party as a full-time professional. I've been working for it now for sixty-one years.

"I went to Detroit in 1928, where I became the secretary of the Young Communist League of Michigan. This was a period when the automobile workers there were not organized. They had a small union that did not command much attention, the Automobile Workers Union. The union was originally in the hands of the Socialists, and it came under the control of the Communists when I was there. So one of my jobs was to help organize strikes. The union was not large enough to have paid organizers, and what we did was print signs, walk picket lines, and we tried to be effective in the face of whatever the management people would throw at us.

"By this I mean it could be dangerous. There were no laws to protect strikers then, and there wasn't much public sympathy either. We had to struggle against the place and time. The authorities were intolerant, and when we set up a line the police might come right in and knock hell out of us. The strikers could try to protect themselves by putting up a fight or something, but you could not go to the courts, you could not go to the government; they didn't care. We had to do the best we could, and be satisfied with little victories. We never forced management to bargain, but working conditions did get better.

"And that was the idea. We did this same kind of thing all over the country. We took everything step by step. I don't think I had any illusion about what was happening. I did not believe we would see the transformation of the United

States to socialism in a few years, in twenty-five years, or anything like that. But I was convinced that it would happen eventually. And I looked on everything I did as part of that development. That's why I stayed with the Party. Other people got discouraged; many of them left, but I knew we would start slowly and then make a tremendous step. I still believe that as much as I ever did."

Philip Bart is a thin man with large ears that are pointed at the lobes. He also has big eyes, and a Charlton Heston nose. He lives in the New York suburbs, and he does not smile much.
Are you married, Mr. Bart?

"Yes. I've had two wives. My present wife is a Communist too."

Family?

"One child. From the previous marriage."

So, a normal life in that respect?

"I think I've had a normal life in most respects. I have just had different dreams. Of course, I have not earned much money—the party cannot afford that—and there's also been the risks."

What about the risks?

"It has never been easy to be part of a minority movement in this country. There are always persecutions. Communists have all had some difficult moments, and I am not only a Communist but a Jew. I remember one time in Pittsburgh, I was speaking on a street corner, and some men drove up. When they got out they yelled 'Get that godamned Jew bastard," or something like that. They did not say 'Get that Communist!' They said 'Get that Jew!' As it turned out they didn't get me. My friends threw me in a car and got the hell out of there. But that's how it's been generally. I have been arrested many times and pushed around from here to there. Others have had worse things done to them.

"And we haven't even touched on the 1950s yet. That is when the persecution reached a peak. I think it took place for the same reason as the problems in 1919 and 1920: the end of a war created frictions between the United States and the Soviet Union. When the Second World War ended the Russians were our allies; they were part of the Four Powers. You will recall that less than one year later, the president of the United States invited Winston Churchill to speak in this country. When Churchill came he said that a so-called Iron Curtain was descending in Europe, and that started the whole thing again; the United States and the Soviets became estranged once more.

"There also were labor troubles right after the peace. The trade unions did not have the right to strike during the war, and so when it ended they wanted to do some catching up. Some of the largest walkouts in American history took place then. Close to five million people were on strike during one period. And the Communists were right in the thick of it. I was in Chicago in the late 1940s; I was very active in a packing-house strike. So people resented that. Politicians picked up on it. McCarthy picked up on it. The Communists were to blame for the labor turmoil, it was said, and the reason was that we wanted to bring the nation down. I'm not surprised McCarthy got an audience."

What do you feel about McCarthy, Mr. Bart?

"I don't have the words to explain."

Were you personally affected by him?

"We all were. The Party was still legal, but that was about all. By law, all of us were supposed to register, and if you registered it was like wearing a red letter on your forehead. Besides this, members were regularly picked up for questioning. The leaders in Ohio were picked up. The leaders in San Francisco were picked up. It got so no one knew who would be next. You were afraid of every knock on your door."

Did you register?

"Not at all. I wouldn't consider it. Members of the Republican Party did not have to register, so why should I? It was a matter of conscience."

Then were you arrested?

"Not for failing to register. I was held for contempt of Congress. I was forced to appear before the House Un-American Activities Committee, and I refused to answer some questions. I invoked my rights under the Fifth Amendment to the Constitution. They would not accept that, even though it is clearly guaranteed in the document. They asked several things about the CPUSA and about my personal involvement, and when they got through they just sent me right down to the Washington jail.

"I was convicted in court on the question of contempt, and I stayed in jail for about a week before I was released on bond. All of this was against the law, so the Party took the case to the United States Supreme Court. We argued that the wording in the Constitution is unmistakable—no one can be forced to testify against himself—and therefore I had been held for something that was unconstitutional. We felt I had the same right as anyone else to the protection; my party affiliation did not matter; and we were right. We won on that appeal."

In time, the party would also win the right to unfettered organizational activity. Registration was lifted, congressional persecution ceased, and political participation was duly regained. That's not to say the party recovered altogether. Its image was indelibly stained and its motives were more or less permanently put in suspicion. The party lost its credibility as well as its momentum during the Cold War and, as a result, the revolutionary fires were all but extinguished. In 1987 the party membership was reported to be less than 40,000, probably much less, and Communist influence in America was nominal.

Phil Bart retired from the CPUSA in the 1970s, after reaching the executive position of organizational secretary. He thereupon edited a history of the party in the United States. He still puts in volunteer time at the party's dreary building in Manhattan, where visitors are searched by an aging gateguard.

There is a story Nikita Khrushchev used to tell about socialism. He said the whole thing requires the suspension of habit: in the Soviet Union people keep on looking in the barn for their horses even after they have given them over to the collective.

"It's true the Communist idea has not yet evolved in this country," *Bart says, sitting on a straight-back chair and running his hand along the lapel of a serviceable jacket.* "But we have worked for many things that have been achieved. Now, what is that? One is Social Security; we fought for it long before it was adopted. The Communist Party also demanded unemployment insurance compensation before it was accepted. We took up the first struggles for black liberation in the South, which is now a reality; we helped attain power in the trade unions; and we have worked for many of the benefits now available to the poor.

"So we consider all of these gains important gains. It is part of the development we seek. We are not failing. We have not lost the struggle. We still have mass support. We will still overcome. Now I don't know when, and I don't know how. It may take the form of Communists elected to government, or it may take the form of a constitutional convention. I continue to believe it will happen, positively. I do not waver in that conviction."

Gus Hall, the longtime secretary of the Communist Party USA, has not had a very successful run in matters political. His party has atrophied, he has been defeated in his half-dozen presidential campaigns, and there is not at this writing a declared Communist serving in any elective office in the United States. Yet the seventy-five-year-old Hall says he has not fallen into despair; and, through it all, he's retained of a sense of humor.

"When I was a young man I used to work in a lumber camp in the north woods. And the facilities were not very good. We didn't have such things as indoor plumbing. Now that was all right in the summer, but when winter set in we did not want to get up in the middle of the night and walk all the way in the snow to the outhouse. So we just went to the bathroom right outside the door. Night after night. In the freezing weather. By the time spring came we had the biggest yellow mountain you ever saw."

PAUL GANN

Paul Gann has dedicated much of his long life to the pursuit of a proposition that some might say cannot exist. He is a conservative do-gooder, a right-wing advocate of the people. His adversaries charge that the terms are an oxymoron, that the adjectives and nouns are contradictory, but Gann will have none of it. He says Republicans practically invented the modern idea of promoting human progress, when they brought about abolition, and he is therefore and indeed a child of tradition. He has fought for the right of people to protect themselves from criminal abuse. He has earned a national reputation as a antitax crusader. And he has bolstered the happy supposition that power in America comes fundamentally from the population—the grass roots, if you will, where every man and woman is a force.

He has not always been applauded for the efforts, to be sure. It is easier to be a Whig than a Tory in the circumstances. In 1987, for example, Gann took on the most important cause of all, the right to life, and there are many who now wish he had not.

"This fight began after I came down with a strange sickness," Gann explains. "We didn't know what it was, but at first we thought it was just the flu or some other kind of bug, and I started taking antibiotics. But it didn't help. I felt very weak. I was running a temperature, and I dropped from 155 pounds to 135 pounds within about ten days. My doctor changed the antibiotics, and changed them again and again, trying to find one to do the job. Finally he said to me that if I lost any more weight he would have to put me in the hospital.

"My wife said no to that. She thought I needed a thorough examination, and she made an appointment for the next day, not just for me but for the both of us. When we got to the doctor's office, she said, 'What is killing my husband?' She said, 'We've been married for fifty-five years, and he is dying day by day, right before me, and I want to know why.' And the doctor said, 'Well, Nell, we have done extensive testing; we think his kidneys are good, his heart is good, his blood pressure is good, his bladder and liver are good, and the fact is we don't know what it is.'

"And she said, 'My God, what could it be?' Then she made a reference to surgery that I had five years earlier. It was open-heart surgery in 1982. I had several blood transfusions, and Nell said that when I got the blood there was no way to check this thing called AIDS [Acquired Immune Deficiency Syndrome], and now it was well known, it was all over the media, people were dying. So she asked if I had been tested for AIDS. The doctor said I had not, and then she told him to do it, and he said, 'Okay, Nell, we'll do it only for your peace of mind.'

"I tested positive. I was very shocked and bitter, of course. I felt it was very unfair, and I hated the person, whoever it was, who had donated the blood I was given. But I got over that stage as quickly as I could, and I decided to do what I've always done, and that is to launch a campaign. I decided to start what may be my last battle as an activist. I am going to spend the rest of my life, however long that may be, trying to protect others from falling under this deadly spell. I want to identify people with AIDS, like we identify people with other diseases that are life-threatening and contagious. I know that idea does not set well in some circles. So be it. We have to control this thing, and I don't know any other way to do it."

Paul Gann, mossback activist, is seventy-five years old, and he knows something of mysterious sickness as well as the promotion of the public good, because he was born to a part-time minister and spent his first years crippled with osteomyelitis. That was on the flatlands of Arkansas, where he says it was no fun for a boy in the country to be confined to his bed and unable to walk.

"Osteomyelitis is an inflammation of the bone marrow. But the doctors did not know what it was then. They called it 'white swelling' or 'tuberculosis of the bone.' It didn't even have a proper name until I was twenty, and so, before that, all I could do was to regret I had it. It struck me in the leg when I was five, and the leg swelled up to where we had to cut my trousers because I could not otherwise get them on. Then as the leg grew larger, it also drew back and around me, until my heel was right on my buttocks. It stayed like that for a long time. I could not walk for five years. I was completely housebound. I could not get out to play or to go to regular school, like other children.

"The treatment was more or less backward. The family doctor came to the house once a week and lanced the leg to relieve the pressure, but it didn't work and it may in fact have done more harm than good. I remember that when he lanced, small bits of bones would work their way out of the cuts, and my mother would pick them up with a toothpick and keep them in a matchbox. Then we decided to go to another doctor, a specialist you know, the experts on everything, and we took the box of bones along so that he might get an idea what was happening. So what he did was take my tonsils out, and my adenoids—I'm telling the God's truth—because he thought that would stop the bones from fragmenting.

"I was fortunate in having a very fine family, however. We were poor, but we were not allowed to think we were poor, or my mother would have taken us behind the woodshed. The way to say it was we didn't have much extra money. My father was a timberman and a minister and he did some farming. My mother was a grand woman who nursed me, and worked with me; she taught me reading and writing when I could not go to school, and, in retrospect, I must say she also taught me the wonderful lesson of helping other people. My father too. I was raised to believe that we are responsible for one another; we are a free people, and we have to work together to keep it that way, so that we all benefit."

Gann moved to California when he became an adult. He married his childhood sweetheart, Nell, put osteomyelitis behind him with the advent of penicillin, and fashioned a mediocre career in what he refers to as sales and promotion. He says he has sold everything from automobiles to real estate and promoted everything from ideas to political candidates, and, as it would develop, that became spadework for a second, public, career.

"Looking back, I think I was always active in something or the other. I was a Nosey Rosy and interested in what was going on. The first time I ever did it formally, trying to fight city hall, was to oppose a bond issue here in Sacramento. That was in 1955. The government wanted to pass a new bond, which meant people would have to pay for it, and I felt strongly enough against it that I decided to stop it. I was the Lone Ranger then—I didn't even have Tonto on my side—but I threw myself into it. The city council supported the bond; the downtown merchants supported the bond; but we went on the air, we got in the newspapers, and, in the final analysis, we managed to defeat it.

"After that I guess I became known as a scrapper. And I got into one issue after another. And people started to come to me for help with their problems. One group of black people, for example; they lived in a bad area for crime, and they asked me if I would help them do something about it. So we formed what was called The Sacramento Parent Patrol. It was all volunteer; we got a building to work out of; and people in this area started patrolling their own neighborhood. They did not carry guns, but they had two-way radios and Polaroid cameras. If they saw something funny going on they would take pictures, and call in, and then the regular police would be notified.

"So they became their own protection. And, believe it or not, they made the neighborhood into one of the safest areas in Sacramento County. The idea has since spread to other communities, and in fact all over the country, and it proves a couple of points that I have been trying to promote for a good many years. One is that law enforcement in this nation is no stronger than the people who support it. The other point is an extension of that. The responsibility of a good government does not stop with the bureaucrats and the elected officials. It rests with the people. That is, we are the government, not the officials, and it's up to us to make it as good as it can be."

An interruption, Mr. Gann. Have you ever run for public office?

"Yes. Twice. I ran for the Sacramento city council one time, and I ran for the United States Senate in 1980. I lost both campaigns. I got a good forty-five percent of the Senate vote, however."

Who did you run against for the Senate?

"Alan Cranston. I did not want to run, and that's sincere. I didn't have any money, I only had a staff of about five people, and I think I signed up to run twenty or thirty minutes before the deadline. But I didn't like Cranston's politics. I still don't think he could beat me with a butcher knife in a fair fight, where both of us had money, and, besides, it was part of my fundamental conviction. We all should get involved. We shouldn't just leave things to someone else. Especially someone like Senator Cranston. I am not an antigovernment conservative; but I do want it controlled by the people.

"There are lots of people who feel like that. Howard Jarvis was one of them. He has died now, God bless him, but we made a good team while he was still here. And it's interesting how we got together. It started in the 1970s. I had given up my vocation then, because I wanted to spend full time as an advocate, and my people were after me to do something about high property taxes in this state. But I didn't think we were strong enough to do it alone. Well, Howard Jarvis was also an activist; he had an organization in Los Angeles and he had been fighting for tax reform for many years. So we just got together on the issue.

"The issue was called Proposition Thirteen. That was the state initiative we devised to cut the exorbitant property taxes in California. Now I was not then, nor am I now, against property taxes, or any other kind of taxes, providing they are fair and reasonable. It's like my minister father used to tell me about the money he collected in church. Some of it was used to pay his salary, and he was very particular about how the family spent it. I used to go to the store, maybe, and want some candy, and he would say no; he said people weren't making offerings so we could buy candy, we had to spend it wisely.

"I feel that was the case with California property taxes. They were set very high so the state could buy things it didn't need. That was abusive. The rate of tax that was laid on the people was such that many of them were losing their homes, because they could not pay the assessments. I would get calls like this: 'Mr. Gann, I'm seventy-seven years old, and my husband and I worked for years to get our home. And before he died, he said, Honey, at least the home is paid for, and no matter what happens to me you will always have a place of your own. That was years ago. Now the property tax is more than our payment was.'

"The state claimed that it needed all the revenue. It was too bad about people like the seventy-seven-year-old woman, but the bills had to be paid. Yet the truth was that the state did not receive any money from property tax, not a single dime, because it went to the counties and the cities and the other districts. Besides that, the state of California at that time had eight billion dollars worth of surplus funds in the treasury. And I don't think they ever gave a thought to where it really came from. They sit in their comfortable bureaucratic offices and forget that it comes from folks who are trying to keep their heads above water.

"So Howard and I got Proposition Thirteen on the ballot. We also got a lot of heat for it. When we started campaigning we became very visible, and both of us were threatened many times. I got calls about how they were going to make my wife a widow. One reason for the hatred was that the state was fighting us with everything it had, including fabrications, and the whole thing became a very emotional issue. For instance. You have a six-year-old who comes home from school one day with a note in her hand. The note says 'Don't vote yes on Proposition Thirteen, because if you do there will not be enough money next year to keep the schools open.'

"The state voted on the initiative in 1978. We got two-thirds of the ballots, and the measure became a constitutional amendment—and happily so. The first year after the enactment, the average taxpayer saved about sixty percent on his property tax bill. It varied, depending on which part of the state you were in, but that was about the average. I think property tax overall dropped seven billion dollars in 1979, and since then the numbers have been much greater. I have been told by the California controller that in the first nine years, Proposition Thirteen has saved the people of this state 228 billion dollars in taxes."

Gann says schools did not close the following year. And Proposition 13 triggered similar tax-cutting measures nationwide. Jarvis went on to the cover of Time *and to other levy wars before dying at eighty-four in 1986. Gann would also continue to wrestle the revenuers before turning his attention to AIDS.*

"I helped to put four other initiatives on the ballot after Proposition Thirteen. Two of them are also laws today, and I think one of them, Proposition Four, is the cap on Proposition Thirteen. I started it because soon after Thirteen was passed the state began to look for ways to get around the amendment. And I became convinced that they would eventually find a way to render it useless. So I told my people that what we had to do was to force the government to live, the same as the taxpayers live, according to inflation and population. What Proposition Four said was that government could not increase its budget from one year to another in excess of the rise in inflation and population.

"Proposition Four passed with no difficulty in 1979. It got seventy-five percent of the vote. And one reason it did was that we added something else to the measure to make sure the state could not maneuver around the intent of the initiative. The amendment says very simply that if the government has funds left over after the budget year—in other words, if it has collected more taxes than were needed to run the departments—then the surplus would have to be returned to the taxpayers. It's one of the only laws like that in the country, and in 1987, I'm proud to say, the state of California had one-point-one billion dollars left over, and they had to return it to the people; it worked out to a hundred fifty to two hundred dollars per taxpayer."

That rebate was the good news for Paul Gann in 1987. The bad news was AIDS. He was advised that he was not suffering from the full brunt of the disease, that he instead had what is called the AIDS-related complex, but he was also told that the complex is normally the precursor to the real thing. Gann says he was "absolutely frightened to death." At about the same time United States medical authorities reported that they expected domestic deaths from AIDS to grow tenfold by 1991, when at least 179,000 of the 270,000 predicted victims will have perished.

Mr. Gann, how many have gotten AIDS from blood transfusions?

"No one knows, but twelve hundred of them have already died."

With respect to that, what are your chances?

"No one knows that either. That's why I want to do whatever I can, in whatever time I may have, to make people listen to reason about this thing. My position is simple. The only way we can hope to get a grip on the disease is to find out who has it and prevent them from passing it on. I believe everyone in the country should be required to be tested for AIDs. Look at my case. I contacted the disease in 1982 and didn't find out about it until 1987. That is five years that I could have been passing it on to others. If I would have known, of course, if it had been diagnosed, I could have taken the proper precautions.

"I think we must face the fact that by now millions of Americans may be harboring this thing. And it doesn't matter if one has AIDS or the AIDS-related complex, these folks are still dangerous to others. The state of California takes the position that if a person has the AIDS-related complex it is not contagious, but that is a damn lie. If you are affected, you are a threat if you are not cautious. And the number of people who are affected may be many times what we think. I know a woman, a doctor in the East, who says that she has a patient who has had the virus for nine years. Nine years! But at least they know about it.

"So I'm offering myself as a public example. And I'm doing it for the same reason I've done these other things in my life; it's in the best interest of the people. I was told by friends that it would be a mistake, that it would embarrass my family and I might destroy the thing that I've worked to build, which is the support of the people. But I can't pay attention to that. I have the idea that California and other states are trying to sweep this disease under the rug; they are bowing to the homosexual lobby that says mandatory reporting is an infringement—and that just flies in the face of the facts.

"The state of California has something like fifty-eight contagious diseases that require mandatory reporting. If the doctor says you have one of them, he has to report it to the state department of health, and after that you are immediately investigated by the department. You know what my doctor said to me? He said, 'Paul, if you want to get something that has to be reported, then go out and get yourself a good dose of syphilis.' Now think about that. The state says a doctor will not abuse my civil rights if he reports my syphilis, but he will if he reports my AIDS. That's how strong the homosexual lobby is on this matter.

"I'm going to beat them, you can bet. One way or the other, I'm going to beat them if God lets me live long enough. I hope I can influence the legislature to live up to its responsibility and enact legislation on its own, but, if not, then we will go to the people, we'll put a measure on the ballot. The measure would say that everyone would be tested, and if a doctor finds you have AIDS he has forty-eight hours to notify the health department. And then the department would be required to do what they do with the fifty-eight other contagious diseases: investigate the carriers, find out who they got it from, and stop the spread."

Paul Gann lives with Nell in a small house in the California capital. He works out of an office maintained by his organization, People's Advocate. He says this about activism: Too many uninvolved Americans get up in the morning and start criticizing the world while they are shaving. Then they nick one of the careless sons-of-a-bitch who is responsible.

"The homosexuals say that if we have mandatory reporting of AIDS it will drive the victims underground. The thing is, many of them have been already driven there—six feet under, actually."

The last time the United States conducted an all-out assault on a sexually transmitted disease was in the early part of the century, when it was estimated that one in ten Americans was suffering from syphilis. The problem was initially recognized during the First World War, when 13 percent of the military inductees were found to be infected, and the lines were drawn when the government detained upwards of 30,000 prostitutes, isolating many of them behind barbed wire. Major progress was made when Congress funded a venereal-disease-control program and all states followed up on that by mandating blood testing for marriage licenses. Today the disease is comparatively rare. In 1986 fewer than 21,000 cases were reported to federal offices.

MAGGIE KUHN

In some ways Margaret E. Kuhn seems very much like the stereotyped little lady that she prefers to think is fable; she is in the autumn of her life, as they say, ick, and she is obediently small, gray, perky, gentle, solicitous, soft-spoken, and lovely. So it was probably natural, some years ago, for the president of the United States to be solicitous upon their meeting. The occasion was a bill-signing ceremony in the White House. President Gerald R. Ford was formally enacting new pension legislation, and Kuhn had been invited with others to witness the proceedings. They were introduced, they shook hands; Miss Kuhn was a Norman Rockwell picture of elderly joy; Mr. Ford was as friendly as he was awkward, and after he had formally put the measure into law, the President tried also to be cute.

Miss Kuhn:
"He leaned across the table and said, 'And what would you like to say, young lady?' So I said that I would like to say that I am not a young lady, Mr. Ford. I am an old lady and proud of it."

She is indeed. Old and proud. The poet Thomas Sterns Eliot once wrote that he did not believe people grew older, he felt that at a certain age they "stand still and stagnate." Maggie Kuhn gives the lie to that theory. She believes that aging is growth, that the worst deformities of long life are those imposed by underestimations, that contribution need not inevitably concede to time, and she has spent all of her own senior years trying to make the philosophy

*contagious. She is the founder of the Gray Panthers, a spirited group that pro-
mulgates the outrageous concept the old are readily as valuable as the young.*

*She is eighty-two. And it is significant to note that she has been battling
for the interests of her generation all of her life. She did not start off to be a re-
former, though, She was the daughter of traditional parents who said she could
be anything she wanted to be so long as it was in teaching, and she set out early
on that course. She enrolled in the women's college at what was then Western
Reserve University (Cleveland, Ohio), and she studied to be a school mistress
until she was diverted by circumstances.*

"My life was changed by an eraser fight. You know, where kids grab the
erasers from the classroom blackboards and throw them at each other. This one
took place when I was a student teacher. The class I was assigned to teach was a
grammar class, and I had them structuring sentences on the blackboard. I was
very much enamored with the John Dewey theory of education, that you learn
by doing, and I felt it was necessary for the students to stand up at the blackboard and parse sentences. They would highlight the subject of the sentence
with an underline, then the subject modifier, and so on; you get the picture.

"Anyway, I thought it would be fun to have a relay, or competition between teams. We chose up groups, and they had to rush back and forth to the
blackboard to parse their sentences, and it all went very well right up until a
photo finish. Then there was a little altercation at the end, and just in a wink the
class got out of the control. The erasers began to fly. Back and forth, off the
walls, off the ceiling. Well, I jumped to my feet to stop it. I stamped my shoes
and I yelled as loud as I could, but nothing happened; so I grabbed an eraser
myself and threw it at the biggest kid in the class.

"Just then the regular teacher walked in the door. And that's when my life
was changed. The teacher was angry, of course. But it wasn't just the eraser
fight that upset her. She said that she did not like my methodology, that I may
have been too free to experiment, and that I would always have trouble in class.
She didn't think my students would learn anything, she went on, and so she
only gave me a passing grade. That meant I couldn't be a teacher. You had to
have straight A's at that college to get a teacher's certificate, and therefore I was
knocked out of the profession and had to get into something else for a living.

"That turned out to be the Young Women's Christian Association. My
mother had a friend who was associated with the group, and that friend asked
me to do some volunteer work. And I did. And this was quite a change. I was
from a middle-class family, a woman who wanted to be a teacher, and all of a
sudden I was with the YWCA. You have to know that the YWCA has always
had a very different purpose from the YMCA. The men's group has been ori-

ented toward exercise and recreation, but the women have always been activists. The YWCA was founded [in 1855] to help women cope with the changes of the Industrial Revolution.

"And that's essentially what I did. I worked with women who had these low-paying, marginal jobs in business and industry. Those were the years of the sweatshops; workers could be mercilessly exploited, especially women workers. A good salary for a woman then was six dollars a week for six days of work, a dollar a day, nine hours a day. They had no protections. There were no unions for women. There was no medical insurance, no unemployment insurance. I used to go to where they lived, and it was shocking; they were dreadfully poor, they lived in small rooms in the ghettos, and no one seemed to care for them.

"I was fascinated and horrified by it. It was my first exposure to this kind of thing. I had taken sociology courses in college, and so I knew it was going on, but now I could see it for myself. And I was radicalized very quickly. These poor women were at the bottom of the society. I used to go down to their jobs and eat lunch with them. It was very sad for me. They had no education, and no hope. There were very few jobs in those days that had career possibilities for women. They couldn't be managers, or administrators, for the most part. They started in menial jobs, and they were normally expected to stay in menial jobs.

"So I found my niche. Social work was just beginning in this country. You had Jane Addams houses in Cleveland where I was. You had some community centers, and some settlements that were also interested in helping people. And you also had church agencies, and a few organizations like the YWCA. The whole field was just opening up, and I graduated from volunteer work to full-time employment with the YWCA, at nine hundred dollars a year, I remember [about three dollars a day]. I also went back to school to get a master's degree in sociology, when they were just starting to teach social group courses, and I was hooked; I got addicted to helping people."

Miss Kuhn says she became so addicted that, from then on to now, she has subordinated most of her personal considerations to her devotions. She has never married, for one thing, or had children to raise. Gerald Ford might well wonder about that: "A pretty little thing like you?"

"I have had great love affairs, and I am glad that I have, but there has always been the conflict of social work, I have always been too interested in what I was doing to take time for other things. When I was in college, I had a very passionate affair with a young man, and it detracted from my studies, and I never forgot that. I've thought about marriage. I've lived with one man, at a time when that was brazen, and I've been engaged a couple of times, yet no, I couldn't do it. I think the decision has been the right one. I've had the best of both worlds. When I am asked why I've not married, I say I've been lucky."

Miss Kuhn went from here to there in social work, through middle age and beyond. She served on the YWCA national staff in New York; she was on the staff of the General Alliance of Unitarian Women in Boston; and she was for many years an associate secretary with the United Presbyterian Church, where she was involved with weighty issues regarding racial justice and world peace.

"Mother Bountiful. That was the name."

Were you at all political?

"I voted for Norman Thomas. He was a giant."

Socialism?

"Yes, it's the only way. I used to have an aunt who lived with us, Pauline. She had been married to a man who was an engineer with the New York Central Railroad, Uncle John, and he was killed in a terrible train wreck. The train had hurled through a closed switch and tipped over. Well, my aunt did not even get funeral expenses from the railroad, because industries did not have those responsibilities. So my aunt took the matter to court. She lost because the court decided that the switchman was at fault, and not the railroad management. Now, that kind of business has been changed over the years, by the Democrats and the Republicans, but I think Socialists would have done it sooner."

Miss Kuhn worked for the Presbyterian church in New York. She commuted from Philadelphia, where she maintained a home, first for her parents, whom she cared for until death, and thereafter for herself and her cats. She says she grew old on the 8:10 commute, and, in 1970, after more than four decades of social activism, she found herself very near mandatory retirement.

"There were others I knew who were in the same predicament. And six of us had formed a small group that got together for lunch and that kind of thing. This was New York, so these women were all very active and sophisticated people. One of them had worked in the Department of Labor; one of them had worked in the student movement of the 1960s; and there they were, there *we* were, getting together in the cafeteria and wondering what we were going to do after we retired. None of us wanted to retire. But the boom was about to fall on us. So we tried to think in a collective way about what we would do for the rest of our lives.

"We were not doddering old fools. We were all well, we were all trained, we were all good organizers, and we developed a kind of an ultimatum for ourselves, a grand agreement that we weren't going to sit around and do nothing from then on. And we decided that we should get into the argument over the war in Vietnam. That was really hot then. Also, there weren't a lot of older people involved. And that is what we were really talking about; we were talking about older people doing something constructive. We were free now to pick and choose our battles, and, initially, we decided to fight for the young.

"One of the first things that happened was that one of our women got arrested. That was Anne Bennett. She went to represent us in a demonstration in front of a New York draft office where the protesters were blocking the entrance of the building, and the police pulled her in. She was taken to jail, where she was kept overnight and strip-searched by the police matron. Oh, she was really infuriated! When she got out of jail she was literally a tiger. She was in her middle sixties, and I don't think she'd ever been arrested for anything before, and that made us all think, Well, great, we must be doing something right.

"Later, we held a meeting at Columbia University. Each of us had our own networks; we all had our contacts, and so we made phone calls to everyone we could think of. To our absolute delight, seventy-five people attended the meeting. They were all older people, and it showed us that we weren't the only ones feeling this way. It was a June day in 1970. A very hot day. We chose a very unwieldy name at the time, The Consultation of Older and Younger Adults for Social Change, and we declared then that we would lobby formally against the war in Vietnam; I think it was the first older group of its kind in America."

The name was changed on the suggestion of a New York television station. A reporter said all the members were like tigers, or panthers—yes, that was it: like the Black Panthers, only gray. They concentrated on Vietnam for a short time, then expanded their purpose to focus on the problems of long life. A primary goal of the Gray Panthers is to challenge and eliminate ageism, the discrimination against the old. No one is old as long as they are seeking something, as it's been said; in this case, justice.

Miss Kuhn continues:

"We were quite something at first. People were not used to old people ranting and raving. The idea was that we were supposed to stay in our homes or our gardens. And we were left-wing. That was another surprise. We had no support from the government. Richard Nixon was the president then, and he had no use for us at all. I recall that he convened a White House Conference on Aging, I think it was in 1971, and we were purposely not invited. We weren't surprised, and we decided we would go to it anyway. We didn't want to be left out of something of that scale, so we conspired to more or less sneak our way in.

"One of our founders, Eleanor French, organized a citizen's group that wrote preparatory material for the conference. We had a United Church of Christ minister who was a member in New Jersey, and he got himself named to lead that state's delegation to the conference. So we did it. We couldn't get in the front door, but we got in the back door, and we had a ball at that conference. We had a big demonstration; we complained about this and that; we handed out leaflets and position papers, and, in general, we tried to promote a whole different view regarding the problems of aging, a view of militancy and of confrontation.

"We also held a sensational protest against the exclusion of black people at that White House Conference. We found out weeks before that no blacks had been involved in the planning and that the data to be used at the conference was screwed up because it did not include much data on the minorities. So while the White House Conference on Aging was being held at the District of Columbia armory, we held a Black House Conference on Aging in a Presbyterian church on New York Avenue. That church is the one Abraham Lincoln used to attend and that lent to the occasion; we had a thousand people attend that meeting.

"We marched on the White House from the church. There were blacks and whites and Puerto Ricans, and we wanted to give a message to Nixon. It got a little messy. As soon as our line got near the White House, there was a police band that arrived; they were on horses, and they drove right in on us. They arrested several people, and some of us were knocked about. I was knocked down by one of the horses. I was just bumped to the ground, and it was awful. They did it deliberately, I think. I think the police were acting on orders from Nixon. I believe he was watching from the window while all this abuse was going on."

In 1973 the Gray Panthers merged with Ralph Nader's Retired Professional Action Group. It has become accredited to participate in discussions and meetings at the United Nations, and in 1987 it was said to have 60,000 members in 100 chapters. The budget in that year was about $600,000. The group is headquartered in Philadelphia and has a branch in Washington.

Maggie Kuhn lives in the Germantown home she has owned since 1958. The parlor is decorated with fine old furniture and copies of the Gray Panther Media Watch. The Media Watch grumbles about the popular depiction of the aged: frail, toothless, cranky, intolerant, quivering, sexless (or, contrarily, lecherous). The Gray Panthers insist that the generalizations invite ridicule.

Miss Kuhn is neither frail, cranky, intolerant, quivering, or sexless. Her teeth are her own affair. She wears her hair in a variety of styles, dresses with varied dignity, and peeps over a pair of stylish reading glasses. Friends call her a wrinkled resource. Critics admit she has charisma. She has written two books, one of which is provocatively titled You Can't Be Human Alone, Let's Get Out There and Do Something About Injustice.

"I think we have been effective through the years. We started out of my house and we've come a little way. We did some nursing-home research in the early 1970s, and we did it very well. We published a comprehensive package of our findings. We also called for reforms and we had a list for citizen action. There were many abuses in the nursing homes before that. Things like neglect and bad treatment and poor health care. It's better now. It's not as good as it should be but, as a result of our work, nursing home ombudsmen were established in every state.

"We also made a very important contribution to end mandatory retirement in this country. At one time, we were the only ones who were working for that. I mean, why should someone have to give up a job just because he has reached a particular age? People can still think when they are sixty-five; they can still roll up their sleeves. We testified from the first on that one. Now it is federal law. Nobody who works for the government can be forced into retirement when he or she gets older. Some states have also adopted the law, and we think that everyone should.

"We have helped strengthen Social Security. We have helped moderate discrimination in housing. We have helped promote positive attitudes toward the elderly. And we have pioneered in establishing an ongoing relationship between the old and the young. We do not want to be just a gray lobby for our own special interests. We want to be thought of as elder models of the tribe, because we are concerned about the tribe as a whole. We want peace for everyone, justice for everyone, and good government for everyone. We want good lives for people of all ages."

There is a joke about the elderly man who marries a woman half his years, then complains to his doctor that they have not had any children. The doctor says, hey, it's no wonder: "Look at your age. If you want your wife to have children you should take in a boarder." A few months later, the old man went back to the doctor to announce that his wife was expecting. "Oh," the doctor said, "so you took my advice about the boarder." Yes, the man replied, thank you very much. "She's pregnant as well."
Miss Kuhn:

"Johnny Carson used to tell a lot of jokes on television about older people. He doesn't do it much any more. He's over sixty now."

7. Morality

REV. ORVILLE CARTER

Morality, as Napoleon knew it, is what keeps the poor from murdering the rich, and that is as good a definition as any. E. H. Chapin said it is the vestibule of religion; John Locke believed it is full knowledge; Ralph Waldo Emerson argued that it is the deep root of high civility; William Paley complained that it is whatever is expedient; Plato wrote that it is the authority of reason over desire; George Santayana said it is the passion of the primitives; James Martineau said it is whatever people glory in; Martin Luther King, Jr. said it is unarmed truth and unconditional love; Jean Rostand said it is what's left of fear forgotten; and the lexicographers, not so poetic, say it is a system of conduct and provide no further editorial explanation.

Everyone has an opinion about morality. Few are in agreement. Perhaps because the rules of behavior are particles in the shifting soil of history. All is change, including fashion, and the only thing that is absolute in this regard is that vices and virtues rise, fall, or amalgamate on the tides of time. Will and Ariel Durant note this in their slim but engaging summation of The Story of Civilization. *They say that, to survive, early man had to be greedy, belligerent, brutal, and sexually abandoned, qualities that have since been subject to question. The Japanese look on suicide as ritual; the English-speaking world thinks it is a crime. What is morality? The best answer is that it is above all personal.*

Here is the Reverend Orville Carter:

"When I was the young man I was what you call wild. I did things that I shouldn't have done. I formed a small musical band, which was probably all right; I played the piano; but I booked the bands at events that were not wholesome. We played at rowdy dances, and we also played at cheap theaters. There were silent pictures then, and they had to have accompanying music, so my band would do that. In other words, we provided the audio excitement. Well, you know, movies depict some rough stuff, so what I did was to play for that and be a part of it.

"After a while, when I turned to God, I knew what I had done. I joined the Assemblies of God, and it does not believe in motion pictures. The films are too suggestive, you see. They are made to titillate. There is lovemaking, and bedroom scenes, and today there is cursing and outright pornography. I gave up going to the movies when I was in my twenties. I watch television now, things like the news, or Andy Griffith, but I will not watch a movie. I haven't been to a theater since silent pictures; I have never seen a talking picture in my life."

Reverend Carter is an eighty-four-year old resident of Rochester, Minnesota. He was born at a moment when the Protestant ethic of the eighteenth century was being replaced by the more malleable values of the 1900s. When Reverend Carter was a boy the nation looked on the hesitation waltz as dirty dancing; women wore carapace corsets to protect themselves from enterprising men; lipstick was not advertised until 1929; physicians warned that masturbation would lead to dementia; and one could be imprisoned for gambling, lasciviousness, and the public use of profanity.

All gone.

There is a witticism about modern women chatting at a houseparty. "Did you hear that Roberta is going to get married?" one asked. "No," another replied. "I didn't even know she was pregnant."

People may not agree on a definition of morality. But they know it when they see it. Dice have been found in the excavations of what were the caves of ancient Assyria. The Durants say that early Greek humanists wrote about homosexuality with "scholarly affection." Governments have been astoundingly depraved from the first; Martin Luther complained that students were offering free love at the University of Wittenberg in the 1500s; and there has been a trade in obscene literature since the days of Jesus Christ.

But that's nothing. Reverend Carter says it's gotten ever so much worse in his lifetime. Conventional wisdom probably concurs. The twentieth century has been an ethical revolution. Some observers say it began about 1910, although Darwin may have started it with his theory of evolution, when theologians were for the first time forced to conclude that parts of the Bible could not be taken literally. The biologist was begged to define a heavenly consideration in his findings, but he said he found it impossible to persuade himself that an omnipotent God would have created creatures that were designed to feed inside the living bodies of other creatures, and the clarification was generally convincing.

World War I followed. Prohibition. Radio. The Trendy Twenties. Inno-cence was lost and experimentation was found. State legislatures prohibited bobbed hair as late as the 1930s; knee-length skirts were banned in some places; but Americans, newly liberated from old constraints, technical as well as philo-sophical, began to do what would become Whatever They Wanted. Emily Post said chaperons were no longer necessary for single ladies. James T. Farrell wrote the first mass-produced foul language in his trilogy on Studs Lonigan. Automo-biles. Jazz. Sigmund Freud. The rate of divorce, when compared with the rate of marriage, doubled between 1910 and 1928 alone.

There's another side of it as well. The devil, after all, also makes use of mo-rality. Unmarried women in a family way were still and often driven from their homes when Reverend Carter was a child. Abortion was an even worse alterna-tive. The change of values in the century did away with the hoary understanding that human beings should be bracketed within universal orthodoxies, that reli-gion had the franchise on virtue, and that, as Oliver Goldsmith has said it, rec-titude that must be ever guarded is scarce worth the sentinel. Margaret Sanger was arrested when she tried to open a birth control clinic in 1916; today she's popularly revered.

Still, Reverend Carter is right. The conduct of United States society is dif-ferent than it has ever been. And unfortunately so in many respects. Studies in the 1980s indicate that as many as 30 million Americans may consume illegal substances (cocaine, marijuana) with some regularity, that employees steal as much as $150 billion a year from their places of work, that one in ten people is victimized by violent crime in the course of any year, and that a quarter of the taxpayers cheat on their returns. Salvation Army officials were accused of tak-ing kickbacks from rag merchants in 1985. The Pentagon at the same time an-nounced that it was investigating forty-five of its top hundred contractors for bribery, false claims, bid-rigging, and billing irregularities.

A poll in 1985 suggested that only 17 percent of the people questioned trusted their clerics. The same poll revealed that 18 percent admitted padding their expense accounts, 33 percent had on occasion used an invented illness to skip work, 40 percent would vote for a homosexual presidential candidate if he or she was qualified, and six out of 10 believed in premarital sex. The average age when boys and girls lose their virginity in the country is presently about six-teen; a Yale University study notes that almost half the nation's marrieds may cheat on their spouses; and, if it means anything—Reverend Carter thinks it does—students who graduated from high school in the 1980s spent more time with television (15,000 hours) than with teachers (12,000).

Ariel and Will Durant quote Voltaire's view of history: a collection of crimes, follies, and misfortunes. Yet they do not lose heart. They say statistics are a poor measure of life as it is actually led. "Behind the red facade of war and politics, misfortune and poverty, adultery and divorce, murder and suicide [have been] millions of orderly homes, devoted marriages, men and women kindly and affectionate, troubled and happy with children." The telling of the twentieth century, then, should include the charities, the kindnesses, the stabilities, and the moderations. "Who will dare to write a history of human goodness?" the Durants ask. If it's done, Orville Edward Carter can be a source.

"I was anything but religious when I was young. My mother and father were members of the Methodist Church, and I was too, in a way, but none of us attended church with any regularity. I believed in God, but I had other interests at that age. I was obsessed with baseball. I played it in school, and I played for semiprofessional teams, and if I may say so I was pretty good. I was a pitcher; I had a good curve ball. The fact of the matter is I thought for a while that I was good enough to play in the big leagues. My dream was to play for the St. Louis Cardinals; that was the team that all my heros played on.

"I never realized the aspirations, however, because I got hit on the head with a ball when I was playing for an independent team during my last year of high school. We did not wear helmets in the games, and my skull was fractured along a six-inch line. It was a serious injury, I was hospitalized for many weeks, and I had a lot of time to think while I was laying in the bed. I decided that the injury would always affect me. I knew that I would never be able to pitch like I should or hit like I should to play in the majors. I knew what it took to get into the big leagues, and I concluded that I would never be able to do it.

"That's when I started to go down in life, and I became a rough young man. When I got out of the hospital I started to barnstorm in baseball. It was not a very good influence on me. I traveled from town to town, playing any team that was willing. The money was certainly good; I'd get fifty to seventy-five dollars a game sometimes. But we got into a lot of bad habits. I drank a lot, and I mean a lot, and I caroused around with the girls in the different towns. One week it would be one place, the next week it would be another. We traveled by cars. We stayed wherever we could. We'd get into arguments with another team, maybe, and there would be fights.

"I also formed the band. We played in night clubs, and that meant there was more drinking and more carousing. I'd play in the band for a few bucks on Friday and Saturday nights, and I'd play baseball on Sundays. I was only in my teens at first, and I became a young alcoholic. I was also breaking the law, because prohibition was in effect, and alcohol was illegal. But I didn't care. I was always looking back, feeling sorry for myself. I really had wanted to play professional ball, and I would have if it hadn't been for the injury. It seemed like drinking was the only out for me, and I went down and down.

"I hit bottom in the late 1920s. I was married by that time and I had become an absolute drunk, and I decided I had had enough of it. My wife was worried, because I was ruining my whole life. So one day some friends and neighbors talked to me. They saw what was happening to me, and they invited me to a Methodist lady's home. That was in Wisconsin, and I lived there before I came to Minnesota. There was a woman in the home who opened her place to religious services. Her name was Mrs. Carson, and there was also a preacher there. So I was converted to Christ; my wife and I were converted together.

"I remember the whole thing very well. I even remember the text the preacher used during his sermon: 'Come unto me all ye that labor and are heavy laden, and I will give ye rest.' That's what I had been trying to find in the world, peace. But it had been like trying to find the pot of gold at the foot of the rainbow; it was never there. I just kept on going astray, and here was a man telling me that I could find rest if I could turn my life over to what he was talking about. I did, and after that I stopped barnstorming right away, I stopped the dance band, and I never took another drink of alcohol, not once."

The young man started preaching within two years. He went back to the same towns where he had played baseball, this time with the New Testament in his hand. He started his first church in Minnesota; he followed Methodist principles for a while; and then he drifted toward Pentecostalism, a new movement in the nation.

Pentecostals organized initially in 1901, in Kansas. They were at one time known derisively as Holy Rollers. They adhere to charismatic leaders, spiritual baptism, evangelical fervor, participatory services, the immediate presence of God, and the literal translation of both parts of the King James Bible.

Hallelujah:

"I was contacted by the Assemblies of God when I got to Minnesota. I did not know about them at the time, but after I started my second church they got hold of me and asked me to take an examination for their ministry. That's the way it was done then. Today it's more complicated—there is Bible college and a period of apprenticeship—but it was not like that in the 1930s. They set me a form to fill out, which had many questions concerning my faith, and they then gave me the examination. The test consisted mostly of biblical questions, and when I passed [with a ninty-six], I was an Assemblies of God pastor.

"I don't know about this Holy Roller name. I never heard it applied to any church where I ministered. But we are holy, that's for sure. The church was started in 1914, and there are over two million members today. We have rousing services; we don't believe in drinking, gambling, dancing, or movies. None of these things are Christian. They do harm to the spirit. You can't worship the Lord if you are drunk. You're not serving him if you gamble, and dancing and movies lead to objectionable behavior. I remember the silent films—it was always a three-way street, a man and a woman, and another man or woman.

"We also believe in the speaking of tongues, or glossalalia. I have done it many times. We believe it came from the time when Jesus gathered his disciples in Jerusalem and told them that they were going to go to all of the world to preach the gospel. Speaking in tongues is therefore communicating with God. It takes place when a person is filled with the Holy Spirit, and it's a time of seeking the Lord, it's a time of prayer. Each person does it differently. I can't understand what others say when they are doing it, and they can't understand when I am. But the Lord knows. It is a very emotional and personal activity.

"I know it seems odd to some people. I can't help that, but it has been a fact throughout my ministry. Some people think we are wild men in the church. Maybe it's because some ministers in some churches have shipwrecked these things; someone is always perverting something that is right; but, be that as it may, I have been laughed at, I have been persecuted, I have even been threatened. I started a church in Dodge Center, Minnesota, and when it became successful and many people were converted, there were local people who didn't like it. They had different ideas about Christianity, and they let me know it.

"In fact, these people said they were going to run me out of town on a rail. They didn't believe in fundamentalism; I wouldn't want to put a mark against any one personally, but they did get pretty angry. One night some of them came to my home and knocked on my door. They handed me a note, and told me to read it and act accordingly. The note said that if I went into my pulpit on Sunday, they would be there to take me. I was still a rather green preacher, and this was a first for me, and I don't mind admitting that I was frightened. I didn't know if they meant they would shoot me or beat me up or what.

"But I went to the pulpit anyway. And those people came into the church forty strong, and sat down in the front rows. I still can see it now. I had an evangelist with me in the church that Sunday. He was a cowboy evangelist from Wyoming, and he was using his lariat as an example of the Holy Spirit. He said the Holy Spirit, or the rope, would seek out those who were lost, and he tossed it out into the congregation. Naturally, he got one of these fellows, and the fellow started fighting the rope, and there I was not knowing what on earth would happen. I figured the rope would only make them more angry.

"When the service ended I asked this big burley friend to stand by me. When those men filed past they refused to shake my hand, and then the word got around about what they wanted to do. The gratifying thing is that when that happened the town turned against them. Some people boycotted their stores, other people wouldn't talk to them, and so on. So the point I am trying to make is that, yes, there was persecution, but I think God always brought some good out of it. Later on, some of those very folks who had condemned me asked my forgiveness; they were converted to our church and became some of the best members we had."

Reverend Carter says he earned ten dollars a week when he started preaching. He also says he could not even have eaten regularly had it not been for private charity. He says he worked his way up, however, ahem, moving from church to church until his salary mushroomed to $135 a week, $7000 a year, the most money he has ever made in religion and the most money he has ever wanted.

He says there are other successes besides income. He has built seven churches and revitalized a host of others. He has also become a local personality in Rochester, where he has constructed three houses of prayer, converted thousands of people, and where he has been a radio evangelist for thirty-three years.

"I have a half-hour program every Sunday morning. It's called the Hour of Revival. The church sponsors it. There is no salary involved, but it is very important to me and I hope to my listeners. It's always been on station KROZ, and the format does not vary much, if at all. I tape a fifteen-minute sermon—I do it right here in my home during the week—and then I give it to a man who works with me, a schoolteacher in Rochester (who is a Methodist, by the way), and he adds to it. He puts the music on for me, and he does the announcing and takes it to the station.

"I don't know how many listeners we have. We get some mail, and it comes from an area that extends far out from Rochester. I've just got a note from a bartender who works in one of the towns. I wrote back to say that I hope he can someday get out of that kind of work. We also get a lot of listeners who are bedridden. You know Rochester; we call it the Sick City. There are many nursing homes here, and [200,000] people come every year to places like the Mayo Clinic. They listen, and they write, probably because they are lonely and helpless.

"I base my message on trying to be optimistic and encouraging. And I answer every piece of mail that I get. I have to be careful, of course; there are lines I don't cross. There is a fine line between helping and going too far. Many of the listeners are older, many of them are discouraged, some of them are dying, and I can't talk about them getting well, because I don't know that. There are some preachers who go out of bounds on this. They make promises they can't keep, always in the name of God, and I don't believe in that in any way.

"I do believe that God heals. I've seen it many times, and my wife is an illustration. She had two and a half years of chronic bronchitis almost forty years ago; she was in bed for five months, but she was cured in one night. I brought a Canadian preacher in to see her. He was a man of strong faith, and he said 'Mrs. Carter, what do you think the Lord would do if he was here?,' and she said, 'He would cure me.' When he left, my wife's voice came back instantly (she couldn't even talk above a whisper before), but she got up, dressed, and she hasn't had the problem again."

Reverend Carter does not solicit money on his radio program. He says preachers should not charge for their service. He thinks God will provide if it's necessary. "There are charlatans in every field. Religion is no different. I've never supported a ministry that begs for money, or collects it through phone banks or computers, and I would not advise anyone else to do it."

He has been a minister for more than half the century. He's been married to the same woman for sixty years. He has three children, two of whom are pastors, and he lives in a humble home across the street from one of the churches he built, where he continues to exhort conduct consistent with traditional order:

"I don't know why things have gone so wrong in society. I suppose the standards have simply deteriorated. People used to have higher standards, and they used to insist that the standards be observed. There was a man here in Rochester some years ago. He had some nude pictures that he was showing around, and he was sent to Stillwater Penitentiary for a good stiff sentence. I visited him there. He was terribly sorry for what he did, and I don't think, after jail, he would ever do it again.

"I feel in a way that the church is partly responsible for the deterioration. Some ministers have not kept faith with the old values either. When I was converted I knew that every answer was in the Bible. And I think we should just go back to those answers. The Bible says that 'If My people, which are called by My name, shall humble themselves, and pray, and seek My faith, and turn from their wicked ways, then will I hear from heaven and I will heal their land.' That's the answer.

"Let's stop trying to figure everything out for ourselves. Listen to the Lord. He doesn't want filthy pictures; He doesn't want crime and brutality and greed, and any of those things which are so prevalent today. I used to see bedroom scenes in silent pictures. Now you can get much worse on home video cassettes. Life is too short to squander. People don't have any time to lose. Paul said to be absent from the body is to be present with the Lord. That means we have to decide now if we want to live in Heaven. You can't fool God.

In 1986, Reverend James Aker of Lynchburg, Virginia, claimed he was 115 years old. If true, it would have made him the oldest man in the nation at the time, and certainly the oldest minister. He said he was born on February 12, 1871, while the nation was recovering from the Civil War, five years before the Indians dispatched George Custer and company at the Little Big Horn, and he said he had been preaching the prophecy for more than a hundred years.

Aker said he began preaching when he was nine. He then took to itinerant evangelism in 1893. He said he was the first pastor of the Cave Rock Baptist Church in Troutville, Virginia, a piece of the rock that in 1955 celebrated its centennial anniversary, and members there claim they had great-great-great grandparents who had been introduced to word of the Lord by the modern Methuselah.

The Reverend said that word still goes: "It's repent. I believe that the Bible says what it means. You have to be baptized in the water, I mean all the way under, and you have to pay the price, that is all there is to it. Fire and brimstone, brother. If you ain't born again, you ain't going nowhere."

BUD SHELTON

In the beginning God created heaven and earth. And the earth was void and empty, and darkness was upon the face of the deep, and the spirit of God moved over the waters. So the spirit of God said, let there be light, and there was light, and he divided it from the darkness, and there was evening and morning one day. And God said, let all of the waters be gathered in one place, and let dry land appear, and it was done. And God said, let the land bring forth the green herb, and such as may seed, and the fruit tree, and it was done. And God said, let the waters bring forth the creeping creature having life, and the fowl that may fly over the land, and the beasts of the earth according to their kind, and it was done. And God said, let us make man and woman to our image, and let him have domination over the fishes of the sea, and the fowls, and beasts, and the whole earth, and it was also done. And God saw all the things that he had made, and they were very good, and on the seventh day God ended his work and rested.

The Bible.

"When I was a boy I was taught that God created the world, and He made man in his likeness. My mother and father said so, my friends in school said so, and the people at church said so. I never thought there was any other possibility. I didn't know what the word evolution meant. That's the way we all were."

Bud Shelton.

There's no doubt about it; matters were simpler when Genesis one was on the master bureau in every home. Preachers can arguably say that the decline in public morality began when the good words no longer rang true. The theory of the Supreme Architect was initially disputed by French scientists of the seventeenth century and was to be effectively discarded by the eighteenth-century publication of Charles Darwin's study on the origin of species. Finally, in America, in 1925, the religious account of creation suffered one more pensive leveling; it was made comic by the case of Heaven versus Earth in the so-called Monkey Trial.

Harry Jackson (Bud) Shelton was a witness at the trial. He may also be the last surviving participant. He was between the sophomore and junior years of high school when the proceedings took place, he testified for the prosecution, which is to say for the chaperons of creationism; and he recounts the historic business with a thoroughly considered sense of proportion:

"It was a rigged affair. I think it was all done for the publicity. But I didn't know that at the time. I was just a kid; I would rather have been playing baseball, or swimming. The trial was held during summer vacation. They asked if I believed in the Bible, and I said yes. They didn't ask if I objected to being instructed in evolution, but I would have said no. I don't think the trial ever settled anything. It was all hoopla."

The trial took place in Dayton, Tennessee, which was then and is now an outback community located at a lazy turn on the Tennessee River. The principals included an obscure biology teacher named John Scopes and a pair of the most famous attorneys in the nation. Tennessee was one of three states to outlaw the teaching of evolution at the time. The law forbade "any theory which denies the story of the divine creation of man as taught in the Bible." Scopes ignored the prohibition, the state prosecuted, and the trial turned into a theatrical confrontation between William Jennings Bryan, thrice a God-fearing presidential candidate, and Clarence Darrow, an agnostic counsel from Chicago.

Did you meet the lawyers, Mr. Shelton?

"I met Bryan in a local law office, where he asked me some questions. I did not talk to Clarence Darrow until the trial."

You were in your teens?

"Seventeen."

And religious.

"Yes, in the way kids were then. My father was a Methodist, my mother belonged to the Church of Christ, and I was expected to follow in their footsteps. I was not fanatic, but I did not believe I came from a simian, and I was comfortable with that."

How did you get involved in the case?

"John Scopes taught at Rhea Central High School, the only one in town, and I was in his class. He was actually a math teacher, and the football coach, and athletic director, but he was substituting for the science teacher at the time."

What kind of man was he?

"He was a nice fellow, a very personable fellow, well liked in the community. He was twenty-four years old, fresh out of the University of Kentucky. And he was just a scapegoat in the whole thing."

Scapegoat?

"Whatever you want to call it. He was no criminal, that's for sure. The way I remember it was that the law against the teaching of evolution had just been passed in the state capitol, and there hadn't been enough time that year to change the textbooks. The old textbooks still contained references to evolution, and Darwin, and the survival of the fittest, and Scopes continued to teach it. I don't know if he did it in defiance of the law or because it was still in the books."

"At any rate, he was not singled out for prosecution. He volunteered for it. The reason was that the American Civil Liberties Union in New York took cognizance of the Tennessee law and thought it would be a good idea to force a test case in the courts. The ACLU put an ad in the newspapers calling for someone to protest the law, so it could sponsor a defense. Some local citizens saw that item, and they asked Professor Scopes if he would be willing to take the action against the statute."

Professor Scopes?

"That's what they called him. It was an honorary title. It was out of respect. I don't believe he knew exactly what he was getting into. I don't think for a minute that he wanted to humiliate people who believed in the Creation. I think he thought the law was too strict, and he felt there should be a freedom to teach all theories, and that's why he volunteered."

Do you remember the textbook, Mr. Shelton?

"It was called *Hunter's Biology*."

How about the parts regarding evolution?

"There were two pages on it. Maybe three."

Was there anything about creationism?

"No, not that I remember. That was in the books at Sunday School, but I personally didn't object to the omission in the high school. I don't think that Scopes was trying to force anything on us. He was just following the lesson. He didn't change my mind about anything; I still believed in Genesis."

Scopes was recruited in May 1925. The trial was set for summer. Shelton says controversy surrounding the development probably started before school let out, but not among his classmates. He says Scopes did not mention it, nor can he recall his parents talking about it; after all, no one could have been aware that the community was on the verge of universal attention.

What kind of town was Dayton?

"Small. A few thousand people."

And when did the attention begin?

"When Bryan and Darrow came to town. They were followed by news people from all over the world. H. L. Mencken was one of them. He was a very caustic fellow. He didn't have very much good to say about Dayton, or about anything else that I recall."

Did you know who Bryan and Darrow were?

"Oh, yes. Bryan was well known in the town, he had been secretary of state in the Woodrow Wilson administration, and he was a favorite in the Bible Belt. I had heard of Darrow too, because he had just come off that [Nathan] Leopold and [Richard] Loeb case; that was the famous 'thrill' killing case."

When did the trial begin?

"In July. I was what was known as a student witness. They subpoenaed ten of us from the class, most of whom were favorable to the prosecution. I had one friend who wasn't. His was the house where Darrow stayed. I don't know one way or the other, but I think he was coached; I would assume that fact anyway."

Did Bryan coach you?

"No. He asked me some questions, as did the attorney general. But nobody told me what to say. I had no preparation at all."

What was your feeling about it?

"I was in awe, I suppose. But I was not much concerned about the legal business. I was not what you would call studiously interested in whether evolution should be taught. I was not concerned with that question, and I don't think many kids were."

Adults were, however. Shelton says the streets of Dayton filled with arguments and demonstrations. Preachers pounded their Old Testaments; visitors carried signboards; vendors sold lemonade and home-made cookies; and Joe Mendi, a Hollywood chimpanzee, was put on conspicuous display, dressed as a human being. Shelton says a radio station from Chicago set up equipment at various places in town, and that was as exciting as it got, back before television:

"We had all heard radio before, but it was hard to listen to because there was so much static interference."

So what happened?

"The trial was held in a small courtroom. It was very hot, and people used fans to keep cool. I don't know how many people got in to watch. Most were kept outside, however. People would bring out news now and then, and there was constant discussion."

Where were you?

"I was called in a couple of days after it began, and I waited in an anteroom for another day or two. The other student witnesses were there, and some adults. It was probably more interesting outside; that was where everything was going on."

When was your testimony?

"On the fourth or the fifth day. The Attorney General did the questioning, Bryan was just a volunteer assistant; I was never questioned by Bryan, and I don't think any of the students were."

What did the attorney general ask?

"He wanted to know about the biology book. He wanted to know when we studied the part on evolution, and all about that."

How did you reply?

"I told him that we had reviewed the whole book that April. But he didn't ask me for any opinion on the matter of evolution."

Did Darrow?

"Yes. The important question he asked was whether Scopes' teaching of evolution had affected my religion in any way. He asked if I still attended church and Sunday School and believed in the Bible. I said I was still religious."

What was the point in that questioning?

"He wanted to prove that a student could read about evolution without being converted to that particular way of thinking."

And did he?

"Maybe in my case."

And that was it?

"I was not on the stand very long."

What was the judge like?

"Well, he was all right. But I have an opinion—I've thought about it from time to time—that some of the things in the trial might have been a little over his head. He was a circuit judge, and I don't think he'd had much experience with these kinds of issues. The scientific testimony might have been a little confusing to him; I know that it was to most other people."

The trial lasted just over a week. Darrow called Bryan to the stand, humiliated him with withering and loaded questions, and subsequently rested his case by admitting that Scopes had indeed violated the restrictions against evolutionary instruction. The jury found for the prosecution. H. L. Mencken said the proceedings had been full of queer and unlovely things. The Honorable Mr. Bryan never got a chance to go on the offensive. "The trial ended before Bryan could rebut Darrow," *Shelton says,* "and he was left with having to print up copies of what he would have said."

Bryan died soon after, is that right?

"Five days after, I think. He was staying in the home of Dayton's druggist. He made a couple of speeches in the area and he died in his sleep, I believe. It was quite a shock here."

What happened to Scopes?

"He was fined one hundred dollars, which was paid by the ACLU. The Tennessee supreme court eventually overturned the conviction, on technical grounds, but it upheld the statue against evolution."

Did Scopes stay in Dayton?

"No, he was a celebrity by then. He got a scholarship to the University of

Chicago, to study geology, and then he went to South America for one of the oil companies. He finally wound up in Shreveport, Louisiana, where he died in the middle 1960s."

Could he have remained in Dayton?

"Probably so. Some people were mad at him, but others understood. He came back one time, in 1960, for the premiere of the motion picture that was made, *Inherit the Wind*."

Fredric March and Spencer Tracy.

"Yes. They did a good act. It was a gross exaggeration, however. The movie made Bryan look like a buffoon, and he wasn't that way. No, no, he was a very distinguished man."

The film continues to show on late-night television.

"It's made Dayton immortal, if that is the word. People pretty much forgot about the trial once it was over, but the movie changed that. The reporters come here every anniversary. There have been several books printed. The tourists also keep coming; there is a Bryan Hill here now, and Bryan College, and the Scopes Museum is kept down in the basement at the courthouse."

And you, have you become a celebrity?

"People say: 'This is Bud Shelton, he was a witness at the Scopes Trial,' although I don't know what difference it makes."

Bud Shelton went on to become a first-string center on the high school football field, afterward serving five years in the army. He married twice, has not had any children, and worked as an accountant in Dayton before retiring in the 1970s. He is seventy-nine. And goes to church most Sundays.

"I am more broad-minded now. I don't take the Bible literally any more, not in every instance. I don't believe God created the world in six days, I think it took longer than that. And I can't quite figure out how all of those dinosaurs could just come and go. But I do think God had a hand in everything, regardless of the exact details, and I'm too old now to think any different."

Is evolution still against the law in Tennessee?

"That was repealed [in 1967.]"

What do you think about that?

"I never thought the law was right. Students should be taught a variety of ideas. I don't think I ever met anyone who was sorely injured by those two or three pages in *Hunter's Biology*."

By the way, what grade did you get that year?

"I wasn't a brilliant egghead. I barely passed Scopes' course."

The world according to Charles K. Johnson is not only the place of men who have been made in the image of God, it is likewise home to logic and reason. There is an up, a down, and a beginning without end. The retired aircraft mechanic is the president of the International Flat Earth Society, headquartered almost inevitably in California, and from this view he thinks heaven is 4000 miles away, just beyond the 32-mile-wide sun, and the planet is a disk at the center of it all, infinite in size.

"I put it together when I was a kid in school. The globe in the classroom did not look right. And this stuff about gravity is garbage. If people in Australia were actually on the other side of us, they would all be standing on their heads. I don't care what the scientists say; they are brutes with two feet who have lied about an number of things. If the world was really round, the big rivers would run two ways, and there would be a great big hump in the Suez Canal. God knew what he was doing."

Johnson says he has 2000 members in the Flat Earth Society. They pay ten dollars a year in dues, and receive in return all issues of The Flat Earth News, *where debunking is editorial policy. The* News *sniggers at stories of an infinite cosmos. It claims space exploration is a hoax. Johnson says he has taken measurements that* "put the greaseball theorists to shame," *and it doesn't matter if nobody listens.* "I believe, and my wife believes, and that is all it takes. Millions will lie, or be deceived, but here are two people, before God, who know the truth."

ALICE DOE

When Alice Doe was a young girl, in the opening lights of the century, a working synonym for public morality was intolerance. It was a time when there were great pressures to reject reality, as one scribe explained it, and to dislike mankind as it is. People thought they were moral when they were only callous. The church made sin too large and understanding too small. And the government, parroting Nietzsche, insisted on a pious conformity in order to lead the nation, and especially the women of the nation, around by the nose. Mrs. Doe says women of respect were expected to conform to a stiff sterility. They could not smoke, cuss, or drink alcohol in the open; they had to hide their underwear, pass up cosmetics, and sit down in front at church. And they also kept off the streets after dark; worried about the nonprocreative amusements of sexual relations; and did not show any leg.

She adds with enthusiasm that it was absolutely wonderful:

"I was walking home from school one day and the girls decided to go rolling down a hill. That was something for us. We did not wear jeans, we had dresses; and there we were tumbling about, and the skirts coming over our heads. One woman looked at us out of the window of her house and told us to stop by pounding on the glass. I felt really terrible. It was one of the few things I ever did like that. Now I don't want that published. I would die if anyone read it. I want anything you write about me to be squeaky clean; because that's how I am."

Alice Doe is eighty-nine. She is also protected with an alias here. She agreed to be interviewed for this historical perspective in the belief that, so she put it, anything appearing in the book would be suitable for Reader's Digest. *The interview took three hours. Mrs. Doe was amiable, animated, and pleased as the parish treasurer on Easter Sunday. Then some weeks later she read one of the author's other books. It contained slang to which she objected. "Frankly," she wrote, "I was horrified at the foul talk," and she no longer wanted to be identified in this work.*

I thought about eliminating the segment altogether. But there is a purpose in retaining it. Mrs. Doe is a simple woman. She has had a life that's been less than she would wish; she therefore believed that appearing in a book of history would be "the best thing that's ever happened to me," and yet she gave it up on principle. That's uncommon. It may represent one of the qualities of her generation, however. People of great age were raised to value such things as moderation, civility, and ethics; many of them are still anchored in that harbor. Mrs. Doe is a tough nut. She may be laced uncomfortably tight, yet she stands her ground, and that in the society of the present is estimable.

"I was not raised in a religious way," she says, "not as those things are known. My father was a good man, and my mother was the same, but they did not recite from the Bible or say prayers. I went to church, but that was what everyone did, and I wasn't the first one to arrive or the last to leave. Church was a social event. We lived in a small town, and there weren't many other opportunities for people to get together. The church would have picnics once a month, everyone would attend; the women would bring the food, the men would set things up, and the kids ran around. It was fun. I had a lot of fun growing up.

"We were poor, there's no doubt about that. My father was a caretaker, and my mother took in washing to get extra money. We lived on one end of a double house; it would be called a duplex today, or maybe, ha, a townhouse. The toilet was outside, but I don't want that mentioned. We did not have any electricity, or even an icebox. The people who lived on the other end of the house kept their food cold in a well that was on the property. The well had a rope and a bucket, that's how we got our water; and the neighbors used another rope to hold a boxful of food, dairy goods, and meat, just above the water level.

"Can you picture the germs? That food box got very dirty, and things had to fall in the water we drank, but nobody thought about it. We kept our water in a big basin on the kitchen table, and everybody used the same cup. If one of my sisters had a cold, I would get it, or the other way around. I sometimes wonder how I lived to be eighty-nine. Did you know they used to put yellow signs on the door when you got a contagious disease? If you got measles, or the mumps, the health authorities would come and put a yellow flag on the door, which was a quarantine. Then they fumigated, which must have done no good at all.

"I don't want to have you think we were shabby people. We were just poor, which was not unusual in our town. I never had a dress of my own, they were always hand-me-down. I used to sleep in the same room with four sisters, and on the same bed with one. If we went to the store, we might get a piece of candy, but we would have to cut it up in equal parts for six kids. I remember I used to envy the rich kids; they would always call their parents 'Mother,' and 'Father,' while it was just 'Mom' and 'Dad' for us. I used to think about having a lot of money. It didn't work out that way. Maybe it would not have mattered.

"I went to something called a 'free school'; it was donated by a wealthy man who lived in the area. I hated it. The teachers did not treat us very good, maybe because most of us didn't have very much. One teacher used to give us pencils each day, and when she came to me she would say 'A little pencil for a little girl.' Then we had to give them back after class. I don't think they were very good teachers, either. And they were very harsh. One boy got in trouble in the singing class, and the teacher took him down on the floor and punched him. I don't know what the boy did, but I can see that teacher hitting him.

"Home was different. I have nothing but good memories of home. Something was always happening. Those were the days of the Hokey Pokey man, for instance. He would come into the neighborhood selling little bits of ice cream wrapped in paper. We called them Dew Drops, and they cost a penny, but we splurged. There was a rag man too, he came around yelling 'Rags, rags,' and he bought and sold. The scissors grinder came. The meat man. The milkman, and the baker. They all had horse-drawn wagons. The baker would stop, pat the dust from his sweating horse, and then hand over the bread. More germs. Germs, germs, germs.

"And, say, the doctor made house calls on a bicycle. If we got sick, he would put this gray paste on our chest, and when he took it away there was a wet spot on it. That spot was supposed to be where the inflammation was. The doctor also delivered babies. I had one brother, and when he was born the doctor came riding up on that bicycle of his. I didn't have any idea what he was doing with my mother. I didn't even know she was pregnant. They kept stuff like that from the children; it was none of our affair. I didn't know enough to tell by looking at her. Babies came from the stork, that's all we knew, and it was enough.

"I didn't want to know about it. I didn't like any kind of talk like that. I used to hear jokes that were slightly off-color, and I laughed, but it wasn't right. I always thought things should be right. I thought people should be decent. I loved my father, and I respected him, but there was this one time he got drunk. The poor man, I don't think it was his fault—he went over to visit someone who gave him a few drinks and he just got silly. When he came home my mother made him go into the bedroom so that no one would see him. It wasn't his fault. Yet I never felt the same about him after that."

Alice Doe was a child for a time too brief. She says she quit school in the tenth grade to go to work. That was the routine, especially for young females. "I was just getting to appreciate school," *she says,* "because I think I was learning things," *but one day her father came home and said he had found her a job.*

"I was fourteen or fifteen years old. The job was at an asbestos factory in a nearby town. It was three miles away, and I had to get up at dawn every morning to get there by walking. I think the shifts lasted ten hours. I made gaskets. They had some rubber in them, but they were mostly asbestos. Asbestos was considered to be a wonderful thing then. It was used in all kinds of construction, and nobody knew about any risk. There were people at the plant who were covered with the stuff every day; they had it on their clothes, and in their hair, and on their faces. I never heard that it hurt any one of them; it didn't hurt me.

"So that was it, I started to work, and I didn't like it any better than school. I worked in a laboratory where we made things like eyedrops and vaccines. I worked in Woolworth, or what was then called the five-and-dime store. I had to stand on my feet all day at Woolworth. They had stools under the counter to rest on, but nobody was ever allowed to sit down. I worked in a toy store once, and I liked that, but the rest of my jobs have been terrible. I was just a teen-ager when I started. I never even heard the term *teen-ager*. The rich kids may have been teen-agers. I never made very much on any job I have had.

"Maybe I thought I'd get a rich kid to marry. That didn't turn out either. I wasn't very much for the boys. I was awfully bashful, and I don't remember meeting a lot of them that I was interested in. I didn't date anyone until I was eighteen, or not quite eighteen. That young man wore a bowler, if you know what that is. An old, round hat. It was an ordinary date. He walked to my house, and he brought candy, and we went out on a 'Beau Night.' Wednesday and Saturdays were Beau Nights. We went to the movies, and saw something like *The Perils of Pauline*, and we went on to the ice cream store. Then he took me home and shook my hand.

"I didn't like boys to kiss me. And there was never anything more than that. I did have one favorite beau. I liked him more than anyone, but I was too shy to get anyplace. It wasn't right to make any advances toward a boy, and I never did; that was my attitude. But I did like him. He was a very nice young person. He had a beautiful speaking voice. He took me on an excursion once. We walked to the railroad station, and rode to the boat, and took it down the river. I will never forget it. He married a schoolteacher, and I was happy for him; I think he did a lot better than if he had got stuck with me."

Mrs. Doe asked for the recording tape to be turned off at this juncture. She said she was getting too private, and there should be no record.

"I don't like to talk about the man I married," *she explained;* "he was no good." *She introduced him hesitantly. Later she would refer to him intermittently and on tape. Some of what follows, therefore, is entirely reconstructed:*

"I was married one time, when I was twenty-six. The man was a chauffeur, and he worked for rich people. He had some good traits, or I would not have gotten tied up with him. He had a good mind. He could read something and remember it forever—how much the pyramids weigh, or vital statistics. He also had a wonderful personality. He was cheerful and friendly, and everybody loved him. You would have loved him. He stopped being a chauffeur after we were married, and he got a gasoline station and for a while he did very well. I thought it was going great; I thought we were going to be on top of the world.

"But he was a Jekyll and Hyde. He was a terrible drinker, and was always going crazy. He would be out drinking, and maybe roll into the house at two or three in the morning, and you wouldn't know him. He might get nasty. Or he'd just sit down, morose and stinking like a pig. I don't like to say what he did when he was nasty. He'd want to get in bed with me, smelling like that, and swearing, and I just couldn't stand it. He'd get angry, and knock me around. I used to sit up waiting in fear. I used to pray to God that he wouldn't be so bad. It was a terrible period. To make a choice like that, that man—I was ashamed.

"And of course he ran around. He was a chronic adulterer. Everybody liked him, and he spent his time and whatever money he had with other women. Oh, I was so hurt. I knew where he was, usually, and sometimes he would tell me about it to hurt me more. I used to think about that young man who had married the schoolteacher; I used to wonder how it would have been with him. People talked about my husband. I know that the neighbors knew. Women would call up, sometimes, and I had to take all that stuff. Is he in? When will he be back? I learned to hate him, God help me; it wasn't Christian, but I couldn't stand it.

"We were married for fifteen years, and after we were separated I lost touch with him for a long time. I never got a divorce, however. I didn't think it would be right. 'Whom God joins together, no man shall put asunder.' I never dated since then either. I've always been too effected. Also, I don't think people who are still married should date. We never had children, and I used to think that was a good thing, but since I've gotten old I regret it. I wish I had something good from the marriage. I hate thinking it was all a failure. I heard he died a couple of years ago, in a nursing home; I did not go to his funeral."

Mrs. Doe is now in a nursing home herself. She has a modest room at the end of a hall filled with chattering women. The interview was taped shortly before Christmas. There were greeting cards stuck to her door, and she wore holly on a pretty sweater. She looks twenty years younger than she is; she wears a square jaw and horned-rimmed glasses; and grim as she may be in conversation, she laughs freely, and periodically bends her head to her knees, chuckling as if it's all relative, which it is.

"I do not drink, smoke, or use profanity of any kind. I think it is insulting and wrong. I smoked two times when I was little. My sisters and I got hold of some cigarettes and we lit up and puffed away. Then I thought that this was the silliest thing I had ever done, and I never did it again. I don't like gambling either. They tried to get that in this state, and I was totally against it. Why do people have to do these things? Why do they have to abuse themselves and each other with sins? I'm for total abstinence in all this. Keep away from it, and that goes for crazy sex stuff as well.

"What is that woman's name, Dr. Ruth? Have you heard this Dr. Ruth? I think she is a terrible woman. She should be put away somewhere. The things that woman says! One of the newspapers carries her column, and I got so mad at it that I wrote the editor to tell him. I said she's corrupting the morals of young people and that she did not belong in the paper. Well, he wrote back. I have his letter here. He said she was filling a need. He said there are things about sex that people do not want to ask their doctors, and Dr. Ruth is valuable for that reason. Valuable? I think she is doing great harm.

"I also wrote to a newspaper columnist. I do a lot of writing of this kind. He had written a column about his wife being mugged by a teen-ager, in New York, and he was furious. He wrote that he did not normally swear in print, and he did not like other people to do it, but he could not help himself this time. He wrote: 'By God, that kid broke all the rules of decency' or something like that. So I wrote to him and I said you also broke a rule; I said you broke the third of the Ten Commandments, you took God's name in vain, and I said 'Promise me you will not do it again.' So he wrote me then, and promised.

"See? I've kept his note to me."

It says: Never Again.

"Isn't that cute?"

It is.

"May I ask your religion, Mr. Tiede?"

I'm Catholic.

"That's nice. I'm glad they finally got together."

Who?

"The Catholics and the Protestants."

Alice Doe has lived in the nursing home for a decade. She says she was homesick when she arrived, but she has gotten over it. She reads a good lot. She quotes from books and magazines. She says she has no income save Social Security, most of which goes for her room, board, and care—which, she notes, is all that she requires anymore. She says she gets lonely, having no children to visit, but perhaps it's just as well:

"I would not like to have children in the world the way it is now. The drugs and crime and the sex, it's ugly. Young people have babies before they are married. They should know better, and that's all."

Someone opens the door to say Merry Christmas.

"I have many friends in the home, and they love me. One of them, poor soul, has cancer. She used to live in a nice room on this floor, and now she has to stay in the infirmary. That's what we all fear, that we get sick and be incapacitated. It happens. It's the last thing you have to think about in life. I have donated my body to medicine, because it might do some good, and because I won't have to leave any money for a funeral. I've also made out a short Christian memorial service, mostly Episcopalian, with hymns on the organ; that will save my relatives from wondering what to do with me."

Have you been satisfied with your life, Mrs. Doe, or not?

"In between."

I see.

"I would like to read your book. But I really don't want to live until it's published. Is that shocking? I've had enough."

Let's go back to the time when Alice Doe and the nation were younger, and the subject of morality was less complex. The following is adapted from the book This Was Sex, *by Sanford Teller, who in turn borrowed it from a book called* Nature's Secrets Revealed, *written by Professor Thomas Shannon, 1914:*

Should the unmarried spoon?

In the human family, spooning belongs only to the married life. If indulged in by married people beyond reasonable limits, it leads to sensuality, physical, mental and moral injury. If indulged in, even to a very limited extent among the single, it is fraught with the gravest of temptations.

"While a goodbye kiss might be indulged in occasionally near the end of an engagement, by pure minded people without any apparent harm, it is not necessary to their happiness or [their] love.

"True love will find expression. Intelligent love, love guided by moral convictions, will find the channels of expression that are safe. If young people would meet each other at the marriage altar with unkissed lips, there would be fewer blighted lives."

MERRILL HOLSTE

One of the annoying characteristics of the religious view of morality is the notion that it must be thrust down the throat of man at the point of a threat. And in the case of Merrill Holste, the warnings of the wages of sin began before he knew full well what the devil was being discussed. He says he was an adolescent when it happened. The year was 1920; he had been taken to hear a traveling preacher conduct an evangelistic revival in a camping grounds not far from St.

Paul, Minnesota; and he still remembers everything that occurred, including his own revulsion:

"The evangelist was a large, fat man. I did not pay attention to what he said exactly, but I watched how he said it. The general theme of the sermon was that people in the audience should 'come and hit the sawdust trail,' which meant get right with God, and he hammered away on the idea of what would happen if they didn't. They would be severely punished, they would go to hell, they would burn in the everlasting fires, they would suffer throughout eternity in the dark underworld of the damned.

"I was very interested in the technique. I was too young to know what he was doing—I didn't begin to understand it until I studied psychology years later—but he was effective. The man's scheme was to scare the people, in a hypnotic way, and that would distract them from what he was really up to. What he wanted was to take their money. He had people standing all around with pails. Collection plates were too small for the tens and twenties that he wanted, so his people circulated with buckets.

"He also discussed his health in detail. He said it was precarious. He said his heart was about to give out on even the slightest exertion, and the only thing he had going for him was this great God in heaven. He said this great God was protecting him. He said God wanted him to continue saving people from damnation. Gradually he started walking about the stage a little faster, and after a while he was prancing back and forth, ranting and raving, sweating and breathing very hard.

"I don't think he was sick. He was overweight, but the rest of it was just part of his show. The idea was to frighten the people first, and then rivet their attention on his strenuous antics. The people no doubt were wondering if he would drop dead at any moment. So they were rendered less alert. They were more receptive to his demands and suggestions. And when he called for them to renounce their wicked ways, they obeyed, and when he asked them to empty their pockets they did that too."

Holste says that by the time the sermon ended a dozen or more in the audience were converted to Christianity. For his part, however, he was converted first to skepticism and subsequently to complete disbelief. He decided the preacher was perpetrating a fraud, trying to subordinate people to anxiety and theatrical suggestion, and he came to believe that it was the way of religion as a whole. He says he organized a small society of "freethinking friends" when he became an adult, and he has been an atheist now for almost sixty years.

"I don't believe there is one thing looking after every leaf that falls. I don't believe people who are good go up in the clouds when they die. These are stories, they are myths. I think people have each other; there is nothing else."

Atheism *is a word from the Greek a-theos, "without god." It is a philosophical position as old as humankind, and it has been held in contempt from the earliest records. There was a time when Merrill Holste might have been hanged for his convictions. There was a more recent period when he could not commit them to print. Atheists are history's niggers. Theologian Paul Tillich said the godless believe that "life has no depth, it is shallow"; Bishop Fulton Sheen said they are people with "no visible means of support." What they meant was that they are thick, scabrous and menacing.*

The evidence is overwhelmingly otherwise, of course. Good minds of every age have rejected theism. Friedrich Nietzsche was an atheist. Thomas Henry Huxley and John-Paul Sartre. The poet Percy Bysshe Shelley was publicly disgraced when he wrote a pamphlet entitled "The Necessity of Atheism": he was expelled from his university and the publication was burned. A British legislator was denied a seat in Parliament when he refused to swear on the Bible. The intolerance has not been as severe in the America of the twentieth century, except perhaps politically; Karl Marx was a humanist, don't you know?

Holste says the Revolution was the taproot of atheism in the United States. He points out that European tradition held that royalty ruled by divine guidance, if not by divine right, and that included the hated King George III of England. Holste believes some colonials thus equated religion with oppression and looked on the fight for independence as an antireligious act. He says these Americans were at the same time disillusioned with the strict observance of Christianity on these shores, and that contributed to the implanting of new thinking and doubt.

The doubt has become widespread in the 1900s. It's gone hand-in-hand with the sophistication and universality of education. Many of the nation's philosophers, scientists, and artists have rejected religion, and while they have not generally done so in an organized way, atheism has developed into a genuine movement for a few. Group atheists initiated the litigation that prevented the forced recitation of prayers in the public schools; they have battled against religious fanaticism and persecution; and they are almost entirely responsible for the wholesale revival of the Founders' argument respecting the separation of church and state. Merrill Holste insists the atheists are not the hideous bogeymen of legend. He says they are in many ways moral champions.

"For example, I have always hoped for the best for everyone. I knew what it was like to be on the bottom at one time, and I was sensitized to it. My parents were homesteaders in South Dakota, at the turn of the century and beyond, and I was in fact a poor farmer boy. We lived in a one-room tarpaper shack at one time and we had to work to scratch out a living. My father owned a hundred sixty acres in South Dakota, but we barely made it. We only had three out of ten years where the crop was worth harvesting.

"The poverty may have been one reason my parents were religious. They may have thought God would help them, or feel sorry for them. They were Methodist people and tried to raise me the same, and I started to go to church when I was very young. The services were held in the local schoolhouse, the same one where I started school. I didn't pay too much attention to the services, but the sermons were loud and ripsnorting, and I knew right away that it was silly and a waste of time.

"I read the Bible the first time when I was in the seventh grade. I thought the 'word of gawd' might settle my doubts. It did. After reading the first three or four segments, I decided I didn't believe a word of it. There was a lot of vulgarity for one thing. Someone was always killing someone else; God was always angry; and so on. I started reading other things, too, about history, and mythology, and I saw the connections. The Bible was a pack of lies; and the preachers were also lying.

"Dad kept trying to make it at farming. We moved from South Dakota to Minnesota, and he worked for my grandfather. One time he took some hogs to market and the prices were so bad that he sold them for the cost of hauling. Same with corn. There were years when it was cheaper to burn it in the stove than to sell it and buy coal. Dad inherited my grandfather's farm when the old man died, but he was encumbered by a heavy mortgage. Then my mother died of tuberculosis. God didn't help out at all.

"I left home when I was nineteen. I had saved a hundred and fifty dollars and I wanted to work my way through college. I started the University of Minnesota, then I got a job working on the Minneapolis transit system. I did it part time and went to school the rest. I cleaned up the cars; I was a conductor and other things. The cars ran on tracks and were powered by overhead electricity. When the trolley poles separated from the overhead wires, I got out and hooked them back up—five hundred and fifty volts.

"I started to get atheist literature in college, and I talked it up. There was a newspaper called *The Freeman*, and there was *The Progressive World*. I sent away for twenty copies of *The Little Blue Book*, which was the gospel of skepticism in the thirties, and that proved to be interesting. I was no longer just skeptical, though; I was fully disbelieving. I met my wife just before I graduated from college, and married her after making sure she was not a Sunday School teacher; we've stayed together now for fifty-two years."

Generally speaking, there are at least four philosophical justifications for atheism. One is that the idea of a benevolent God is compensation for the inev-

itability of world misery; the second is that there is no rationally tangible verification of a supreme being; the third argument is that religion is a betrayal of the natural sense of human destiny; and number four has to do with the inconsistencies that are the unlit side of many religions.

Holste holds with all of the justifications, but he is particularly attracted to the last question. He reminds that Christianity sponsored the Inquisition, and popes have ridden enthusiastically to war. He says the Bible is likewise cruel and unusual in this regard, and so, when he took a place in the workaday world, he felt it was necessary to develop this theme and encourage others to also think about nonreligious alternatives.

"There were not a lot of national atheistic organizations when I got out of school [with a degree in business administration]. Joseph Lewis was a well-known atheist, and he had a group in New York City, and there were also organizations founded by William McCarthy and Gus Horack and others. They were far away from Minneapolis and St. Paul, however, and I had to start my own little society. At first I called it the Twin City Rationalists, and then I changed the name to the Twin Cities Secularists.

"It was a small group. I'd say we might have had thirty people at a good meeting. And we weren't activists in the sense of the word today. I might write a letter to the newspaper, or someone else might debate a preacher, but that wasn't the real purpose. We met for the same reason that all people with minority opinions join together. We kept each other company. It was nice to have shared views. Churchgoers gather for that same purpose; you do not feel so lonely if there are people around for support.

"It was social in a way. But we also studied our positions and discussed them. I picked the Bible apart, personally. I have never understood why decent people believe in this junk. I have a pamphlet that calls it 'the most vile, brutal, obscene, and false book in the world.' It is full of polygamy, and rape, and murder. It advocates slavery. Sarah advised her husband to rape their maid. How can such things be read in a church? I don't think any righteous god would have anything to do it with it.

"Listen to this: 'Moses stood in the gate of the camp, and said, Who is on the Lord's side? Let him come to me. And he said unto them, Thus saith the Lord God of Israel, Put every man his sword by his side, and go in and out from gate to gate throughout the camp, and slay every man his brother, and every man his companion, and every man his neighbor. And the children of Levi did according to the word of Moses [who said] consecrate yourself to [God], that he may bestow you a blessing this day.'

"It goes on and on like that. God ordered the murder of thousands of people? Why would murdering friends and relatives cause one to be consecrate?

Yet that's what the Bible says. How could our loving and all-wise God order such frightful and vicious stupidity? You can read it in Exodus. Then you can read in Deuteronomy that Moses told his people to 'utterly destroy' the residents of the Promised Land [Palestine] so that the Israelites could move in and take over. Why would a god want to commit genocide and boast about it in his autobiography?

"The answer is that there is no God. And God did not inspire the Bible. The book was written by priests so that, primarily, they could increase and solidify their own position in their society. In other words, they invented the Christian religion so that they could control it and the people who believed in it. This is the reason they made God such a wrathful figure. It was a way of forcing people to submit. Nobody wants to make God mad, because the Bible points out that he can cut off their heads."

Holste worked for many years for Minneapolis transit. He later became a municipal printer and acquired a reputation for challenging the church, often in printed tracts. For instance, quoting Epicurus: Either God wants to abolish evil, and cannot; Or he can, but does not want to; Or he cannot, and does not want to. If he wants to, but cannot, he is impotent. If he can, but does not want to, he is wicked. If he never can, nor wants to, he is both powerless and wicked. But if God can abolish evil, and wants to, then how comes evil into the world?

Holste says he did not encounter very much social exclusion. He would be condemned by clerics, but in those encounters he could give as good as he got. He debated all critics, usually by the pamphlets. He wrote ponderous pamphlets: on fables in the Good Book, on the similarities between ministers and African shamans, on the history of oathtaking, which is to say "so help me God," which he claims is a modern version of the same superstitious ceremony that Joseph used when he placed his hand on the penis of his father to summon fertility forth as witness.

"Then there is the treatment of women in religion. They have always been the principal attendants at and supporters of the church, and I've never been able to comprehend why. The Bible orders the subjugation of women to inferior status. Some churches have always denied them meaningful roles. It started in Genesis. Women were an afterthought. She was supposed to be created as a 'helpmeet.' It turned out she would be nothing more than chattel. If the Bible is true, if every word is gospel, then women are second-class people.

"We read in the Bible that multiple marriage was okay for men, but not for women [Genesis 16:1-3]. We read that women were required to be virgins at marriage, but not men [Deuteronomy 22:13-21]. We read stories where it was okay for men to pass their wives off as prostitutes [Genesis 12:1-16]. We read that women were 'unclean,' according to the Old Testament, and that men could get a divorce merely by sending their wives from their homes [Deuteronomy 24:1], and Jesus said in Matthew 5:17 that men who married divorced women were committing adultery.

"Women are also bonded in the history of religion. Religion has been big on slavery. Parents could sell their daughters to satisfy debts; husbands taken into slavery could force their wives into accompanying them. What kind of philosophy is this? How can the preachers and the priests and the theologians still say the Bible is God's work? There was only one way a woman could get out of slavery, the Bible says. 'If a man smite the eye of his servant, or of his maid, that it perish, he shall let him (her) go.' That, I'm afraid, is in Exodus 21:26-27."

Merrill Holste lived in Minnesota until 1975. He worked hard, paid his taxes, raised three children (the godless do not necessarily have horns), and, on retirement, moved to an adult community in New Mexico, where he has instituted the Albuquerque chapter of a national organization called American Atheists.

He sometimes writes opinion for the American Atheists' magazine. The name of his column is "The Angry Old Atheist." One reason he is angry is that he is a registered Republican who deeply laments the emergence of an evangelistic wing of the Grand Old Party and the concomitant lack of atheistic representation:

"The truth is, religion has grown in my life and atheism has stayed about the same. I think there are many reasons. Most people do not like to admit they are godless, so they don't get out there and fight for the truth. On the other hand, the religious sects are well organized and financed. They have a tremendous propaganda effort. You can't turn on the radio on Sunday without hearing their lies, and it's gotten to be much the same for television. That's a lot of advertising. They just brainwash the people, and that is all there is to it.

"I still do what I can. I pass literature around, and I still write to the newspapers and the opinion-makers. I wrote to the Republican National Committee once. I said there was too much talking about God in the party, and too many preachers. I talked about a preacher in California. He said God should smite anyone on the Supreme Court who supported legal abortion. I don't know if the guy is Republican or what, but can you imagine that? That's what these religious freaks are like. They are always talking about God getting even with sinners."

Which brings up a point, Mr. Holste.

"Yes?"

You're seventy-nine. Do you worry about God getting even with you?

"Not me. Some people may think about that when they get older. I don't. The preachers say good Christians will be rewarded in heaven. They will sit at the foot of the Father. I think that would be very boring, even if it were true: singing hosannahs all day long. No, I think what happens when we die is that we go to sleep. And that's all I want to do when it's my time."

A Gallup survey taken in 1987 indicates that nine in ten Americans share a fundamental belief in God. The survey also said that eight in ten believe God works miracles, eight in ten are "sometimes very conscious of the presence of God," and eight in ten are convinced they will face the Lord on Judgment Day.

A 1987 Gallup poll said the convictions differed significantly according to the education level of the respondents. Ninety-four percent of those with less than a high school education said they never doubted the existence of God; 90 percent of high school graduates felt that way, while 78 percent of college graduates agreed.

Ninety percent of the women interviewed believed in God, as did 86 percent of the men. Eighty-seven percent of the whites polled said they had no doubts. Ninety-three percent of the nonwhites went along too, plus 91 percent of the Hispanics.

As for age categories, the percentage of those who said they believed in God are: 84 percent of those eighteen to twenty-four; 88 percent of those twenty-five to twenty-nine; 84 percent of those aged thirty to thirty-nine, 90 percent of those aged forty to fifty-nine, and 90 percent of those aged sixty and over.

"If only God would give some clear sign. Like making a large deposit in my name at a Swiss bank. (Woody Allen)

MOTHER HALE

In 1969, when she was sixty-four years old and understandably weary of a life of work and worry, Clara Jean Hale was ready to resign from everyday concerns and spend the rest of her life in a quest for leisure. Then, as it's said, there was a knock on her door.

"Who is it?"

Are you Mother Hale?

"Yes."

Well, you don't know me, but . . .

Mother Hale. That's what they called her even then. And for fair reason. She had a pair of children of her own, and she had raised scores of others as a sort of surrogate parent. She had adopted one boy; she had taken in a small legion of day-care kids; she had been the neighborhood nanny; and even though she'd loved every one, drying their eyes and kissing their smiles, enough was enough, it was over; she was going to take it easy.

Knock, knock.

"There was a young woman at the door, and she had an infant baby in her arms. And they were both addicted to drugs. The mother used heroin and other things, and she had passed it on to her child. She said she couldn't take care of the child. She didn't have work, and she spent most of her time trying to get money to get drugs. Then she asked if I would please take the child, because otherwise it would die. I told her I didn't want to take care of children any more, that I had given it up, but she sat the baby by the door and left, and I was in business again."

The business would come to be known as Hale House. It is the only private facility in the nation that cares for narcotically afflicted children. Mother Hale provides a home for the infant kids of junkies, nursing and curing them while the mothers are being assisted elsewhere. She is now eighty-two. She has rehabilitated hundred of kids and healed almost as many damaged families. Earlier in this chapter there was a listing of the varied definitions of morality. Add one more: Delivering the helpless.

None are more helpless than addicted babies. They have been brought into the twentieth century on the point of a needle, and, saving intervention, they are doomed from the first breath. There is nothing particularly surprising about it, either. The tragedy is one for the ages. The use of drugs in America is almost as dated as America. Native Americans got high on peyote cactus buttons; white settlers smoked Jimson weed, and when ether was discovered, in the 1800s, people could purchase it at traveling medicine shows for a few cents a gasp, whereafter they would laugh, dance, and otherwise make morons of themselves.

The drug culture did not take full bloom until this century, however. One reason is that in the beginning it was tolerated, and even encouraged. Cocaine,

for example, used to be thought to have a whole spectrum of beneficial qualities.
At one time the surgeon general of the United States endorsed it for casual con-
sumption. People could buy it over the counter for two or three dollars an ounce.
The nation imported a wine laced with cocaine that was so popular it was said
to be used by the pope. Coca-Cola was brewed with cocaine until 1903, when it
was replaced with caffeine, and so were some teas, cigarettes, and chewing gum.

The nation began to reconsider the use when it was discovered, early in the
1900s, that anywhere from 250,000 to four million Americans had become
narcotically addicted (out of a total population of 80 million). Cocaine was also
blamed for fueling crime. And rumors were spread that drug-sodden Negroes
might be a threat to the white social order. The first national control laws were
passed in 1914. Yet the door could hardly be closed. Marijuana was introduced
on a large scale by Mexican laborers in the 1930s; soldiers came back from
World War II with amphetamines and other chemical stimulants; and, in the
1960s, a new drug binge took hold and continues late into the century.

In 1987 it was estimated that one out of every other American adult had
used an illegal narcotic on at least one occasion. And there were thought to be
three-quarters of a million addicts. The addicts were mostly in the urban areas.
Perhaps the largest concentration was in the New York neighborhood known as
Harlem. Harlem is a historic resource in many ways. It is also a mean scar
where drug addiction is ten times higher than it is in New York as a whole and
where the gentle Mother Clara Hale resides:

"I did not start out in Harlem. I grew up in Philadelphia. My father died
when I was a small girl, and my mother raised four of us alone. She ran a board-
inghouse in Philadelphia—it was by the waterfront—and she supplemented our
income by selling meals to the longshoremen on the dock. My mother would
cook the meals and we children would carry them over. We did not have much
money, I have never had much money, but we had a sense of family, and that
was important; my mother insisted on that.

"I idolized my mother. I always wanted to be like her, but I didn't even
look like her. She was the daughter of a white man who had been in the slavery
business at one time, and she had fair skin. She did not look black, except that
she had knotty hair. And she also knew everything. You could ask her any question; she always had the answer; and she was just brilliant, I thought. I never
knew how she came to be so smart, because when she was born, usually, black
girls were not put in school.

"She died when I was sixteen. As I think back on it, I think she knew she
was going to die. She kept telling me that I was going to be on my own one day,
that she was not going to be around, and she wanted to prepare me for the outside world. So she did it in every way she knew. She taught me how to be reli-

gious, and how to believe in God, and how to work, and everything. She said I would have to be a little forward, a little pushy, and she said I should live decently and show care for other people.

"I was still in high school when she died. And I had to find a place to live and continue my classes. I moved into a room with a friend, I paid a dollar a week and she paid a dollar a week, and when I graduated from high school I went right to work. At that time they only had black people doing domestic work, and that's what I did. I worked in a white person's home, cleaning and all. I worked for a quarter a day. I think I was a good worker, because my mother taught me well; I always had a job.

"My social life was limited. I had girlfriends, but I did not like boys an awful lot. I was real thin (they used to call me Stringbean), and I don't think the boys cared about a skinny thing like me. I finally met one nice boy, his name was Thomas, and he took me to Harlem. I married Thomas in the 1920s; he was a floor waxer, he had his own business. We stayed in Philadelphia for a few years and then he wanted to get more education; so we moved to New York, where he went to night college.

"We had two children, Lorraine and Nathan, and I also started taking care of other children. I was the superintendent of our apartment building, I did the janitorial work, and it meant that we did not have to pay any rent. After a while some ladies in the building asked me if I would keep their children when they left for work. And eventually that became what they did. They knew I would help. If they needed a place for their child they'd say 'Call Clara.' It was really very nice, because their children were company for me, and they were also company for my children, both of whom were still quite young.

"Then Thomas died too. First my father, then my mother, now my husband. I was only twenty-seven, and it was very hard to take. I had to quit the superintendent's job because I couldn't do it without Thomas, and so I got a job cleaning Loews Theater. I did that from midnight to seven A.M. so that I could still be with my children during the day. The children sustained me. I also kept on caring for other boys and girls. That kept me from being lonely, and it gave me a purpose. I always thought that God had a purpose for me; I thought He had a plan. He took my husband, but not me; He still had work for me."

Mother Hale continued to do janitorial and domestic work through her middle years. And she expanded her day-care obligations. She also picked up her nickname. She says the children she took in began to call her Mommy; she thought it was nice, but she didn't want the other mothers to be hurt, so she asked the kids to call her Mommy—or, as it's become, Mother—Hale.

She put her own children through college. Dr. Lorraine Hale is now a specialist in early child development and the director of Hale House. Mother Hale also cared regularly for forty other children who were also to go to college, and they are today doctors, lawyers, dancers, businessmen, singers, and so on.

There were, however, other children in Harlem who were not faring so well. Mother Hale says they lay beside their drug-addicted mothers in the streets and the alleys. The addiction of the children took place in the womb. Babies can be either nourished or poisoned during gestation. Physicians say they are affected by the common utilization of blood and other fluids.

"Lorraine sent that first woman and baby to my door. She saw them on the street; this woman was nodding away, and my daughter felt bad for them. Lorraine walked past them at first, but then she came back and she watched them as they were sitting there. It was night, I think, and Lorraine eventually went up to the woman and she told the woman where I lived. She said my mother lives down the street, you can ask anybody about her, and I'm sure she would be able to help you if you would go and see her.

"So the woman came. And she had a very beautiful little baby. But I was alarmed when I met them. I had never known a drug addict before. I had never been around them, and I was afraid. But Lorraine told me that I had to help the baby. She said it wasn't necessarily the mother, it was the baby. She said there were children like that all over Harlem, they were drug addicts from drug addicts, and they were dying like flies because there wasn't anyone who bothered to take care of them.

"That first baby was a month old. She was just a little bit of a thing, and dirty and all, and she was sick in that she was withdrawing from addiction. She cried and screamed and made all kinds of faces. I had taken care of a lot of children, but I had never seen anything like it. I didn't know what to do at first, so all I could do was clean her up, give her as much food as she could take, and love her. It took four to six weeks of that, and the little baby got well and started to be normal.

"Meanwhile, the mother had come back. She thought I would take the child to the police or something, and she was happy to see that I hadn't and that her baby was so much better. So the way it was, she started telling some of her friends what I did, and other mothers started showing up at the door with other babies. The mothers were all addicts, and the babies were the same. One or two on one day, two or three on the next, and before you knew it, three weeks later, I had a total of twenty-two addicted children.

"This was in my old apartment. I had five rooms, and I had lived there for thirty-one years. But when the city heard about all these addicted children, I was told that I would have to move. The city said the place was too small, the elevator was broken most of the time, and I had a month to find something else. I didn't have any money, and I didn't want to just get rid of the children, so I went to Percy Sutton then, he was the borough president, and he promised to help. Then Lorraine wrote to get a grant from the city, and after that we found this five-story building here on 123rd Street and named it Hale House."

Hale House is in the center of Harlem. It is fast by sidewalks littered with debris, and people around the clock. Cops walk the beat in pairs. Burglar alarms accompany the noise on the boom boxes. And the by-product of the density is exorbitant conduct. Dope is available in small shops that otherwise peddle cigarettes and magazines; pimps control their produce with nods and hard gestures; small people are extorted by big; bluster is the sport of choice; and good people hurry behind closed doors after hours.

"We had one problem of this kind here. Two men robbed us with guns one time. There was a girl who was working here, and she told the men when everyone in the house got paid. So they waited until everyone had cashed their checks, and they came in and held everybody up. They meant business. They shot one of the chairs because one lady did not get up as fast as they wanted. Then they took all the people downstairs and made them get undressed in the kitchen, so nobody could go after the police. They didn't hurt anyone, but they took all the money.

"Then something nice happened. When the story got out, people started sending us money to make up for what was lost. Everybody got their salaries back, and we had some left over. So I think some good came of it. It showed that people supported us. And we haven't had any trouble since. Some of the mothers have boyfriends who keep a watch when they are around, and people in the neighborhood also help out. I walk out on the streets, I think I'm perfectly safe. People call out 'Hello Mother Hale, how are you?,' and it seems that everyone knows what we do is good.

"What it is, we try to save the children and the mothers. We want the mothers to get treatment for themselves. That is important. We don't want the families to break up for good; we want to encourage mothers to get back with their children. So we take the child here and we send the mother to another agency for adults. The mother is then given a social worker, and she joins a program, and she gets rid of her addiction. It is very difficult—it usually takes a year or a year and a half—but she can take the child back when she is free of drugs.

"The children stay here all the while. We put them together according to age and try to make it just like a regular home. We have to get them off the drugs first, of course. We do it cold turkey. We don't give any medication except intensive care. They have their own beds, or cribs, and we watch them carefully through this withdrawal period. They holler, they bounce around; it's not good to see. We feed them a lot during this time. A baby may normally have a bottle every two hours or so, but we make it every half hour or so. It seems to help them.

"I keep the children in my bedroom when they first come to Hale House. I have two cribs there and that way I can keep a close watch. I love each and every one of them, just as if they were my own. I pick them up when they cry, and I walk them around, and I sing songs to them. My voice cracks now, so I don't sing very well, but I think they like it. They stop making faces, and they smile. They stop hurting for a while. They are so lovely then; they are drug addicts, but they are beautiful children, and it's just that they've gotten a hard start."

Mother Hale says she has nursed more than 600 addicted children (1987). And the success rate has been exceptional. Five hundred fifty have been reunited with their mothers; others have been given to near relatives; and only fourteen have had to be given to the city for adoption. Mother Hale says three children have died. She got them too late. They were too sick to survive.

"Now we are starting to get babies with AIDS. So we will probably be losing some more. It's started in the last few years. Their mothers share contaminated needles with other addicts, and everything is passed on to the children. It is so sad. They are not only addicted, they have this incurable disease. You wouldn't know it to look at them. When they come in they just look like the rest of the children. Then they run high temperatures, and they show other symptoms, and we have their blood tested for confirmation.

"I haven't been able to keep these children in the house. Some of the people who work here are afraid to handle them, and so I've sent them to the hospital. They all stay together there, and some of us go over to feed them and do other things. I don't worry about picking them up, and snuggling them; that's not the way the disease is transmitted. I wouldn't worry even if it was. I feel so sorry for them. They just lie there in their beds, they don't know if it's sunshine or rain outside. They are my children, like all of the rest, and I love them."

Mother Hale is still a Stringbean. She has white hair, good health, and a soft voice. She is called a saint in Harlem. Not bad for the granddaughter of a slave. She was named the American Mother of the Year once, and she has received 182 other citations. It's a change from domestic work in Philadelphia.

"The children and their mothers often come back to visit. On holidays and other times. I remember them all. I'm proud of every one. That first addicted baby, she is eighteen years old today and she was here not long ago. She said, Mother Hale, I have gone through high school, but I don't think I can make it any higher. I said, Sweetheart, don't you worry, that doesn't matter: you've learned things they don't teach in college."

8. Making It

LES STAUDENMEYER

The advantages of wealth can be greatly exaggerated, at least according to those who are in a position to know. And maybe that's why L. G. Staudenmeyer does not like to talk about his own tidy fortune. He began accumulating money, or those things that can be converted into money, at a time when it was popular to believe that nothing is so comfortable as a small bankroll, because (according to Wilson Mizner) a big one is always in danger. And, as we have seen again and again in this book, the original children of the twentieth century tend to cling to their first principles. The early editorialists claimed wealth is a matter of temperament, not income. They said God does not make the well-to-do, He only devised the curse. They also said a rich man is merely a poor man with money. And Les Staudenmeyer believes it.

How much is all this land worth, Mr. Staudenmeyer?

"Oh, God, hard telling."

Well, how much land do you have?

"Four ranches now. Forty thousand acres."

And how much is an acre worth?

"This and that. It depends. I know 640 acres I could have got for two thousand one time. Now they are asking for one hundred thousand."

Okay. Now we're getting somewhere.

"We are?"

I want to buy everything you have. Name your price.

"There's all the equipment, you know, and the cattle."

How much?

"I'd have to think on that."

Staudenmeyer takes a pinch of chewing tobacco from a can. He puts his thumbs in his suspenders and holds his belly. He remembers someone telling him that he is richest who is acquainted with discretion, and that (as sociologist Robert Lynd put it) if one browses in a dictionary of quotations he will find little reason to cheer wealth. Besides. Besides. It's better for a man to tell how he made himself than how he made his fortune:

"It was hard work and plenty of it. Yes, sir. That's the way I see it. Hell, you had to work. That's all there was to it. You couldn't go to the courthouse to get your money then. Noooo. Food stamps weren't available. They didn't give away welfare checks, and all the rest of it. You rolled up your sleeves, you stuck your nose down in it; if you didn't it was just too bad.

"I bought my first ranch when I was twenty-five years old. You bet. That's when we rode horses. You didn't go around in a fifteen-thousand-dollar pickup with a heater in it, and the upholstered seats, and the mats on the floor, and the windshield washers. I was out in a wagon, summer or winter. If I couldn't make it back to the house, I'd put down a bedroll, a blanket, and sleep on rocks.

"Sure it got cold. This is Montana. And the wind blows and the snow drifts, and the creeks ice up. It didn't make any difference. I didn't have a thermometer for thirty years. What did I care was the temperature was? It didn't change anything. The cattle. The fences. The repairs. You see what I mean? There wasn't any other way back then. Noooo. We had to work."

So there is another first principle. Staudenmeyer agrees with his generation that hard work and success come from the flames of the same campfire. The conviction is naïve, it would seem. For every man who has become rich punching cows in the West there are armies of others who have just gotten by or gone broke. Staudenmeyer could have been eaten by a bear in his bedroll before he made his first million. Success is not simply labor, or all the farmers and watermen would be able to pay their bills. Or Perry Como would still be a barber. Success is a crap shoot.

Just the same, the dice have been exceptionally kind in the 1900s. Americans have prospered as have few others in any society, in any period, and as no others in terms of numbers. The United States as late as 1925 was a nation where half of all farm families earned less than $1000 a year, where almost half of the rest of the people earned less than $1500 a year, and where only 10 percent of the population could fairly be considered middle-class. Now see: More

Americans had more money in 1987 than may have been good for them, an average of $33,000 apiece when considered against total personal income of $409 trillion.

Les Staudenmeyer is still the exception. But increasing numbers are having affairs with the bitch-goddess Success. In 1987, Americans owned 95 million homes, 170 million automobiles, 175 million telephones, 90 million television sets, 14 million recreation boats, and $2.1 trillion worth of savings accumulations. The Internal Revenue Service said that, in 1986, about one in every sixty tax returns reported adjusted gross income of $100,000 a year, and—pay attention, Mr. Staudenmeyer—estimates suggested there were more than one million millionaires. How did it happen? It wasn't all hard work. The century has been blessed with the fuels of growth. There have been new inventions (the automobile), new sources of power (electricity), and relatively new techniques of stimulation (mass advertising). Samuel Eliot Morison, the historian,says the first two fed the third. He has written that the maturation of salesmanship gave new meaning to the rule of rising expectations. The billboards introduced an epidemic of greed. Dad wanted a Ford, Mom wanted a washing machine, and Baby had to have everything. On credit, of course. Ergo, private debt rose to $2 billion in 1929.

Then the stock market crashed. Yet World War II followed closely. If there is anything that is coupled with success in the flames of a campfire it is military conflict. The government spent $360 billion to defeat the Axis. Most people who survived shared the pot. Between 1940 and 1985 the gross national product grew from $100 billion to almost $4 trillion, a rise of over 3600 percent, and average disposable income went from $570 per capita to $11,000, a boost of a factor of nineteen. Beyond this, the GI Bill of Rights redefined United States education; average schooling was 8.6 years in 1940 and 13 years in 1987.

The Soviet Union once described America as the Kingdom of the Dollar. It is, what's more, the citadel of man's faith in himself.

Les Staudenmeyer is a large, gruff grizzly. He lives in Dillon, Montana, where the Beaverhead County Museum displays the bleached skulls of kilt Indians. He likes to drink, chew, play cards, and avoid church. His friends call him the Last Real Cowboy.

A note. Staudenmeyer talks like there's still no heater in his pickup. He chatters briefly and then stops. He is therefore hard to interview. What follows is pieced together from frugal fragments. It's five hundred answers to a thousand questions.

First, a telephone interruption:

"Yeah?"

"Yeah."

"Nooooo."

"You bet."

Staudenmeyer relaxes in an overburdened swivel chair. He wears good leather boots, soiled, and a Stetson. The Stetson is felt. Only the hands wear straw. Staudenmeyer calls his employees "hands," sometimes Mexican "hands". The hands are all legal, he says. All good men too. He had an Indian hand once, who drank some, yes, but the old boy could do anything with a horse.

"I have always liked horses, since I was a kid. I came from Wisconsin, the southern part, where my dad was a farmer. I rode horses from the start. I was the only boy. I had six sisters, three older and three younger. Four of them are still alive. Two are in their nineties, and two in their eighties. I was born in ninety-eight myself, I'm eighty-seven now, soon to be eighty-eight. I went to high school in Wisconsin, and I stayed there until 1918, the year the war ended, and then I left.

"I wanted to get into the war, but my folks didn't like the idea. They kept me out, so I left to get on my own. My mother gave me forty dollars and I took the train west. I didn't know where I was going. I wound up in Butte at first, because it was the biggest railroad stop in this corner of Montana, and then I came down to Dillon. I don't know why. I was looking for a job. I spent most of the money my mother gave me; I had eight or ten bucks, and I came on down and went to work on a ranch here.

"I never finished high school. If I'd have stayed in Wisconsin three weeks longer I would have graduated, but I didn't. I was pretty smart, though, there's no question I was smart. I went to work at the Diamond O Ranch, as it was called, and I learned more in a few months than I ever did in the books. I learned how to work, for one thing. I didn't get paid at first, I worked for nothing; and I learned how to work the cattle and shovel the ditches, sunup to sundown—sometimes longer than that.

"I would have stayed there, but I got the flu. You heard of the flu of 1918? You bet. People dropped like flies. [Twenty million died worldwide]. I was sick as a dog. So was everybody else. They put us in the bunkhouse (you know what a bunkhouse is, don't you?), that's where you slept, and an old lady from the house took care of us. She gave me something. I guess it was medicine. I was so far gone I would have drank it if it was poison. I made it, though, I got through the whole thing."

Staudenmeyer says he went back home after that. He married a Midwestern sweetheart and returned to Dillon to put down permanent roots. His face gets red at the word sweetheart. *He talks freely of udders, however. He makes points in his conversation by raising his voice, freezing his face, and looking surprised. You know what a bunkhouse is, don't you!*

He started ranching for himself in 1922. He raised beef, which, at the time, was the last breath of the Wild West. Open range. Cattle drives. Buckaroos. Frederic Remington, you bet.

> With my feet in my stirrups,
> And my hand on my horn,
> I'm the best damned cowboy,
> That ever was born.
> Come a ki-yi, yippee,
> Come a ki-yi, yea,
> Come a ki-yi, yippee, yippee yea.

"I bought small that first time. I didn't get a herd with it, but I picked one up here and there. You didn't need much capital back then. You needed a good banker. The ranch was a little ways from Dillon, which was not much of a town in 1922. There was part of a house on the spread. We didn't have any money to talk about, me and the wife lived off the land to get started. You bet. Nobody gave you anything. Noooo. You borrowed money, you bought and sold; that's how you got along, I told you that.

"Bad days came, it didn't matter. That was when you worked even harder. Some people gave up in the Great Depression, everything went all to hell. I stayed on. My wife stayed on. She never complained. You want my honest opinion? They thought it was tough during the Depression, but's tougher now that it was then. You could hire a hand for a dollar a day in the Depression; I had one and I had to cut his wages down from that. Today you pay seven-eight hundred dollars a month for a Mexican.

"And I'll tell you something else. Do you go to the movies? You see John Wayne? Those cattle drives weren't so tough. We had to drive our herds to our summer range every year, which was about seventy-five miles. It took about ten days with cows and calves, about four days with the older ones. A thousand at a time. It wasn't much. It was like a vacation. People worked in the mines in Butte, you know what they did? They would leave their jobs and come down for the drives. They were paid pretty good.

"I saw John Wayne's outfit in California. Did you know he owned a ranch; did you? He was a nice fella. Then I saw Lawrence Welk's ranch. I've been all over. My wife and I, we went to Florida, we took the Love Boat. I didn't like it. My first wife died, what, thirteen years ago. I married again.

What? No, this ain't snuff. Look here, it says 'smokeless tobacco.' I used to smoke cigarettes; I rolled them myself. John Wayne did it one-handed in the movies; you don't see that in Montana.

"I never wore a pistol in a holster. I always had a Remington rifle in my saddle, thirty-thirty, but I never had to shoot anybody. I might have wanted to, but I never did. That was when there wasn't so much law. Oh, there was law—we always had law—but sometimes it wasn't available. If a man stole your cattle, he was in big trouble, big trouble! They'd be hung. Sometimes they were hung on the trail. There's some cattle rustling even now; the son-of-a-bitches come in the night with pickups.

"I used my gun to get game sometime. And to protect the herds. I raised sheep for a long time, I had a lot of them at one time, and you had to keep them from the wolves. There were also bears. Grizzly bears some. I shot my share of them. Now you know what, they want to bring the wolves back, and they want to bring the grizzlies back, the Fish and Game Department? If you shoot a grizzly today you will be arrested. You bet. What do you think about that? You can't shoot a bear any more on your own land.

"Oh, yeah, I tended sheep. I wish I had some now, because I made money on them. Some people didn't like them to start. They said they ruined the range for cattle, and they objected to the fences. You don't hear any complaints about barbed wire today. The cattlemen must have learned to like it, because everyone's got it now. There's no open range no more. That's gone. The government has land we can use, but that's all. When I came here you saw nothing but wild grass; now it's private property."

Staudenmeyer owns some of the property, or lots of it. He says he "did pretty good pretty fast" growing meat, and he eventually accumulated the 40,000 acres. They are each and every one in Beaverhead Valley, at the foot of the Bitteroot mountain range, a mile above sea level. A monument to Lewis and Clark is nearby.

Right. Forty thousand acres at, let's say, a hundred dollars apiece, is $4 million. Add another million worth of buildings and equipment.

Five million dollars, Mr. Staudenmeyer?

"I have no idea. All I know is that we keep busy. I've got five thousand head of cattle, or around that. Course, you can't make anything on them now, but we're still operating. Same old way, too. I don't believe in a lot of this new stuff. You bet. Artificial insemination? Nooooo. I put the heifers with the bulls. I'll get maybe two thousand calves a year. I don't believe in vitamin supplements, either. We grow our own hay, sixty-five hundred or seven thousand pounds of it a year, and there are plenty of vitamins in it.

"I've got six or seven men on the payroll full time, and most of them are Mexican hands. I couldn't run it without them. They work hard, we don't hire nothing else, and we pay them good. You got to pay them good. I got a Mexican hand who's been with me for years, and he gets nine hundred dollars a month. Plus you have to give them a house, and lights and heat. You have to do it get anybody good. That's where it's all changed from before. People don't work for nothing, like I did. Everything costs today.

"I think the best time for ranching was in the 1940s, during the war. Taxes were nothing. Overhead was nothing. I paid twenty-five hundred dollars a year in taxes during the war. You know how much I pay now. I pay fifty thousand dollars a year. It's terrible, the bills. It's three thousand dollars a month just for fuel. It's sixty thousand dollars for a tractor, and I got a dozen of them. I don't know what's happened. It's sixty dollars for a new tire. That's why I don't have artificial insemination. It costs too much.

"I have to have a bookkeeper to look after it. She is a certified public accountant, and I guess she has a computer. I don't like computers. It's just more paperwork. Paperwork, paperwork, paperwork. Taxes, government regulations; it's bad for us. You're supposed to tell them everything, but I don't do that. It's nobody's business but mine. The government didn't buy this land. I did. I'm the one who's kept it going. I've been a rancher now for, hell, it's been sixty-five years. You bet.

"It's nothing fancy. I see in Texas they get around their spreads by airplanes and helicopter. You don't do that here. I know three people who tried it and they went broke. I watch the pennies. I used to belong to the National Cattleman's Association, and I also belonged to the state association, and I did that for thirty years. Then one day I took a look at it, and I realized I was spending eight hundred dollars to a thousand dollars on memberships. So I quit. They came here and asked me, but I told them I won't join again.

"We operate at a loss, many times. It's true. You can't turn a profit the way things are. We got trucks and tractors, and you can't make a dime. You can't just let the herd eat the grass today; you have to send them to feed lots in Kansas City. All the way there and back by truck. People in the city, they don't think about this. I don't know where they think the steak comes from. It's still the Depression on the ranch, I say that all the time, and I'm old enough to know."

It is twenty-five degrees below zero in Dillon. Staudenmeyer has spent the morning making rounds. He says he still walks the fields, he still rides the fences, and, for all of his grumbling about the cost of operation, he still sells awesome numbers of cattle a year.

Still got the bedroll?

"Damn right, and I use it."

He is hard of hearing. But his voice is like the crash of timber in the high country. When he coughs, the horses shy. He is quiet when referring to his land, though. He is not so tough about sentiment. He would not give up an inch of the holdings.

"I love the land. I live in town, but my home is out there. It's all I know. It's all I want to know. You have land, and it's all that's necessary. I'm lucky in that way. I was a pretty smart kid, I did the right thing. I worked and I built it up. Ten, fifteen, a hundred years, my ranches will be here."

You're not the last cowboy, then.

"Nooooo. There are plenty left. Young and old, all around here. The way things are, they can't afford to quit any more."

Writing in THE WALL STREET JOURNAL, *Donald G. Smith has given one reason why so many Americans have been successful. They were, as children, educated in proprieties by the town drunk.*

In Smith's case, a man named Irish Bill:

"He was a big man, loud and crude, and reputedly dangerous, but I am hard pressed to recall any damage that Irish Bill ever inflicted on anyone. He slept under porches and in garages, and occasionally he did odd jobs for merchants and people in the neighborhood. His chief social function, however, was in serving as a horrible example for the children. The consequences for any transgression were that [one] would 'turn out like Irish Bill.' "

Donald Smith goes on to note that the nation doesn't have town drunks any more, "probably because we have so little regard for the doctrine of personal responsibility." He writes that there are still drunks, for certain, but none of them are any longer allowed to be just bums; they are rather people with diseases, and, what is more, they may well be victims of a careless world.

"I rather regret the passing [of the town drunk]," Smith concludes. "He served a purpose. We did our homework because we didn't want to wind up like Irish Bill. We minded our parents, did our chores, saved part of our allowance money, and memorized the Gettysburg Address for the same reason. These are things that one doesn't do for the victim of an uncaring society or someone with a disease. We do them only in the presence of someone who had a choice, and blew it."

DELLIE NORTON

Hello. Are you Dellie Norton?

"I am."

I called you this morning. The book interview?

"I remember. Come on in."

You didn't tell me it was snowing here.

"I told you the roads were bad."

You did say you lived on the side of a mountain.

"I told you the roads were bad."

You didn't tell me you had a dog.

"Oh, he won't hurt you. Fool thing. Want a drink of water?"

Water?

"Best water in the world here. Comes from a spring. That's why I live in the hills. You can't get good water anyplace else."

Thank you. It's, ah, cold.

"I use to make moonshine when I was young, with my husband. Folks raved about it. It was the water; that was the secret."

Mrs. Dellie Chandler Norton. Eighty-eight and wonderful. She is a national treasure. She was raised in the traditions of the Appalachians, one of which was social singing, and she is now one of the last of the living museums of traditional American music. She learned the tunes on her mother's knee, she kept them alive with spirited if isolated practice, and whereas no one used to pay much attention save the echoes in the high country, the early ballads have of late received their due. They are the songs of the people, simple and historically poignant jewels.

I used to have a father, but now he's gone.
He's gone to his home, on high.
Prepare me, oh Lord, to sail on that ship,
That ship that sails by and by.

My days are so long, so long and dreary,

They seem like weeks to me.
And the months are so long, so long and dreary,
They seem like years you see.

Prepare me, oh Lord, to sail on that ship,
That ship that sails on high.
Prepare me, oh Lord, to sail on that ship,
That ship that sails by and by.

She clears her throat. And pats her chest. She says she is hoarse and can't sing, and she stops as abruptly as she started. Applause. How long have you known that song, Mrs. Norton?

"I don't know. Seventy, eighty years maybe. People sang it when I was a girl. We didn't have no radio, or nothing like that, and the songs were all we had to enjoy ourselves."

And where was that?

"Right here. I've lived in Madison County [North Carolina] most of my life. I left a couple of times, with my husband, to see if we could do better. Tennessee and all over. But it wasn't no good. You can't get a good drink of water anywhere else."

Mrs. Norton lives in what the mountain people call a hollow, in this case Sodom Laurel Hollow, a navigable place between the worn hills. Some years ago a British ballad scholar named Cecil Sharp came to the United States to collect songs in the colonies and claimed that there was more traditional American music in Sodom Hollow than he could find anywhere else in the Appalachian chain.

Mrs. Norton, what can you recall of your childhood?

"I was born in t'other hollow over there. No, that way. My father had twenty-five acres, and he worked in the coal mines for a time. There wasn't much work. I had four brothers and sisters; they're dead now. One of them died when she was ninety-three years old."

Did you go to school?

"There wasn't no regular school. There was a Presbyterian school, where you had to pay, and I went there a little, not more than three months. I learned at home, though. I learned to read and write, but I can't write no more because of arthritis."

Go on.

"I used to hunt, there is deer and small animals all through the woods. I raised 'bacca [tobacco], and I had cows that I took care of."

Did the cows have their legs shorter on one side?

"You mean for standing on the hills? No, they just leaned."

When did you start singing?

"Oh, mercy, We sang as soon as we could talk. Someone had a banjo, and maybe there was an accordion—I used to play the accordion—and in the summer we sang on the porch. Other people would come. Everybody did it. That's all we did for entertainment. Someone would start, and the rest joined in."

Ballads.

"Old stuff. Sometimes gospel music."

How old?

"They say hundreds of years. People been here who tell me some of the songs go way back, to that George Washington, I expect."

Will you sing another?

"My voice is no good any more. It's old now, and cracking."

Young Emily was a pretty fine miss,
She loved the driver boy,
Who drove the stage from the olden gate
Way down on the lowland road.

Be sure you don't tell my father,
He's not to know your name,
That you are the driver boy Edmund
Who drives on the lowland road.

Young Edmund fell to drinking,
And from drinking into sleep,
He did not know what my father had said,
To cut off Edmund's head.

Young Emily rose in the morning,
Putting on her clothes,
She said I'm going to find my driver boy,
Who drives on the lowland road.

Oh father, oh father,
I'll have you hung in the public square,
For the murder of my driver boy
Who drove on the lowland road.

Did you say "cut off his head"? Those are some kind of lyrics.

"Lots of them are like that. They tell about things that go on. Family problems, hard work, wives who cheat, husbands who drink."

Speaking of husbands.

"I married when I was nineteen or twenty. That was Ross Norton, and he was the only one. He drank a lot. Sometimes he was good to me and sometimes he wasn't, just like it goes in the songs. But it don't matter none any more; he's been dead over twenty year."

What did he do?

"He was a logger."

Did you have children?

"We had five children. Three are living and two dead. The boy died when he got stuck in his car in the snow. It was gas from the engine [asphyxiation]. My oldest girl had appendicitis."

The old woman looks down at her hands at that. She folds them and lifts them from her lap. She is delicately small, sitting on a worn cushion in a rocking chair, and not at all accustomed to private expression. She says she wanted to leave the mountains at one time, despite worry of the water, to sing professionally, but her husband would not let her leave home.

"I don't know why."

Maybe he thought you'd get a boyfriend. Look at Dolly Parton.

"I would say so."

So you had to wait?

"I was seventy when I first sang for money. David Holt ask me to do it. You heard about him. He has been on *Hee-Haw* and other TV programs [Holt is a ballad preservationist and entertainer]. He heard about me from somebody, and he came up here to tape some songs. We've been all over since he came, out and around."

Where was your first performance?

"In Durham. He took a whole bunch of girls from the hollow, and I got a hundred dollars. It was the most money I ever made at one time."

A whole bunch of girls?

"People what had sang together here. Evelyn Ramsey, and Sheelah Barnhill, and I don't remember the rest. Most of them are dead now. We were the Sodom Laurel Ballad Singers. We sang in auditoriums . . . and in festivals."

Television?

"Yes, plenty of times. David Holt made movies of us. I've got video cassettes here, and look at all of them tape recordings."

Let's listen to a tape.

"I'm not in on every song."

What's that one there?

"It was made at a festival. Where is the start? I don't know if I'm at the start. I had a cold that time; I didn't sound good."

Who is that singing?

"Some man there. He was half drunk. I think I'm singing next."

My father heeee was a rich old jay,
My mother sheee was a lighting fire,
And me a girl the only heir,
Which has brought me to despair

And when I wore my long suit gown.
He followed me from town to town.
But now my apron will barely tie,
He'll pass my door and go right by.

He'll take another on his knee,
And he'll say to her what he did to me.

I wish to God my babe was born,
And standing in his papa's home,
And me a poor girl, were dead and gone,
And the green grass growing all around.

The old woman's voice does crack. And she must lift her chin to hit high notes. She has style, however. And a bit of the ham. She works a syllable beyond its given length, and she rolls over the sentencing, up and down, now quiet, now loud, as befits an artist used to the hills. She seems personally involved, too; life is normally trying, and she shows it.

She has made one commercial recording. She has been featured in the National Folk Festival in Washington. She lives in a weathered home, which leans away from the wind, with a man she adopted. The man was abandoned by his mother when he was young, and Mrs. Norton took him in. She says he is retarded, and no one knows his age, "and I learned him to work; he's a good boy."

But can he sing?

"He just listens."

Does the dog always bark?

"Only when he's not sleeping."

How high up the mountain are we?

"There are three more homes before the top."

It's a good place for a kid on a sled.

"I did that as a girl. On a piece of lumber. Getting so I can't do anything these days. I can't hardly work no more."

One more song, Mrs. Norton?

"I'm so hoarse. Hak, hak. You should just read this one."

I looked down from a distant window,
On a far and distant shore.
I looked down from a distant window,
To where I am no more.

A young man courted a handsome lady,
He loved her dear as he loved his life.
Unto him, she made a promise,
That she would be his lawful wife.

As soon as the parents came to know this,
They strove to part them night and day.
Son oh son, don't be foolish,
She is poor, they would say.

As soon as the lady came to know it,
She made up what she would do.
She wandered forth and left the city
The green wilds for to view.

There she took a gleaming dagger,
And pierced her own good heart.
Let this be a youthful warning,
No true love should ever part.

At night, temperature falling, Dellie Norton's home is as dark as her ballads. There are four rooms in the place, small windows, and coal dust. She squeezes into a corner opposite the television and keeps a blanket around her shoulders. She wears athletic socks over dark brown hose. Print dress and apron. Bobby pins in the hair. It is five miles down a goatpath to a filling station, it's twenty miles over a mountain pass to the nearest town of any consequence, but it's not far from heaven.

Do you still sing at festivals, Mrs. Norton?

"I don't do it much any more. I ain't got my voice."

Privately, then.

"I sing to myself . . ."

Yes?

"When I'm not so hoarse."

There is a knock on the door. The adopted man with no age admits a local resident, wrapped in disaster wear, who has the most powerful four-wheel-drive vehicle on the Eastern Seaboard.

My sleigh has arrived, Mrs. Norton.

"Have some more water before you leave."

Gerald and Bonita Davison were married in "nineteen and twenty three." They lived on a 640-acre farm north of Texhoma, Oklahoma; they raised wheat and cattle, for the most part; and everything went pretty well until, as Mrs. Davison recalls, the "black dusters" arrived: "The dirt would boil up in the distance, you could see it coming for miles, and it would roll over the farm like you couldn't believe. If it was daytime we had to turn on the lamps. You looked outside and couldn't see the barn. If you had to go to town, you drove on the edge of the road, and used the fence lines as a guide. It was just like a biblical plague."

The black dusters blew over the southern portion of the Midwest during the 1930s. They were the result of a combination of calamities and technical ignorance. The farmers of the time stripped their land of the natural grass of the ages, and the customary winds then teamed with a severe drought to transform the unprotected area into what was to become known as the Dust Bowl. More than 150,000 square miles were affected, including parts of Oklahoma, Texas, Colorado, Kansas, and New Mexico.

Mrs. Davison:

"The dirt was very fine, and you could not fight it. It got into everything. The house, the food, the well water. One of my children was born in 1933, and we couldn't put her on the floor until she was walking; it was that filthy. I couldn't see the color of my linoleum. You'd wash one minute and be gritty the next. One night my husband and I were sound asleep and we heard a big crash outside the bedroom door. The wind had come up, and the dust blew into the attic, and the ceiling just caved in. We just pulled the blankets over our heads and went back to sleep.

"And the fields were ruined, of course. You might see shoots up one day, and the next they would be covered. We had a neighbor who worked for us sometimes, and one morning he went out to plow up listers [eight- to ten-inch ridges that are supposed to protect dry furrows]; things got so bad he had to quit by noon, and a few hours later the ridges were all leveled. I kept a small garden, and I got a few things from that, but otherwise we couldn't grow a crop. My husband tells people that we didn't grow enough to take care of our milk cow."

Bonita Davison says many of her friends and neighbors gave up and moved out. In fact, half the population of the Dust Bowl relocated. The Davisons hung on, however, and still today live in the Oklahoma panhandle. They have turned their farm over to their children and have taken residence in Texhoma, where they wonder what would happen if the Dirty Thirties returned:

"The young people today could not make it. They don't know about that. What would they do if they couldn't see their video recorders? Well, we didn't even have electricity until the 1940s. And we didn't have running water; we got it from the windmill. Young people can't picture that. We had to fight; the Dust Bowl was just one of many things we went through."

TIP WARREN

Tip Warren is one of Dellie Norton's Appalachian neighbors. They are not close neighbors; they are separated by 150 miles of woods and wilderness, but he's right next door in terms of mountain concord. He lives in Gray, Kentucky, on the other side of the Cumberland Gap, which is not far from Stinking Creek. The community is bound by Round Knob, Bailey's Switch, Black Snake, Flat

Lick, and Beulah Heights. It's flanked by the Daniel Boone National Forest; it's likewise in the vicinity of the Great Saltpetre Cave; and it is jurisdictionally incorporated in Knox County, which has all during its 188 years of existence been one of the dreariest and most impoverished places in the nation.

Did somebody say poverty? It certainly was not Tip Warren. He thinks the only thing wrong with not having any money is the sympathy it engenders. He was born poor, he grew up poor, he married poor, he raised his own poor family, and he has grown old in the same condition; yet, please, no condolences. Success has many fonts. It's one thing to survive in America with abundance; behold with wonder those who make it with nothing.

Or almost nothing:

"The first time I lived in a house with electricity was in the 1940s, I believe, after they finished with the war. I got a radio a little before that, but it was second-hand, because I couldn't afford to get anything right from the store. Then I got an icebox in the 1950s, and that was a dandy, because before that we kept things cold in the dug well, or maybe we tied them down and just left them sit in the running water in the creek.

"We didn't get indoor plumbing until later. Everybody used to have outhouses in the hills, and some still does. They were pounded together with boards, and they were sat over holes that were cut out in the ground. I had one for a long time that I kept by the creek. When it got full and the rains came, the stuff would wash in the water. People downstream might have drunk it, I guess. Anyway, we were glad to get the icebox."

Tip Warren is ninety-two. He was born in a log cabin the year after Thomas Edison gave the first public showing of the invention he called the kinetoscope (motion pictures), but he was not to see films himself until he was well into middle age. He says everybody was destitute then in rural Kentucky. Indeed, most people were wanting to some extent or another throughout the United States. The wage-earning class had expanded by a factor of four during the nineteenth century, but it was still a time of high unemployment (1.4 million jobless in 1905) and mass privation (the infant mortality rate in 1901 was one in ten births).

Better things followed. Success against the odds of the past has become the collective specialty of twentieth-century America. That doesn't mean for everyone, however. Indigence has continued to rest beyond the opening of the national cornucopia. In 1985 the census bureau estimated that 33 million Americans were living below the officially designated poverty line (measured as $11,000 worth of income per annum), and that included T. Warren, who could tell the Census Bureau a thing or three about it.

"It's never been anything else for me. It's all I've ever known, no money,

and make do. And my daddy didn't have nothing before me. He did some farming, and he was an old-time healing man, I guess that's what you'd call him.
They didn't have a lot of doctors in the hills, and he was one of them that went
around helping people that got sick. He delivered babies, and he could set a
bone or pull a tooth. He didn't go to school, not for doctoring, but he knew how
to do it. He had medicines and powders that he made himself, from roots and
other things.

"My daddy was an old man by the time I was born. He'd fought the Civil
War, what was a long time ago. He was discharged in 1864, I believe it was. He
went to it from Kentucky, but I don't know if he volunteered or was called. He
told me the stories about it—he fought with a musket—but I didn't listen much. I
was called myself in 1917, in the World War, but I didn't have to go. I was ex-
amined, and I passed, A-1, but I had two children of my own by that time, and I
was let go. I was just as happy as I could be for it; I didn't want no part of a war.

"Now that I think about them, my mother helped my daddy with the doctoring. She'd go along and sit up with whoever was sick, all night if there wasn't
no one else to do it. And she never expected a dime for it. People did for each
other; that's the only way we knew how. If you got sick, the neighbors came in.
If your house burned down, everybody would get together and build a new one.
I remember people taking time off from their work to build roads together; if a
man was in the woods or something, he'd soon have a road to his place.

"There wasn't no other way. The government did not do it like it will today. Anyway, people were scared of the government, or they were scared of the
law part of the government. When a government man came around it meant
some kind of trouble; the man with the badge was up to no good, or so we
thought. It's not like it is now, where there are programs for this and that. The
fact is the government paid to insulate my house not long ago. But when I was
young, it wasn't common to go to a courthouse and ask for help, even if it would
have done any good.

"For sure you couldn't ask for any money. There wasn't none. What we
did was live off the land. My daddy had forty acres or so, hillside land, in Chop
Branch Hollow. It wasn't much good for growing things. The soil was good,
what there was of it, because it was made up of all those leaves what had fallen
for hundreds and hundreds of years. But it was too steep. We'd put down corn,
and the rain would wash if off, or the sun wouldn't hit it most of the time. We
got some crops, things to eat, and for the animals, but it didn't get too big.

"I remember clearing it. That was another hard part. It was called grub-
bing. There wasn't no tractors, or machines—what you would call bushhogs today. We had a team of mules, and we cut the trees and then had to pull the
stumps out with the team. It was work. We'd start soon and quit late. I won't
forget that good soil, though; it even had a good smell about it. It was good and

rich, and black as night, not like it is here lately. I don't know what's happened to it. The good stuff has all washed off—it don't last, I guess—I'm not an expert.

"The first house was made of logs. Then my daddy traded it for another one, further back in the hollow, and that one was logs too. We had windows but no screens, and in the summer it got hot and the doors and the windows were kept open. That let the flies in, and there were a lot of them. There were more fleas, though, and something called cinches [bedbugs]. They left red spots on you when they bit. The women would boil water now and then, and splash it all over the inside of the house, and that would kill them. My mother, she would pick them out of my hair.

"The fleas wouldn't stay on your body much, because when you got to walking around they would hop off. We had to take baths when they didn't. The bathtub was a wooden barrel. My daddy cut a barrel in half, and you could store things in it or use it as a tub. The women would haul water from the well and heat it over a fire. The water didn't come to the tub, like now; we took the tub to the water. We had homemade soap; it was made with animal fat, and there were big bars of it. There wasn't no special time for those baths, you know; whenever my mother caught us.

"There was a school at the bottom of the hollow. It was called Rock Springs. We only had it for six months at a time, and I didn't go but to the seventh grade. My people didn't let me. Kids quit to help out at home. I had a brother who went on past that, because he wanted a higher education. One day I went with him to Frankfort, because he was going to take a test to get into a bigger school. But there were all these intellectual scholars there, he had to compete with them; and so he gave it up and we came back home, because he knew it wasn't no use to try."

Warren suggests the brother's attempt to break away from the hills was a presumption. The normal order was to accept the cards as they were dealt, in this case miserably. And there was one consolation in this resignation. The old man says the mountain folks did not usually care that their hands were atypical. He says he never went hungry; he had shoes in the winter; he had the security of his family; and, in addition, he had the traditions. He saw pictures in the schoolbooks and magazines of outside riches, but he did not have any regrets:

"I expect it's hard for some to believe, but most of us, we thought everything was pretty good. When I got older I knew I didn't have much, but it didn't bother me none. I had most of what I wanted. We got to hunt and fish, and we'd sneak off if somebody got some corn liquor. There was also the girls around, and we knew what that was about. We'd take the girls to church, or maybe a dance if someone got one started, and then, afterwards, the boys would get together and talk about the girls, and the girls would do the same thing.

"I met my Ida when I was no more than a boy. She lived in the hollow and I knew her for years before we got married. We got married in 1912. I was seventeen years old, and she was younger than that. It wasn't out of line, I don't think. People got married soon back then, and there wasn't too much formality, either. I got a license from the county, which cost two dollars and fifty cents, and they said a few words to us. I didn't get dressed up—I wore my everyday overalls—and neither did Ida. Here's Ida here; she's dead now, but I still got her picture in the house.

"Nothing changed when we got married. My folks were old by then, and Ida and I stayed on the farm to help out. Daddy didn't die until he was in his eighties, and it was just old age that got him. My mother went first. She was wore out by then, and it was a heart attack. One day she just raised up in bed, and looked around, and that was it. I heard her go. She was buried on the farm; that's where we put my daddy later. There was rocks to pile up to mark the graves; the place was sold a long time ago, but the stones are still there.

"There wasn't no money at all on the farm, except some little bit I might make by selling something or other. We raised everything we ate. There were cows for sweet milk and butter, and hogs for meat; we didn't have a flat place to grow hay, but we had some corn for grain. I'd take the corn to the mill to get flour. There was certain days they'd do it, maybe on Saturday, I don't remember. I'd put the corn in the 'mill sack' and take it over on the back of a mule. The mill would keep some of the corn—it was called a toll—and that's how I paid for the flour.

"We did need to get some things from the store. A little salt and things like that. There was a little country store, but it wasn't big enough to keep much in it, so we had to go to town every three or four weeks. Barboursville was sixteen miles away, it took a couple of hours both ways, and we'd get candy too; I have always liked candy. I used to buy stick candy for me and Ida and keep it in jars. I still get it now, but I keep it in the refrigerator so it don't get sticky. I still get peppermint and caramel; the only thing different is it's more expensive.

"I bought my first suit in Barboursville, at a store there, and that was when I bought what we called Sunday shoes. They were like slippers. My regular shoes were all made of thick leather and they were put together with nails and that, but I gave a dollar and a half for that lighter pair of shoes, and I thought I really had something. The suit was five dollars, I believe. I only wore it on Sunday too. I'd go to church, and then when I got home I'd take it off so I could feed the pigs. I kept it a long time. The women would brush it and keep it nice.

"Ida [he pronounces it Idee] had six children. Two of them were twins. Four of them are still alive, but two died when they were young. There were measles and smallpox—they were the dreaded diseases, like cancer is today—and that got them. There wasn't no hospital to go to, and we couldn't afford it, and the medicines didn't always work. One of the boys got whooping cough. We put things on his chest and kept his bowels open, but it didn't do any good. He'd cough, or he'd go 'wooooop, wooooop,' trying to cough; it was bad to hear."

Warren sold the family farm in the 1930s. It was the last piece of land he would own. It was also the first and the last time he moved out of Knox County. He took his family to Harlan, Kentucky, a hundred miles east, where he found a job mining coal.

Bloody Harlan?

"It was a rough place. Rough people."

Gunfights, I hear.

"That's true."

Why?

"When I went to work there was no unions in Harlan County, and you knew better than to say anything about it. If you did you lost your job, or maybe you get thrown in jail. The trouble was when the men tried to organize, they would go on strikes, and the companies would send in people to break them up. It got bad at times. There was bad feelings, and people got beat up. The company might shoot first, and the men would shoot back; maybe there was people that was killed like that on both sides.

"What I did was stay away from that. I just shoveled coal. It was all deep mining, and all by hand. There was those who blew the rock apart (I knew how to do that myself) and the rest of us shoveled it up. We went down first thing in the morning, and stayed ten to twelve hours, and there wasn't much money. You got paid for what you shoveled, so you had good days and bad. Sometime there was bad management, and they put you where things were slow, and maybe you'd only make a dollar or two.

"One thing that was wrong was there wasn't no masks. The companies did not think about the dust. I started spitting it up right away when I worked there, and after a while it was all the time. I got black lung today. I get attacks. I went to the hospital not long ago, in Corbin, and the doctors worked on me day and night. They take the fluid out of my lungs, because sometimes I can't breathe good. I get $328 a month [in compensation] for it, and it's more than I made in the mines."

A lot more. Tip Warren was born too fast. He grew old before the advent of skyrocket salaries. A good wage in his prime was $150 a month, and he says he did not reach that very often, if ever. Consider this: The old man worked half the century in an assortment of jobs and he did not make as much in total as a middling professional football player makes today in a month.

Not that he failed. That judgment depends on perspective. Warren says he lives better now than at any time in his life. He has taken the rocky road from the nineteenth century, but he lives in a tidy house that he rents from his daughter; he has a flush toilet and an electric range; and nothing light should be made of it. Ida is gone, but he says she made his life rich, and no man who has had a good woman has lived for naught.

"Ida died in 1971. And it didn't suit me to get married again. I had some hances, but I didn't want to, and I'm not lonely anyway. One of my sons comes by every day, and my daughter, Ethel, is in the house next to this. I go over there and visit or she comes here and visits. Maybe I'll go off in the hills. Maybe I'll go to town, if I can get a lift on the road. I got two television sets, you can see, one atop the other; I don't watch them much because it hurts my eyes after a while.

"I'm doing all right. I get $186 a month in Social Security, and with the black lung check it makes about $500. I only pay thirty-five dollars a month to Ethel for rent, and lights and heat and the rest don't come to a hundred more. There's food after that, and I eat good, but it means I always got some money left over. Not much, not a lot, but a little. I can buy something if I want, and I don't have to take welfare. I've gotten some government help, some surplus commodities, but not much more than that.

"My daddy didn't have anything. He had mules and some poor land is all. I've had automobiles, and an old Chevrolet truck I bought from a man. I've had $300 to $400 in the bank at a time. I've been to Florida, to Tennessee, and other places. Sometimes I wish I would have had more; I could have used it plenty. But I never wanted to live in a big house, like you see on the television, and everybody else seems to have, and I never wanted to dress up like they do. I like it here in Kentucky."

The old man turns on his stove to make breakfast. Bacon and eggs that come in cartons and packages. There is a cane against the kitchen wall. There are plastic flowers in a vase. There is a calender from the Huff Drug Company "Wishing You a Happy New Year," and there is a picture of family members framed in glass that reflects a bare bulb hanging from the ceiling.
There is also a stopped clock, which is apropos.
Tip Warren does not want to be completely up-to-date.

"I just like to sit and think. When I do it's about how it was. I don't care that I'm better off. I liked it when there wasn't so much. That's my opinion. I paid twenty dollars for a heifer once and got milk for ten years. You remember that suit I talked about? I wish I still had it. I thought that was a fine thing."

A study completed in 1987 suggested that elderly people who live alone, such as Tip Warren, are five times as likely to be poor as those who live in pairs. The study (by the Commonwealth Fund, an organization that specializes in health issues) said, however, that, unlike Mr. Warren, most of the singles are women. The research indicated that of 27 million Americans who are sixty-five or older and not institutionalized, one-third live alone, eight in ten of them are widows, 10 percent of the total are poor (against 4 percent of couples surveyed), and impoverished female singles outnumber impoverished males by 20 to 15 percent.

The study suggested that the number of elderly widows will quintuple by the year 2020, to 7.5 million, and, in a reversal of the time-honored lifeboat protocol, they— along with children under eighteen (13 million in poverty in 1987)—will most probably and demographically constitute the poorest people in America.

EDNA GARDNER WHYTE

Depending on the point of view, Edna Gardner Whyte was born one year before the advent of powered air flight or one year after. She thinks personally that it was the year before. She says the venerable Orville and Wilbur Wright took the first motorized flight in December 1903, at Kitty Hawk, North Carolina, but she and many others of this opinion may be in error. There is substantial evidence that a German immigrant named Gustave Whitehead got off the ground in 1901, several times actually, piloting a monoplane with butterfly wings near Long Island Sound.

Quibble, quibble.

In either case, says Mrs. Whyte:

"I was a child of this new invention. I grew up with it and became enthralled with it. People could get in a machine and go to the clouds. Wasn't that something? I got in my first plane when I was twenty-two. As soon as I touched the stick and saw the controls I knew that I was in love. I also knew what I wanted to do in life. I wanted to fly. I wanted to be part of it. I took an initial ride in 1926, and after that I took lessons so that I could get a private license.

"There was one problem. This was a long time ago and I was a woman. Women didn't fly, not very many of them. The men were in charge and they didn't think we should be up there. When I went to get my government license, the man said, 'What do YOU want a license for?' When I told him that I wanted a career in aviation, he said, 'I've never given a license to a woman before, and I'm not sure that I want to start doing it now.' He was so big, and so grouchy, and so intimidating that I got scared, and I had to beg him to give me the test.

"It was ridiculous. He was a government employee, and I paid my taxes, and that should have been all there was to it. But I was a woman, he could have stopped me; and back then I had to beg. I said, 'Please, give me a chance, give me a test run, let me take the written,' and I started to cry. Tears came down my cheeks because I wanted it so much. So he looked down at me, and he said 'Oh, all right, come on,' and he took me up and gave me my check ride and, probably much to his surprise, I passed."

Edna Whyte's birth day was in 1902. By then people had been trying to fly for thousands of years. The mythologists put Icarus en route to the sun on wings of wax. Leonardo da Vinci contended that a bird was merely an instrument and worked according to mathematical laws which man might reproduce. The French went up in balloons in 1783; American gliders were sent soaring in the 1890s; and, whoever built them first, gasoline airplanes were introduced just as automobiles were beginning to proliferate.

Never mind the Wright brothers here. They have already received their historic due. Gustave Whitehead, on the other hand, has not. He was a Saxon seaman who came to the United States in 1894 and settled into tinkering, odd jobs, and building aeroships in Fairfield, Connecticut. One ship was 36 feet long and anatomically correct. It had fixed wings, a fan tail, a fuselage, landing wheels, and an adjustable propeller. It wasn't sleek but it was revolutionary, the same as Whitehead himself.

A Connecticut newspaper reporter wrote that Whitehead made his maiden flight on August 14, 1901. The journalist said that Whitehead rolled out before dawn and went aloft when the sun came up. The story indicated that the airplane soared as high as forty feet for a distance of a half mile, but, alas, few took note of it. Whitehead may have had a brilliant mind, but he was an uninspired salesman. There were only two witnesses present. And skepticism lurked about. No other newspapers bothered to attend the launch.

Whitehead is said to have made subsequent flights before the Kitty Hawk incident. Yet he died broke and in obscurity at about the time E. G. Whyte got her license, and history since then has ignored him. The Wright brothers said the Whitehead flight was a myth. The Smithsonian Institution says there is not enough documentation to consider the claim seriously. A replica of the Whitehead plane was built in 1985, however, and flown 330 feet in 1986; that was 210 feet farther that the first Wright Flyer.

Nineteen eighty-six was also the sixtieth anniversary of Edna Gardner

Whyte's initial venture aloft. She's been at it now professionally for almost as long. She has watched aviation develop from pusher planes (engines in the rear) to moon flights; she has flown for a total of 34,000 hours, more than any other woman ever; and, at eighty-five, she still takes off daily. Iron Edna.

"I was very lucky when I was young to be influenced by a pair of women pilots named Katherine and Margery Stinson. I read about them first in 1915 and followed them from then on. Katherine was a 110-pound girl flying air shows all around the world—in Japan, in China, and over the English Channel. And she and her sister were both teaching flying down here in Texas, getting lots of publicity, when the men of this country didn't think women had brains enough to even vote in elections.

"The stuff about brains got me. I could not understand how I could go to school with these little boys, and get higher grades in most cases, but they still didn't think I had the intelligence to vote, or to fly, especially to fly. You don't know what it was like growing up like that. When I cried in front of that government man to get my license, it was not the first time I cried because I was a woman. I went to bed many a time crying my heart out because I was a woman in a man's world.

"Maybe it made me more determined, too. I was convinced I was as good as any man, and I wanted to prove it. That was one reason I got into flying. I wanted to get into a man's field to show I could do it. I didn't want to beg any more. During the First World War, President Wilson asked Katherine and Margery Stinson to teach men to fly for the military, and I thought that was wonderful. I figured that if I became a pilot I would be like them, and I wouldn't be left behind by the men.

"But there was another problem. Flying was expensive in those days. It's expensive now, but it used to be worse. There weren't many planes around; it was hard to find instructors to take you up; and they charged what the market would bear. I paid thirty-five dollars an hour for my first lessons, in 1920 dollars, and I was not flushed with money. I had to go into nursing so I could pay for it. I became a nurse in 1926, and I made seventy dollars a month. If I spent more than one hour a month in the air, I couldn't eat.

"I was in Seattle, Washington, then. I had been raised in Minnesota; I went to the Pacific Northwest to nurse; and I'll never forget the first instructor I had. He asked me 'Have you ever been up in an airplane before?' And I said 'No, I've never touched one, but I want to very much.' So he took me up the first time on a Saturday. He had an OH5 Jenny; it was an eight-cylinder World-War-I trainer, the kind you see in the films, with the pilot exposed and his scarf blowing around.

"I took a couple of lessons from that man. And it was a rough start. He would take off badly, and he would land even worse. We would come in all crooked, and we would bounce around on the ground and turn 45 or 180 degrees. I figured that was the way you did it. But on the third lesson we landed and ground-looped, and took the lower wingtip off. And when we got out to look at the damage, another man came up to me and said, 'Edna, you better find another pilot. This guy has only flown for eight hours.'

"I took the advice, and I got a more experienced pilot. He could at least land without bouncing around so much. Still, it was trial and error in the 1920s. There wasn't much ground training, and you learned by going up and doing it. The pilot would sit in the front seat, and he would yell something back, and you'd try to do what he said. I took ten hours of instruction by 1928—that was two years after flying licenses became mandatory in the country. My private license number was 4013, which meant I was the 4013th person to get one."

In 1929 Iron Edna took her nursing abilities and her fetish for flying into government service. She was commissioned in the Navy Nursing Corps, where, she says, she was given three meals a day and free time at the airport. She says she would have liked to have joined the military outright, as a pilot, but it was not allowed, and all she could do in exasperation was to grumble:

"I wanted to fly the mail on one of those beautiful military planes, but they would not so much as let a woman touch them. I talked with the Army several times, but it was no use. So the only recourse I had was to get even in my own way. I had started to teach flying by that time, and every time I took someone up for a lesson and we would see other planes in the sky, I would say: 'See that nice straight stream, that's a girl pilot, but see that crooked one, that's a boy pilot.'

"Well, word got around what I was doing, because I used to talk about it all the time. Every time I got some of those men in their fancy uniforms together, wearing the chickens and the stars on their shoulders, I told them that story. So I guess they finally decided to shut me up. One day they invited me out to fly some of their planes. Oh, I had a ball! And I apparently did all right, because the fellow who went up with me said that Edna Whyte was one woman who could become a combat pilot.

"I never did become one, but you can say I've done everything else. I've flown everything from cloth planes to helicopters. I've filled thirty-four log books with trips. I bought my first plane in 1932, when I paid six hundred dollars for an Travelair. The payments were thirty-nine dollars a month, which was a lot of money, but it was more than worth it. I've never been without a plane after that. I've owned more than fifty altogether. I've also owned two airports. I've still got several of the planes today, and I've got one of the airports.

"I kept that first airplane at an airport on Cape Cod, in Massachusetts. That was during Prohibition, when people were shipping all the illegal liquor along the East Coast and other people were picking it up and selling it at tremendous profits. So one day this man came up to me at the airport and asked me if I would fly out to Martha's Vineyard and identify the color of a flag that was anchored in an inlet. I said okay. I went out and saw that it was blue, and when I told the man he gave me twenty dollars.

"I thought that was great. And the next time he asked me to do it, he gave me another twenty dollars, and so on and so forth. Twenty dollars here, twenty dollars there, and I thought I was getting rich. I could make my airplane payments, I could pay my hanger bills and my gas, and I still had some left over. But after a few weeks someone called me aside and said 'Edna, don't you know what you're doing?' And I said no, what? And he said, 'You darn fool, you're spotting the pickup points for the rumrunners!'"

Iron Edna says she gave up the payoffs reluctantly. Yet she soon found another way to pay for her flying. Barnstorming. She says the word comes from the days when itinerant actors performed in barns, when no theaters were available, and the term went airborne after World War I. Some pilots barnstormed at fairs and air shows while others, like Mrs. Whyte, one of the few ladies to take the risks, did it at every Middlesex village and farm.

"I started in the 1930s, when barnstorming was getting a bad reputation. There weren't many safety regulations and there weren't many good fliers, and that meant there were a lot of accidents. But I knew what I was doing, and I did it in a good aircraft. I had a Stinson SMA-8, which was a big cabin plane, and I used that in Mississippi and Louisiana, and through there. Then I barnstormed in a J-5BI south of Norfolk, along the Atlantic, down into North Carolina and the peanut patches.

"I would simply drop down into a field along a big highway and wait for people to stop for a look. Airplanes were still unusual in, say, 1935 and 1936, and they always attracted attention. Particularly if they weren't at an airport. So I'd land and wait. Pretty soon the cars would stop, people would come over and start asking about the plane, and I would offer to sell them rides. I could take four people at a time in the J-5BI, and I charged them three dollars a piece, until no one was left.

"I think I also attracted people because of my sex. It turned out there was something good about being a woman after all. I didn't play on it, though. I didn't promote myself, and I didn't try to play the part of the dashing aviatrix. I didn't wear the flowing scarf or anything like that. People have always said that Edna Whyte is one woman who flies in a dress. I did too, sometimes. Other times I wore slacks, and I wore the old flying cap, the leather one, the one with the chin straps and goggles.

"I made sure the rides were brief. I wanted to make money, and I had to get as many people in the air as possible. I got them seated quickly, I took right off, I'd circle the pasture or something, and then I'd land to pick up another load. The more people there were, the shorter the rides. We would get them up and down in just a few minutes, and that was the way it went, hour after hour; I don't think anybody ever thought they were being short-changed. I think they all got their money's worth.

"There was one time, however, I landed near the Virginia border and about a hundred cars stopped. There were so many people, and we sold so many tickets, that I got to worrying if I'd have enough gas. So I cut the rides even shorter than usual. I took off with one wing down, so I would leave the ground in a turn, and I'd go right around in a circle and sideslip it, and then land. Pretty soon people began to complain. They said I didn't even know enough about flying to keep my wings straight."

Mrs. Whyte says in hindsight that the merry-go-round tours were not the wisest flying she's done. But she adds that, with courage, danger has always been a cockpit companion. She's flown in weather where engine oil had to be thawed out before using, and she's made landings where there have been more holes than earth. She says in six decades of it, she has crashed twice.

"The first time I was flying a Waco F, and it was very windy day. You can get kind of cocky when you're lucky, and I was always pretty lucky. I probably shouldn't have tried to take off in the wind, but I did. I taxied down to the end of the runway, and when I got there and started to make my turn, the wind was going thirty-eight to forty miles an hour, and it picked me right up and turned me over. It was good it happened on the ground and not in the air; still, the plane took six months to be repaired.

"I was not hurt in the crash. But let's face it, plenty of women have been killed in planes over the years, and sometimes I don't think we remember that. Everyone has heard of Amelia Earhart [lost in the Pacific in 1937], but she has only been one of many. I counted it up once, and there were thirteen pioneer women who gave their lives for aviation. There have been a lot more since then, but in the early days, in the days of Amelia Earhart, there were thirteen killed in planes, including Amelia.

"Personally, I don't think it's fair to remember Amelia and not the rest. I don't want to belittle Amelia, but a lot of her story was promoted. She had a husband [George Palmer Putnam] who was the heel who promoted her. Amelia was a great loss to aviation and she was a great loss to women in general, but she was used by George Palmer Putnam. He would promote something for her and she would do it even though she may not have been qualified, bless her heart, and people don't realize that.

"I hate to talk this way, but Amelia did very little flying other than what her husband promoted. She didn't instruct, for example, and she was not the greatest flyer of the time; that was all promotion. Meanwhile, and here's the way I look at it, other women have been lost and they have been completely forgotten. Mildred Dolan was lost over the Pacific, for example, and she's been forgotten. We had Marjorie Miller and Harriet Quamby, who went down on other flights, and they've been forgotten.

"Thirteen women. And I want to say one more thing about this same thing. There was my friend Laura Ingalls, she was a flight instructor on Long Island, and one year she flew a Lockheed Orient to Mexico City, to Peru, and back up to New York, and she didn't get anything for it. The New York papers gave her a few inches and that was all. But a year and three months later Amelia flew to Mexico City and back, and was lost for a couple of days, and her husband put it in every newspaper in the world.

"I don't know. Maybe I shouldn't say that. But it does make me mad. Women have taken their share of the risks. The second time I crashed I had a passenger with me, a student. That was more recently, in 1985, when I was eighty-three. We were in a OX5-Waco 10; it was on the runway then too. My student turned and went between two trees, and there was a big electric cable there; I pulled the plane up but the front wheels caught. We tipped over. The student was okay, thank God, but that time I broke my nose."

Iron Edna got out of nursing in the late 1930s and became a full-time flying instructor. She trained military pilots during World War II, married a co-captain after that, and built an airport in Roanoke, Texas, near Fort Worth, in 1969. She says she has taught more than 4800 students, many of them women; she is now the oldest surviving female instructor in the land and the last of what used to be called the powder-puff pioneers.

She lives in a home that is attached to a hanger at the Friendly Aero-Valley Airport. She has 127 air-race trophies; she belongs to four halls of fame; she won the Charles Lindbergh Lifetime Achievement Award in 1987; and she still flies seven days a week.

"There's a story I tell about building this airport. It goes back to this thing about male versus female. I was just getting started, and I needed five thousand dollars to complete some construction, so I went to the Small Business Administration for help. They said 'What did you say you wanted the money for—an airport?' Then they said I'd have to wait a few days for an answer. And finally they just said no. They said I was too old, for God's sake—I was seventy—and they said a woman couldn't build an airport.

"That reminded me of the good old days. But I built the darn thing anyway. I started with thirty-four acres, and now the whole place covers 220 acres. There are seventy-seven hangers and about 400 planes, and we have more business than we can handle. I wish I could get the Small Business Administration to take a look. They wouldn't give me a measly five thousand dollars, but if they would go down to the courthouse and take a look at the tax rolls, they would find the airport they thought I couldn't build is assessed at seven million dollars.

"Maybe that's why I keep flying. Maybe I'm still trying to prove myself as a woman. But also I'm grateful. I'm grateful for the sixty-one years, and I keep trying to pay something back for it. I thank the Lord every year when I pass my flight physical. It means I can keep on teaching this wonderful way of life. I don't think I would last six months if I had to retire. Oh, maybe I would. Maybe I could find a little old ladies' home that had a landing strip, and I could stay alive by taking the gals up now and then."

Mary Hougas says that it seemed like a good job at the time. She was a young woman in Ottawa, Illinois, looking with others of her group for what opportunity there was in the small community, and she was hired to do detail work at a radium-dial company. "You know the clocks that glow in the dark?" she says. "The hands used to be coated with a radium substance, and we did the painting. They gave us the stuff in little jars, and we used regular artists' brushes, all day long, every day. Everybody thought it was great. We didn't know much about radiation then."

We do now. Mrs. Hougas and others believe the work was the death of a substantial number of the dial painters. Mrs. Hougas keeps a list of employees who have died of cancer, seventeen of nineteen from one group alone. She says she has had bouts with the disease herself, including the necessity for a mastectomy, and she links it to the radium:

"You had to see what we did to believe it. We got that paint all over everything. Some women would paint it on their fingernails to impress their boyfriends, and some women would lick the bristles of their brush to give it a nice point. The room I worked in was covered with the stuff. It was on the floors, on the walls, on the doors. If you spilled it you wiped it up with a rag, and then you used the rag for other things. I washed, naturally, but I couldn't get clean. My kids used to ask me to get in the closet at home so they could see me shine.

"I didn't work for the company when it started. Back then they didn't have rules at all. But even when I was there, beginning in the 1930s, there weren't many protections. Nobody really warned us. And nobody for sure said that it was any kind of a threat to our lives. There was some talk, and the company just said it was lies. One day one of the supervisors said the paint was so safe he could drink it, and so he did. He mixed some of it in a glass of water and took it in front of us. He's one of the people who have died since, from cancer, the poor man."

Mrs. Hougas worked in the dial factory for thirty-one years. She says the original painting building was closed when the risks began to be known (1968), after which it was used as a meat locker (some customers of the locker have also died of cancer). Mrs. Hougas says the government investigated the circumstances at one time, but it did not issue any condemnations, and lawsuits have been filed that have also failed officially to fix blame. Meantime, many former workers who are still alive have nightmares about their futures.

Mrs. Hougas:

"I don't like to talk about it any more. Some of the ladies won't talk it all. What's the use? Who do you go to? What can you do? We had a mortician in town who said people could take a geiger counter to our graveyard and hear it tick over the dead."

BEANE KLAHR

Given allowances for age perhaps, and other variables, there is someone like Beane Klahr on the main street of every small town in America. They own a store, a shop or an agency; they carry family names well known in the vicinity; they open their doors when the rush hour is still in progress, then they do not sit still for a moment all day. Friendly but proper. Wizened and a bit wan. They wear white shirts with pocket protectors; they wave from behind plate-glass windows; they hear the mysterious invoices of routine, it is said; and they have been around, at the same stand, remarkably, since anyone can remember.

Good thing.

Beane Klahr has been a jeweler for longer than most people have been people. He started in his father's lap, when diamonds were much younger and gold was twenty dollars an ounce, and he has been in the same store in Middletown, Pennsylvania, since stickpins were in vogue. Who says the world turns? Klahr Jewelry was established in 1885; it has a print on the wall of Abraham Lincoln, who had only been dead twenty years when the store opened, and it still has the safe that was installed in 1910. One of the businesses of business, in this consideration, is to provide an implement of constancy.

Mr. Klahr is eighty-eight. He is much the same now as always. He is punctual, skilled, efficient, and determined. He is likewise professionally adjustable. He has weathered every economic storm of the century, and then some. He has remained solvent through floods, depressions, wars, and even a nuclear disaster:

"The Three Mile Island power plant is just east of downtown. You've heard of it, I assume. I can see the cooling towers from one of the rooms above my store, and people always ask if that doesn't make me nervous. No. Not at all. I didn't like it when the accident took place, but I wasn't really worried about the plant itself. I was worried about business. I've always felt like the plant was perfectly safe, even when the meltdown happened, but others got scared, and everything went flat.

"There was this one girl who comes to the store regularly. I have a little photo-finishing business here, where people drop off their film, and this girl comes by to pick it up for the developer. She's very nice and does her job, but she got real concerned during the radiation scare. People were jumpy, and the radios were giving warnings, and she just stopped making her rounds. Even now, when she comes to town, she'll come to the store but she will not drive past Three Mile Island."

The old man shakes his head. You can never tell about people under eighty. He sits in a chair aside a jeweler's bench. He has a magnifying glass clipped to his spectacles. The cash register rings in the background, as do chime clocks when the hour hands are straight up, and he says without being asked "We deal in American merchandise only; we think it's best in the long run."

There are about 360 licensed businesses in Middletown, most of them small. There are more than 7.3 million businesses in the rest of the nation, including farms, most of which are also small. Small business is defined here as those entities that employ fewer than 100 employees, but otherwise the term in a misnomer. Small business is big business in the American twentieth century. Places like Klahr Jewelry employ three of every four people in the workforce (74 million out of 111 million workers). They form the spine of the economy.

And Beane Dean Klahr was born to the manor, literally. He says he was birthed in an apartment over his shop, back when watch fobs and brooches were hot items—and still lives there today.

You have an unusual name, Mr. Klahr.

"It's Pennsylvania Dutch. We are old Germans."

What about the given names?

"My father took my middle name from a local doctor he knew."

And Beane?

"Some people pronounce it Bean-iee, but don't repeat that."

Klahr says he was given his first jeweler's glass when he was a schoolboy and was delighted to see what everything looked like at 2.5 power, but he had wanderlust. He joined the army at seventeen.

"That was the First World War. I never got to it, however. They put me in the cavalry, so my means of transportation was a horse, and they sent me to Fort Bliss, Texas, right down on the Mexican border. The United States was worried that the Germans might try to invade this country through Mexico, and they sent us there to keep watch. Fort Bliss is a missile base now, it's connected to the White Sands Missile Range in New Mexico, but you wouldn't have believed the place in 1918. There was nothing but desert, and El Paso was like a little village.

"I was in the Fifth Cavalry, and we did some things with the Seventh Cavalry, which was George Custer's old outfit. The Seventh was a legend even then. It hadn't been that long since the Indian wars, and they were tough fellows. I guess we were all tough. You had to be tough to sit on a horse all that time. We didn't have Jeeps and trucks, and we didn't march; the horse was still the thing. We rode two-by-two in columns; the horses pulled the artillery; and we were taught that one of our jobs was to take care of the animals.

"As a matter of fact, we were taught to take care of the horses before we took care of ourselves. If we were out in the field and we stopped to eat, we had the feed the horses first; we had to give them water before we could drink. When we finished for the day and got back to camp, they had to be groomed. You'd brush them, to get rid of the sweat and dirt, and check them over to see they weren't injured. They were kept in stables which always had to be clean, and there was a stable sergeant to make sure everything was done right.

"I had two horses to take care of. There were more horses than troopers, so some of us got double duty. I don't know if any of them had names, but they all had numbers. I remember riding horse number 1, for some reason, but I don't think it was mine. The number was branded on one shoulder, and the initials U.S. were burned into the hooves, to identify military property. Some of the horses had a third brand as well. If the animal wasn't any good any more, or got too old, they would brand it IS, which meant it had been inspected and condemned.

"I was at Fort Bliss for almost two years. The Germans never tried to come across the border, but we did have some trouble with Pancho Villa, the bandit. Mexico was not a republic yet, and Pancho was still making raids and causing trouble. One time he came into Juarez, Mexico, and shot up the town, and some of the bullets came into El Paso. The United States didn't like it, so we were sent across the Rio Grande to hunt him down. It was like an invasion, only no war was declared. We chased Pancho all the way to his camp, but we never found him.

"That was after the World War had ended. But I was still in uniform. I was nineteen. Then I found out that my father needed me at home. The man who was working for him in the store had left and became a competitor, and my father asked me to get out of the army, which wasn't easy. I told my commander that I had enlisted for the duration of the war, and I wanted to leave because the war was over. He said no, I didn't enlist for the duration of the war, but for the duration of the emergency, and he said the emergency was not finished. I finally got out at the end of 1919, and I went back to Middletown to stay."

Middletown is a town of 10,000 people. It was named because it has half-way between Lancaster and Carlisle on one of the original trade and travel trails that joined eastern and western Pennsylvania. It is also just beyond the suburbs of Harrisburg, the state capital, and sits on the northern bank of the Susquehanna River at a bend that incorporates Three Mile Island.

"My father learned the jewelry business from his brother. And he passed the lessons on down to me. See my fingers; do you notice anything? There's no sweat. Jewelers and watchmakers, they should not sweat. Sweat contains acid—most people don't know that—and when you touch something you leave it behind. It's usually no problem, but it's bad in the jewelry business, where you don't want to corrode gold or silver. So my father taught me how to keep from sweating. I've learned to control it.

"I lived above the store when I got back from the army, and then I got married and moved out. When my father died in 1937, I took over the business and moved back in. There were still gasoline lights in the place then. I had to rework the wiring and everything. I tried to rent the apartment on the third floor, but nobody wanted it, and it was probably just as well. I raised four kids of my own here over the years, and it's been convenient; when I go to work I just slide down the banister.

"Other than the remodeling, the store is pretty much the same as it always was. It's not very big, but it's about right for this town. In the old days, when we didn't have air conditioning, we used to raise the big window back here, then open the front door, and we got a very nice crossventilation. Ask Agnes here. She's my right hand; she's been working for me for thirty-one years. Agnes, didn't we use to open the window? It was nice and cool, wasn't it? Yes, it was; that's how I kept from sweating.

"I think I still run the business like my father. It's not fancy, but we make a living. I have never made the jewelry we sell, because that's not necessary. There are too many people to buy it from. I have gem men and watch men and others, and we sell everything from necklaces to trinkets. I didn't used to take the photographic film, but it's in demand now. If a person comes in and wants something special, we can get it. You don't stay in business if you don't, and we try to stay in business.

"I shouldn't have said we don't make jewelry. I've done it from time to time. Someone can show me a picture, and I can do it. And we also do a lot of repairs. Or when we sell a ring, we probably have to fit it to size. We can work with gold or silver. I remember when gold was thirty-eight dollars the ounce; I remember when it was twenty dollars and sixty-seven cents an ounce; and I remember when it was a thousand dollars an ounce, which was during that completely crazy time in the late 1970s; the most I ever paid for an ounce of silver was fifty dollars.

"I have to turn down some of the stuff that comes in for repair. It's just not good enough to fix. But I can do anything else, and it doesn't matter how expensive. People in this town don't like to go anywhere else with their good stuff. I had a lady call me today with a Tiffany ring, and she said I just had to take it because I was the only one she trusted. She didn't want to go to Harrisburg, she didn't want to go to the mall, because she thinks the jewelers there are nothing but a bunch of crooks.

"That's how we have continued. There have been a lot of ups and downs since this store was opened, but we have built a reputation. The shopping malls have hurt very much; they are all around today; and they have all these signs on the window: FIFTY PERCENT OFF, SALE, SALE! But people still come back here, because they know we'll treat them right. They know we're more expensive, but they know we'll give them the best price we can, They know when they come in the store, we won't look at them as if they are going to steal something. And they know we'll be here tomorrow; people in the malls tend to go out of business."

Klahr says he has not in sixty-five years worried about going out of business. Good times or the opposite. He says the government closed a nearby military base after the Spanish-American War and it closed another one during the combat in Vietnam, yet the Klahr family coped by diversifying. He says the store stayed open during other misfortunes by cutting prices. "I recall the river flooding to where you could hardly see Union Street, but I was still here, bright and early, in case anyone was interested."

As for Three Mile Island, same thing:

"I always approved of that power plant, even when they first started talking about its construction. I knew about the dangers of radiation, because my first wife died of it. She got sick and the doctors gave her radioactive treatments, and she got cancer from that. But I didn't worry about it in the plant, and I thought it would improve people's health. Before TMI was built, they had a coal-burning plant on the river. They brought the coal in railroad cars, and crushed it, and then burned it to make electricity, and you couldn't breathe without inhaling soot."

The Three Mile Island accident occurred on March 28, 1979. It was caused by human and mechanical error. Gas was permitted to invade the vent-

ing system, and a large hydrogen bubble formed at the top of one of the plant's two reactor containment vessels. The result was the worst nuclear-power scare in United States history. The reactor lost much of its coolant, and the heating material cooked to the point of partially melting. Pennsylvania declared a local emergency; the entire East Coast of the nation was transfixed; there was concern that the uranium would burst its bounds and many people would die from the radioactivity.

Mr. Klahr:

"The first news came during the day. I happened to be talking on a radio station at the time. One of the stations came in to ask me about the history of the town and put me on the air. When I got done the mailman was in the store, and he said he liked the broadcast, and little stuff like that, and then he said that something had gone wrong down at Three Mile Island. I said, what? And he repeated: there was something going on at the plant. That was a Thursday, and there wasn't much news as yet.

"Everybody knew about it by Friday. And this town started to turn upside down. People got frightened, you know how they are; well, many of them went overboard. I didn't. And I told people I wouldn't. I had heard Paul Harvey talk about it on the radio. He said someone had put a geiger counter along a public building in Washington, D.C., where there was natural radiation in the stone, and Paul Harvey said it measured more leaking radiation than was occurring at the Three Mile Island reactor.

"But you couldn't tell that to some people. They just panicked. Everybody had a rumor—the cows were dropping dead in the fields, or the milk was ruined, or the plant would explode. I kept drinking milk right through it, from a local dairy, but some other people wouldn't even buy local food. Then the state put out some stuff about evacuating, and thousands of people packed their clothes and left. I knew a lot of them. I think half the town went someplace else before the whole thing blew over.

"I opened the store every day, as usual. They told us to stay inside if we didn't leave, and not open the windows, and I went along with that. But I kept the store open. I had a friend from whom I had bought a lot of jewelry, and he was in Japan at the time, and he called his office and told them to help Beane Klahr any way they could, give me anything I needed, and take me anyplace I wanted to go. He thought the whole place had been destroyed and there was nothing but a hole left in Middletown.

"There's no doubt about it that business was hurt. People still came in; I still made sales. But the climate was bad. They had ambulances running all around taking the old people out of the nursing homes, and the police cars were driving in and out, and the reporters were everywhere. I know people who just threw things in their cars and left without locking their doors. The mayor here, he said that if anyone was caught looting homes, they would be shot. He meant it, and nobody lost anything.

"And the cows were okay. The thing went on for a couple of weeks before it died down, and after that there were all these stories about the cows aborting and chickens laying green eggs. It never happened. I have a friend who has a farm within a half-mile of Three Mile Island, and he said everything was normal. I think most people here came to know that. There weren't very many who moved away permanently. Today, you hardly know the plant is there. One of the reactors is producing power, and they are still working on the one that went wrong. Nobody thinks about it any more. All in all, it's been a good neighbor."

Beane Klahr is the oldest merchant in Middletown. He runs the oldest family-owned business in his county. He is a member of the Chamber of Commerce, Rotary International, and when he stands on a chair to reach the merchandise he keeps on the top shelf the second Mrs. Klahr holds him steady by pushing against his rear end. Pewter plates. Gold chains. Pens and pencils. Dodads and thingamajabbers. "I used to appraise jewelry also, but I don't do it any more. Suppose I appraise a ring for thirty-five hundred and the owner takes it someplace else where it's appraised for forty-five hundred; well, the fellow may sue me, and it's not worth that chance."

He is a cheerful man. His suits are too large. His wife says, "You know what people do with Beane, they buy something someplace else, then they show it to him to get his opinion, and he always tells them yes, it's nice." *He nods at that. True.*

He takes a business card from his pocket. It reads: "If I die tonight my soul will be in H _____ tomorrow, signed _____ . *Fill in the right word, sign your name, and carry this card with you so that the preacher can tell the truth at your funeral."*

He rubs his dry hands.

"Three Mile Island was nothing. Taxes are what hurts. They put a new tax on business recently—it was a surcharge on electricity use—and I tried to fight it. I got hold of a list of more than 350 business people in Middletown, and I wrote to all of them to have a meeting. You know how many showed up? Only twenty-three showed up. They won't stay in business very long that way."

9. Growing Old

FINIS MITCHELL

In 1975, when he was seventy-three years old, or maybe it was 1981, when he was seventy-nine (history does always not have to be certain to be instructive), Finis Mitchell fell into a crevasse as he was crossing a glacier in the Wyoming portion of the Rocky Mountains. He confesses that it was a witless blunder. The crevasse was covered over with powdered snow that he had not adequately probed, and when he dropped through he twisted a leg.

"The heel came all the way back up to my ear and the toes went in the other direction, and these ligaments in here was all busted. The knee hurt like the devil. I managed to pull myself out of the hole, but I couldn't stand up. The leg wouldn't take it. I took a step or two and fell down again."

So there he was. Crippled on a piece of ice in some of the most merciless wilderness in America. Seventy-three or seventy-nine, and let's not get into that again. Younger men with both legs working have perished under better conditions. But there is something to be said for experience—it is, as the Belgians maintain, the comb that nature gives man when he is bald—and Mitchell had long before learned the rules of survival. He crawled over the snow to a forest, where he nursed his knee with an icepack made from his underwear. When the swelling subsided, a day later, he turned a tree branch into a crutch and limped to the safety of a road that was eighteen miles and forty-eight hours away.

Mitchell says his mother had said it years before, and she was right: the Wind River Range can be intimidating.

"My dad brought us out here in 1906. We had a farm in Missouri, and Dad traded it for a hundred and sixty acres at the foot of the mountains. My mother didn't much like it. We chartered a boxcar on the railroad, and we put everything we had in it. My dad put all of the household goods at one end of the car and all the livestock on the other end. I've never told this before, but between the livestock and the furniture there was quite an opening, a space, and that's where Dad put the mattresses and the bedding stuff, and it's where we all lived on the way out to Wyoming.

"Now here is what is secret about the story. We weren't supposed to be living on that boxcar. My dad had permission to stay with the livestock, to keep them quiet and such, but it was against the rules for the rest of us. So we had this big trunk, and it was supposed to be filled with clothes and things, but that's where we hid whenever the train was stopped. It worked okay until one time when we were stopped, in Denver, and an inspector came around and heard me cough in the trunk. My dad said it was a cat, and the inspector let us go.

"Oh, how Mother hated the whole business. I'm sure she'd rather have stayed in Denver than come to Wyoming. This was still the frontier then. And my dad's hundred-sixty acres was way out in the wild, right up against the Wind River range. The guy who traded it was a shyster. The land was bleak and it wasn't worth a dime. It was sagebrush and sand. There wasn't a house, there wasn't a road, there wasn't any water. My mother took one look and she just sat down and cried. She said 'Reese'—that was my dad's name—she said, 'Reese, please, let's go back home.'

" 'Home?' my father said, 'this *is* home.' "

Pinedale, Wyoming. The population then was fifty to one hundred. It is situated midway between Yellowstone Park and the Flaming Gorge Recreation Area, to give a hint of the ambience, and it is the western gateway to the ferociously splendid Wind River Range.
Finis Mitchell is the lord of that range.

"I climbed my first mountain in 1908. My dad decided to hunt for elk, and he took the entire family along. We had a team of horses and a wagon, and we went north of New Fork lake. My dad went high on a ridge, and I went along as his shadow. We walked all morning and didn't take a shot, and so I got restless and I asked him if we could see anything if we went to the top of one of the mountains. He said he didn't know, but we went up, and it just took my breath away. We were at the top of the world. We looked over the trees and the rivers; it was spectacular.

"I've been climbing over the Wind River Range from that day to this. I've climbed 229 of the mountains, and I've been all over the glaciers and the lakes. I've climbed some of the mountains many times. I've been up my own mountain many times. The United States Geological Service named a mountain after me in 1973. They weren't supposed to do it, because the rule is that you are supposed to be dead before they do it. But I told them I was half dead, anyway. Mount Mitchell is on the south end of the range. It's 12,482 feet high; all told, I've climbed it twenty times."

Half dead? The Lord of the Wind River Range is not normally so humble. Nor that much in error. But in this case he is just playing along with an old tune. There is an onerous conception in the nation that a person of eighty-five is washed up. The whimsy is that there is not much future in old age. Stephen Leacock said that the only good thing about being elderly is that it is better than being postelderly, and who was it who said "First one forgets names, then one forgets faces, then one forgets to pull the zipper up, and finally the zipper down"? What did he know?

All right, there is some truth in it. Given alternatives, growing old would be outlawed. It leads to limitations. George Burns says that one problem with aging is that "a lot of us have had arthritis since it first came out." The wicked witch is always doddering, while Snow White is in her teens. In 1987, there were 1.5 million retired people living in nursing homes; there were 3.5 million below the poverty level; and one in four required help in performing some daily activity. And of course there was this: people born at the first of the century who had survived to 1987 had an average of from five to eight years to live.

Yet the easy characterizations of the elderly are careless. And the stereotyping is normally misleading. The first children of the 1900s have not only been fighting war, pestilence, and famine; they have been battling the debilitations that have always been associated with growing old. When Finis Mitchell was born, there were only 360,000 Americans over the age of eighty-five, almost all of them enfeebled, chronically ill, and housebound. There are now three million men and women over eighty-five; the group comprises one of the fastest-growing segments of the population; and the majority are not so dreary as the fairy tales suggest.

Generally speaking, in the late 1980s only a quarter of the older olds fit the stereotypical embodiment. For every one in a nursing home, two others were not. For every one in poverty, two were not. For every one living alone, two were not. According to the National Center for Health Statistics, 74 percent of men over eighty-five were married, 70 percent were living with their spouses, 72 percent of both sexes had homes "within minutes" of their children, and, to go on: 60 percent had no difficulty walking, 72 percent had no difficulty bathing, 74 percent had no difficulty preparing meals, 76 percent had no problem managing money, and 77 percent did their own (light) housework.

The poets say there can be a second bud in advanced age. Easy for them if they've never caught a seed under their dentures, but they are entirely right.

Ronald Reagan was president at seventy-seven, Xavier Cugat started his band again at eighty-seven, and Finis Mitchell still climbs peaks at eighty-five. Gag writer Robert Orborn says that the first thing people should do when they turn sixty-five is to plant a pair of acorns, ten feet apart, and buy a hammock. Scarlett O'Hara said tomorrow is another day. Since 1900, the average lifespan has grown by a quarter of a century, almost as much as had been accumulated in the previous five millennia; and, good to say, the extra time is often used wisely.
   Look at Mount Mitchell.

"I would have liked to have spent every day in the wilderness, even when I was young. But I got married to a wonderful woman, I met her at a picnic, and I had to support my family. So I worked like everybody else. I worked for the railroad, and I was also in a sawmill one time. There was a sawmill on Little Boulder Creek. My dad had taught me how to fall a tree in any direction, even away from where it was leaning, and I went to work at it. The fellows who owned the mill figured that two of us should cut three thousand board feet of lumber a day, but we did better than that. We did twice that. Boy, we really went to town!

"Then one year the fellow who packed the mail in our area, he froze to death on the trail. That was between South Pass and the Big Sandy stage station. I was a pretty husky young kid, and that's what they needed for the job, so I was hired. I did it with a horse and a toboggan. There was another fellow who packed the mail in the summer, in a dilapidated old automobile, but it had to go by horse in the bad weather. And it could get bad, boy! Eight feet of snow was nothing back in the hills. When the wind blew and the stuff got to drifting, you could stand between the telephone poles and reach up to the wires.

"The mail job was a doozy. I only packed it about eight and a half miles, but it could get mean. The Big Sandy stage station had a cave dug into the steep side of a hill, where there was a draw come down off the mountain, and we'd stay in it all night. There were two of us. The other fellow brought the mail from Elkhorn, and I brought mine from South Pass, and then we'd exchange it. It was a little like the Pony Express. I had a first class sack, and it was locked with a padlock, and it was very important stuff. I had to sign an agreement that if anything happened out there I had to keep possession of the mail.

"Things did happen. That's why the guy who had the job before me froze to death. When it was stormy we had some terrible blizzards, and there wasn't any shelter for miles. I got into it once. It got so bad that my horse couldn't stay on the trail. I could feel my way through the snow, but the horse slid off the ice, and when he did that he hurt himself. He wrecked his damn leg at that time, and I had to kill him. I'm not supposed to say damn, but it was bad, it was the only horse I owned. Also, I couldn't just throw the mail sack away, because of the rule, and I had to cart it on foot all the rest of the way.

"Others froze out there too. People had to have their feet cut off. It's rough country on the range, but I loved it; I have always loved it. It's a place where a man can be his real self. I've told people that for years. I print it on post-cards so it's down in black and white: 'The Wind River Range is a place designed by God. Here you can speak the language of the wilderness. Here you can rejoice in nature. . . . The glistening of the moon on a glacier, the music of waterfalls, the eternity of the mountains. . . . You can trod the mountains and recognize that this is a prayer; God bless those who preserve the wilderness.' "

The Wind River Range defines the Continental Divide in the Bridger-Teton National Forest. It runs for 125 miles in west-central Wyoming and includes the highest peaks in the state. The mountains are relatively young (they were cut to their present shape by glaciers that moved in 9000 years ago), and ten of the glaciers continue to be the largest formations of the kind in the contiguous United States. There are several hundred mountains. The United States Geologic Survey says there are 3000 lakes. There is an Indian reservation to the east, an elk refuge to the west, and 2.2 millions acres of federal set-aside.

Mitchell moved into the range itself the year of the Great Depression. He had been working for the railroad, putting money away for a house, when he lost the objective and the savings to the crash. He says the railroad laid him off, the bank closed down, and he was forced to turn to the land for sustenance.

Forced?

"Actually I was freed. I always wanted to become a mountain man. Like Jim Bridger and Jedidiah Smith. I was twenty-seven years old, and the first thing I did was to start trapping. You could get a federal permit for five dollars a year, and I knew how to do it because I had grown up doing it. Catch muskrat and mink. Jim Bridger did it when he was alive [1804-1881]. He lived in this part of the state. He had a fur company here, and he was a guide. There's a Fort Bridger now, it's west of Rock Springs; he was one of the men who brought civilization to the mountains.

"I got a dollar for a muskrat pelt, and maybe three or four dollars for a mink, so I was partial to the minks. I set traps every week, and I'd get three or four at a time. The nature of a mink is to walk along the edge of a stream, that's how he fishes for his food, and that's where I trapped them. I looked for places where the water ran against a high piece of bank, and I laid the trap a few inches in the stream. It was steel spring. You can bait the trap if you like, but you don't need to. If you got it in the right place, the mink will walk right in, and, pop!

"Then my wife and I had a friend who steered me in a different direction. He said, 'Finis, why don't you get you a tent, and some horses, and set up a fishing camp right there in those mountains, because there are a lot of tourists starting to come up here, and they'll pay you to take them out.' And that's what I did. We rented some horses and got some old saddles and pitched a tent at the Big Sandy Openings. It was on the edge of the range, and we called it the Mitchell Fishing Camp. There's a big lodge there today, right on the same spot.

"That tent became my home and my business. My wife and I lived in it for years. It was twelve by fourteen feet, and it had three-foot walls, and it cost twenty dollars. We had a little sheep-wagon stove in one corner, and a table in another corner, and a bed in the back end. And that's all we had. It was all right; I had lived in a lot worse places than that. It was good and dry, and the stove kept it warm. Then if you opened the flap, there they were, the mountains, just as God made them. I thought it was great, and all these people would come up and pay me to do exactly what I wanted to do: take them into the range.

"Everything went fine. I was in heaven, boy. But there was one thing that was wrong. We only had fish in three lakes up there. The fish were native cut-throats, and they couldn't migrate from one lake to another, because the mountains were too high. Fish travel the streams, but they can't swim straight up, and we are talking about waterfalls that are three hundred and four hundred feet high in many cases. So the fish congregated in just a few lower lakes, and that wasn't good for business. So what we did was to transplant them ourselves; this was in the 1930s, and we carried the fish from one lake to another all over.

"I don't even know if it was legal to do that. I'm sure today they would throw you in jail. But we made a deal with a fish hatchery, where we got the fish for free, and we carted them from lake to lake in five-gallon milk cartons. We didn't get paid. We just thought it was the right thing to do. And we did it for years. There were only three lakes that had fish when we started, and I think we moved them to at least three hundred others. Now it's a good feeling to remember things like that. We moved over two million of the trout, and that's the reason people can go up there now and get fish anyplace they want."

Finis Mitchell was named for a friend of his family. He says Finis is pronounced like highness, which is fitting for the Wind River lord. He was less than royal in the fishing endeavor, however, going out of business even as the trout population grew, and he went back to work for the railroad. He retired in 1967.

He speaks from underneath a baseball cap which proclaims that he is the Greatest Grandpa. He wears bib overalls habitually, a plaid shirt, and Montgomery Ward shoes. He has ruddy cheeks, clear eyes, and a limp that dates to that 1975 (or was it 1981?) tumble on the ice. Age? He says he won't stop climbing because he grows old, because he'd grow old if he stopped climbing.

"I went from retirement back to the mountains. But I never really left them. I've taken pictures in the range for almost fifty years, and I've been map-ping the place even longer than that. Both of these things are important. The range is so rugged that it's never been completely explored, so that's what I tried to do. I've taken pictures of four thousand lakes, where the federal people say there are only three thousand, and I have done what I can to name the various places and make corrections on the official maps.

"Here is an example, on this map, where the federal government had it wrong. They would send me maps like this, and I would make corrections all over the face of the maps. You see that mark, that is the Klondike Mountain, and the government showed it right on the Continental Divide. But I went up there one time, walking around, and I discovered that it wasn't on the Divide at all. You see here, this is the Divide, and the mountain is over here a little bit. So I told them about it, and gave them the map I corrected, and now they got it in the right place.

"Oh, there've been many things like that. Hundreds. And when I see something that isn't recorded at all, or doesn't have a name, then I do that. I suggest names all of the time. See this glacier, hitting the mountain and bending around? I named it J Glacier. And this lake had no name, so I recommended that they call it Berg Lake, and they call it Iceberg Lake. Back here, there was a big peak on the Continental Divide, and I named it Yukon Peak, and all of these things, they are on the maps today.

"This is Suicide Lake, I named it in 1952. I was going over some glaciers, and down a gorge toward the Freemont River, when I came to a cliff. So I looked over and saw this big pine tree, and I decided to jump down to it and shimmy to the bottom of the cliff. It was a great idea, boy, until a branch broke, and I dropped way down the slope. I was lucky, because my pack broke my fall, and when I got up I was looking right at the lake. I said right then that it should always be known as Suicide Lake.

"That wasn't the only time I was lucky. You have to be lucky to go up there for as long as I have. The blizzards come up in a few minutes, and there are avalanches. I've been trapped under rocks; I've been frostbit. When I went out on that 1952 hike, I got into one area where I couldn't get out. The mountain had slid in and blocked the canyon near Pine Creek. I had to crawl under this blockage, and it was slow going. I thought I'd be gone for a few days, and I had to stay out for two weeks.

"It didn't matter. My father said the mountains were our home, and that's what they've always been for me. I remember being stuck in a storm once. And there was another fellow stuck a few miles away. I didn't have a tent or anything for shelter, but I had a good sleeping bag, and I got in it and was very comfortable. I was there for three days waiting for the storm to end. I let the snow act as part of my insulation. I walked out very content with myself, and with nature, but that other fellow I mentioned to you before, he died of hypothermia."

Finis Mitchell lives in Rock Springs, Wyoming, still with the woman he met at that frontier picnic. He is not so bold as he was, nor as sure of foot, but he remains a legend in his time and place. He has taken 124,000 slide photographs of the Rocky Mountain wilderness; he has explored his region as no other man has been able; and, fully disciplined if ony partly schooled, he is assuredly the foremost living authority on the Wind River Range.

He wrote a guide to the range in 1975. It is ripe with high-country homilies: "A mountain is the best medicine for a troubled mind." "Never gamble with your life because you can lose only one." "This is your wilderness. Take nothing but pictures, leave nothing but footprints, and kill nothing but time." *He has served two terms in the state legislature.*

"There's acid rain in the mountains now. And I can see, over my life, how the weather and the other elements work to take the edge off the peaks. But it's still like it always was, in most ways. You can drink clear water in the streams, you take a breath and it is so crisp that it almost hurts, and you can sit in places where no one has ever sat before. You can learn to live with yourself in a place like this—not by yourself, but with yourself—because you have to respond to your own thoughts.

"I've learned this, too. The mountains get steeper as I get older, but not too steep. I still have some to climb. I'm going for a hundred years. That's not a long time in Wind River Range."

According to figures released by the Metropolitan Life Insurance Company in 1987, the average American life expectancy has reached 75 years. Life expectancy was about 46.5 years in 1900 and grew to 65.6 years in 1950 and as of this notation, using newborn babies, it is 71.5 years for men and 78.5 for women. The Met said the figures were even greater for older people: of those age 65 in 1987, men had an average 14.7 more years to live and women 18.9.

If that's not enough, there is cryonics. The American Cryonics Society claims that 100 people have been frozen after death in the 1980s on the chance they might be revived one day by science.

Remember Digger O'Dell, "the Friendly Undertaker"? He enlivened The Life of Riley *radio program during the 1940s and 1950s. "Well, Riley," he would say, "I've got to be—shoveling off."*

WILLIAM HILLCOURT

The way William Hillcourt tells it, the whole thing started as a Christmas present. The year was 1910, he was a young tad in Denmark, and Santa Claus gave him a book called Scouting for Boys. *A book? For Christmas? When you are nine years old? That might be as lovely as getting suspenders on one's birthday, but not on this occasion. Hillcourt says he was very much pleased.* Scouting for Boys *was the rage throughout Europe. It had been written by Robert Stephenson Smyth Baden-Powell, a British baron, who was also a celebrated military hero. Baden-Powell, destined to be General Baden-Powell, later to be a knight of the Queen, won renown for commanding a British redoubt during a 217-day seige in the South African War, and his* Scouting for Boys *was a call to arms for children whom he thought should be organized into more peaceful for ranks: the Boy Scouts.*

"I got all excited about the book," Hillcourt says, "because Baden-Powell wrote that if I wanted to have fun, if I wanted to learn new things and participate in wonderful adventures, all I had to do was to get enough boys together for a patrol, and pick a patrol leader, and go out and do scouting."

And you did, Mr. Hillcourt?

"Yes. I became a Boy Scout in January of 1911, in Copenhagen. That was a little over two years after the organization was formed. And in one way or another I've been a Boy Scout since."

How old are you, sir?

"I'm eighty-six."

You've been a Scout for seventy-seven years."

"Yes."

Do you recall your first day?

"It was a very serious occasion. We started by taking the Scout Oath, which was the Danish Scout Oath. Translated, it was 'I promise to do my best, to be faithful to God and my country, to be alert, brave and clean, and to obey the Scout Law.' "

The Scout Law?

"We were required to learn ten parts of the law. The first one, in Danish, was 'En spejders ord staar til troende.' "

What does that mean?

"A Boy Scout's word stands to be trusted."

William Hillcourt was introduced earlier in this book. He is the man in the first chapter who pointed out, with patience, that the twentieth century began on the last day rather than the first day of the year 1900. He is nicely educated; he speaks well on many subjects; he has a Continental quality that betokens dignity and sophistication; and he may be the oldest and no doubt the longest continually active Boy Scout in all the universe.

God love it. He has a photograph of himself in full uniform, and it is enough to make a stone smile. Here he sits, gray and wrinkled, a great-grandpop of the classics, in epaulets and short sleeves and a bandanna around the neck. Immensely satisfied, moreover. How many times has he raised his three fingers, flags waving, and promised to obey the Scout Law? There is a patch on his shoulder in the photograph. It's the numeral one. Indeed.

How did the Boy Scouts come about, Mr. Hillcourt?

"It was a combination of Baden-Powell's efforts and the way things worked out. When Baden-Powell returned to England from the [Boer] war, he was sent around that country to reorganize the military calvary, and he saw a lot of things that he didn't like. He saw a lot of boys standing around idle, smoking cigarettes, and there was also an drug problem in those days."

Marijuana?

"No, not then; it was opium. And cocaine, too. It was fashionable. Even Sherlock Holmes used seven-percent cocaine."

Kids used it?

"It was like the American situation that we went through after the war in Vietnam. And Baden-Powell started to get concerned. He was worried about young people, and their future, and in that respect he was worried about the future of England."

What year did he start the Boy Scouts?

"I don't think at first that he had any intention of starting the group. He wanted to direct young people to the existing organizations of the day, such as the Boy's Brigade. But one thing led to another, and the Scouts began in 1908."

Hillcourt says he rose to the equivalent of an Eagle Scout in Copenhagen. He also received a college degree in pharmacy and worked in the business for a time, but he could not shake his attachment to the patrol. He attended the first international Boy Scout Jamboree in 1920, in London; he wrote the first of what was to be several books about the organization, in 1926; and, using the money from that publication, he decided to take a look at the scouting organization that had been formed in America.

"I got my original look at the Statue of Liberty in 1927. That was sixty years ago. I saw it from the ocean side, and she wasn't too friendly from that side. She turns her back to the ocean, and it's only when you sail past her that you get the opportunity to see her as the symbol of welcome that she is."

Did you intend to immigrate?

"Not then, really. I just wanted to see more of the world. I was working part time for a Copenhagen newspaper, and they would pay me for articles I sent. But one of the things I wrote about was the Boy Scouts of America, and eventually I decided to stay."

What did you write?

"The good things and other things I saw."

What were the other things?

"That's what the Scout organization wanted to know. And it's how I really got started with the BSA. One day I went to Scout headquarters, and I met a man named James C. West on the elevator. West was the chief Scout executive with the BSA, and we had a short conversation, and he asked me casually what I thought of the Boy Scouts in this country. I took the question seriously, and I went back to my room and wrote an eighteen-page document about what I thought. Then I sent it to James West."

Yes?

"He called me in. He said he was interested in my criticism that the BSA was not using the patrol method. I wrote that the fundamental idea of the Scouts was that it was an organization of boys under the leadership of boys; in America it had become an organization of boys who were under the leadership of adults."

You were hired on the spot.

"Almost. I told West that in order to get the BSA back to the patrol method, the organization needed a handbook for patrol leaders. After that I gave him an outline for the handbook. And then he asked me if I would be interested in writing it myself."

Did you?

"I was worried that my English was not good enough at the time, but I did it. As it turned out, it was just right. I had a limited vocabulary, but so does the average fourteen-year-old boy, and it was in the language of the boys who would read it."

Handbook for Patrol Leaders.

"It was the book the Scouts had until 1970, when it was revised. Over the years, I believe, two million copies were printed."

You were a best-selling author.

"You can figure out what it would have been at a 10 percent royalty. But I did it for the Scouts instead of for the money. I was a salaried employee in 1929, and I received a hundred fifty dollars a month."

Hillcourt was to write several other manuals for the BSA, including a couple of versions of The Boy Scout Handbook, *one of the most popularly read publications in history. He also became an editor of* Scouting *magazine and an editor of* Boy's Life *magazine, where he began writing under the nom de plume of Green Bar Bill, a nickname that has followed him for half the century.*

Tell me about Green Bar Bill.

"In 1932 we were in the middle of the Depression, and a lot of boys' magazines went out of business. *St. Nicholas* and *Youth's Companion* and a whole bunch of them. But James C. West didn't want that to happen to *Boy's Life*, so we decided to change it, improve it, put in more stuff about adventure and physical fitness, and I thought it would be also be different to write under a sort of mysterious title, and I hit upon Green Bar Bill."

Which means?

"Back then a patrol leader's badge consisted of two green bars."

With that, William Hillcourt became one of the most recognized Boy Scout officers in the nation. Green Bar Bill would advise entire generations of kids to be alert, brave, and clean (as the Danish say it) or to be mentally awake and morally straight (as it's suggested in the U.S. of A.). He would write on everything from Tenderfoots to tourniquets, he would encourage leadership and locomotion. Merit badges. First Aid. Self-improvement.

He would also participate in the best and worst times of the BSA. He watched the Scouts expand from 756,000 members in 1925 to more than six million in the early years of the 1960s. Then he watched the membership tumble drastically after that.

"We lost about 40 percent of our boys in one seven-year period."

What happened?

"Some of it was just the world we were in. Young people started to rebel in the 1960s, and it continued into the 1970s. They turned away from the traditional ways and institutions and organizations. The birth rate also fell off during that period."

What else?

"The Boy Scouts made some mistakes. We got far, far away from the fundamentals of Baden-Powell. We got caught up in that national trend toward managing everything. It was the 'Days of Management,' as I call it. Everybody had to be trained to be a manager. Everything had to be 'relevant,' and all that. As a result, unfortunately, we changed the Scout program completely."

How?

"For example, the BSA decided that the scoutmaster should be the manager of learning. That had nothing to do with scouting, because the truth is that the boys themselves should decide what their learning is to be. But the idea was adopted, and that led to such things as a new "advancement" program where a boy could be rewarded for minor things or, on the other hand, where the organization actually complicated his advancement."

Complicated?

"I'm thinking of the merit badge for citizenship. It had always been relatively simple and fun. But then the BSA tried to make it more 'relevant.' They told the boys to go out and meet the political leaders in their towns, such as a mayor, and to interview him. Well, that was a complication. Young people join the Boy Scouts to have adventures in the outdoors, not to interview politicians, and so we were straying from our purpose."

And that is?

"Doing right for the boys. It was as if the organization had said: 'Stop, there must be a more difficult way to do things.' "

In the name of being relevant.

"That was what was so frustrating. The Boy Scouts of America hired a polling firm to survey public attitudes on the Boy Scouts of America. In other words, we went outside the group to find out about the group, and what we supposedly found was that the public thought being relevant meant being in tune with the times."

You disagreed.

"I asked whether scouting should be in tune with the times. Because it had never been in tune with the times. It always followed its own course and plowed new ground. When Baden-Powell established scouting, he would take the boys out camping, even though everybody knew that 'night air was bad for you.' You got malaria and other things from night air. It was only for soldiers and explorers. And there was no good sitting around a campfire when you had a perfectly good kerosene lamp at home. And there was no sense cooking your meals when your mother was willing to do it for you. That was the tune of the times."

Did anyone listen to you?

"Not at first. I had retired by that time. But while I was away they revised the *Boy Scout Handbook* that I had written, and the sales went right down. My books had been selling about 650,000 a year, and the new book dropped to about 360,000 a year. I told the BSA that it was because the program had changed too much, that the *Boy Scout Handbook* was no longer telling boys about the excitement and romance of scouting. I also told them that I would like to write another *Boy Scout Handbook* myself."

That was in 1978.

"Yes. They never changed a word in it. And sales have gone back up. So has membership. It is now about 5.1 million boys."

Green Bar Bill lives in Manlius, New York, outside Syracuse. He has retired his flag again, but he remains a consultant to the BSA. He has in fact become known as the conscience of the BSA. And he is without argument the living embodiment of the BSA.

Seventy-seven years.

"I've loved every minute of it. It is a wonderful organization. You know, we have had a total of seventy million members in this country alone."

John Kennedy was a second class scout.

"And Gerald Ford. He was an Eagle Scout. And there have been so many others, leaders in every field, people in all walks of life. You can look around the world and see many things that are wrong, but I think it would be worse without the Boy Scouts. I see it at the jamborees I still attend. I see blacks and whites, and Jews and Arabs working together in scouting."

You still attend jamborees?

"I go to whatever I can. I was in Cincinnati recently. Seventy thousand people went there to watch the boys show their stuff in a big auditorium. Handicrafts, equipment, first aid—especially first aid. One of the little girls in the audience got a candy stuck in her throat, and a fellow with Boy Scout training administered the Heimlich Maneuver, and she was all right."

The Heimlich Maneuver. There's another change.

"Well, there has to be change. I've never been against it when it is good for the boys. But some things must remain the same. When I wrote that *Boy Scout Handbook*, the most important page I had to write was page nine. That's where I had to tell the boys what they can expect in the Boy Scouts, and what we expect from them. We are in so much competition today, with television, and computers, and everything else under the sun, that I had to be sure that what was on page nine was just what the boys wanted in the BSA, and that to be sure if they joined they would get it."

What is it that boys want?

"They want to be helped to become men."

And how to do that?

"Motivation."

William Hillcourt is a member of the National Council of the Boy Scouts of America. He looks as if he can tie a heck of a knot, and he sounds like Victor Borge. It is estimated that fifteen million copies of his Boy Scout books have been printed and sold.

"There is a story about a banquet for Eagle Scouts that was sponsored by leading members of a community. And the boys were paired up with and introduced by these men. So one fellow got up to say he was an engineer, and he was proud to introduce the Scout who was going to follow in his footsteps. Then another man got up to say he was a doctor, and he was proud to introduce the Scout who would follow in his footsteps. Finally, one man got up to say that didn't have the faintest idea what his Scout was going to be, and that was the best thing of all, because in all probability the profession had not yet been invented. I like that story. The moral is Boy Scouts are trained for tomorrow."

Those old Scouts who believe the weather used to be better yesterday may be right. A search of selected records conducted in 1987 revealed that when the period 1900-1939 was compared to 1950-1982 the first years were 10 percent less cloudy. Researchers William L. Seaver and James E. Lee said that they looked at statistics for forty-five cities and found the weather in all but one— Fort Worth, Texas—has deteriorated. They blamed increased pollution.

JOE AND ELNER BLUMLE

It was in some ways a storybook way to begin a life together. And in other ways it wasn't. Joseph Blumle was the roughhewn son of one of the town's leading merchants, loud, spoiled and untamed. Elner Spellingberg was a petite girl from the outlands, born in a log cabin to fewer peccadillos. They lived on the opposite sides of the tracks in the scarcely peopled northwestern corner of Pennsylvania, one to howl in the ways of the young, the other to whisper, and when they met, on a wintry afternoon in 1913, there were predictably competing emotions.

"I went down to the ice pond, and there she was," *Joe says, using his hands, palms facing, to form a figure from the past.* "I thought she looked pretty good, and of course I started to show off a little. When you think you're in love with a girl you try to get their attention that way. I threw cattails on the ice in front of her. The pond was in a marsh, and the cattails were right there, and I pulled them up and tossed them. Puff. They break up like powder when they hit. It was a mess. And instead of making headway, I guess she got mad at me."

Elner?

"Yes, that's right; I didn't like it. And I didn't like him. He had a reputation like that. He was from a wealthy family, he lived in this great big house, and he had it too easy. I thought he was a smart alec, and he was somebody you avoided. Besides, I was only sixteen then, and I wasn't supposed to think very much about boys. I had a very strict father. He was a good father, but very strict, and he wouldn't allow me to date up to then. So I just kept skating that day. I may have said a few things to Joe, but nothing nice. He was making me angry."

Joe again. He is still sandy on the edges, and provocative, perhaps even now to get Elner's attention. He lets her talk for a moment or two, but only a moment or two, before taking over:

"I had one problem for sure. My dad had a beer business, and I worked for him, and it made for an awful time with the girls. I'd go to a dance, for example, and I couldn't help it, because I had to taste the stuff in the business, but if a girl smelled it on your breath, ooooh, that was terrible, ooooh, you've been drinking the evil stuff, and they wouldn't have anything to do with you. It's not like that any more. Today if a girl smells booze on you, well, you can't get rid of her. But Elner didn't like it; it's the way she was raised."

"Joe . . ."

"I was a bottler for my dad."

"Joe . . ."

"It was what we called raw beer. Lager. Three-point-two."

"I . . ."

"But we got together. We dated for quite a while. I had an old Maxwell car, like Jack Benny, it had two cylinders and twelve horsepower. People would say, ooooh, you have a car; ooooh, you drove to St. Mary's; ooooh, what will they think of next? We went to dances, and the movies. We only did the two-step and the waltz. There were slide pictures at first, they didn't move, and I think it was mostly travelogues and that kind of stuff. And then they got moving pictures. We'd sit in the back with our girls. When they made popcorn you could hear the steam whistle."

Elner?

"Yes, Joe has always dominated."

Joe and Elner Blumle have been in love for seventy-five years, somehow, and married for sixty-seven. They therefore represent yet another unusual factor of the twentieth century, permanent fidelity. Zsa Zsa Gabor once said that people are incomplete until they are married, "and then they are finished," and the sentiment has grown large in the 1900s. Marriage is now the chief cause of divorce. The rate of matrimonial division increased 700 percent between 1905 and 1985; there were 1,159,000 splits versus 2,400,000 weddings in 1986; and half of all marriages are said eventually to fail.

Yet Joe and Elner remain hitched. Incompatibilities be damned. They can still give each other looks, as Ring Larder would put it, that might be poured on waffles. And it's still not entirely unusual for their age grouping. Marrieds who have survived everything else in the century seldom break up. Women too often lose their husbands, because as a rule they live longer, and only 25 percent of them who are seventy-five or older still have spouses; yet three-quarters of the men over seventy-five are married, and more than seven in ten males over sixty-five room with their women.

Old love lives. So does tolerance. Elner Blumle says she learned it on the edge of her mother's apron.

"My father was the king in our house, and my mother's job was to cook and to sew and to help him. Joe's father was also the king in his home, and his mother was second. I'm content with that. It is undemocratic, but I don't think I would have it any other way. Well . . . "

Joe: "I grew up in Emporium, Pennsylvania. Elner was from a little town outside there. My dad was from Germany; he came to this country with other people who knew how to brew beer, and that's what he did. He also had a farm, and he was in the state legislature for a while. He built a great big house in Emporium that is still standing. It cost forty-eight thousand dollars, it has twenty-nine rooms, and there are tons of hand-cut slate on the roof. He called it The Homestead. Elner and I lived in it after my parents died. You can see it today right there; it's a hotel with a dining room.

"My dad started the beer business with Peter Straub, and Straub Beer is still around today. But they went separate ways when my dad came to Emporium. He started brewing his own stuff in the 1800s, it was a tiny small operation then. All he had was an earthen cellar, and he brewed the beer just like people might make home brew now. He could only brew in the winter, because it got too hot the rest of the time. We put the beer in white bottles—we didn't get the brown bottles until later—and that stuff would spoil right off if the sun got it.

"Then he started buying raw [not pasteurized] beer from the bigger breweries and putting it in his own bottles. We sold it anywhere from ninety cents to a dollar for a case, twenty-four bottles, sixteen ounces to a bottle. Have you ever seen one of those old bottles? They had porcelain caps. We bottled the beer by hand, and we put the caps on by hand. You snapped it on with a rubber washer. We used to give a penny to get the caps back. Then the kids started breaking the bottles to get the caps; okay, we wanted the bottles too, so, after that, we only paid for capped bottles.

"It was good beer, there's no question about that. But the whole thing went blooey at Prohibition. We were modern by then and had machines to do everything, and it was pasteurized stuff, but my dad got a letter from the government. Ooooh, they said, you have six months to get rid of your stock. You could still sell it until the middle of the summer in 1920, then that was it. Some of the breweries continued to sell, but my dad didn't. He closed the business as directed. I don't think he was mad, except at some of it; he never reopened."

Elner says the Blumles tried to send Joe to college so he could prepare for other work. He ran away every time, which she continues to believe a mistake. She says she'd liked to have had the opportunity herself.

"My parents were poor, however. We had a two-story log cabin. There were a couple of rooms down, and one up. I did finish high school; Joe only went through the ninth grade, because he thought he knew everything by then. When I graduated I went to work for Sylvania, making electric bulbs."

Joe served stateside during World War I, and Elner says he has told her every detail of it, many times. "I had an exemption," *he interrupts*, "but I went because people started calling me a slacker." *The two were married in 1920, and moved to Detroit.*

"Automobiles were becoming very important," Joe says, "and we went to Detroit because that's where the jobs were. We stayed at the Cadillac Hotel for our honeymoon, for twelve dollars a week, and then I got on with the Hudson-Essex company. I did different things. One day the foreman asked me if I wanted to be an inspector. I thought, ooooh, an inspector! So the next day there I was. He put me on the assembly line and I inspected truck pumps. I took the pump and hold my hand over the opening, to hold the air in, and then I put it in a tub of water to look for bubbles. Ha, ha. I came home to Elner and I said, ooooh, I'm some inspector."

To which Elner shrugged. "I hated Detroit," *she says.* "I was a small-town girl, and I had never wanted to leave home. But Joe dragged me off. All the noise, and the crowding, I didn't like it. Yes, we spent a few days at the Cadillac Hotel, but after that we moved to a downtown apartment. The building was so full that we had to live with the landlady. There were four rooms, and we shared the kitchen and the living room. If she had company, we shared that too. It was not a good situation.

"And I got very homesick. And, really, it was so bad that I really did get sick. I couldn't eat, and I didn't sleep well, and so Joe saved up enough money to send me home on the train. I thought that if I ever got there, I would never leave the place again, and I was very excited to get back to good old Emporium. That's where all my people were, and the good memories. But after I visited with my father and mother for a while, and my brothers and sisters, I was ready to go back to my husband."

Meanwhile, Joe was not captivated by Detroit himself. When his parents died in the middle 1920s, he took Elner to Emporium to take over the Homestead mansion. There was an initial attempt to sell the building, but the Depression had set in, hence he borrowed $5000 from a bank to turn it into a restaurant and inn.

"We operated it for twenty-seven years," *he says, barking and laughing and enjoying the memory.* "We lived in part of the building and rented twenty-one rooms, some for permanent boarders. It worked out. I think we got a good reputation there. The Sylvania Corporation was in town, and there was a lot of business from that. It was a good clientele, ooooh, the best people in town. We got all the big parties, and all that. On Sundays we would entertain and gave a good dinner. We charged seventy-five cents or a dollar for a plate, and people would come from all over to get in on the deal.

"And I was shuffling a little beer around. I belonged to the American Legion, and I'd make it for our big celebrations. We had a big sauerkraut pot, and I'd brew it in that, anywhere from twenty-five to thirty kegs of beer. Then I'd age it in the cellar until it was ready. And when we'd bring it out we used to put ice over all the kegs. It was wonderful beer. It was as clear as it could be. The only thing was the ice would freeze the yeast, and that stuff was left over, and some of the help would always take this yeast and drink it, and, God, they'd really get loaded.

"Then, later, I really made a killing on booze. I had this buddy in the Army who was high up in rank, and he had something to do with intelligence, and he put a bug in my ear. I don't want to say who it was, but he became a big general, and just before World War II he told me that I should buy all the liquor that I could. He said the war was going to start for sure, and when it did alcohol would be rationed. Right after that I went out and borrowed seven thousand dollars, and I bought all of the stuff I could; we put it in our attic, and I made a lot of money on it."

Elner looks at him with a wan smile. They are sitting in their favorite chairs, respectively. Hers is orange velour. His has a sheet for a cover. You are not supposed to swear, she thinks, neither should you go on eternally about that gosh-darned beer:

"The Homestead was very nice. It was a fine place for a man to take his wife to dinner and dance. We had some opportunities to turn it into a hideaway and that kind of thing, and Joe was always trying to bring in things like slot machines, but we both wanted a respectable place. Our friends would come to dinner, and we wanted the best for them. We knew everyone in town, because we'd been raised there, and the friends became our family, because we couldn't have a family of our own.

"I tried to have children, but it wasn't physically possible. I had been injured by a very bad epidemic of Spanish flu. Many people were affected by it. The men would get it so that they would bleed from their nostrils, and the women would bleed vaginally, and that was supposed to be good. They said that if you bled you'd be all right, and if you didn't it meant you were going to die. Well, I bled, and I survived, but it did enough to me internally that I just couldn't have a normal pregnancy.

"I didn't know that when we were first married. Women were kept in the dark. I got pregnant three times, and none of them were successful. I didn't have a live birth. I shouldn't have tried again after the first time, because one of my fallopian tubes burst, and it was dangerous for me from then on. The doctors didn't tell me that. I don't know if they knew or what. The other thing was that Joe and I were Catholics, and the Church was against birth control.

"I wish I could have had children. I remember that I always regretted it whenever I saw other women with their babies. But we did help with some of our relatives' children. And we raised one girl as our own. She belonged to a relative, and there was some trouble in that family, and she asked us if she could live with us. She was in the seventh grade, and we said yes, and we kept her until she was an adult. She was a wonderful girl, and we loved her and took care of her."

The Blumles remained at The Homestead until 1948, when Joe's health deteriorated and they were forced to sell. Joe had diabetes, and they walked away with seventy-five thousand dollars, stopping eventually in central Florida. Joe says the same military general who told him about the coming of World War II also mentioned the likelihood of a space agency on Cape Canaveral. The general said a man would be wise to invest money in the area. He was right again. The Blumles now live on the water near Cocoa.

Joe: "When we came here there was nothing. We lived on Cocoa Beach and there were only nine houses. Plus the cockroaches. Elner calls the roaches Carmelites because they look like they are wearing brown habits. It was all trees and scrub brush here. U.S. 1 was deserted. You'd see cars, but there weren't any stores or gas stations. Look at it now; it's what the space business did. When the government came here, so did everybody else. We were pioneers. *[In 1987 there were more than 100,000 people living on the 40-mile edge of the Kennedy Space Center].*

"I bought my land for $5000. There are seven acres, with 550 feet on the Indian River and 550 feet along U.S. 1. Elner says that was about ten dollars a running foot. I remember people back home said, ooooh Joe, you're building down there, ooooh, what do you want to do that for? And now look. We had this house put up in one month. It's all made of cement block, and that way it doesn't rot in the heat and the salt air. Then my brother built a house, and there was another building. Elner says it's worth at least a thousand a foot now; I could get a half million for it."

Elner: "I've never liked it here. I'm still a Pennsylvania girl. Florida is a man's world. They fish, and they fish, and they sail their boats. Joe used to go on the water all the time. I don't like the nudity, either—what I call nudity. People go into the stores wearing practically nothing, even the women. I think a woman should always be nicely dressed in public. I can't get used to it. Joe and I used to have big arguments about it. Still do. I've always wanted to go back home to Emporium."

Conflict. Richard Taverner said that the only way the wedded can avoid it is if the husband becomes deaf and the wife blind. Elner jokes that her hearing is fading, and Joe has cataracts.

Their home sits near the river under thirty-year-old trees that have grown

high and wide to block the sun. The house is pink, and is shrouded with drop-
pings of Spanish Moss. The living room faces the spaceport across the river. The
two watched the first sounding rockets go up, then the advent of manned flight,
the trips to the moon, the space shuttle flights, and, in 1986, the detonated
death of seven astronauts aboard the ship Challenger.

"It was too bad," Joe says, "but they made too much of it. When I was a
kid, before I went in the Army, I worked in a powder factory in Pennsylvania.
We made the stuff they used in the artillery shells, and that was more dangerous
than the rocket ships. We had explosions all over. Five, six people would be
blown up at a time. We had to go out and pick their meat off the trees, that's
how bad it was. It didn't cause a big fuss, though. There were no investigations.
People should know that."

He is shaped like a beer barrel. He wears a stocking on one hand because
his fingers get cold in the air conditioning. He is ninety-two. Elner by contrast is
thin as a tulip stem and has been worn by sprinkles rather than storms. She is
two years the younger.
She is also worried:

"I never used to think about us growing old. We were always too busy
working and staying active. And we were healthy. When we had our fiftieth
wedding anniversary we just went out and did the town, and twenty-nine couples came down from Pennsylvania to join in. Then when we were married sixty years we were a little more quiet, but we still felt good, and we had a dinner
party. Now it's going on sixty-eight. Joe's diabetes is bad, and he has other problems. He can't get around any more, and I have to take care of him.

"I can still do it. But it is getting harder and harder. I don't want to put him
in a nursing home, because I would not want to go to one myself, but we are
reaching a crossroads. We don't have any children. Most of our friends have
gone on. There's no one to help out. I would like to take him back home; I
would love to go, we still have people there. But he can't take the cold any
more, so there is no sense thinking about that."

Joe: "I've got to go to the bathroom."
Elner: "Can you make it?"
Joe: "This is my speed. I've got no speed left."

"He hates that walker," *she says.* "But it's the only way he can get around.
He gets depressed sometimes. It's too bad."

Is he difficult to live with, Mrs. Blumle?

"I don't know. I've never lived with anyone else."

Have you ever wanted to?

"No. I haven't. And I want to stay with him as long as I can."

Arthur Harkins, a futurist at the University of Minnesota, says that people may shortly begin to "marry" robots. He says those who can't find companions in the human ranks—burn victims, perhaps, or the elderly, or just the very fussy— may have the option as soon as the 1900s yield to the next century. He thinks the advent of computerized artificial intelligence, as well as improved materials, will give machines new levels of acceptance.

Harkins says the marriages would not be civilly legal, and the relationships would undoubtedly be met with religious and other resistance, but the development would have real advantages. No one would need be lonely any more. And individual emotional choices could be assured. Men would be able to order robots programed to serve breakfast in bed, and women could purchase decided hunks who would also never complain about taking out the garbage.

"I'm leaving you, John. I've fallen in love with an IBM."

J. WAYNE SIPE

Now, how to put this? One is reluctant to say that when he reached advanced age of his own, J. Wayne Sipe had an old dream. Dreams do not get old. People do, dreams don't, perhaps because, when everything is working correctly, the latter are intended to compensate for the former. That is most certainly how it has been in the circumstance at hand, anyway. When Wayne Sipe retired from the pursuits of commerce in the 1960s, he met friends who had airplanes, and he naturally accepted invitations to fly; from then on, over the years that followed, he says he nurtured what with everything considered was an impossible yearning—he wanted to jump from the heights by parachute.

"Gee, Wayne, that's crazy," his barber said, in so many words.
"I don't think so."
"You're in your late seventies, man."
"So?"
"And you have a heart condition?"
"It doesn't matter."
"You'll never do it."

304 · AMERICAN TAPESTRY

"I will."

"You're just blowing smoke."

"I'll tell you what I'll do. I'll bet you fifty dollars."

"You're down."

Parachute? Wayne Sipe had never done anything more than fall off a roof or two. But let's not get ahead of the story. Who is this fellow and why doesn't he act his age? He is a twentieth-century American original who is convinced, along with the writer Arthur Miller, that an era, a nation, or a human being can be said to reach the end of effective life when illusions are over.

Sipe started his life in Fort Scott, Kansas. Like so many of his generation, he was a farmer's boy. His father raised everything from grain to cattle on a spread near the Missouri border. That is on the periphery of the region that dried up in drought during the 1930s, became known fearsomely as the Dust Bowl, and coupled with the Great Depression to bury great expectations.

That's another thing about dreams. They can also miscarry:

"I wanted to be a farmer like my dad," Sipe says. "I got married, and I got a farm of my own, and I was doing all right. I had a hundred sixty acres of good land, and I was running a small dairy. There were thirty-seven cows—some of them gave up to eighty pounds of milk a day, which was a lot for the time. I figured that with the land, the cows, and the machinery, the whole place was worth seventy-five thousand dollars. And I wasn't all that much in debt, at least not before the drought and the Depression. Then when the bottom fell out, I borrowed to keep going, and everything was plastered to the hilt.

"It's real hard to describe. The only thing was that everyone was in the same boat. Nobody had any money, you couldn't sell what you produced—not for more than a few pennies, anyway—and it got worse and worse as time went on. I started getting eighty cents per hundred pounds of milk, if you can imagine that. Oh, yeah. Before the crash I was getting two or three dollars. Then I had to pay twenty cents a hundred to get it hauled to the condensary [dairy]. I lost out all the way. It got to be a thing where the more milk my cows gave, the more money I lost.

"I stuck with it as long as I could. I borrowed on everything I had, but it wasn't any use. I got two cents a pound at the hog market. And then I had to sell some of my cows, and I got eighteen dollars apiece. Eighteen! Today, cows of that caliber go for eight hundred. So one day I was with my wife in the barn. I had just thrown some milk in the strainer and I turned to her and said, 'Let's rack it up, and move to Oregon.' She said 'All right, when do you want to start?' We sold the place at auction, and when all the debts were paid, we had less than a thousand dollars.

"We went to Oregon in a 1929 Model A. I built a box on the back, and we took all the belongings we could, and our two children. We had some friends in Oregon. They said things were better out there. They painted a little brighter picture than it was, I guess, because when we got here we found that it was pretty much the same. But we had to go somewhere. There was nothing in Kansas. I remember my banker, Tom Givins, he said he thought I was making a mistake. He said he'd help me get started again if I ever came back, but I never did.

"I worked wherever I could in Oregon. There weren't many jobs. Fact of the matter, I worked for WPA [the federal Works Projects Agency] at one time. Glad to get the job. We built roads, with wheel-barrels and picks and shovels, and I got forty-nine dollars a month. Oh, yeah. We lived in a little house; my rent was five dollars a month. Then, oh, I guess I had been on the job for a couple of months, and they made me a foreman, which they raised me up to sixty-one dollars. That's the way it's been. I've never gotten rich in Oregon, but I made up for losing the farm."

Sipe eventually became a roofing contractor in Salem, Oregon. That's how he received initial parachute training. At least he learned how to land. He owned the contracting business for several decades, nailing thousands of roofs together, and when he retired in 1972 he did not want to go quietly over the hill. "I had to keep busy," *and so it was, as he says with some misgiving,—*"I might as well tell you all of it"*—he did a stint in professional gambling.*

Cards, Mr. Sipe?

"Poker."

Hey, you are *a dreamer.*

"Oh, yeah. I had played since I was young. So I started playing with the big boys, here on the West Coast, all around. My wife was not happy with it, and I didn't blame her, because I'd be gone for several days at a time, and, besides that, these are not the kind of people you want to bring home for dinner. There are some strange people playing. You can drop a lot of money doing it (one time I lost eleven thousand dollars in one night), and your ordinary, everyday fellow doesn't get involved. But I liked it. I can't take retirement; I have to do stuff, anything.

"I didn't have to go to Las Vegas, or even the real big cities. The games are going on everywhere, if you know how to find them. Here in Salem, and Portland of course. I'd play a couple of times a month, at least. Big stakes. Sometimes I knew the people, sometimes I didn't. That wasn't important. All you have to have to get in is the money. The usual thing was to start during the afternoon, two o'clock, something like that, and then we'd play all night long. You could quit whenever you wanted, or if you tapped out, otherwise it might go on for twenty-four hours.

"The secret of playing poker is to know how to evaluate your hand, and at the same time know how to evaluate the people you are playing with. There is just as much difference in the way people play cards as there is in the people who play them. Everybody plays a little different from everybody else, and you have to be able to determine what the difference is. It's important to have a good memory; you have to remember the cards being played, so you know how your own hand stacks up, but the big thing is to figure out the guys across the table.

"I'll give you an illustration. There was one man that I played with who had a peculiar habit. And I had it pegged pretty quick when the game started. When he was buying—you know what I mean, when he had a good hand and he was trying to jack up the pot—he would put the little finger of one hand in a certain position. Oh, yeah. He did it every time. He didn't know he was doing it, if he did he would have stopped, because it proved to be very expensive for him. The other fellows never caught on, so I had a great opportunity there, and I beat that man consistently."

Isn't that unsporting, Mr. Sipe?

"Poker is not baseball."

Did you have any peculiar habits of your own?

"The only thing I did was to project my thoughts sometime. I don't mean by my mannerisms or the expressions on my face, but I projected my thoughts mentally. I've always done that. Lots of times I will be thinking of something, and my wife will answer me without my saying a word. So if I got into a game where I was up against a player who could receive the thoughts, I got out."

Sipe says he won more than he lost at poker before acceeding to his Significant Other's request to get back on the road of righteousness. But don't get the wrong notion. The man is in the main straight up. Harry Truman played seven-card stud. What's a little Hold 'Em? There are 2,598,960 possible poker hands in a fifty-two-card deck. Isn't that fascinating. Well? Well?

Wayne Sipe belongs to the Fraternal Order of Eagles, if that is any better. He has been a member for forty-seven years and is currently employed as a secretary at the eyrie in Salem. He says the FOE was founded in 1898 as the Order of Good Things, and the name change occurred in 1900. He says it is a charitable organization that raises and contributes money to a list of worthy causes.

One cause in Oregon is called the Hearing Aid Fund. The Eagles have established it for underprivileged children who are hard of hearing, and in 1987 Sipe had an idea to meld it with that longtime dream mentioned a few pages back. He wanted to parachute; he also wanted to help the children hear; and he decided to raise money by making his first jump in public.

Right. People would pay to watch the old gentleman bounce.

"Well, right away my wife didn't like it. I was going from poker to parachutes. She reminded me that I had a couple of health problems, and she made me at least consult with the doctor.

"Doc said, 'Wayne, you know you've had two heart attacks.'

"I said, 'Sure.'

"He said, 'You were also hospitalized with inner-ear infection.'

"I said, 'Yeah.'

"Then he said, 'My advice would be not to do it.'

"All right. I said 'Thank you, doctor.' He was absolutely correct. I do have an irregular heart. It goes out of rhythm. I was in the hospital a week with it one time and four days the other. It doesn't just miss a beat or something like that; it flutters like a butterfly. They can't tell me what it is—nobody has ever said what's wrong—but it gets pretty bad. I might wake up some night and it's pounding so that it hurts.

"But I'm otherwise in good shape. I think I'm fit. I do a lot of hunting in the mountains, and I have a nineteen-foot skiff for fishing in the ocean. Besides, I did not only dream about parachuting, I wanted to prove something. You don't have to retire and be done with everything. I suppose you'd call me elderly. I don't feel it, but I guess I am, and I wanted to show that people my age could still do most anything they wanted.

"Anyhow, my wife asked me later if I went to the doctor.

"I said, 'Yeah.'

"She said, 'What did he say?'

"I said, 'He said I should go for it!'

"So I fibbed to her a little. And not long after that I went out to an airport in our area where they have a parachute club, the Pacific Sky Divers, and I told them what I wanted to do. I wanted to go up on my birthday, so it would make it more interesting for the people who would be watching, and I needed the proper training. They didn't discourage me at all. They said they had never instructed a man of my age but that they were willing if I was, and if I was really serious about it.

"I said I was serious; I had already made all the preparations. So what they did was to show me what the parachute was and to give me a rundown on what would be happening, and, mostly, the instructions concerned what I should do if something went wrong. I would be using a static chute (that means it would open automatically), but if it didn't there was also a second chute. Every parachute has a back-up chute—it's called a pilot chute—and they taught me how to get it open in case of trouble.

"And that was about it for training. It only took a couple of hours to get through everything. They taught me how to guide the chute; you can go one way or the other by pulling here and there. There are two places to put your hands—they are called toggles—and you can guide it to the left or the right. That was important because you don't want to hit a tree on the way down, or maybe a power line, and you also have to aim for a target. There's a mark on the ground when you jump, and you head for it."

Sipe was contacted by the media. There had to be publicity to raise money for the charity. CODGER TO JUMP FROM PLANE! *No, that's not what the stories said, it was what they suggested. Parachutes are as old as the sketches of Leonardo da Vinci, successful parachuting began in 1789, but it had as a matter of accepted wisdom been a young person's perversion. Sipe had fallen from a roof one too many times. Dreaming is all well and fine, yet it is castles not coffins that are built in the air.*

It was raining and overcast early in the designated day. Sipe had his daughter come with him to the airport, because, as he puts it carefully, "I might have been too excited to drive myself back home." Or too something. He rented a plane for $100. He took off in midafternoon, when, the weather cleared.

"The plane was a Cessna one-eighty. The plane is built especially for skydiving. The door on the plane is not an ordinary one; it is wider and when you open it up it slides over your head. I had a jumpmaster; he was from the diving club. We went up forty-five hundred feet, which is a little less than a mile, and we flew over a landing area that was in a little valley, and there weren't a lot of trees. There was only one electric line there too, so that was not a worry.

"It's a funny thing. I was not nervous at all. I just sat on the floor of the plane and waited for my jumpmaster's directions. His first command was 'Feet out.' That meant I put my feet through the door and on a little rail outside the plane. Then the next command was "All out," and I pulled myself up to stand on the rail, and I held on like that. I didn't pay any attention to the ground then. I was too busy holding on. I don't have any strength in my arms, and I had to fight the wind.

"Then the jumpmaster slapped me on the thigh, and I jumped. I couldn't have held on anyway, to tell the truth, and so I had to go one way or the other. It was a rare sensation, and the chute opened when I was down about thirty feet. There was a little jerk, but it wasn't as bad as they told me it might be, and I wasn't thinking about that anyway. I looked up to see that beautiful canopy pop out above me and fill with air, and I was swimming back and forth, and I knew that I was home free.

"The trip down was—it was sort of indescribable. I was just floating around. The sun was shining, and the sky was blue, and I just felt real nice. My heart wasn't pumping a bit. I didn't have a thing in the world to worry about. They gave me this sweatshirt, one of those that has a message written on the front, and it said 'Only Skydivers Know Why the Birds Sing.' And I guess that's it. I drifted down for six or seven minutes, I was having a good time, and I was sorry when I hit the ground."

Wayne Sipe landed within 200 feet of the target. He said the bump was significant but he did not so much as get a bruise. Other skydivers came on the field to collapse his parachute; spectators gathered around with glad greetings; and the barber, "you remember my barber? He was there with the fifty dollars in his hand."

Sipe raised $1400 for the Hearing Aid Fund.

He was eighty years old exactly.

Before he died in 1986, J. Douglas Brown said that "with the exception of constitutional amendments, the Social Security Act was the greatest piece of legislation in United States history." He would be expected to be proud, having fathered the law. Brown was the director of the four-person task force that created the America idea in 1935, having borrowed its parts from longtime German tradition, and, despite the original criticism that accompanied the enactment, he defended it all his life:

"There was one Republican critic who shall remain nameless. He was in Congress, and he said that we had destroyed the idea of America, the idea of self-sufficiency and making it on one's own. I said we certainly did not. I said we only made that more possible. That Republican retired about the same time I did. We both began to get our checks in the mail, and to my knowledge he never sent any of them back. I know I never have. It's easy to be tough when you are young; you need something else when you're old."

The first social security tax was 1 percent of earnings, and in five years 220,000 Americans were receiving $50 million in annual benefits. The payroll bite was 7.5 percent in 1987, and more than 38 million people were receiving $200 billion a year in various benefits. As of 1988, the total amount passed on to social security recipients since 1935 has exceeded a trillion dollars.

ADAM DALESSIO

Adam Dalessio pronounces his name "Da-less-eeo," and, given to such things, he goes on to say, in an exaggerated accent, "Da-lessa-you-know of me the better." Ho. What a character. Yet he's too modest in this instance. Which is actu-

ally out of keeping. He is but of course fascinating, and he knows it. He is Latin, after all (Browning: "Open the heart and you will see, graven inside, old Italy"). And he is also the eighty-year-old mayor of Follansbee, West Virginia, which is of some interest in itself. Follansbee is in a five-mile stretch of hills between Ohio and Pennsylvania, and Dalessio suggests that if you get tired there you can lean on it. What a character.

"The town grew up around an old steel mill. The Follansbee brothers out of Pittsburgh built the mill, and in those days the Welsh were in charge of everything. The Welsh and the English. They knew how to make tin plate, and the Follansbee brothers brought them in from Europe and from New York. I give them credit, they knew how to roll tin plate. But they didn't like the rest of us who were Italian, and German, and Polish, and Russian. They were running things, and we were following. It was tough to get a good job if you weren't Welsh or English.

"That's why I ran for public office. I was like a foreigner in my own town. We had three wards, and when I campaigned in the Welsh ward they looked at me down their nose. I went to about six houses the first time. I had a brand-new hat, and a vest with a watchchain, and I knocked on a door, and there was an old English lady. She looked at my card and she said, 'Adam Da—how do you pronounce your name?' So said, 'My name is a-Adam a-Dalessio, you unnerstanda me.' I was just carrying on. But she said: 'My God, you want my vote and you don't speak English?' "

He won the election anyway. A city council seat that time. Later he would become mayor—over and over and over, and over, matter of fact.

There have been good times in office, he says:

"We needed a place for the low-income people. So I went to Washington to lobby for money for a federal housing project. Richard Nixon, you'll remember, he froze the funds for things like new housing, but I still went there to bug them about it. I wanted a high-rise building and, luckily, I got the congressman from this area to stick with me. The congressman had a friend at HUD [Housing and Urban Development], and that turned out to be the clincher. I got the money in 1980: a million and a half dollars. The high-rise was built for forty-eight families, and it was named after me."

There have also been bad times:

"I've made one or two enemies in the job. I probably shouldn't say this, because the legal part of it is still going on, but one guy, he got pretty nasty about things. He was a good friend at one time, and then he started to oppose me, and then he just went wild. He made threats. He loosened the lug nuts on my son's automobile tires, and the wheels damn near fell off. Then somebody shot a shotgun blast through a window, broke down doors, and I don't know what all. The guy died before we could get him to trial. Too bad. I wish he had lived to face the music.

Adam a-Dalessio was born in Maine. His father was a tradesman who migrated to the West Virginia panhandle to roll steel, in 1912. Follansbee was and is a steel town, and Follansbee Steel was the center of the known world. There were calendars: "Home of Follansbee Steel." Then the mill was sold. Then it was sold repeatedly. Then finally it went out of business, on Mayor Dalessio's watch, and he had to do something about that.

But we are moving too fast.

There were ten children in the Dalessio home. Most of them quit school to work in the mill. Young Adam included, after seven grades:

"I was fourteen, or fourteen and a half, and I went up to apply at Follansbee Steel. They didn't want to give me a job, because of my age, but my dad was working there, and he was a good friend of the man who was the superintendent. My dad used to make a little home brew, and invite the man down to the house, and you know the rest. The man called my school, and said, 'Boy, this kid is a big one, he's big enough to beat me up, he may be fourteen, but he looks nineteen or twenty'—and so I started working in the mill in 1922.

"It was quite a thing then. That was before all the rules and regulations. We worked in the summer and were laid off in the winter, because that's how it operated. It was hot, I can tell you. If you worked in the hot mills it would get 150 to 160 degrees, maybe more. We could stop to take water, and there was this little container there, full of salt tablets. We'd eat them all through the shift. Still, people couldn't always take it. They would pass out in the heat. They'd drag them out until they were better, then put them back to work.

"I did everything in the mill at one time or the other. I worked in the hot places, and I rolled for a while, everything but the good jobs. They kept the good jobs for the Welsh. The Welsh were in charge of everything, and they stuck together. One time I went in and I asked this Welsh boss for a better job. His name was Jake Jones, and I wanted the screwboy job. When they start rolling sheets, they go through big rollers, and the screwboy turns the screws on the rollers, and I wanted the job. Did I get it? No. Jones gave it to an English kid.

"I worked my way up, however. I cut bars for the hot mills at one time. In other words we cut them with shears. We had what we called a big hammer, and we would take a ingot out of the hearth, I'd say twenty inches in diameter, and they'd press it down under the hammer until it got down to the size where it would fit it the rollers. And then they'd roll it out into a smaller bar, and we would cut them to size with the shears. The bars would be red-hot, and then they would fall into a bucket of water to cool. They'd be sent from there to be rolled into tin.

"We had fifteen hot mills. And we made everything from electrical sheets to the stuff for tin cans and roofs. You name it. I made bullet jackets for the military. I had been moved to the rolling mills by that time, and I'd roll out a copper-clad bar that was at least forty to fifty feet long. A sheet of the stuff, in other words. Then they would take it upstairs and cut it into shape, and that's what they put in the bulletproof vests. For the soldiers. They were old-fashioned by today's standards, but I guess they did the job, and that's what counts.

"It was good work, and it was a way of life for us. I even worked for the mill when I went back to school. I was a big, husky guy, and the football coach asked me to come back, I worked the midnight turn, from eleven P.M. to seven A.M. Then I went home to eat a bowl of milk and bread. We broke the bread up in the milk and sprinkled sugar on it, like cereal. Then I went to school. I didn't think it was unusual. Today you couldn't do it, but we were in the dark ages. You had to work. You had to help. I did that until I quit school again in 1927."

This time Dalessio quit to get married. To Genevieve. "Her father owned a restaurant in town." He reflects on the betrothal with joy and sorrow. They were together for fifty-three years before she died of emphysema, at which time he says he did not have enough money to bury her. That is another side of early life in the mill. The pay was not substantial; Dalessio never earned more than $700 a month; and when he retired, after more than five dedicated decades on the job, he was pensioned off to the ever-so-bleak realities with a impudent $1644 per annum.

And then there were the strikes.

"We had one strike in the middle 1930s, just before the war, where we were out a year and a half. People don't believe it when I tell them today, but I used to have to shoplift bread to get by. We had a family, and we lived in a small cottage behind my mother's house, and they stopped the electricity, they shut the water off, and there was no credit. I used to get up in the morning, look for someone's garden, and then crawl on my hands and knees to steal vegetables. I used to follow the milkman around so I could get a chance to grab a quart on a doorstep. You couldn't earn any money. The mill was everything. I'd shovel a little snow in the winter, and get a quarter."

The old man chokes at the telling. It reminds him of Genevieve.

"She was real good, real good. It was real bad when she died."

He cries.

"I'm sorry."

There's a break in the conversation, followed by a change of subject. The mayor is big and loud, but soft as an ingot in the hearth. You want a housing project in Follansbee? Ask Adam.

"Don't forget, I worked fifty years up at the church. I volunteered at St. Anthony. Anthony is my middle name. I worked a lot with the older people. I ran their Bingo games, every Tuesday night, and all of their bazaars. The priests gave me the key to the safe. I called the numbers and then put the loot away. My wife says I was a fanatic about it. She said, 'You know, if I die on a Tuesday night, you'll go to Bingo first before you think about it.' And it damned near happened. She died on a Monday. What a lady she was! Real, real good.

"But it wasn't just Bingo. I've always had a lot of things to do. I used to run the horse book in town. I took bets. I worked out of a building downtown—it's still there—and every day I'd mark the races down on a board. From New York, from Cleveland, from Churchill Downs. I marked the horse, the jockey, and the odds. Then we had a ticker-tape machine that called the races. We got customers from all over. I used to keep six hundred dollars sewn into a pocket in my pants, and that's what I used to pay off. That's right, I admit it. I did it for years."

Dalessio says the book was illegal. And he was raided once. He says he was serving on the city council then, and, fortunately, he grabbed the money and scrammed before he was pinched. He says the police were not fooled, however.

"After I got rid of the money i went out on the street, and the police were still cleaning up. They had arrested some people and were taking them in, and one of the cops came over to me and said: 'Boy, councilman, you run pretty fast.' "

Da-lessa-you-know was elected to the council in 1941. He says he wanted to introduce ethnic diversity into the Welsh establishment. He felt that if the Italians and the Germans started to be treated as equals, well, the damn fools would begin to believe it. He had a ripe sense of social outrage. He also wanted to build some ballparks, and new streets, and so make Follansbee a better place for the kids and the elderly, and, kaf-kaf, Bingo players and bookies.

"I was on the council for three terms. I wanted to run for mayor right after, but a friend of mine was in the office, and he didn't retire until 1969. Then he said, 'Adam, you should run,' so I did. I didn't do much campaigning. I had everybody at St. Anthony on my side, and I used to sit on a downtown bench and talk with people. I even got a few votes from the Welsh ward. You remember that old lady I mentioned? She didn't think I could talk. I told her, 'I'll-a tell you a-what, lady, when I get-a elected, I'm a-gonna learn to speak English a-pretty good.'

"That whole Welsh business has been changed since then. When I took office I wanted to get some of those damn Welsh people out of the government, and I did. But they would have left anyway. They only had control of one ward, and they couldn't stand in the way of everybody else. And today it's all different. We've got five Italians on the council. We've got other nationalities in other offices. We don't operate like we own the place, though, and I think the Welsh will agree. We get along now; everybody seems to understand everybody.

"And we've done some good things. The town is much better than it was. One of the things we did, in 1976, we annexed a very important piece of land. It sits on a hill, and there is an industrial park, and there is a coke plant and a chemical plant. Some of them didn't want to do it, but I kept after them. I told them, 'Listen, you need water up here and if you agree to the annexation, we'll sell you the water.' Then when they still hesitated, I said 'All right, don't annex; we'll sell you the water anyway.' They liked that, and so we got the land.

"It was a big break. The tax revenue was terrific. The new homeowners did not contribute a whole lot, but the corporation tax increased the Follansbee collection by more than three hundred thousand dollars a year. All new revenue. We had so much money it was almost coming out of our ears. We went from a budget of about five hundred thousand dollars a year to damn near a million, and so at the end of that first fiscal year we couldn't spend it all. Now, the law said that if we didn't spend it all, we had to give the surplus back to the corporations, and so I figured out a few things we needed.

"I spent some of it on downtown revitalization. We tore out all the sidewalks for three blocks and put in new ones for the people; we made handicap ramps; we planted trees on the streets and corners; and we built a little minipark. Then I got a new garage for all our trucks, over by the sewage plant. I also upgraded the water plant by buying new motors, digging a new well, and putting in a new filtering system. Then I beefed up the police department. When I started as mayor, we had three policemen and a chief; now we have seven men and the chief."

Very nice, mayor.

"That's nothing. The big thing we did was to get this new plant on the Ohio River. The one the Japs are operating."

Japs?

"Yes. The Nisshin Steel Company of Tokyo. It's just happened. They are going to come in here with this computerized coating operation. It's going to be in combination with Wheeling Steel. Wheeling Steel had the plant going for many years, and then they closed it down in 1981 or 1982. They had been making the same stuff that this new mill is going to make, all along, and so when I heard that the Japs were looking for a place to make their stuff, I decided that the town ought to go after it.

"I'll start at the beginning. I saw in the paper that Nisshin wanted to find a spot to start this coating work. I called the governor right away, which was Jay Rockefeller, and he agreed to help. Then I started to meet with Wheeling Steel, and I reminded them that they had this empty mill here, it was three blocks long, it was plenty big. We also have railroad sidings; we have river barges; we have good roads. Lots of other towns wanted the new operation, but we thought we had a good shot.

"The way we got it was to go along with the one big thing that Wheeling and Nisshin wanted. They wanted to borrow twenty million dollars to get the plant all ready and equipped. The state said okay at first, because they had money for that purpose, but then the state had to renege because the Japs didn't have a credit rating in West Virginia. Well, it was panic then. But then Wheeling Steel suggested that I apply for a federal grant of ten million dollars, and that would be enough. So I did, and we got it.

"That's not all. When I got the federal money, in 1986, they had a stipulation. They said Wheeling-Nisshin would have to repay the loan to the town of Follansbee. Now, the government didn't want the money back itself. It said Follansbee must get it, and at eight percent interest to boot. So we not only got the new coating plant, which is good for eighty jobs here and more jobs elsewhere in the area, it also means the plant will be repaying us a million dollars a year, beginning in 1988, for fifteen years.

"It still knocks me over. A million a year in additional income! The federal government will not let us put it in our budget, but we can use it for any kind of community development we want. So we're talking about new industrial parks, bringing more business into town, putting more people to work at good salaries, and increasing town revenues even more. I've already got my eye on one piece of land. I'm already thinking about new programs for the poor and the elderly. They live in dilapidated buildings, and it's a shame, and we are going to fix them up. We got the money now. We have plenty of money. We have so much money I don't really know what we can do with it all."

The mayor turns suddenly modest again. He says getting Wheeling-Nisshin was a cooperative effort among many people. That is true. It is likewise true that His Honor, seventy-nine at the time, was the major player. Most towns in the 1980s lost steel mills; Follansbee was the only one to gain one. The mayor receives a salary of $300 a month in office. He earns it. He has put his community on an economic easy street until the twenty-first century.

Adam Dalessio has been mayor of Follansbee for ten terms. He is also the municipal judge, but he presides primarily in traffic cases.

"I tell my police force, look, the yellow light is only on for a wink. If a guy is going through a yellow light it will probably turn to red. Give him a chance.

Don't bring him in here. I'll just have to dismiss the case." *He also tells his friends* "No, I won't fix your ticket. Whatta you think? I could have you arrested for this." *Hard.*

The mayor lives in a home he purchased for $6000 directly behind the municipal building. He says he goes to his office every day, and then to Dalessio Manor. That's the housing project he built. He says he goes there to spend time with the "old ladies." One of them used to nurse his wife when she was sick. He says she never took a dime for the effort. When Dalessio Manor was finished, the mayor moved the woman into the first room available.

"Eleventh term? Sure, I'm going to go for it. I've been at it too long to quit now. Besides, I've got a lot of money coming in here, and I want to stick around to see how it's spent. We just bought a new fire truck, you know. Three hundred thousand dollars, with a seventy-five-foot-ladder on it. I wasn't in favor of the ladder. We need a seventy-five-foot-ladder like we need wings on the wheels. We got good firemen, but I don't mind saying that the truck is a big toy. The tallest building we have is forty-five feet.

"But I didn't say much about it. This is a small town and you have to get along. Which is okay. I like it, and I think it likes me. When I stopped doing the church work because it got to be too much, they called me up during Mass and presented me with a plaque. Then the priest asked me if I wanted to say anything. Here's what I said: 'If and when I die and I get up to Heaven, Saint Peter is going to greet me at the gate and say 'Oh, Adam Dalessio! I know you. Go down the hall, turn right into the big room. Bingo starts in ten minutes.' "

What a character.

—

10. Discovery

CLYDE TOMBAUGH

If Clyde Tombaugh were a young man again and beginning a professional life under the conditions that existed the first time he did it, he would not likely be given the opportunity to join the vocation in which he has singularly distinguished himself—and, indeed, in which he has made history forever and ever. Tombaugh is an astronomer. When he entered the field in 1929 he was a modestly educated farm lad whose only academic qualification was the time he had spent, after working in the fields, looking at the heavens through a telescope he had constructed from instructions that were set down by a backyard handyfellow writing in a Sunday school newspaper.

Astronomy today would chuckle. This is science, my boy. One must have a degree, a background, a base of authority. Where did you go to school? What have you written? Who is your reference?

Clyde Tombaugh is eighty-six now.

He discovered the planet Pluto when he was twenty-four.

"I think one reason I got that first job, at Lowell Observatory, was that nobody else wanted it. At least nobody who had been to college and had any credentials in astronomy. The observatory was well known, and it did important work, but most astronomers thought that it was a waste of time to look for the ninth planet. The last planet discovered was Neptune, in 1846. And Uranus was supposed to mark the boundary of the main solar system. Many visiting astronomers would scoff when they learned what I was doing. 'Young man,' they would say, 'if there were any more planets to be found, they would have been found long before now.'

"I didn't believe that. The sky is a big place. Even today, things are easily overlooked. We know that there are at least ten billion galaxies in the universe.

The average galaxy contains about one hundred billion stars, or suns. Some of them contain many more, but one hundred billion is average. Now, let's use grains of sand as an analogy. If we say that a particle of sand is about one millimeter and we carry this out mathematically, comparing it to ocean beaches, we find that there are one hundred stars for every grain of sand on all the beaches in the world, and we still haven't found the end to the universe.

"I wasn't looking all over this enormous expanse for Pluto. But I did cover a lot of space. I took my photographs with a thirteen-inch telescope at Lowell. That means I was recording images with the intrinsic brightness of the sun to distances of six thousand light years. A light year is the distance that light travels in 365 days at 180,000 miles a second. Think of it! I was really getting a tour. I took photographs on fourteen-by-seventeen-inch plates, and each plate contained from 50,000 to 150,000 star images. I had to look at every one of those images to find the ninth planet, millions and millions. You can't find Pluto today if you don't know where to look."

Yes, one must know where to look. Tombaugh thinks that and curiosity are the only truly important qualifications for science. Education is grand, experience is beneficial, yet direction is a near-imperative of discovery. Building bricks were conceived by laborers; the telephone was put together by a speech therapist; and Christopher Morley said high heels were invented by a woman who had been kissed on the forehead. Clyde Tombaugh at twenty-two was a field hand but he had eyes to see, and did.

Still, there is much to be admired in the scholarly sophistications of science. Alfred North Whitehead said the greatest invention of all has been the invention of the method of invention and its various ramifications. The training, the organized discipline, the institutionalization of genius. Thomas Edison was a self-taught tinkerer when he created the stock ticker in 1869, but he started a commercial laboratory after that, and most of his patents to 1931 were the products of a well-schooled staff.

Therefore the twentieth century has been blessed with educated regimentation. The first patent in America was issued by the Colony of Massachusetts in 1641 to a planter who devised a new way of making salt. And George Washington granted the first United States patent, in 1790, to another farm boy, who had a better idea to produce "pot ash and pearl ash." Yet there were only 700,000 more patents written until 1900—when, given academic institutionalization, discovery began to deploy as never before.

Six times as many American patents have been awarded in the twentieth century as in the previous 200 years. Learned men have said that more knowledge has been created in the latter decades of the period, worldwide, than in all of the time gone before. It is probably not fundamentally right to say that inven-

tiveness has therefore increased exponentially through history, because early inventions were only the distinct products of an overwhelming array of lesser discoveries, few of them recorded, and the fact is we are keeping a better score now.

Yet genius has had remarkable proliferation in the 1900s. Men like Tombaugh have not only left their children with roots, as the proverb wants it, but wings. The airplane. Plastic. Radar. Rockets. Transistors. Turbojets. Nuclear energy. Fiberoptics. Also, uh, television. And Pluto. Exceptionally Pluto. The computer on which this book is being composed is merely a convenience. The writing could be done with a stone on the wall of a cave. What Clyde Tombaugh discovered was, in 1930, the impossible, and, although he was initially untutored himself, he taught us the word was not good English:

"I had an interest in astronomy ever since I went to grade school. That was near Streator, Illinois. I was a bookworm, and I loved geography, and I was in the sixth grade when I started wondering about geography on other planets. I had an uncle who owned a three-inch telescope, and he would lend it to me for weeks at a time. The telescope wasn't the best; it was crude and it had all these false colors, so it didn't give much definition. Yet I was able to see the larger craters on the moon, the ring of Saturn, and the phases of Venus.

"My uncle also lent me a book on astronomy. It was small but informative, and I read the thing so many times that I knew some of the pages word for word. I knew the statistical figures of the planets by heart; I found out about the sun and some of the stars. I also read about Galileo Galilei, who proved that the earth revolved around the sun instead of the other way around; I read about Sir William Herschel, he discovered the planet Uranus; and I read about Percival Lowell, who became a hero to me and founded Lowell Observatory.

"Percival Lowell was a member of the famous Lowell family from Boston. They were rich and influential, and he became a rich and influential astronomer. He was also an outcast among astronomers, because he had theories that got him into trouble with his peers. He studied the canals on Mars, for example, and he believed they were created by highly intelligent beings up there. And then he got this idea that there was a ninth planet. That's why Lowell Observatory started looking for the planet; Lowell wanted to show he was right.

"I never knew Lowell. He died in 1916. But it's interesting that he was my boyhood hero and one of the reasons I got into astronomy. Between jobs on the farm, of course. We moved to Kansas in 1922, where my father had a large wheat farm. He couldn't afford to hire anybody to help with the work, so I was the one. I can't say I enjoyed it. I was far more interested in books and in machines than I was in crops. One year we got hit with a terrible hailstorm, we lost everything, and I vowed then I would get off the farm just as soon as I could.

"I built my first telescope in 1927. I still have it, a nine-inch reflector, out on the lawn. I used to keep it in a storm cellar. It is a very good telescope. I even ground the mirror by myself. I used it to make some early drawings of the markings on Jupiter and Mars, in 1928, and I sent the drawings to Lowell Observatory. I wasn't looking for a job, but that's what it led to. Dr. V. M. Slipher was the observatory director, and he liked the drawings, and he wrote almost immediately to ask me if I would be interested in doing night work that would involve long exposures in an unheated dome. I didn't know what that meant, but I accepted a 'few months' trial' and stayed on for fourteen years."

Lowell Observatory was opened in 1894, chiefly to study the crisscross markings on Mars. (Incidentally, the theory of purposely constructed canals was not conclusively set aside until the advent of space probes, three-quarters of a century later.) Percival Lowell also used his institution to look for what he called a Trans-Neptunian planet, and what others came to know as Planet X. Lowell wasn't the first to suspect the existence of a ninth body. Astronomers had also searched for a Planet O and a Planet P, et cetera. But Lowell spent the most time and money looking. And he was roundly hooted for it until his death.

Tombaugh says the derision should be considered in context. The common wisdom about astronomy, if one will forgive the comparison, was very much limited in scope. The science in the 1920s was still largely confined to Milky Way concepts. Astronomers were beginning to peek at other lights beyond these limits, but no one was certain there were additional nebulae until the nearest galaxies were precisely measured with the first 100-inch telescope in the 1920s. Quasars were unknown. Black holes were fifty years away from interpretation. Another planet? Next they'll say the steady state theory is dated.

"I arrived in Flagstaff, Arizona, in January of 1929, and went right to the observatory with Dr. Slipher. He showed me my room in the administration building, a very small room, and told me a little of what I would be doing. Keep in mind that I was just an untried young man from nowhere. I had to stoke the furnace, for one thing. It's cold in Flagstaff [elevation 7250 feet], and the administration building was heated with a wood furnace. I had to go down every couple of hours to keep it going. I also had to remove snow from the domes, and there was a lot of snow in Flagstaff; three feet at a time was not uncommon.

"My main job, though, was to participate in a renewed search for the Trans-Neptunian planet. The original search had been called off when Lowell died. He had looked for the planet with a five-inch telescope, which means he didn't have a chance of finding anything because he couldn't see far enough out. Then he looked with a nine-inch telescope that he borrowed, but the search was very sloppy and he failed again. When Lowell died he left a lot of money to the observatory, but his widow tried to break the will. There was a ten-year legal battle, at which time the observatory was forced to go on hold, and the planet search stopped.

"Lowell's widow did not win out, but it cost the observatory a lot of money. So when I started I knew right away there was a pressure to produce. Dr. Slipher had bought a new thirteen-inch objective-lens telescope for the search—it was a beautiful thing, and very expensive—and it was obvious that he wanted to prove that it was worth the money. There was also this lingering doubt about the project in the scientific community. So I knew Slipher expected results. I think maybe he was a little too anxious sometimes. Be that as it may, I spent the first few months learning how I was going to search for Planet X.

"How would you do that? The object was to search for a very dim point, the planet, among millions of other points, the stars. How do you pick out one from the others? Only by its motion. Stars are fixed in place, but planets move around the sun; that's one of the things that make them planets. So I was to take a photograph of a particular area of the sky, and then, in a little while, take another photograph of the same area. Then I was taught to compare the photographs to see if any of the thousands of images had moved. That was the whole of it. I was to take the pictures, night after night, of prescribed areas.

"Actually, I didn't compare the photographs at first. Not personally. Slipher did, and others, because I think they wanted to find the planet right off. I didn't think that was a good idea. I didn't think it was good to make quick searches, because that was a way to make mistakes. You have to be methodical. You have to look at every image, thousands and thousands and thousands, and not miss a one. If you miss one, it might be the planet. That happened, you know. I took some early photographs at Lowell of Pluto, when Dr. Slipher was making the comparison. He didn't take the time to do it right, however, and he missed the image.

"We did have mechanical help making the photographic comparisons. We used a blink-comparator machine. We took the photographs on fourteen-by-seventeen-inch glass plates, which I would develop in a darkroom, and then the plates would be placed in the machine, where one would blink on, then the other would blink on, back and forth, so that you could make systematic comparisons without moving your eyes from one plate to the other. The blinking was very rapid; I found that three alternating views per second was the best rate. It still took several hours to scan a plate, but it could be done thoroughly.

"I took my first plate in April of 1929. Plate number one. It was a nice night, with a breeze, and freezing temperatures. It might be interesting to note that it was the first of 362 pairs of plates I took at that observatory over fourteen years. I continued to search after I found Pluto. I was a perfectionist in that way. I took photographs over thirty thousand square degrees of the sky, everything that could be seen from the observatory latitude, and, if you add it all up, I spent seven thousand hours at that blink-comparator, and I looked at ninety million star images. I don't think anyone else has seen as much in such detail."

Tombaugh says it was the most tedious work he has ever known. And exacting. Day after day. Week upon week. The glass plates would break. The telescope would not hold the guide star. The clouds could ruin an entire night's schedule. Then there were the inevitable self-doubts. Tombaugh says asteroids move like planets (they are known as miniplanets), and he was tortured that he might claim one as Planet X. He was twenty-three. Kids foul up.

He came eventually to the blues. The dome was cold, the hours were endless, and he was making ninety dollars a month. He still wanted a career in astronomy, though, and he knew this might be his only opportunity. Moreover, he was the only man in the world who was paid to look for Planet X. That was something. He decided to redouble the effort. He fixed the mechanical problems, he solved the worry about asteroids; he would scan the whole damn galaxy, if only to prove there were only eight planets after all:

"In January of 1930, a year after I came to the Observatory, I began taking new photographs of the Gemini region. That was Percy Lowell's favorite location, and Dr. Slipher also favored it. I had taken plates of the area before, so this was another go-around. I worked my way across the region, until on January 21 I fixed on Delta Geminorum, and it started out to be a good night was in the offing. But then the wind came up, bad, and I lost sight of my guide star. I thought about stopping, but I hung on through a full hour's exposure.

"When I developed the plate later it was a mess. The star images were puffed up, and I'd lost a lot of the clarity. I lost about one and a half magnitude. I didn't pay much attention to the plate for that reason, not until later. But actually, that plate was the first one I looked at that showed Pluto. The January 21 plate. Some people have said this means that the planet was actually discovered January 21, but I don't go along with that. I didn't see Pluto then. I didn't recognize it for another month, on another plate, so that was the discovery date.

"I photographed that Delta Geminorum region again on January 23. And then I photographed the comparison plate on January 29. Then I put them in the blink-comparator on the morning of February 18. I viewed the plates for several hours, until I had covered about one-fourth of the images. This is what I mean by tedious work. It took all day of very concentrated effort to compare all of the images, tiny little dots, most of them the size of periods in a sentence. I always worked from right to left on the plates so that I would remember where I was in case I left the machine.

"I always marked a north-south center line on the last plate taken. That was also for viewing reference. And I had just returned to it, and scanned a few fields to the left, when I saw an image of the fifteenth magnitude pop in and out of my view. That's the way I could tell something moved. If it was in one place on one plate and not in the same place on the second plate, it was moving. I said 'That's it,' and I think that's all I said right then. I checked to make sure the movement was to the east. It was, and I knew I had found a planet.

"I had to make absolutely certain, however. I was very excited. I measured the shift of the image with a ruler, and it was 3.5 millimeters. Then I replaced one of the plates with that January 21 plate, the one that had been distorted by the wind, and I found the image on it was 1.2 millimeters east of the January 23 position. That was exactly the way it should have been. I knew for sure then, there was no question, and I had complete confidence in my work. So I stopped, and sat back to relax, and I was so thrilled that I was actually shaking.

"It was about four o'clock in the afternoon. I was so excited I forgot to look at my watch to record the exact time. Some people have criticized me for that. A lot of astronomers since then have been angry about it. They've said 'Well, why didn't you record that?,' as if I had done something terrible, and I've said that it didn't make a darn bit of difference. The planet had been unknown for hundreds of millions of years; why worry about a few seconds? Four o'clock was close enough. And it was closer to five by the time I had confirmed it.

"Then I went down the hall to see Dr. Slipher. I paused before I went in so that I could act as nonchalant as possible. When I walked in he was looking at some papers on his desk, and I said, 'Dr. Slipher, I found your Planet X.' Well, he rose right up out of his desk with a look of elation and also of reservation. I said that I would show him the evidence if he wanted. So he raced down the hall, and I could hardly keep up with him. He was excited. Boy! You can see how these people felt. They'd been laughed at for years; this was vindication."

News of the discovery was not released until March 13. That was the seventy-fifth anniversary of Percival Lowell's birth. The observatory sent a cable announcement: "Systematic search begun years ago supplementing Lowell's investigations for Trans-Neptunian planet has revealed object which since seven weeks has in rate of motion and path consistently conformed to Trans-Neptunian body at approximate distance he assigned. Fifteenth magnitude. Position March twelve days, three hours GMT was seven seconds of time west from Delta Geminorum, agreeing with Lowell's predicted longitude."

"The planet was not named for several months. We didn't really think about it very much, because we were so busy at this time, but the public began clamoring for a name. So we discussed it. A lot of names were suggested. Lowell's widow wanted it named after her, which was ironic since she was responsible for stopping the original search. We also thought about naming it for Lowell himself, but that would not have been in keeping with custom. It's customary to name planets after mythical gods.

"The trouble with the mythical gods, however, was that most of the names were already in use. We would have liked to have named the planet Minerva, the goddess of wisdom, in honor of Lowell's insight, but the name had already been assigned to an asteroid. So it came down to Pluto and Cronus. Cronus was suggested by an astronomer nobody liked, so that was out. Pluto was suggested by a child in Britain, and it stuck. Pluto, god of the underworld. Also, the first two letters in Pluto are Lowell's initials."

The discovery of the ninth planet created international delight. But also a permanent dilemma. The planet is so far away, between 2.69 and 4.65 billion miles from earth, that it remains very difficult to study. And it is so small, no more than 1500 miles in diameter, that there is continuing disagreement whether it is in actuality the littlest planet in the solar system or the largest asteroid. At any rate, it now has its own moon, Charon, discovered in 1978.

Clyde Tombaugh lives with his wife next door to his nine-inch telescope in Las Cruces, New Mexico. He is short, and bent some, a professor emeritus of astronomy at the University of New Mexico. When he looked at those ninety million stars during his stay at Lowell University, he also discovered a globular starcluster, a super cluster of galaxies, several lesser clusters, five open galactic star clusters, one comet, and an estimated 775 asteroids. He counted 3969 asteroid images on the plates he took, 1807 variable stars, and 29,548 galaxies.

"There is still a question as to whether there is another planet out there. Or two, or three, or whatever. It's possible. But it would have to be very small. I would not have missed anything big. In fact, I would not have missed anything small either, not within the limits of my plates. I am a perfectionist. When I looked at the ninety million stars, I saw every one of the ninety million stars, and I guarantee there is no planet in my plate limits.

"So someone would have to start all over and use a more powerful telescope to pick up fainter lights. And I don't know whether anyone would want to do that. A larger telescope would increase the number of star images by about twelvefold, and that would be just overwhelming. I spent seven thousand hours studying my plates over fourteen years, but a man with a larger telescope might have to spend fifty thousand hours over forty, fifty, or sixty years. Who's going to do it? When I think about it sometimes, I can't even believe I did it."

On June 24, 1947, an acting United States deputy marshal named Kenneth Arnold was flying a rescue mission over the Cascade Mountains in the Pacific Northwest when, as he put it, he was startled by "a tremendously bright flash of light" bouncing off the skin of his plane. He said he looked around, to see where it had come from, and he noticed a cluster of nine objects racing across the sky in an inverted echelon pattern in the vicinity of Mount Rainier. He later told an

Oregon newspaper the objects "looked like a saucer would if you skipped it across the water."

That newspaper announced the moment to the world. The first flying saucers had been seen, traveling at about 1350 miles an hour like geese going backward. Skeptics said the objects may have been weather balloons, but millions of Americans wondered otherwise, and Unidentified Flying Objects took a place in the lore of the land. And in that of most other lands. One computered calculation estimates more than 100,000 reported sightings worldwide since 1947, about 10 percent of which have not been assigned to known circumstances.

In 1966, a George Gallup poll indicated that 34 percent of American adults said they believed in flying saucers. By 1987 Gallup said that 50 percent believed, with one in eleven people saying they had seen them personally.

JOE MCKIBBEN

Joseph McKibben would agree with those who say that "history is the short trudge between Adam and the atom." But he would not agree that since this is true, since man is finally beginning to understand his journey, he must now and suddenly contemplate the prospects of its fiery end. McKibben is a physicist who helped develop the first nuclear detonation. He is in this respect one of the few of that group who is still around to defend the enterprise. Yes, he admits, it was frightening what the scientists had in their notebooks; yet there were no Frankensteins in New Mexico in 1945, only men on the moving edge of the inevitable. The bomb was going to be born. The need to know was the midwife. McKibben thinks it was everlastingly fortunate that the delivery took place in America. And if he is going to go to hell, he continues, it won't be for stealing thunder from the gods.

"The thing that people tend to forget is that we were called to New Mexico because the nation was in a world war. And when we started working on the original bomb, it was because we worried that the people we were fighting were working on it. The Germans had been experimenting for many years [they were the first to split the atom on purpose, in 1939], and you have to appreciate how we felt. Nobody wanted Adolf to get the first bomb, because everyone knew what he'd do with it if he did. Our job was to prevent it; the morality considerations came later."

Joe McKibben is a tall man, thin, and, if it's not stretching it to say, he has a Strangelovian laugh. (Remember Peter Sellers in the war room?) A tight smile, teeth together, to filter actual whimsy. And the noise. Like a nervous bleat. On the oddest occasions.

McKibben is seventy-five. He has been engaged in nuclear research for fifty years. Early in the morning of July 16, 1945, he helped arm an atomic explosive on a 103-foot tower at a site near the Rio Grande, and just before 5:29 A.M. he threw the switches that, at 5:29:45, ignited the world's first nuclear blast.

"There was some concern about it, that's true. Enrico Fermi had brought it up years before during his work with reactors at the University of Chicago. I guess he had made some back-of-the-envelope calculations—or, not really calculations, but looking at the possibilities of a reaction getting started in the atmosphere. He concluded that the possibility was remote. He decided the reaction could be contained and controlled, and I was pretty convinced he was right. But I could not be totally convinced. I felt the odds were less than one in a thousand of something like that. But no one knew absolutely what would happen—blow up the world or something."

There is the laugh. Joe McKibben uses it when he is uncomfortable. He does not like to speak to the risks at the creation. He does not like to speculate about dramatics and emotions and other ancillary topics. He is a scientist, dry and exceedingly careful. He spent the night before that first explosion sleeping under the shot tower. There was a rainstorm in progress, and electrical disturbances in the atmosphere. What would have happened if lightning had hit the tower? McKibben says simply that the bomb might have blown. So what? It didn't. Naturally, he notes, "We didn't know everything."

Yet the scientists at the beginning did know a great deal. The atom was enigmatic but familiar. The countdown in New Mexico actually began in the Greece of 2400 years before, where a philosopher named Democritus decided that all matter is made up of invisible particles. The theory was instantly buried—no one knew what the great man was talking about—but it was revived in the seventeenth century by Isaac Newton. The particles were then linked to electricity (electrons) in the eighteenth century, and the study of atoms was popularized by subsequent research in X-rays, uranium, and radioactivity.

The studies came of age in the 1900s and changed the visage of human thought and interaction. The initial fruit was picked in Europe, where it was cooked in the cauldron of the Third Reich. The Nazis created large explosions when they began to split the atom in their laboratories, creating the equivalent energy of 200 million electron volts at one point. Then, ironically, A. Hitler made a telling contribution to the American bomb. His regime drove many of the great European scientists to America—Einstein, Fermi, Neils Bohr—and the refugees were married in America to bring about the New Mexico progeny.

There were natives in on it also.

"I was raised on a farm in Missouri. I went to a one-room schoolhouse in a small town north of Jefferson City. It was a place where you could take advantage of the classes, and I went through eight grades in six years. I didn't have any ready goal, except I wanted to be a mechanical engineer or a scientist. I remember being very interested in the theory of relativity, and maybe that did it, because I majored in physics at Park College, near Kansas City. I graduated in 1933, and did graduate and post-doctorate work at the University of Wisconsin.

"I was a post-doctorate fellow when the Japanese bombed Pearl Harbor. That's when I got started in what was going to be the bomb project. I worked with a couple of Van de Graff machines [electrostatic generators] at Wisconsin. I built one of them myself, and I was asked to make some tests. There was a man named Gregory Bright—he was one of the first organizers of the bomb project— and he asked me to use the Van de Graff to make fission cross-section measurements. I don't recall the exact dates now; it was after we had gotten in the war.

"It was secret work. But I knew exactly what I was doing. It was generally known then that a fission bomb was possible. We called it a fission bomb, the word atomic is a shorthand invention, but as I say most of us thought it would work. I was the senior man with the Van de Graffs, even though I was just out of graduate school and I hadn't actually been working with neutrons, but there was no mystery about anything; I was told all along that we wanted a detonation from a controlled chain reaction, the biggest explosion of all time.

"Not many people know it, but Gregory Bright was in charge of all this research at one time. And the original name of the project was the OSRD, I believe, the Office of Scientific Research and Development. But Gregory never could have directed the thing all the way through. He was a Russian, and he had the personality we often associate with Russians, and he was let go. The government hired that military general then [Leslie Groves], and he brought in [J. Robert] Oppenheimer, who was in charge in New Mexico.

"I met with Oppenheimer the first time in the fall of 1942 at the University of Chicago, when he called in all of the representatives of the various research arms. And we had a mild disagreement there. I understood his point of view; he didn't think we were getting a good reaction picture; he said there was a resonance in it that might be trouble. But I said I didn't think it would bother us, and—what the hell—it was all we had. And he accepted it. He was a good diplomat. He was good at many things. He put all of the pieces together."

McKibben went to New Mexico with a wife and child. He also took his Van de Graff machine. It was the spring of 1943. The tide in the war had turned. The German offensive had been stopped at Stalingrad. The Allies won the North African campaign. The Axis forces were soon to be in full retreat. The

*bomb was still to be built, however, under the code name Manhattan Project,
and hundreds of soldiers, laborers, technicians, and scientists were assembled at
a location that had once been used for a boy's school: Los Alamos.*

*An aside. McKibben is a physicist and talks like one. His eyes light up with
recollections, but his tongue can wiggle in the dark. Much reconstruction has
therefore been necessary here. The memories are his. The words, not always.*

"At first we just plunged into the job of setting things up in Los Alamos. It
was all built from nothing. There weren't many roads, there wasn't very much
asphalt of any kind, actually, and we had to get settled before we could work.
We set up our shops—some of the buildings were already there—and we got
homes for our families. Some people lived in quonset huts. My wife and I were
in a quadraplex built for the purpose. There was a commissary; the government
furnished coal for heating. It wasn't so bad. It was rather close, but we got by.

"The security was strict. I could not tell anyone where I was. If I wanted to
write my parents, I had to send the letter back to Madison, Wisconsin, where it
would be postmarked and forwarded. Mail was censored; we couldn't travel
without permission; and what few phones we had were tapped. One time my
wife got a call about her brother. He had been in the Army and went batty or
something, and her family called to ask her to come to see him. She said she
didn't know if she could get permission to leave for that reason, and, just then, a
voice on the line said 'It's okay, Mrs. McKibben, you can go.'

"I could not tell my wife what I was doing, naturally. I think she had a suspicion we were building a big weapon, but nothing more than that. My young
son wondered why I didn't come home some nights. He became frightened because of that. I told him that he didn't have to worry, that I wasn't in any danger,
but he got worse and worse. After a while my wife had to take him way, back
East. Neither one of them were when we actually set off the bomb. I suppose
that was okay, however. I worked all the time, and I never really had time for
them."

*McKibben worked in his laboratory until he received a new assignment in
March 1945. He says he was promoted to more critical work just prior to a test
run of the first nuclear shot. He says 100,000 tons of conventional explosives
were taken into the desert then, at what was to become the White Sands Missile
Range, north of Alamagordo, and stacked for detonation. The idea was to test
instruments, to "get everything lined up." Then it was learned that, Good God,
the firing mechanisms were not ready:*

"The government had hired a guy to do that job. I've forgotten his name,
but he was a person who had a lot of experience working on railroad relays
[electromagnetic devices that can be used to activate switches]. Here, I have a

relay here. It's like the ones we used. Solenoids. Contacts. See the contacts there? Anyway, the guy was hired to set these up, and two or three weeks before the conventional test, well, he asked for a delay. That was when the shit hit the fan, if I may say so. He wasn't ready by any means, and that was a setback.

"So they started to look around for somebody to replace this guy, and their eyes fell on me. I had a simple technical ability; I had built a Van de Graff; and, in addition, I was a group leader. They asked me to get something ready, and I did. We had all the circuits and the relays, and we had the boxes all made, so it was a matter of arranging it. We took it down for the hundred-ton test. There were some difficulties; not everything worked as well as we wanted it to work, but from then on I was in charge of the timing and for the real thing."

Put another way, he would blow the bomb and at the same time set off the experiments and cameras necessary to record the blast. Everything had to be synchronized. McKibben was the man to do it. He says today that he "didn't do anything—throwing the switch was not important." The truth is he wired the system when others could not, and he detonated it before it might otherwise have been blown. That was most important. The war in Europe was over, but not the one in Asia. The bomb was consigned in July; Japan gave up a month later—any delay would have cost lives.

The bomb was put in place on July 14. It was fastened inside a sheet-metal enclosure on a oakwood platform atop a metal derrick. It was fat, black, and festooned with cables and wiring, some of which were connected to an aluminum firing unit. The bomb was over ten feet long, slightly more than four feet in diameter, and weighed 10,000 pounds. The device was originally designed to fire at the urging of a gun assembly that would shoot its parts together. It was ultimately modified to detonate by an implosion; the nuclear material was wrapped in chemical explosives that, on activation, caused chain reaction.

The desert site at White Snads was designated Trinity. The explosion would be so fierce that the floor of the earth would be fused into a green composition named trinitite. Windows would blow out of houses 200 miles away. A 1200-foot crater would be dug. The tower would evaporate. Life to one mile would cease.

"I was not paying all that much attention to anything except what I was assigned to do, but I can give you a fair description of Trinity. It was set in a large valley between a pair of small mountain ranges, and, being July, it was hot. There were insects, and snakes, and spiders. We set up experiments everywhere, and we had three main administration bunkers plus a small unmanned bunker for materials. The big bunkers were about ten thousand yards away from the tower, or about five miles.

"A rainstorm came in the day before we were scheduled to go. And while we worked through that someone got an idea about sabotage. There was a security group, but three of us decided to spend the night under the tower. Ken Bainbridge was in charge of the test shot itself; George Kistiakowsky was in charge of explosives; and I was there for the timing. We were the arming party. We stayed up all night, but I did doze a little, and, in the rain, I dreamt Kistiakowsky was squirting me with a hose.

"Norris Bradbury was also out there. [He later became the director of Los Alamos Laboratories.] And there was some lightning flashing around. So at one point I said 'Well, I wonder what would happen if lighting hit the tower?' He didn't say a damn thing, but his face got an inch longer. Then he drove away in a Jeep, and later he called me on the phone. He said, 'Did lightning hit yet?' and I said 'No, we're still here, and I wish I'd not brought up the question.'

"Actually, I wasn't too concerned with it. I was concerned about the rain. It set us back a bit, we were supposed to have gone off earlier than we did, and I worried what the water was doing to my wires and my connections. But the decision was eventually made, and we started getting ready way before dawn on the sixteenth. There were some technical pressures to get it going; we were on the same radio frequency as Radio of America, and we had to get off the air before they came on.

"I was stationed in the South 10,000 [bunker]. Oppenheimer was there, Bainbridge, Donald Hornig [later the science adviser to President Kennedy]. I can't remember who else. Kistiakowsky certainly. There wasn't a big crowd, because it wasn't a big place. The bunker was made of heavy timbers, and there was dirt piled up outside the walls. There was an open door in back, facing away from the tower, but there weren't any slits in the walls, so we could not see anything at the tower without going outside.

"I was not nervous, not at all. And I was too goddamned tired to think about history being made or things of that nature. I had made all of the last-minute connections at the tower and at the 800 yard station, and now I was working on my lock box. That's where the main switches were kept. There were nine switches inside: they weren't the basic switches, they were safety switches. I also had four meters there, with a camera on them. This was forty-three years ago, and it didn't look like NASA control.

"The switch that activated the bomb was on an automatic timer. The timer was a little drum five inches in diameter, and it had little pegs on it that operated microswitches. And the way I activated the timer was with a toggle switch. Once that switch was on, the automatic timer took over. The only way it could be stopped then was by Don Hornig. We had had an electrical problem during a dry run, so we put in a protection: Hornig could throw a switch that would stop the operation down to the last second.

"That wasn't necessary, though. Everything went all right. We had a public address system coming into the bunker, and I was told in that way when to activate the automatic timer. There was a guy named Sam Allison on the PA, with a good senatorial voice, and he did the countdown. He told me later that he thought he was the first man ever to count backwards for something like this. I threw one switch at minus twenty minutes, one at minus five minutes, and then one at minus forty-five seconds.

"I also threw a switch at plus ten seconds. By then this great flash of light had come into the bunker through the open door, and everything was like daylight. After that I went out to see it. By that time the brilliant flash of light was gone and I could look directly at the blast without hurting my eyes. At that moment it was very colorful; it had picked up a lot of iron in the soil. Red. Turbulent orange. I can still see it today, sort of. It was the only atomic explosion I ever saw in person, and I still see it.

"While I was outside, I kept looking at my watch. Because when the shock wave arrived I got behind the bunker for protection. I didn't know exactly how it would come, but somehow or the other I felt it was going to be big. Actually, I didn't feel too much. Someone said it knocked Kistiakowsky down; I'm not sure of that. Then I looked out again when the wind went by, and the mushroom was forming, a great huge thing. And I knew it had been big; it was ten times bigger than we thought it would be."

The public was not advised of the test until after the United States dropped a similar device on Hiroshima on August 6. Three fifths of the city was wiped off the face of the earth and 20 percent of the population was destroyed. Another bomb was dropped on Nagasaki on August 9, killing or mutilating 100,000 people, and, forty-eight days after Trinity, the Second World War ended.

Joe McKibben never left Los Alamos. The crude quonsets of the Manhattan Project were to yield to the most advanced nuclear laboratories on earth, and McKibben stayed on to become an old hand and reluctant luminary. He lives with his wife in a ranch home, where he is working on what he call a revolutionary "new field of force theory" that nonetheless sounds dull as he tells it, and, good for him, he says he will win the Nobel Prize yet or die trying.

He notes that most of his colleagues at Trinity are dead. McKibben is therefore their spokesman now, and, for this reason, careful with hindsight.

"There were discussions that began immediately after we set off the bomb. The controversies and so on and so forth. But I wasn't part of that, and I've never gotten into it much. When the shot took place at Trinity, my immediate reaction was, okay, we have won the war. That was the goal, we succeeded, and I've never regretted it. I've always had the feeling that we were lucky to have done it. If we hadn't someone else would. I think the Russians would have gone ahead with it, and if that had happened, the world today would be different."

The United States nuclear arsenal contained nine warheads in 1946, the only ones in the world. The number in 1987 had grown to almost 55,000, with a total yield equivalent to 16 billion tons of TNT, or about 2660 times the firepower released in World War II.

What is it that conceives this kind of business? The human brain as it is now constituted is a three-pound, 40,000-year-old instrument that contains approximately 100 trillion nerve connections. If it were a modern computer of a comparable capacity it would be 100 stories tall and as wide as Montana.

RUTH BECKER BLANCHARD

On the first day of September 1985 a team of French and American scientists came upon magnificent buried treasure in the dark and frigid depths of the North Atlantic. The researchers had for several weeks been combing a 150-square-mile area south of Newfoundland, finding naught but exhaustion for their troubles, but all of a sudden, very early that morning, the team's pilotless submarine made contact with a large metal object settled in muck at 41 degrees 56 minutes North latitude, 49 degrees 56 minutes West longitude, which proved to be the boiler of one of the largest and most tragically controversial passenger vessels that ever sailed and sank on the sea.

The steamship TITANIC *had been found.*

In two pieces, which is some satisfaction to Ruth Blanchard:

"Yes, that's right, I have been trying to tell people that for years. I have been saying all along that the ship split in two while it was going down. I could see it distinctly from where I was, in the lifeboat. The boat was going down very slowly, it wasn't dashing into the water at all; and it was breaking apart, probably at the place where it hit the iceberg. There was a tremendous hole there. It was plain to see, even though it was night. And it split in half. I'm glad to see we know that now."

Mrs. Blanchard is eighty-seven. Her maiden name was Becker, and she was a girl of twelve when the ship that "God himself could not sink" did anyway. It was April 14-15, 1912. Some 1500 of the 2227 passengers died. One book, by Walter Lord, called it A Night to Remember.

"It was a beautiful sight," Mrs. Blanchard says.

Beautiful?

"Yes, the lights and all. So big. I remember it as beautiful."

Ruth Becker Blanchard was born on the East Coast of India, to American missionaries. It was a period when the imperial British star was beginning to descend in world affairs, partially in the shadow of the streaking American comet, and the word on the playing fields of the Commonwealth was that this new ship, built in Belfast, would put the ebullient upstarts to the West in their place. It was conveniently overlooked, if known at all, that the Titanic *was almost entirely financed through United States banks, and was in effect American property.*

"We lived near Madras," Mrs. Blanchard says, "which is just north of the island of Ceylon [now Sri Lanka]. My father taught missionary school, and all of us kids were raised over there."

How many were in your family?

"My father, my mother, a brother, sister, and myself. I might tell you that the reason we were on the *Titanic* was my brother. He became quite sick in India, and the doctor said that he could not make him well, he would die in India, and we should take him to America where the medical facilities were better."

Through England, correct?

"Yes. Right away my father booked passage on a ship for my mother and we children on a ship from Madras to London, and, also, the *Titanic* was leaving from Southhampton for New York City at about this time, so we got passage on that. Father could not leave his job, and stayed behind. There were four of us on the *Titanic*."

The maiden voyage.

"That's right. It was the first time it was sailing with passengers. And my mother was very dubious about going on a new ship that had never crossed the ocean. She told the purser about that. He said, 'Madam, you do not have to worry about anything, because the *Titanic* has watertight compartments; even if something did happen, the compartments would keep it afloat.' "

"The ship that could not sink." The fact is no one who had anything to do with building the TITANIC *ever said as much, specifically. Shipyard officials said the boat was as safe as 1912 technology allowed. White Star Line operators stressed the remarkably engineered bulkheading arrangements. The talk of guarantees, therefore, was public conclusion. The newspapers played it as nationalistic pride, also to tweak the ever crowing Americans, also and more importantly to caution Germany, an increasingly aggressive European pest.*

The TITANIC *set out for New York on April 10. It was the biggest vessel in history to the time, four times the length of the Statue of Liberty, displacing*

46,328 tons. (Several larger ships were built later, including the 83,673-ton QUEEN ELIZABETH and the 1035-foot NORWAY). The crew was said to be the finest ever assembled on one boat; the captain (Edward J. Smith) was the highest-paid seaman of the day; and the trip was scheduled at a decent time in the North Atlantic, the weather being clear, chilly, and the waters generally calm.

However, the ship's conduct proved to be unhappily ambitious. The captain wanted to get to the United States quickly (read: impressively), hence he ignored the Marconigram warnings of gathering ice, and he pushed on at a reckless 22 knots per hour in the dark, until just before midnight, April 14.

"We were in second class," Mrs. Blanchard says. "There was first class, second class, third class, all the way down to those poor people in steerage. I think we were on deck number two."

When were you first aware that something had happened?

"My mother and I both woke up at midnight, and she was a little bit scared because we couldn't hear the engines. On a big ship like that you can always hear the rumbling of the engines, and since we were not supposed to land anywhere between London and New York, she said, 'Something's the matter—we've stopped moving.' "

Were you scared?

"No. I was just a young girl. I didn't think that way. But Mother got up to ask the steward if anything was wrong. He said, 'Well, it's just a small thing. You can go on back to bed.' And she did. But she did not go back to sleep. And the longer she lay there, the more commotion she heard. People were moving around upstairs, and they were racing around in the halls."

She got up again?

"She did. She went in the hall, and this time the steward said, 'Madam, the *Titanic* has struck an iceberg. Go back to your cabin immediately, put on your lifebelts, put your coats over your nightclothes, and come up to the boat deck and wait for orders.' "

This was now April 15?

"Very early in the morning, after midnight. My mother got us out of bed. I don't think she told us about the iceberg—if she did I don't remember it—but she got us dressed, and after we were in our things, we all went to the top deck as we'd been told."

Was there any panic at this time?

"We went into a great big room on the top deck, and the only thing I saw was that a lot of men and women, mostly women, were sitting there crying, because they didn't know what to do."

No pushing and shoving?

"I never saw any of that. People were sad but quiet. Even my mother, who was very worried. She said to me, 'Ruth, I didn't know it was this cold. Would you go back down to our cabin and bring up blankets to put around you, your brother and sister?' "

How cold was it?

"I guess I was too excited to really notice. I was marveling at everything. It was an adventure at my age. I got the blankets, but I didn't have time to give them to my brother and sister, because the officers came in to say it was time to get in the lifeboats. Then one officer took my brother and sister, and took them up an iron ladder, and put them both in a boat."

How about you?

"They would not let me in then. Nor would they let my mother in. My mother said, 'Please let me in, those are my children,' and when they relented, my mother got in and called back to me to go along the deck right away and look for another lifeboat."

How long did that take?

"Not long. I saw another officer putting people in a boat, and I asked him. He said 'Sure,' and he picked me up and dumped me in. I was the last one. We were all crowded together, we had to stand up in the boat, and there wasn't room for anyone else."

How many were in your boat?

"We had about sixty-five or seventy people. And they started lowering the boat just after I got in. And I'll tell you that was bumpy. You see, the *Titanic* was new, and the paint was like glue on the pulleys that were used to lower the lifeboats. They were stuck, and the boat did not go down evenly. One end would drop, then the other end would drop, and everybody worried about falling out. Then, when the boat was almost to the water, we saw another boat being lowered right over us. We yelled at them to hold it, but they didn't hear. So one of the men in our boat [boat number thirteen], took a knife and cut the rope, so we could get away. Luckily we didn't have far to drop; we made it, but when we pushed off that other boat plopped right where we had been."

What time was it now?

"Oh, one-thirty, I'm not sure. But I do know the first thing I saw when we were in the water. Now this is what I remember seeing. There was a great big gash in the side of the *Titanic*, where the ship had hit the iceberg, and water was rushing in."

Was it going down yet?

"Very slowly. And it was so beautiful. When we got quite a ways away, and we looked back, the lights were on all over the ship, over the whole ship, and it was going down so smoothly. It was terrible, but it was beautiful."

Could you see the people aboard?

"Yes, and I could hear them, which was awful; I didn't like it at all. When the ship started to go down faster, the people on the decks knew it, and they started to shout and to scream. They said 'Help us, please help us!' I could see them on all of the decks. Many of them jumped overboard. Well, I didn't like it, but I don't think I really understood. I think maybe I still thought it was unsinkable and the people would still be saved."

Did any of the people who jumped come to your boat?

"One man did, but we could not take a single other person. The men would not let him in, and the poor fellow just swam away."

When did the ship finally go down?

"Not long after [2:30 A.M.]. The prow went first, dropping away, and the stern seemed to me to stand straight up in the water. It was three, four, five minutes, and it disappeared."

The broken halves of the TITANIC *came to rest at a depth of 12,000 feet. It probably took the great liner ten minutes to hit bottom, at a speed of 20 m.p.h. Later inquiries showed that most if not all loss of life could have been avoided. The ship carried lifeboats for only half the passengers, a gross error, and many of them were lowered away before filling. Also, a potential rescue ship was only ten miles away, but the radio operator of the vessel was off duty and did not hear the SOS, and the captain dismissed the distress flares as a ship-to-ship greeting.*

Mrs. Blanchard says only seven hundred people were saved:

"I still had my blankets on in the lifeboat. And the man who was in charge asked me if he could have them. He said the sailors who were rowing had been down in their bunks when the ship hit the iceberg, and they were called up to man the lifeboats before they had a chance to get jackets."

Did you give them up?

"Of course. There was quite a bit of helping one another in the boat. There was this German lady next to me, and she was crying, and I asked her why she was crying. She said she had a six-week-old baby, and she was separated from it during the confusion of getting into the lifeboats, and now she said it was in a boat by itself, wrapped up, and she thought it might be thrown over."

Thrown over?

"Accidentally. If they just thought it was a bundle of clothes. So I told the lady that I was sort of in the same predicament. I had been separated from my mother and my brother and sister. So if we were rescued I said I would help her find her baby, and she could help me find the members of my family."

And when were you rescued?

"We got off the *Titanic* about one-thirty, and we saw rockets going off in the distance about four or four-thirty. Then we heard the foghorn, and finally we saw a big light shining down on the water, and we knew it was a ship. It was the *Carpathia*. And we were saved."

Still standing up after three hours?

"Yes. They picked us out of the boat by ropes. It was so cold that our hands were frozen, we couldn't hang on to anything. So they tied us in swings and hauled us up one by one, to a big room, where they had brandy and hot coffee and some food. I didn't get any of the brandy, of course, I was not old enough, but I was thankful to be alive, and the first thing I did was to set out with the little German lady so we could find her six-week-old baby.

"And we found it. Oh, my, I never saw anyone that happy in my life! She hugged it and kissed it and rocked it in her arms. Then, a little while later, about nine or ten in the morning, a woman came up to me and asked if I was Ruth Becker. I said I was, and she said 'Your mother has been looking for you.' I said You mean she's safe, and the lady said Yes, and so were my brother and sister. I was as happy as the German lady.

"So we were all okay. But we didn't celebrate, because it was a terribly sad time for many other people. You know, on the *Titanic* it was women and children first, and most of the husbands were left behind. Many of them said they would be all right, that they would be along in later lifeboats, but nobody on the *Carpathia* could be certain. So the women stood at the rail, and looked and looked to see if their husbands would come.

"They never saw them. When a boatload of women and children were rescued, the *Carpathia* would send crews out in the boat to try to find others.

But they all came back empty, so far as I could tell. All those men. Even if they did jump off before the *Titanic* went down, they could not last long in the cold water. So then, when all the boats were in, at twelve noon, the captain announced that the *Carpathia* was going on to New York City. And everybody knew then. All the men had drowned. Oh, my, when he made that announcement, the whole ship went silent."

The governments of both Britain and the United States investigated the disaster. One was inept and the other almost insolent. The Washington probers fussed and fumed, helping nothing, and the London sleuths agreed that someone must be guilty but could not decide who. The English raised a monument to the TITANIC captain, who had gone down with the ship, and several groups were also formed to defend the skipper of the CARPATHIA. White Star Lines eventually paid $2.5 million to the families of the dead, about $1600 a corpse.

Later, some maritime habits were mercifully altered. An international ice patrol was formed. Ships were instructed to carry lifeboats for all passengers and crew members. And radio watching became an around-the-clock operation.

Ruth Becker Blanchard grew up in the Midwest. She married a man in the dry cleaning business. She is now a widow in Santa Barbara, California, where, in 1987, she says someone ran into her automobile, leaving her paralyzed on one side of her body.

The newspapers called her when the scientists found the TITANIC in 1985. She told them it should be left alone:

"The wreckage is a tomb for all those who died. The bottom of the ocean is their graveyard. Please, let them rest in peace."

The impression that the TITANIC could not sink was of course patently absurd. But there's been a lot of absurdity patented in the century under consideration. The flying wing, for instance, never really got off the ground. The jet car was also slowed by realities. Scientists have failed miserably with food pills, 3-D, universal languages, and two-way wrist radios. There used to be X-ray machines in the shoe stores through which customers could look at the green images of their feet, and it's a wonder anybody over fifty has any toes. And how about cocaine soft drinks, breast enlargers, and wheel knobs.

The Museum of Medical Quackery is located in St. Louis, Missouri. It features an array of items that have been idiotically associated with electricity— which in the early 1900s was touted as "life itself." (Where are you now, Boris Karlof?) The museum has everything from electric girdles to electric baths to electric bedroom slippers. There has been an electric machine to analyze per-

sonalities and several to grow hair, and there used to be a penny-arcade box, complete with a shock meter, which, it was said, would cure headaches, rheumatism, and female languidness.

BRUCE MEDARIS

Aviation, nuclear energy, and computer technology apart, the most significant scientific advancement of the twentieth century may have taken place on October 4, 1957, when the first artificial satellite was put in an orbit around the earth. It was a 184-pound ball, 23 inches in diameter, to which were affixed four antennas that lay in one direction as if they were swept by the speed, and it circled the globe every 96 minutes on an elliptical trajectory that ranged between 141 miles and 587 miles in attitude. Beep, beep. The sphere contained a radio beacon and a thermometer; it was referred to by its designers as the ES, elementary satellite, but everyone else called it Sputnik I.

The Russians had beaten the free world into space. Many Americans were flabbergasted, and at least one was exceedingly angry. John Bruce Medaris says it should never have happened:

"We could have gotten a satellite up first and there is no doubt about it. We could have done it weeks before the Soviets. We knew Moscow was working on this thing—they announced their intentions well in advance—but we didn't take it seriously. Some of our people didn't think the Russians could do it. They thought the talk was just more propaganda. Therefore it was never a priority with us; we wanted to launch a satellite, but there was no hurry to do it and we went about it the wrong way.

"Now, let's back up. Let's go through the stages of this thing. The primary purpose of rocketry at that time was military. Both the United States and the Soviet Union had developed ballistic missiles, and the technology was there to start getting into space exploration. The idea started being tossed around in the early 1950s, and it took shape by the middle of the decade. Both nations said they would try to put a satellite up during the International Geophysical Year [an eighteen-month period in 1957-1958].

"The Russians gave the job to their missile people, naturally, because they had the expertise. But the United States turned it over to Navy research—the wrong group, as it turned out. I argued against this at the time. But Dwight Eisenhower could not be persuaded. It was pure orneriness, if I may say so, and the president had bad advice. I don't think Ike really understood the importance of it all. He thought the idea of a satellite was a scientific toy, and there was no big deal to being first to deploy it.

"The Navy had an impossible job. They were assigned to build a satellite-launching vehicle from the ground up. There wasn't enough time for that. But they went ahead, and I always forget the name of that thing they were working with—what was it?—the Vanguard. They renovated a couple of sounding rockets, and they came up with a three-stage vehicle that couldn't do the job soon enough. The Vanguard worked after a while, but that was after the Sputnik shot.

"Meanwhile, I was in command at the Army Ballistic Missile Agency in Huntsville, Alabama, and we kept telling everyone that we were ready to launch at any time. We had developed an intermediate-range ballistic missile, which was a modified Redstone, and it could have easily given us a satellite before the Russians. But we were forbidden to do it. We were not allowed to load the fourth stage [with a package], or we could have put something into orbit as early as September of 1957.

"We tested that missile [Jupiter C] in its full configuration on September 20. I was told emphatically that if I loaded the fourth stage I would lose my job. The government still wanted the Vanguard to be first. So we shot the Jupiter six hundred miles up and three thousand miles downrange, and it was a tremendous accomplishment. We called it Missile 27. And we could have beaten the Russians by more than two weeks. As it was, our hands were tied; and I suspected then that the Soviet scientists might leave us behind."

We have heard from Bruce Medaris before in this book. He is the snappy octogenarian who fought in three wars for the United States, rising in the military ranks from a Marine Corps private to a major general in army ordnance. He started by cleaning rifles, which is another way to say it, and wound up commanding the development of nuclear delivery systems. He also directed the beginning of the nation's post-Sputnik satellite effort and is for this reason often called the father of America's space age.

And one more thing, also repeating the segment in Chapter 3. Medaris is a priest in the Episcopal church who believes in the teaching of Mark that "they shall lay hands on the sick and they shall recover":

"I have had cancer, so-called, three times, plus a number of other things, and there was one time that it was critical. I was told by the best medical authorities that if I had anything important to do I should get it done before Christmas of 1965, because I was dying. It was bone cancer, and it was in the thighs, and in the ribs, and the doctors said there was nothing they could do. They gave me female hormones, but, otherwise, the only thing they promised was to make me comfortable as possible.

"But I believed in Christian healing. And one night I went to a service conducted by a healer named Virginia Lively. I asked her to pray for me, and, believe me, when she put her hands on me I was quite certain something was happening. Her contact with me got very hot; it was like an electric current through my body, and I was transformed. By the fall of that year it was obvious that the disease was going away. And by the spring of 1965 there was no way to tell that I ever had bone cancer.

"People don't believe that, I know. But I'm telling you the way it happened. I went on to become a minister myself, and I've been very active in healing and exorcism and other things. The Lord said He would give us 'comforters'; He said He would not leave us 'comfortless'; and I believe this is a very real aspect of the Lord dealing with His people. I want to make it clear that I myself have never healed anyone, but the Boss has done it through me, just as He has done all the other things through me.

"I can tell you about one exorcism that was rather spectacular. I was in Florida then, and the bishop sent me a student from Rollins College, and after some conversations I determined that the young man was indeed possessed. So we put him on the floor, and I bored in on the exorcism itself. At first I had a hard time getting to the spirit inside the boy, but then the Lord gave me his name, it was the 'spirit of rebellion,' and when I called out the spirit's name and walked toward him with a crucifix, the boy just blew up. It took six strong men to hold him. Then I persuaded the boy to call out for Jesus, and when he did, he collapsed, and he was all right, and it was all over."

General Medaris is eighty-five. He was fifty-four when he was chosen to take direction of what was to become the nation's initial step into space. That step was preordained, he says, and it was the result of many footprints that had already been recorded. When the Chinese invented gunpowder in the eleventh century, they made it possible to shoot crude missiles by the thirteenth. When Isaac Newton outlined his three laws of motion in the 1660s, he said the principles would enable mankind to travel to the stars. When Robert Goddard shot the first successful liquid-propellant rocket in 1926, he laid the foundation of modern astronautics.

Medaris says the next step was the nuclear bomb. The only ones ever used in hostility were dropped from airplanes but, after World War II, the potential led to an intense competition between nations to develop more sophisticated delivery systems. And that was the start of ballistic missiles. Well, check that. The Germans created the first ballistic missiles during the war, the V-1 and V-2 (the initial stood for Vengeance). Bruce Medaris says he was introduced to the V-2 while on duty in France in 1944. One of the missiles landed and detonated near his command post. When he took over the Army Ballistic Missile Agency in 1956, he was to direct the work of some of the transplanted German scientists who had invented that vehicle.

"The Army Ballistic Missile Agency was an outgrowth of the competition between the services to build bigger and better rockets. The Air Force had its facilities, the Navy had theirs, and, until 1956, the Army effort was mostly at the Redstone Arsenal. Then Washington decided to build an intermediate range ballistic missile, and the Army wanted to do it. Looking down the road, the Army also decided to get into the whole field in a bigger way, and the Army Ballistic Missile Agency was formed as a separate command at Redstone Arsenal.

"I was in on the original planning. I had the technical knowledge, and I was the acting chief of ordnance about that time. But I didn't have any plans in this matter beyond that. Actually, I was ready to retire from the service. I had been in the military a long time, and I had given my notice to the Chief of Staff. I had a deal cooked up with [General] Omar Bradley, who was already out of the service and was in private industry. He asked me to start work with Bulova Laboratories, on Long Island, and I thought that it would be good for me.

"Then one Sunday afternoon I got a call from Carter Magruder, who was deputy chief of staff for Army logistics. He went through the whole business about the intermediate range ballistic missile, and how important the new agency would be, and I said, yes, I know all that. Then he said, 'I've got news for you.' He said, 'We have gotten word back from [Secretary of Defense] Charley Wilson that we cannot have the agency unless you are put in command of it. You are the only officer he wants. What do you say to that?' I said, yes, sir.

"I took over in February of 1956. I was the first officer in the Army to have total command of the research, the building, the production, and the deployment of a weapons system of this magnitude. But there was already a lot of work going on at Redstone. The Redstone missile was in operation. Western Electric was working on the Nike air-defense missile. The Army had already deployed the Nike-Ajax, and the Nike-Hercules was almost deployed. We also had the Hawk, the LaCrosse, the Honest John, the Little John, and other systems.

"One reason we had so many missiles was because we had those German scientists. Werner Von Braun and the V-2 people. Von Braun was one of the best of the German rocket scientists. He was hardworking and brilliant and he was thinking about putting up satellites even before the war ended. As a matter of fact, he got in trouble for that. The Nazis arrested him in 1944, because they said he was planning to divert war materials to the space idea. He was later released, and, in 1945, he and his staff managed to get out of Germany and they made their way here.

"I don't know how many times I've been asked about fighting the Germans during their war and then working with their scientists afterwards. They devised the ways for Hitler to try to kill me, and now I was hand-in-hand with the same people. I never looked at it that way. It didn't bother me a bit. I looked on them as people who were now working for the benefit of the United States, and it was a happy thing that they were. We could not have advanced so far as we did with rockets, in the time that we did, if we did not have the Germans.

"I know what people were saying. Some people still argue about it. There was the opinion that some of the scientists should have been put on trial, and the only reason we didn't do it was that we needed them. Von Braun was put in that category, and I could philosophize on that part of it all day long. But I never agreed with the persecution—and that's what it was, persecution. I believe the Justice Department was working with the KGB, trying to scrape up dirt, and the evidence is not worth the powder to blow it up. The Germans were loyal men.

"I became quite close to Von Braun. I taught him my way of doing things, such as how to keep control over the contractors, and he taught me a few things too. I think we were as good a working team as could have been formed at that time. He was the imaginative idealist, and I was pragmatic enough to keep him down to earth. I don't think we've had anyone as gifted in the space program before or since. If we would have listened to him more, instead of trying to persecute him for things that weren't true, our space program would be better off."

Medaris says Von Braun joined him wholeheartedly in the bid to get a satellite into space before the Soviet Union. He says the two men drew up a plan to launch seven small objects between January 1957 and December 1958. The government put its faith in the Navy Vanguard, however, and forbade the use of the Redstone or the Jupiter [a modified Redstone] for satellite purposes.

The Vanguard project involved the amalgamation of technologies from two existing rockets, the Viking and the Aerobee, and the construction of a new three-stage launch vehicle. Initial shots of the first stage were successful, but the Vanguard failed on its maiden launch as a complete system. The first-stage engine lost power at one second after ignition and exploded.

"I was at a cocktail party the night we heard about Sputnik. The party was for Neil McElroy, who was about to become the new secretary of defense, and he was making the rounds of the major military posts. My public relations man gave me the note, and I read it aloud. Von Braun and McElroy and I were standing together, and we discussed it immediately. Von Braun was very angry. He reminded McElroy that we could have done the same thing a long time before. But that wasn't important any more. The question was what were we going to do about it now?

"In that sense, I think, Sputnik may have been the best thing to happen to the American space program. It woke everybody up, and people began to realize the consequences. Everybody was shocked and worried, and our prestige was at stake. So I remember that night at the party, Von Braun turned to McElroy and he said we could put a reply satellite up. He said it wouldn't be the size of Sputnik, but it would be an answer. And he said we could do it in sixty days. I said, 'No, Werner. Ninety days.' That prediction turned out to be right."

Medaris got permission to launch in November. That was after the Vanguard blew up on the pad and the Russians had launched their second Sputnik, this one containing a dog named Laika, who lived in space for a week. The Defense Department initially wanted the general simply to 'prepare' for a launch, because it thought that Vanguard might still orbit a satellite in December. Medaris balked. "I said to hell with that." *The Vanguard was not ready anyway, hence the army launch was slated for January 30.*

"There was a lot of pressure all around. And not just in the technical area. One of our people had some conversations with a Russian scientist who worked on the Sputnik program, and he reported that the Russians were making space their number-one priority. They were going to send up manned satellites, and they were going to go to the moon, and we all wondered what else. If they orbited nuclear weapons over the United States, we had no defense at all.

"We took the Jupiter [called Juno for this purpose] to Cape Canaveral under cover of secrecy. We didn't name the satellite then, because we wanted to wait until it was a success. And we were not able to launch on January 30. The winds at the Cape were too strong at one point, and there was a threat of storms. My launch director was Kurt Debus. We wanted to shoot in the evening, again for reasons of secrecy, but the weather was still bad at nine-thirty that night, and I had to hold the launch.

"The next day, January 31, looked better. We picked up the count in the afternoon. I was in a blockhouse with the good view to the pad. I was struck then, as I was to be on similar launchings, by what a gorgeous and inspiring sight it was. The vehicle was a magnificent human achievement, and it pointed in the direction of divine inspiration. I had a long wait in the building, though. The good of the nation was riding on the success or failure of the shot; I was very aware of that fact.

"There was not absolute secrecy, of course. We didn't want to show too much of the vehicle, because it was a military rocket, but there were news accounts of the event, and reporters were present. I think there were two hundred reporters. The Army Ballistic Missile Agency had prepared a press kit, and there was other information available. No, the space program has been in the public domain right from the start. I'm not sure I agree with that completely, but that has been the agreement.

"We were trying for a ten-thirty-P.M. shot, but we had a pretty bad scare about nine-forty-five. The pad had been cleared, and everything seemed ready, but we had a chemical leak at the bottom of the vehicle. So we had to stop the countdown to check it out. I worried for a while that I'd have to scrub again, and that would mean I couldn't keep my promise to launch in January. Fortunately, the leak was fixed. It turned out to be nothing at all, and we started counting, if I'm right, at ten o'clock.

"Now I was very confident. But the last few moments may have been the longest of my life. In those very last seconds, one of the instruments showed some kind of a failure. No one knew right away if it was serious or not, and there wasn't any time to think about it one way or the other. I looked at Debus and he just turned his thumb up. That did it. I was confident enough to override the negative signal. I said forget it, go ahead, and after that the missile lifted off. 'Go,' I said, and it did!"

The launch occurred at 10:48 P.M. All stages worked as expected, and the satellite was released into orbit about midnight. The official announcement was made at 1:30 A.M. (all times Eastern Standard), February 1, and General Medaris says the satellite was thereupon named Explorer I in honor of balloon tests of the same name that had been conducted in the 1930s.

The nation was to launch more than fifty Explorer satellites before the program was ended. And both military and civilians had a part. The Army Ballistic Missile Agency that Medaris inaugurated became the Army Ballistic Missile Command, also under his direction, and, in 1958, President Eisenhower turned space exploration over to a National Advisory Committee for Aeronautics (NACA), later the National Aeronautics and Space Administration (NASA).

Medaris retired in 1960.

"I lost my last battle in the military. I argued very strongly against taking the military out of space exploration. I thought we should have had a joint military command formed from the three services, and I still do. The military has the most critical use of space science, and therefore they have a vested interest in doing it as well as can be done. NASA does its best. But it's not concerned with national security; if it was, I believe we would have done better in this field than we have done.

"More importantly, the military would classify much of what would be done. They would keep the Russians from stealing all of the advances that we make. That is how the Russians have kept up in space, and in some cases gone ahead of us, by using our information. NASA makes everything public, and the Russians can get anything and everything they want, and it has been worth billions of dollars to them. They don't just use the data for space shots, either; they use it for military reasons."

The general spends much of his time in a wheelchair. He has a small chapel in his home, and he hands out religious literature to visitors and guests.

"I don't know if I'd like to personally go in space or not. But that's the direction to consider. The first man to walk on the moon is now almost sixty years old. It's possible that the first person to go to the stars is already born."

In 1986, the magazine U.S. NEWS & WORLD REPORT asked several futurists and related experts to take a peek at the twenty-first century. These are among the aggregate predictions:

The year 2000: The Soviet Union makes the first manned flight to Mars while the U.S. begins commercialized manufacturing in the zero gravity of a space station. The year 2001: Bioengineers develop vaccines to prevent heart disease, many cancers, and "smart pills" to boost intelligence quotients. The year 2005: The average workday is cut to six hours and the workweek to thirty. The year 2010: Hypersonic planes fly at 12,000 mph and reduce travel time from New York to Japan to 45 minutes.

The year 2030: The oil age ends, as scarce petroleum is replaced by natural gas, solar collectors, and nuclear fusion. The year 2050: The Olympic Games fall into disfavor as sports fans object to the bioengineering and computerized training of athletes. The year 2075: World population reaches 10 billion and the population on Mars is 10,000. The year 2080: The arms race ends as America and the Soviet Union agree to a historic treaty. The year 2090: Somebody cheats on the year 2080.

LAWRENCE STANHOPE

Before he died in 1974, Charles Lindbergh came to have growing doubts about the instrument he worshiped above all else. He said that after three-quarters of a century of engine-driven flight, the stark fact was that "the historical significance of aircraft has been primarily military and destructive." He might have had similar concerns about most scientific achievements of the 1900s. A major and sobering discovery of the age is that if necessity is sometimes the mother of invention, neutrality is almost always the other parent. New things can both create and solve problems. Science kills as easily as it gives birth and promotes as much suffering as comfort. The tragedy of tinkering man, Lindbergh said, is that even as he surpasses miracles he has not yet devised a way to guide his work to a constructive end.

Lawrence Stanhope concurs. He says science is agnostic regarding morality. He says it insists on redoing the world and at the same time leaving the change to chance. He also holds that it won't do any more. The twentieth century is coming to an end even as new machines fastened to old thinking can conceivably prevent the advent of the twenty-first. Stanhope says that man in the past could always hope for a better day, but now he must confront the prospect of having no day at all. Unless:

"I recently read a story about Noah, the man in the Bible with the ark. I am not fanatically religious, but I liked the story. The writer reminded me that Noah lived in a time when the world was full of wickedness, when there was great corruption and violence and selfishness. But Noah would not go along with it. He had integrity. I suppose he could have built his boat just to save himself, but he created it for a bigger purpose. He wanted to save mankind from itself. That is the lesson of the story.

"And it's also the way I feel now. I think someone has got to start doing something to save the world again. That's why I came up with this idea. I don't want to make a dime from it—I'm too old to be thinking about getting rich; my only intention is to give it to the United States, give it to the Soviet Union, give it to England, and give it to everyone else on the planet. I want to use it as a new start. I want to see that all people begin to share in the wonders of science instead of just the terrors.

"I think maybe Providence is guiding me in the same way it did Noah. My idea came almost like some kind of vision. James Watt said he got the idea for the steam engine from a vision; he was walking in a park and he 'saw' the steam engine arrange itself in his mind. That's how it was with me. I wondered what single thing would benefit mankind most. Then it came to me so fast that I could not write it down quick enough. I had to shout it out so I would remember every detail: Perpetual Sunshine. We could grow enough food for everyone."

Perpetual sunshine! Is this man on full power? Well, that's what they asked about Noah. And also Daguerre, Tesla, and Fulton, among others.

Larry Stanhope has patented his hope: Number 4,583,321.

It's never been easy to have vision or anomalous thought. Galileo was condemned to life imprisonment, then put under house arrest, for pointing out that the earth was not the center of the universe. In 1956 the royal astronomer in Great Britain declared that the talk of space travel was "utter bilge." The creative have been needled throughout the ages of civilization, sometimes with justification—city planners in Winooski, Vermont, once talked of enclosing the community in a plastic bubble to cut the costs of snow removal—but more often because it is difficult to modify conventions and rejigger preconceptions.

A man living in the pine woods of Louisiana claims he has invented a device that manufactures more energy than it consumes. Joseph Newman says his generator would revolutionize the fundamental fueling of society. He says cars could be driven for pennies and buildings cooled and heated for small change, and he says scores of engineers who have studied the machine have arrived at the same conclusion. Alas, he can't distribute it because he can't get patent protection. The government says the laws of physics deny the machine's potential, and, having tested it, the patent office also says it plain doesn't work.

Another man, this one in Pennsylvania, insists he has found petrified human bones embedded in slate formations near a coal field. Edward Conrad says the fossils are the oldest animal fragments ever discovered, and they upset most contemporary assumptions concerning the beginnings of the human race. Here again, some experts agree. There is some supporting evidence. Yet here again are the giggles as well. Science says people evolved two million years ago; bones in coal would thus have to be at least 280 million years old, and so it can't be. Conrad, forget it. Leave curiosity to the people who invented the bomb.

Larry Stanhope:

"I always wanted to be a minister or an actor. I grew up in California, where there are plenty of both. I got tired of the organized church, however, and all of that stuff about being holier than thou. And I only did a little acting. I knew Dana Andrews and I worked with people like Orson Wells and Joseph Cotton in places like New York, but I was only a bit player. I remember a line I had: 'Down with the slings, I say.' I've never forgotten it: 'Down with the slings.' I also was an usher at the San Francisco Opera House.

"My real love has been growing things. I've been doing it since I was a boy in the San Joaquin Valley. I was put out on this fruit farm that my grandmother had when I was eleven, and we grew everything. We had forty acres of grapes. We grew peaches and dried them. We dried prunes, and figs. We grew lots of vegetables too. Peas, beans, celery. And we grew different kinds of berries. Strawberries, loganberries. We had two plots of forty acres each, and we had another one of twenty acres. That was a hundred in all, and located near Fresno.

"I was the oldest boy in the family, and I was put out on the farm to help support everybody. That meant I had to skip some of my education. I used to go to school in the morning and then work in the fields during the afternoon. I didn't mind it, though. My grandmother ran the farm, and she was just a tremendous person. My grandfather was not worth anything, but my grandmother was great. Her name was Cornelia Wilson. She was related to President Wilson. Oh, how she could work! She knew everything. She could plow, and cultivate, and harvest.

"And she had great intelligence. She was the brains of the whole outfit. And she was one of the people who started the Sun Maid Raisin Company. That was because the raisin market at that time was not good; in fact it was awful. There were two or three packing companies in Fresno. They all stuck together; they only gave so much for the raisins; and they were the only ones making money on the crops. You see, it took seven pounds of grapes to make one pound of raisins, and the packing companies only paid two cents a pound for the raisins. We were losing our shirts on it.

"So then my grandmother got together with other growers to form the Sun Maid Raisin Growers Association, which later became a company. I think it was the first fruit association in the country. The growers decided that they had to get a seventy-five or eighty percent control of the market in order to get fair prices. And they did it by holding back all of their raisins that first year, which created a shortage and a big demand. And it broke the grip of the packing houses. After that we started getting ten cents a pound, which was a five hundred percent increase."

Stanhope is eighty-six. He was married once, but it did not work out. He wears wide lapels; he worked as a clerk for Montgomery Ward; and he has operated a hotel in Miami Beach. He became a part-time inventor in the mid-1950s:

"It was because of my grandmother. She got me interested in doing things more intelligently, and she taught me to do things that would help people. She was getting older by then, and she couldn't work as hard as before, and she thought I could do something to help her out with the chores she had. There was no idea of making any gigantic profit from an invention, not even at the beginning. The idea was to make something that would help people, that would make their lives easier. That was the philosophy then, and it still is the now.

"The first thing I invented was like a simplified greenhouse. I wanted one that could be built at a minimal cost and also work better. So I designed one that could be put up on a slope, at right angles to the sun, and in that way it could take maximum advantage of the solar energy. The excavation was east to west, and the greenhouse sets in a trench that provides irrigation. It works very well. It catches the very last of the sun's rays each day. I got the patent for it in 1957, number 2,805,518, and I called it the Stanhope Sunslope.

"The next invention was in 1969, and it added mechanization to that earlier greenhouse. Now, this one could be built on three levels. I would grow tomatoes or something on one level, then maybe berries on the second level, and fruit or grapes on the third level. And all of them could be rotated. You have to let things like fruit trees and grapevines go into dormancy on a regular basis, so they could be rotated to the bottom where it was dark. It was a conservation of space, growing more in a small area. The patent number is 3,461,605.

"I got a third patent a couple of years later. I had moved to Florida then, and I thought that fruitgrowers needed something better to help them pick their crops. People were climbing on the trees with ladders, or they were using mechanical shakers which hurt the trees and bruised the fruit. So I invented a platform shaped like an inverted V that can be placed over the trees and rolled along the rows. Several people stand at various levels on both sides of the platform and pick the trees. It's very safe. Patent number 3,568,796.

"That makes everything except my most recent patent, the big one, the one that can help change the world. And I want you to know that I haven't made a dime on any one of them. Anyone can pick up these ideas. They are so simple that no one needs my permission. They could build them in their backyard, with the exception of the second one, and I wouldn't even know it. And that's all right with me. I think inventions should be for the benefit of everyone. I made these things so farmers could grow better crops, and make a good living.

"I also want to show people that I have been here. I was born in 1901, and I've been fortunate enough to survive all of the wars and the diseases and the other episodes of this century, and I want to leave something besides my dust. I have been divorced since I was in my sixties; I don't have any children; many of my friends are gone; my brothers and sisters have all passed on, so who will remember me when I die? That's where Perpetual Sunshine comes in. If I can get this across, if the nations will listen, I'll leave something vitally important."

Stanhope says he devised the notion of perpetual sunshine in 1983. Watt-like. He says today sits on the threshold of blooming space; if there is a tomorrow it will be in the skies. Star wars or peace? Exploitation or unification? New frontiers or more of the same? Somebody said that moon rocks are okay when everybody's eating. Emerson wrote that other worlds are the only light when it's truly dark where we're standing. Stanhope's plan is to join hands on the only frontier of understanding left, before it's too late.

"I call it the Space Garden. I want to feed the world. Millions of people go to bed at night hungry; this is in spite of all the advances we have made in agriculture. The United States has so much milk that the government has to subsidize it to keep the prices up. There is so much butter and wheat and fruit that we can't consume it all. But many children in Africa are starving. I've seen figures that in some impoverished countries one in every four persons are undernourished. This is just not acceptable. The next century must be better.

"Specifically, I want to use existing space technology to grow crops in space. I have designed a detailed greenhouse that would be built high over the earth. Now, it wouldn't be in orbit like a satellite. We don't go with the earth on its rotation. That would mean that it would revolve around the planet and be cut off from the sun half the time. Instead, we power the garden in the opposite direction of the earth's rotation, westward, and that will keep it between the earth and the sun. It would give us perpetual sunshine. And we could grow crops twenty-four hours a day.

"I have made it my life's work. I have prayed over this, and I have struggled for it every day for the last five years. And the thing is that it has been here all along. Nobody picked me to be a genius, the idea has been here for anyone to see, and it just happens I was the only one looking. Think of it. The garden would be way above the storms, way above the hail and the floods. There wouldn't be any insects. There would not be any pollution. We would grow the finest and healthiest crops ever produced. Day in, day out; the seasons wouldn't matter any more.

"What a blessing it would be! I don't say that it would do away with the need for earth-grown products. But it would eliminate the everlasting worry of shortages. If there was a drought in the American and the Canadian plains, the grains could be easily be supplemented from space. If there was desperation again in the Sahel, or freezing weather wiped out fruit in the tropics, it would all be replaced by revamping the schedules overhead. We could grow as much as we wanted. Potatoes, corn, soybeans—you name it. It excites me to talk of it.

"Of course, the size of the crops would depend on how many space gardens we put up. But I have conducted some experiments to scale that give an idea what we could expect from each growing platform. Those platforms would be built with four levels which would encompass one acre of total growing space. During my experiments I worked with levels placed on tables of forty-three square feet. That is a thousandth of an acre. So, using this scale, I calculated that a platform in space, 120 foot by 120 foot, would yield—are you ready?—five million pounds of tomatoes a year.

"Every hungry person on earth could be fed. And probably a good lot cheaper than it costs to do it now. I don't know this for certain, though. I have never tried to figure how much the space garden would cost. The biggest cost would be getting the materials into space. Shooting them up. The platform itself would not be very much. It is not much more than a sophisticated greenhouse. Then there would be fuel for propulsion, the gardens would have to keep moving to stay between the sun and the earth. Once everything was in place, though, expenditures would fall.

"I originally thought that everything could be in place about ten miles over the earth. I didn't want to lose very much gravity. But then I talked to NASA about it. They said I could go higher. Now I believe it could be placed up to a thousand miles. The gravity at that distance is fifty percent what it is on earth, and that would be enough. You have to have enough gravity to hold the plants in place. If it was weightless the roots wouldn't stay down, nor anything else. The soil would float around; you couldn't irrigate. But fifty percent, okay.

"I have covered and sealed the space garden, naturally; it's cold in space. We would bring along some kind of soil, probably vermiculite in an aggregate, and some oxygen. The space garden would also manufacture some of its own oxygen through that wonderful cycle where humans exhale carbon dioxide for the plants and the plants give off oxygen for the people. The gardens would also need water. That could be scooped from rainclouds in special vehicles for the purpose, and the water would be recycled within the self-contained garden.

"Finally, the four levels would be rotated into and away from the sun. I told you about that second invention of mine. This would be the same thing. Plants cannot live under constant exposure to the sun. They must be in the dark at regular intervals. So the rotation would do the job. The rotating levels would also provide economy of space. The space garden does not need to be the size of a football field. It would be the size of a couple of tennis courts. I can see thousands of courts; the more we put up, the more we can grow."

Larry Stanhope worked for three years to patent the space garden. And very nearly failed in the effort. The patent officers wondered if the idea was "feasible and practical" for one thing, and, during an early examination, they rejected the application on 112 counts. The inventor persisted with revised calculations, however. He also impressed the federal officials with his thoroughly contagious personal convictions, and, because of his age, the patent regulations were bent a little (the process was accelerated), and Stanhope prevailed.

Stanhope lives in Lakeland, Florida—where, he admits, he is trying to put the bite on someone, anyone, to provide backing.

"No, I've not had any luck yet in this respect. But I'm working at it. Something has to happen. I am talking about the future. We aren't going to get anywhere doing what we've been doing. We can't have peace by telling the Russians that we have more warheads that they do. And the Russians can't generate any security by thinking they can kill us all. We've got to work together. How old am I? All right, let me tell you what I've learned: If you plant a seed it may grow. If you plant it with someone else, it has a much better chance."